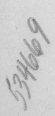

WITHDRAWN
FROM CSUSM

Utopia Ltd

THE STORY OF THE ENGLISH NEW TOWN OF STEVENAGE

Utopia Ltd

The Story of the English New Town of Stevenage

by

HAROLD ORLANS

NEW HAVEN
YALE UNIVERSITY PRESS
1953

Printed in Great Britain

Whatever they preach to us, whatever we may learn, we should still remember that it is a man that gives and a man that takes. It is a mortal hand that offers it, it is a mortal hand that accepts it.—MONTAIGNE

Who plans the planner?—KARL MANNHEIM

Foreword

I N November 1946, the British Government founded the New
Town of Stevenage, thirty miles north of London, as part of a
long-term programme to move over a million people from the
metropolis. This book tells the story of this New Town: the history
of the decentralization policy, of the existing town of old Stevenage,
and of the first four years of the new development; the sociology of
the New Town plan and of the strong local opposition which aroused
nation-wide interest and led to a court case that almost stopped the
project; the nature of the Development Corporation established to
plan and build the New Town and the difficulties experienced in its
relations with other Government departments and the Stevenage
District Council. The book is, therefore, an historical and sociological study of a pioneering Government venture and of its impact
upon a small town. It represents the results of interviewing, observation, and documentary research conducted over an eighteen-month
period from October 1948. (For details of the research procedure, see
Appendix B.)

Montaigne asks if it can be fitting for 'men who combine an exact
and tender conscience with prudence, to write history. How can they
pledge their word on a popular belief? How can they be responsible
for the opinions of men they do not know, and give out their con-
jectures as current coin? Of actions performed by several persons in
their presence they would refuse to give evidence upon oath before
a judge, nor would they undertake full responsibility for the intentions of any man, however intimately known to them. I hold it to be
less hazardous to write of things of the past than of things of the
present, inasmuch as the writer has only to give an account of a bor-
rowed truth.' With all these remarks I concur emphatically.

But if we are all damned no one can escape damnation. It is a
professional deceit of historians that they must wait until 'all the
evidence is in' and a 'proper perspective' is possible. Of course, the

evidence is never 'all in', and there is loss as well as gain in waiting for it; a distant perspective is not necessarily truer than, but only different from, a close one. In any event, although the historian prefers Caesar dead, the citizen must have him alive, and it is the professional conceit of social scientists and historians of the present that they can help citizens understand and cope with a living Caesar (or, perhaps more often, that they can help Caesar rule). Readers may judge for themselves the extent to which this conceit is justified.

Sociology can subsist without names and dates, but history cannot. This book is impaled upon the dilemma. Anonymity was pledged to all informants, and the pledge has been honoured although it necessarily detracts from the historical value of the work. I can only give my word that informants were well placed to judge whereof they spoke; that, so far as I could judge, they spoke sincerely and honestly and I have made every effort to report their meaning accurately; that remarks attributed to an 'informant' and placed in direct quotes were most frequently recorded during the course of an interview or, occasionally, immediately thereafter; often they were written by the informant himself. To avoid the possibility of injury I would have identified no one by name or title if the book could thus have retained any value at all—historical or sociological. (A pseudonym was even selected for 'Stevenage', but it proved hopeless to conceal the site and yet tell the story.) The course generally adopted was to designate no one by name or station below the rank of Council or Corporation Chairman when the source of information was either a personal interview or a private document; however, there are non-specific references on the order of 'an Independent councillor' or 'a Corporation officer'. The intent, of course, is to emphasize that my interest is not in the individual but his role. Judgements of policy and practice are reported, but I have attempted to ignore purely personal criticism. This, again, must depreciate the historical value of the work, since it is scarcely possible to write authentic history without appraising the character of the men who lived it.

Direct quotation has been preferred to paraphrase and, so far as confidences permitted, sources have been indicated and amplified in very full notes. No evidence, aside from that which might have been defamatory, has been suppressed or knowingly distorted. Undoubtedly a great deal has been overlooked because of limitations of time, accessibility, and interest.

The principal claim made is that this is an empirical study begun without bias for or against New Towns and the other planning issues discussed; conducted independently; and concluded as the weight of evidence fell on the balance of each issue. That there are limitations to empiricism in this field, beyond which subjectivity operates, is not disputed. But there is no conclusion I would not willingly change to accord with further evidence.

However, this is not a pacific but a *critical* analysis. It is a study of conflict and tension between rival groups—planners and the planned, different schools of planners, the Ministry and the Development Corporation, the Corporation and the Stevenage Council, etc.—more than of co-operation and harmony; of problems more than the solution of problems; of the failures and difficulties more than the successes of planning. In part, circumstances at Stevenage seemed to warrant such an emphasis; in part, the emphasis is due to my interests and another book could depict these events in another manner. But one can only write one book at a time. The rosier picture provided by official publications is readily available and it would be extravagant to reproduce it here.

In so far as any partisan spirit animates this work, it is a partisanship of the less powerful against those with more power. I have tried to be fair to both sides of every issue, but where a choice was necessary (and in research and writing, as in life, some choice is always necessary) I have presented a fuller brief for the weaker side—the Ministry with respect to the Government, the Development Corporation with respect to the Ministry, the Stevenage Council with respect to the Corporation, the citizen with respect to the Council, and so on. As the policy of those in power is not generally hidden under a bushel and, in any case, carries the day, I have few qualms about this procedure.

H. O.

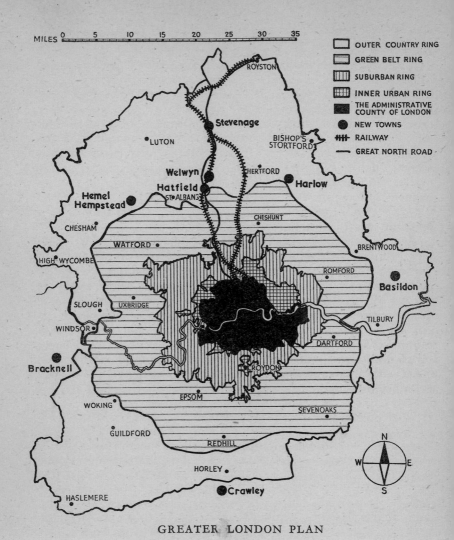

MILES

0　5　10　15　20　25　30　35

OUTER COUNTRY RING
GREEN BELT RING
SUBURBAN RING
INNER URBAN RING
THE ADMINISTRATIVE
COUNTY OF LONDON
NEW TOWNS
RAILWAY
GREAT NORTH ROAD

ROYSTON

Stevenage

LUTON

BISHOP'S
STORTFORD

Welwyn
Hatfield
ST·ALBANS

HERTFORD

Harlow

Hemel
Hempstead

CHESHAM

CHESHUNT

WATFORD

BRENTWOOD

HIGH WYCOMBE

ROMFORD

SLOUGH
UXBRIDGE

Basildon

WINDSOR

TILBURY

DARTFORD

Bracknell

CROYDON

EPSOM

WOKING

SEVENOAKS

GUILDFORD

REDHILL

N
W   E
S

HORLEY

HASLEMERE

Crawley

GREATER LONDON PLAN

This amended version of the map of the Four Rings is reproduced from Patrick
Abercrombie's *Greater London Plan 1944* by permission of His Majesty's
Stationery Office. Of the eight New Town sites indicated, only two (Stevenage
and Harlow) were recommended in the *Greater London Plan;* the others were
chosen subsequently.

Acknowledgements

THE Social Science Research Council and the United States Educational Commission in the United Kingdom made this work possible by the fellowships which they awarded in 1948–9 and 1949–50, respectively. I am grateful to the responsible persons in both institutions for their faith, and to several less responsible officers for their kindness.

Mr. Edward Shils and Prof. David Glass of the London School of Economics took some interest in the research. Believing that sociological research was very important (which was somewhat more than I believed) they supplied a degree of personal encouragement which was most important. However, neither is responsible in any way for this book or has even read the manuscript.

The people in Stevenage and elsewhere who gave the information recorded here could not know (for I did not know myself) the exact use to which it would be put. They were helpful mainly for personal reasons, and, in some cases, these initiated a real friendship. I also profited from the special hospitality given to Americans. It is a delicate matter for a guest to analyse (which often means to criticize) the principles, goals, and, alas, even the motives of his host, but it is along such paths that honesty must sometimes tread. To those who may be offended I should like to say, I bear no malice; and I should like to thank all who helped me so generously. Their names cannot be given because anonymity was promised to every informant.

I want particularly to thank the officers and members of the Stevenage Urban District Council, the Stevenage Development Corporation, and the Ministry of Town and Country Planning, without whose co-operation this research could not have been conducted. The late historian Mr. Reginald L. Hine and Mrs. Hine made available unpublished notes on the history of Stevenage which I have used in Chapter II. The directors of Mass-Observation gave me free access

ACKNOWLEDGEMENTS

to their files, which included an unpublished survey of Stevenage opinion, and were as helpful as they could be.

The following were good enough to read and comment upon all or parts of the manuscript: Gilbert Beaven, Geoffrey Berry, Len England, Ruth Glass, William O. Hart, Charles Lindblom, Sigurd Lorentzen, Michael Lyster, Charles Madge, Chester Rapkin, E. R. Roper-Power, Eva Slover, Gordon Stephenson, Stanley Tankel, Jaqueline Tyrwhitt, and Charles Walker. I accepted all of their corrections and some, but not most, of their advice. None of them can be held accountable for any errors or opinions which remain. Some readers took strong exception to views I have retained—for instance, most English readers disagreed with my view of the flat-house controversy and, in turn, I have had to criticize their views at some length.

I am obliged to the librarians of the British Museum, London University, the London School of Economics, and the Architectural Association for facilities they extended.

The diagram 'The Three Magnets' from Ebenezer Howard's *Garden Cities of To-morrow* is reproduced by courtesy of the publishers, Faber and Faber Ltd., and the map of the Greater London Plan from Patrick Abercrombie's *Greater London Plan 1944*, by courtesy of His Majesty's Stationery Office.

H. O.

London, August 1951

Contents

xiii

CONTENTS

Part Two: The New Town Plan

CONTENTS

Part Three: The New Town Machinery

Part Four: Review and Discussion

Chart

Maps

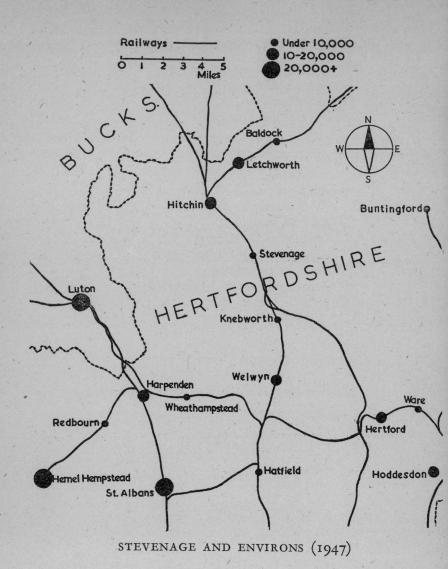

Railways ——

● Under 10,000
● 10-20,000
● 20,000+

0 1 2 3 4 5
Miles

N
W   E
S

BUCKS.

Baldock

Letchworth

Hitchin

Buntingford

Stevenage

HERTFORDSHIRE

Luton

Knebworth

Welwyn

Ware

Harpenden

Wheathampstead

Redbourn

Hertford

Hemel Hempstead

St. Albans

Hatfield

Hoddesdon

STEVENAGE AND ENVIRONS (1947)

Part One
The New Town Idea

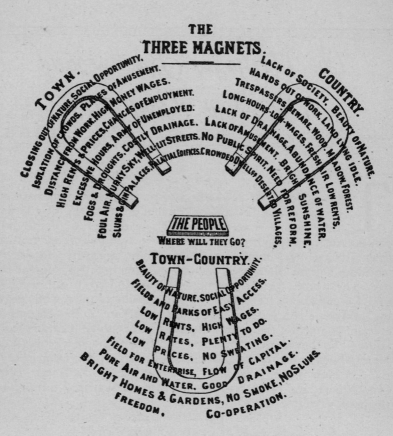

See p. 8. (Reproduced from Ebenezer Howard's *Garden Cities of Tomorrow* by permission of the publisher, Faber & Faber Ltd.)

CHAPTER ONE

The Historical Background of the New Towns Act

THE building of New Towns in relatively rural parts of Britain, established as Government policy by the New Towns Act, 1946, can be understood as the juncture of the most conservative and progressive forces, as the union—and conflict—of town and country, industry and agriculture, capitalist and gentry, working- and middle-classes, Labour and Conservative, present and past. The whole story cannot be told here; indeed, it can never be told, for one cannot learn the story while telling or tell it while learning, and there is no natural end to either labour. In this chapter an account is given of the garden city idea and of town planning legislation—the formal ideological and parliamentary antecedents of the New Towns; there follows the briefest history of Stevenage, site of the first New Town; Chapter III enters in greater detail into recent events there; and other bits of the story are scattered throughout the book.

A. URBAN PLANNING BEFORE 1939

(a) The Urban Crisis

The industrial revolution made her an empire, but is still not fashionable in Britain. The foreign visitor has heard much about the lovely thatch-roofed village, the stage on which so large a portion of English ideology is enacted, but when he comes to England he will search hard before he finds one. The few that survive are indeed lovely, but they are isolated preserves, representative neither of the countryside nor of that England which is the most urbanized nation in the world—nearly half its population living in centres of over 250,000.[1]

Elizabethan or Georgian England may not have been the aesthetic paradise that is often imagined—vulgarity was probably as vulgar and ugly buildings as ugly as today; but damage was undoubtedly on a smaller scale. It was the industrial revolution that gave England the face she now bears and that, in the opinion of those who set opinion, ravaged the countryside and desecrated the city—'the dirt and ugliness' of the English city, it has been said, 'is a subject almost too painful for an Englishman to dwell upon.'[2] The historian R. C. K. Ensor attributes much of the transformation to the growth of railways in the middle of the last century. Before then, the use of local materials had ensured a certain harmoniousness of design, despite changes in architectural styles. 'These conditions the railways destroyed; for by enabling heavy materials, for the first time, to be freely distributed at low cost all over the land, they abolished the cheapness of local materials, and substituted that of national ones. The cheapest walling was found to be brick; the cheapest covering, a low-pitched roof of North Wales slate. . . . The fact that it broke all tradition and was in itself ugly, could not avail against the law of cheapness.'[3] Of course, there were numberless other causes for the urban afflictions that assailed Britain: the rapid increase of population; the decline of agriculture and the rise of mechanized mass production; the triumph of capital and wealth in industry over wealth in land (marked politically, by the victories which Liberals won over Conservatives and the Commons over the Lords, and, socially, by the marked influx of *nouveaux-riches* into the peerage); rampant profiteering by the bourgeoisie and the complementary impoverishment and disenfranchisement of workers; the complacency of the rich and the powerlessness of the poor.

The problems of nineteenth- and twentieth-century cities were not merely ugliness and dirt (how English cities will ever be clean with every room in them heated by a separate soft-coal fire billowing its smoke into the streets is beyond conceiving).[4] All the material and

[1] See M. A. Abrams (ed.), *The Home Market* (London, 1939), p. 38. The date to which this estimate refers is presumably 1931. The density of population for England (Wales and Scotland excluded) has been given as 766 per square mile in 1939, compared to 702 for Belgium, 360 for Italy, and 36 for the United States (Royal Commission on the Distribution of the Industrial Population, *Report*, Cmd. 6153 (London, 1940), p. 13).

[2] E. D. Simon, *A City Council from Within* (London, 1926), p. 135.

[3] R. C. K. Ensor, *England 1870–1919* (Oxford, 1936), p. 153.

[4] One English authority defines the open fire as 'possibly that type of apparatus which involves the maximum of labour, dirt and smoke of any of the methods of heating which are open to us'. As long ago as 1661, John Evelyn expressed his concern 'That this Glorious and Antient City [London] . . . should wrap her

social problems of a rampant industrialism were concentrated there.

'The housing of the industrial workers that was rushed up conformed to a classical pattern: the congested, undifferentiated gridiron that had been used to house slaves in Egypt and Mesopotamia and in the cities of the Alexandrian Empire.'[1] Overcrowding resulted both in houses and neighbourhoods, where sidewalks and streets provided the principal open spaces. Sanitary standards were low and the most densely populated districts were generally the least healthy (a condition aggravated by the frequent location of the densest settlements on the poorest sites, where land values were low). Early working-class housing was usually in the immediate vicinity of the factory, but, as the urban population and the size of factories grew, an increasing proportion of workers had to travel increasing distances to their work—a trend promoted also by the improvement of public transport and the movement of industry to more economic peripheral locations. At the same time, to escape the high rates and low status of proletarian districts, the middle classes moved to the suburbs. So wave after wave of unplanned building welled from the blighted centre over the neighbouring countryside, while the mounting population, traffic, and property values placed an increasing strain upon almost every function of the city, and extorted vast ransom—in high taxes, high prices, and inadequate, expensive remedial services—from every citizen. In every industrialized nation the question arose: *Can Our Cities Survive?*[2]

(b) Utopian Solutions

There were not lacking people who answered 'No: large cities cannot, and, if they can, *should not*, survive'. And it was natural enough in such a period that many (reactionary, liberal, and revolutionary) utopian thinkers, conceiving a world without the evils of the industrial city, should find the spirit of their utopias in the countryside.

'Whereas there was a time in the history of Europe when the word *paganus* was a term of reproach, indicative of backwardness, its place was

stately head in Clowds of Smoake and Sulphur, so full of Stink and Darknesse. . . .' (Both cited by H. Kamenka, *Flats* (London, 1947), p. 99). More recently, it has been estimated that between 200 and 500 tons of smoke-dust fall yearly upon every square mile of industrial towns in Britain (E. W. Smith, in Gilbert and Elizabeth McAllister (eds.), *Homes, Towns and Countryside* (London, 1945), p. 70).

[1] The gridiron pattern 'provided the quickest and most economical covering of the ground, and, moreover, was easy to police' (Jaqueline Tyrwhitt, 'Society and Environment: A Historical Review', *Town and Country Planning Textbook* (London, 1950), p. 135).

[2] José L. Sert's book of this title documents these developments strikingly (Cambridge, Mass., 1942).

taken for the socialist Fourier by its opposite, *civilisé*, for Marx by the *Bourgeoisie*; and whereas during the period of urban expansion in the twelfth and thirteenth centuries towns could be founded with names like Sauveterre and Salvetat, it was "Nature" that was commonly regarded as the sanctuary during the similar period in the nineteenth century. The city had been replaced, as a symbol of freedom, by the country.'[1]

In 1820, the manufacturer and socialist pamphleteer Robert Owen put forward 'a Plan for relieving Public Distress and Removing Discontent, by giving permanent, productive Employment to the Poor and Working Classes, under Arrangements which will essentially improve their Character, and ameliorate their Condition, diminish the Expenses of Production and Consumption, and create Markets co-extensive with Production'. He called for the formation of agricultural villages of from 800 to 1,200 population, which 'in the neighbourhood of others of a similar description, at due distances, will be found capable of combining within themselves all the advantages that city and country residences now afford, without any of the numerous inconveniences and evils which necessarily attach to both those modes of society'.[2] The villages would be 'essentially centres of social life and rational education as well as of productive activity . . . . they would not compete but co-operate one with another, and their aim would be as much to train good citizens as to relieve the necessities of the poor'.[3] In 1845, Moffatt, a London architect, proposed a similar scheme for the creation of villages in the environs of London: 'Air and space, wood and water, schools and churches, shrubberies and gardens, around pretty self-contained cottages, in a group neither too large to deprive it of a country character, nor too small to diminish the probabilities of social intercourse.'[4]

James Silk Buckingham's *National Evils and Practical Remedies* (1849) had a more direct influence upon the subsequent development of the garden city idea. Buckingham suggested that 'The Model Town Association' should be formed

'for the purpose of building an entirely new Town, to combine within itself every advantage of beauty, security, healthfulnes, and convenience, that the latest discoveries in architecture and science can confer upon it; and . . . peopled by an adequate number of inhabitants, with such due proportions between the agricultural and manufacturing classes, and between possessors of capital, skill, and labour, as to produce . . . the highest

[1] W. A. Eden, 'Ebenezer Howard and the Garden City Movement', *Town Planning Review*, vol. 19, 1947, p. 125.
[2] Robert Owen, 'Report to the County of Lanark', in *A New View of Society and Other Writings* (London, 1927), pp. 245, 265.
[3] G. D. H. Cole, in Introduction to Owen, op. cit., p. xiii.
[4] Mass-Observation, *An Enquiry into People's Homes* (London, 1943), p. 27.

degree of health, contentment, morality, and enjoyment, yet seen in any existing community. . . . [1]

The Model Town, 'Victoria', was to be about a mile square, with a population of 10,000. Noxious industries would be put 'at sufficiently remote distances from the residences and workshops, to insure their occupants from any interference with their health or comfort'.[2] Inhabitants would all be shareholders in The Model Town Association owning all land and buildings. The puritanical aspect of the scheme is indicated by Buckingham's prohibition of intoxicating liquors, tobacco, weapons of war, and Sunday work in 'Victoria', and his imposition of strict penalties against adultery. Indeed, one commentator, noting the fort-like layout of 'Victoria', concludes that this 'is a dictatorial plan. . . .'[3]

Owen attempted to realize some of his ideas at New Lanark, Scotland and again at New Harmony in the United States, and a few benevolent industrialists built model towns of their own; 'among the schemes which actually came to fruition were Sir Titus Salt's Saltaire near Bradford (1853), George Cadbury's Bournville near Birmingham (1879), and Sir William Lever's Port Sunlight near Birkenhead (1887). . . .'[4] However, it remained for Ebenezer Howard to formulate and demonstrate the idea of the garden city that had increasing influence upon town planners in ensuing years, and whose success was climaxed by the New Towns Act, 1946.

(c) Ebenezer Howard and the Garden City Movement

'Howard awoke intellectually among liberal non-conformists, freethinkers, land reformers, co-operators, and devotees of many revolutionary creeds.'[5] Henry George had popularized the doctrines of *Progress and Poverty* in a series of lectures in England from 1881 onwards, and his book and Edward Bellamy's utopian novel *Looking Backward* (1888) had exercised considerable influence upon the formative socialist movement.[6] Bellamy gave Howard 'the conception of an ideal town . . . as essentially a "socialist community",'[7] which

[1] James S. Buckingham, *National Evils and Practical Remedies, with the Plan of a Model Town* (London, 1849), p. 141.

[2] Buckingham, op. cit., p. 151.   [3] Eden, op. cit., p. 131.

[4] Mass-Observation, op. cit., p. 27. The Bournville Village Trust's *Sixty Years of Planning* (1944?) gives the history of Bournville village.

[5] F. J. Osborn, 'The Pioneer of New Towns', *The Times*, 28th January 1950, p. 7.

[6] Ensor notes that upon George's 'catchword "unearned increment", much more than on Marx's "surplus value", the thinking of the English socialist movement was based . . . . popular English socialism from its start was Utopian and idealistic, not analytic' (op. cit., p. 334).

[7] F. J. Osborn, in Preface to Ebenezer Howard, *Garden Cities of To-morrow* (London, 1946), pp. 20–1.

7

he expressed ten years later in *To-morrow: a Peaceful Path to Real Reform*.[1]

Rhapsodically, Howard asks 'how to restore the people to the land—that beautiful land of ours, with its canopy of sky, the air that blows upon it, the sun that warms it, the rain and dew that moisten it—the very embodiment of Divine love for man. . . .'[2] Yet he is not unmindful of the disabilities of rural life—the social and cultural isolation, lengthy ill-paid labour, and the absence of many amenities. His solution is indicated in a diagram of 'The Three Magnets', which lists the principal advantages and disadvantages of 'town' and 'country', and suggests that the advantages of each can be retained and the disadvantages eliminated in the 'town-country' of tomorrow. See page 2.

Residents of overcrowded urban centres are to be encouraged to move to relatively self-contained garden cities of about 32,000 population, built by voluntary associations with State help. Howard undertakes to show how, in garden cities,

'better opportunities of social intercourse may be enjoyed than are enjoyed in any crowded city, while yet the beauties of nature may encompass and enfold each dweller therein; how higher wages are compatible with reduced rents and rates; how abundant opportunities for employment and bright prospects of advancement may be secured for all; how capital may be attracted and wealth created; how the most admirable sanitary conditions may be ensured; how beautiful homes and gardens may be seen on every hand; how the bounds of freedom may be widened, and yet all the best results of concert and co-operation gathered in by a happy people.'[3]

Something may be said about the political orientation of Howard and the garden city movement which succeeded him. 'So far as he had any politics at all, Ebenezer Howard was a Liberal. He did not believe in the State or think it right to depend upon State action.'[4] Howard explicitly denied that his scheme was 'a socialistic experiment', observing that socialists believed in governmental monopoly of employment, but 'it is very doubtful whether this principle . . . represents a basis on which an experiment can fairly proceed with the hope of permanent success'. But he did not object to calling his plan socialistic 'if by Socialism is meant a condition of life in which the well-being of the community is safeguarded, and in which the collective spirit is manifested by a wide extension of the area of municipal effort'.[5] His disciple, F. J. Osborn, suggests that his

[1] Republished in 1946, edited by F. J. Osborn, as *Garden Cities of To-morrow*.
[2] *Garden Cities of To-morrow*, p. 44.   [3] Ibid., pp. 48–9.
[4] C. B. Purdom, *The Building of Satellite Towns* (London, 1949), p. 359.
[5] Howard, op. cit., pp. 114, 131.

'bias was always for variety and elasticity of initiative, but he wanted his idea generalized, and in his book foreshadowed some State participation, for example, in acquiring the sites. . . . But Howard did not share Bellamy's trust in State organization. He proposed a voluntary co-operative set-up: a limited-profit association that would own the site, confine its own part to a few specific aims, and leave full play for private, group, and municipal enterprise, the balance of which was, he thought, unpredictable.'[1]

W. A. Eden is of the opinion that Howard's 'Garden City . . . represents a step towards an almost medieval world of limitation and privilege'.[2] Rasmussen places the genesis of the idea several centuries later, suggesting that 'Howard's Garden City idea is an . . . attempt to create a small community, entirely Georgistic within a capitalistic state. . . .'[3] While Howard himself (according to his biographer Macfadyen), felt that the Garden City satisfied the needs and welfare of all contemporary classes:

"the Garden City is a practical gospel for working people—aye and for all people . . . . it is good business for employer and employed: it will help to make the British Empire flourish." . . . [In Garden City] No revolution has taken place. It is a "peaceful pathway to real reform." . . . There is no antagonism to any class. Landlords are not regarded as worse than any other people . . . . the ugly nineteenth century has been wiped off the slate and the country has resumed its natural evolution from the eighteenth century. . . .'[4]

The town and country planning movement that adopted and developed Howard's ideas adhered, of course, to no one party, and included representatives from many sections of British society—landowners, gentry, churchmen, manufacturers, businessmen, civil servants, architects, engineers.

The bulk of *To-morrow* examines practical considerations—revenue, finances, administration, etc.—involved in building a garden city. Shorthand reporter and son of a shopkeeper, Howard was at home in such matters, and it was perhaps because of his greater attention to them that he eventually met with greater success than so many predecessors. As *The Times* remarked upon the centenary of his birth, Howard achieved 'the right blend of visionary aims with businesslike means to capture the mood of the later Victorian social reformers'.[5]

---

[1] F. J. Osborn, 'The Pioneer of New Towns', *The Times*, 28th January 1950, p. 7. [2] Eden, op. cit., p. 135.
[3] Steen Rasmussen, *London: the Unique City* (London, 1937), pp. 370–1.
[4] Dugald Macfadyen, *Sir Ebenezer Howard and the Town Planning Movement* 1933 (Manchester, 1933), pp. 23–4, 29. The words within double quotes are Howard's.
[5] Editorial, 'Old Cities and New Towns', *The Times*, 28th January 1950, p. 7.

First to the heavens he casts his eyes;
Then on his boots they're found;
For though his thoughts are in the skies,
His feet are on the ground.[1]

'Howard's great virtue was that he was able to create a picture that accorded with the ordinary aspirations of the class to which he belonged—the somewhat earnest, chapel-going, or chapel-emancipated, lower middle class which had lately acquired political power, and was destined to inaugurate a revolution by returning the Liberal Party with its huge majority at the General Election of 1906.'[2]

In June 1899, Howard founded the Garden City Association (which had 1,300 members two years later and is still active and influential as The Town and Country Planning Association) to implement his ideas, and, in 1903, acquired a tract of land in Hertfordshire, thirty-five miles north of London, where the building of the first garden city, Letchworth, was begun. In 1919, a start was made on the second garden city at Welwyn, in southern Hertfordshire. Letchworth and Welwyn Garden City, with a combined population of 40,000 in 1950,[3] stand as the fullest realization to date of the garden city idea. Each town was built by a company selling to the general public shares which yielded a maximum yearly dividend of 5 per cent at Letchworth and 7 per cent at Welwyn.[4] In the light of the experience at Stevenage which will be described in Chapter III, it is interesting to note that

'At Letchworth none of the very few original inhabitants except a few farm labourers looked upon the coming of the city with any pleasure. Had a vote been taken, it would have been wellnigh unanimous in rejecting the scheme. . . . At Welwyn Garden City the few original inhabitants with hardly any exception hated the idea of building the satellite town, and the neighbouring small town of Welwyn was solidly hostile, though not one of its comfortable residents was directly affected, and its tradesmen had every reason to be glad.'[5]

Despite their positive achievements, garden city enthusiasts for many years had little influence upon Government policy. Osborn recalls how, in the early decades of the century, he spent much time

---

[1] A verse about Howard recited at a Welwyn pageant in 1923 (from F. J. Osborn, 'Sir Ebenezer Howard', *Town Planning Review*, vol. 21, 1950, p. 222).
[2] Eden, op. cit., p. 134.
[3] The Registrar-General's figures for mid-1938 were: Letchworth, 15,990 and Welwyn Garden City 12,150. In 1949 the population of Letchworth was estimated at 'just under 20,000' (Stevenage Development Corporation, *Stevenage New Town Technical Report* (1949), p. 2); that of Welwyn Garden City, in 1950, as 18,500 (Welwyn Garden City Development Corporation, *Second Annual Report* (London, 1950), p. 203).
[4] F. J. Osborn, *Green-Belt Cities* (London, 1946), p. 58.
[5] Purdom, op. cit., p. 392.

lobbying, lecturing, and propagandizing the garden city idea, only to be counselled by Howard '. . . you are wasting your time. If you wait for the authorities to build new towns you will be older than Methuselah before they start. The only way to get anything done is to do it yourself.'[1]

(d) Planning Legislation

'Town and country planning,' states the Conservative Party, '. . . is no new Socialist invention. Its origin may be found in predominantly Conservative legislation in the second half of the nineteenth century, since when there has been continuous development.'[2] This may be true, but it is also true that Conservative doctrine changed markedly during this period, and that planning legislation initiated at various times by Conservative, Liberal, and Labour Governments commonly testifies to the increasing State control over private enterprise which all parties, whatever their ideology and social base, have been obliged to accept.

From 1848 onward, Parliament ventured to set minimum standards for the housing of the poorest classes, but problems raised by other types of housing and urban growth as a whole were recognized more slowly. Twentieth-century legislation manifests an increasing recognition of the desirability of town planning, first on a local and then a national scale, first in a negative and then in a positive manner. Successive acts covered broader areas and delegated greater powers, but—such has been the case unto the present day—varied interests profiting from the *status quo* united to oppose each change and, as the interests favouring change seldom exerted continuous strength and problems marched on ahead of solutions, each act fell short of achieving its mark.

London philanthropic organizations such as the Metropolitan Association for Improving the Dwellings of the Industrial Poor, established in 1842, pioneered in the improvement of working-class housing. Their efforts and the reports of the Poor Law Commissioners in 1842 and the Royal Commission on the health of towns in 1844 led to the Public Health Act, 1848, which introduced a method for the control of new buildings and new streets soon altered by the Local Government Act, 1858, to control by local authority byelaws.[3] The Labouring Classes Lodging Houses Act, 1851, authorized borough councils and local boards of health to erect houses for

---

[1] F. J. Osborn, *New Towns After the War* (London, 1942), pp. 7–8.

[2] *The Campaign Guide General Election 1950*, (Conservative and Unionist Central Office, London, 1949), p. 488.

[3] See Lewis Mumford, *The Culture of Cities* (London, 1940), pp. 176–7, and the *Report of the Committee on Qualifications of Planners*, Cmd. 8059 (London, 1950), p. 1.

artisans. '. . . powers to control the density of building development were granted under Disraeli's Public Health Act of 1875, which empowered local authorities to make bye-laws regulating the construction of houses and the spaces between them', while the Housing of the Working Classes Act, 1890, was the first significant measure to promote slum clearance by local authorities.[1]

'That byelaw control achieved substantial results in securing that new houses and streets were constructed so as to be reasonably sanitary is demonstrated by the sharp contrast between houses built before and after this control was established. The control was however very limited in its intention. It specified minimum standards which, when taken, as they often were, as a guide, produced . . . dreary vistas of ugly uniform streets. . . .'[2]

It has been observed that private building covenants, which grew up during the second half of the last century, also contributed to the eventual formulation of a public planning policy. These covenants, entered into by individuals who bought or leased plots of land on many private building estates, created, in effect, private zoning ordinances. However, they imposed only negative restrictions upon the use of land. 'A covenant that was positive, requiring a person to do something, could not be made to run with the land unless it had a clear negative implication, such as a covenant to maintain a plot of land as an open space which could be enforced as a covenant to restrict building.'[3]

The first direct planning law, the Housing and Town Planning Act, 1909, passed by a Liberal Government, permitted (but did not require) local authorities to prepare plans for new suburban areas—built-up areas and open country were both excluded. Like the private covenant upon which it was modelled, these plans were negative in effect. 'Although no development could take place which did not comply with the scheme, there was no effective provision to ensure that particular development did take place.'[4] A sanguine view holds that this act 'represented a considerable measure of social progress in that it modified the freedom of a landowner to develop his land in whatever manner he pleased subject only to compliance with Public Health and Building Acts and bye-laws and the common law of nuisance'.[5] Contrariwise, the act has been called 'a masterpiece of the obstructive art. It made town planning schemes nominally possible, but planted such a hedge of deterrent regulations round them that in ten years less than 10,000 acres were brought under planning. At the same time it blocked any real town planning

[1] *The Campaign Guide General Election* 1950, p. 488.
[2] Cmd. 8059, p. 1.   [3] Cmd. 8059, p. 3.   [4] Ibid.
[5] Expert Committee on Compensation and Betterment, *Final Report*, Cmd. 6386 (London, 1942), p. 8.

legislation. . . .'[1] In its provision for full compensation to owners whose property would be reduced in value by the application of a planning scheme, and the free gift to owners of any increase in value resulting from the scheme, the act was 'designed with care for the sanctity of private property'.[2]

The Housing, Town Planning, etc. Act, 1919, compelled towns above 20,000 to prepare suburban planning schemes before 1st January 1926 (a deadline later extended three years, 'but even by then comparatively few schemes had become operative'); removed the local authority's obligation, under the 1909 Act, to obtain the Local Government Board's consent before preparing a plan; authorized the Board to require any local authority to prepare such a plan; and—an important provision—enabled local authorities to form joint committees for the preparation of a more comprehensive scheme.[3] A number of succeeding laws adjusted the planning powers of various local authorities without broadening substantially the range of land over which control was exercised. The Housing, etc. Act, 1923, enabled the planning of areas of special aesthetic or historic interest; the Town Planning Act, 1925, the first to separate planning from housing, consolidated previous legislation; and the Local Government Act, 1929, allowed county councils (previously passed over in favour of smaller local government units) to prepare planning schemes independently or jointly with other local authorities.[4]

Finally, the Town and Country Planning Act, 1932, extended planning powers to almost all built-up and undeveloped urban and rural land (although rural interests protested that 'the Act regarded the countryside as a mere appanage of the town . . .').[5] It authorized 'the making of planning schemes for any land, whether built on or not, and whether in town or country, subject only to the exclusion . . . of built-up land unlikely to be redeveloped and land so remote as not to need planning. . . .'[6] The last important pre-war planning measure, the Restriction of Ribbon Development Act, 1935, was designed, as its name suggests, to restrict attenuated building along

[1] Ensor, op. cit., p. 518. The 10,000 acres comprised only three schemes.
[2] Astragal, in Ian MacCallum (ed.), *Physical Planning* (London 1945), p. 2.
[3] Cmd. 8059, p. 5.
[4] Cmd. 8059, pp. 4–5, and D. J. Beattie, *Hart's Introduction to the Law of Local Government and Administration* (third edition, London, 1946), pp. 546–7.
[5] '. . . it had been the intention to extend planning powers to all land, whether urban or rural: but . . . practical experience quickly proved that it was entirely inadequate for the formulation of country planning schemes as such. . . . The whole essence of the Act is that it is an Act controlling development, and "development" under it means building and similar works, and not agricultural development' (*Report of the Committee on Land Utilisation in Rural Areas*, Cmd. 6378 (London, 1942), p. 40).
[6] Cmd. 6386, p. 8.

major roads, which had been one of the most pronounced, and in many ways undesirable, features of construction in Britain after 1918.

From time to time official bodies investigated the garden city proposal, but no Government initiative was taken in this direction during the inter-war period. In March 1920, a committee under the chairmanship of Neville Chamberlain, appointed to advise the Minister of Health, Christopher Addison, on the best method of dealing with slums, recommended that 'the development of self-contained garden cities, either round an existing nucleus or on new sites, should be encouraged and hastened by State assistance in the early stages'.[1] Even before this, the Housing (Additional Powers) Act, 1919, had granted powers for the acquisition of land for the construction of garden cities, 'enabling the Ministry of Health, had it so decided, to create new towns after the manner contemplated by the New Towns Act'.[2] Similar provisions were incorporated also in the Housing Act, 1921, and the planning Acts of 1925 and 1932, but these powers were never used[3] (although, as will be seen, the Ministry of Town and Country Planning intended to use this 'sleeping' provision of the 1932 Act when, early in 1946, it wished to proceed with the Stevenage development before the New Towns Act became law). The Housing Act, 1921, also authorized loans to private associations for the development of garden cities, but Welwyn Garden City, Ltd. was apparently the only body to utilize this provision.

A Greater London Regional Planning Committee, created in 1927 by Chamberlain, then Minister of Health, expired ten years later having accomplished little beside issuing some reports (the work mainly of Raymond Unwin, the prominent planner who was the committee's technical adviser). Its 1931 Interim Report on Decentralization declared:

'It is desirable to secure that well planned industrial areas should be laid out and equipped in conjunction with .... complete industrial garden cities located between 12 and 25 miles from Charing Cross. . . . The satellite town or garden city seems to offer the most complete and effective ultimate type of decentralisation towards which to work. . . .'[4]

The committee recommended 'a graduated policy of realisation', noting that 'without the co-operation of the owners of land, or the

[1] *Interim Report of the Committee Appointed by the Minister of Health to Consider and Advise on the Principles to be Followed in Dealing with Unhealthy Areas*, March 1920, p.6.
[2] Ernest Watkins, 'The Law of Planning', *Town and Country Planning Textbook* (London, 1950), p. 510.
[3] Cmd. 8059, pp. 5–6.
[4] *Second Report of the Greater London Regional Planning Committee* (London, 1933), p. 109.

extensive purchase of land by Public Authorities, the present powers alone are not adequate for the purpose'. With little avail, it regarded the granting of these powers 'as a matter of urgency'.[1] Another Minister of Health, Arthur Greenwood, established a committee in 1931 'to examine the experiences gained in regard to the establishment of garden cities and villages and satellite towns'. Its report, issued in 1935, was full of 'amiable commonplaces',[2] and its recommendation to establish a national planning board was ignored.

(e) The Failure of Legislation

Altogether, it cannot be claimed that inter-war legislation achieved a notable degree of control over development. At the end of 1941, only a fraction of the land in Great Britain was covered by planning schemes,[3] and it was possible for the Minister of Town and Country Planning to state, in 1947, that 'More damage has been done, both to our towns and to the countryside, through sporadic and ribbon development since 1909, the date of the first Town and Country Planning Act, than in any period preceding it'.[4] A number of reasons have been adduced for this failure:

It has been suggested that 'The subject was new, it was full of technical points of procedure, and before it was fully taken in hand the [1939] War put an end for a time to further progress'.[5] This puts a kind face upon the matter, but can hardly be considered a satisfactory or sufficient explanation. Although the war interrupted building, it also gave, as will be seen, a great impetus to the planning movement. The technicality and administrative complexity of some of the planning law may readily be granted. Regarding the Restriction of Ribbon Development Act, 1935, for instance, a ministerial committee commented that 'what . . . [it] has chiefly achieved is to introduce another Government Department into the field of plan-

---

[1] Ibid.

[2] Purdom, op. cit., p. 367.

[3] At the end of 1941, some 1,056,000 out of 37,339,000 acres in England and Wales were covered by approved planning schemes (Cmd. 6378, p. 40). 'The total area fully planned in the sense of being included in approved planning schemes, between the inception of town planning in 1909 and the 1st April, 1932, was 75,020 acres. . . . At 1st April, 1939, the aggregate acreage covered by schemes which were awaiting approval was 4,027,683' (Royal Commission on the Distribution of the Industrial Population, *Report*, Cmd. 6153 (London, 1940), p. 109). Operative planning schemes covered 1,809,458 acres or 3 per cent of the national total (but a far larger proportion of the urban area) as of June 1942 (Cmd. 6386, p. 9). The total area of Great Britain in 1946 was 56,201,000 acres of which 45,830,000 constituted agricultural land and 1,143,000 acres the principal urban areas (*Whittaker's Almanac* (1949), p. 664).

[4] Statement by Lewis Silkin, January 1947 (quoted in The Labour Party, *Speakers' Handbook* 1949–50 (London, 1949), p. 379).

[5] Beattie, op. cit., p. 547.

ning, to the confusion of the general public and of the planning authorities themselves'.[1]

Parliament's refusal to provide sufficient powers to enforce its purported goals was, of course, a more important reason. 'The story of the 1932 Act is one of high hopes and subsequent disappointment. Many of the powers necessary to put into operation the intentions expressed on behalf of the Government were whittled away as the Bill proceeded through Parliament, and as the Act eventually emerged it·fell far short of the hopes that had been raised by its initial form.'[2] Planning was permissive not mandatory,[3] and the plans that resulted were of negative or restrictive, not positive or constructive effect— i.e., they secured that development could take place only in certain ways, but not that any area would actually be developed:

'The only constructive powers were not under the Town Planning but under the Housing Acts. Under the latter . . . Local Authorities could lay out their new Housing Estates so as to provide for all aspects of life incidental to Housing (e.g. provide shops, community centres, and recreation grounds, and sites for churches, schools, and industries). Few Local Authorities, however, used these powers to the full. . . .

'We may sum up the pre-[1939] war situation by saying that the Town Planning Acts were restrictive in their operation though general in scope and the Housing Acts constructive in operation but limited in scope.'[4]

A major weakness was the absence of central control and policy making. It should be remembered that county councils were allowed to participate in the planning process only after 1932, and that, previously, planning powers were delegated to borough, urban and rural district councils—i.e., in general, to small and weak local bodies whose efforts were, for the most part, unco-ordinated. 'To expect a vigorous planning initiative and the employment of skilled planners from small or poor local authorities is to expect the impossible.'[5]

'The local authorities, responsible as they are to local bodies of electors, naturally consider questions of planning and development largely with a view to the effect that they will have on the authorities' own finances and the trade of the district. Proposals by landowners involving the further development of an existing urban area are not likely . . . to be refused by a local authority if the only reason against the development taking place is that from the national standpoint its proper location is elsewhere,

[1] The Committee on Land Utilisation in Rural Areas, Cmd. 6378, p. 44.
[2] Ibid., p. 40
[3] The provision of the Housing Act, 1919, which made it the statutory duty of borough and urban districts with a population over 20,000 to prepare a limited plan, was repealed by the 1932 Act (Cmd. 6386, p. 9).
[4] R. L. Reiss, 'Redevelopment and Overspill', in Barbara Bliss (ed.), *The New Planning* (London, 1945), pp. 12–13.
[5] W. A. Robson, in Gilbert and Elizabeth McAllister (eds.) *Homes, Towns and Countryside* (London, 1945), p. 144.

particularly when . . . the prevention of any such development might not only involve the authority in liability to pay heavy compensation but would, in addition, deprive them of substantial increases in rate income.'[1]

As the Uthwatt Committee saw it, the central powers of the Ministry of Health 'were regarded by Parliament as regulatory and restrictive of the action of the local planning authorities rather than as positive and constructive. The Ministry has had no effective powers of initiative nor the power of financial assistance. . . .'[2] William A. Robson, however, has placed a great deal of blame upon the Ministry itself:

'The Ministry of Health was supposed to be the supervising authority, but in practice contented itself with an assiduous attention to minute details of trifling importance. It decided appeals against restrictive provisions to which objection was taken by disgruntled property owners or business interests. It issued model clauses. It sent high-sounding messages of encouragement to abortive conferences. It made much ado about nothing. At no stage of its career did the Ministry of Health show any signs of understanding what the planning movement is about. . . . It is, indeed, impossible to avoid the conclusion that . . . between 1919 and 1939 . . . those in control of the Ministry of Health regarded town and country planning as an excrescence of minor importance in the work of the Department. It never attained a status at the Ministry comparable with such services as main drainage or sewage disposal. . . .'[3]

We have only touched upon the vital question of compensation, which, in January 1941, an expert committee headed by Mr. Justice Uthwatt was appointed to review. 'Unquestionably the greatest obstacle to really effective planning,' the committee concluded, 'has been the fear on the part of planning authorities of incurring indefinite liabilities in the matter of compensation if the extreme step of forbidding development is taken. . . . An examination of the Town Planning maps of some of our most important built-up areas reveals that in many cases they are little more than photographs of existing users and existing lay-outs, which, to avoid the necessity of paying compensation, become perpetuated by incorporation in a statutory scheme irrespective of their suitability or desirability. . . .'[4] This was the justice behind the Labour Party's claim that the 1909–35

[1] Cmd. 6386, p. 9.   [2] Cmd. 6386, p. 8.
[3] Robson in G. and E. McAllister (eds.), op. cit., p. 145. Cf. his even more impassioned attack upon the Ministry in his *The War and the Planning Outlook* (London, 1941): 'It is impossible to over-estimate the detrimental effect on the planning movement in this country of the timid and negative attitude of the Ministry of Health during the past thirty years. We owe the Ministry of Health little for the services it has performed as the department supposed to be in charge of central planning functions. It has been a drag on the wheel of progress; it has been preoccupied with incredibly trivial details; its capacity for leadership in this sphere has been conspicuous by its absence' (p. 15).
[4] Cmd. 6386, pp. 15, 17–18.

C

planning legislation failed 'chiefly because the Tories had not the courage to stand up to the landowners over the problem of compensation and betterment'.[1]

'Inclination', however, might have been a better word than 'courage'. The Conservative-dominated inter-war Governments were plainly not interested in planning *per se*; on the contrary, they wished to give private enterprise building and industry as free a hand as possible conducive with the broader needs of the nation. Accordingly, planning legislation tended constantly to lag behind the needs which provoked it, or private enterprise kept one jump ahead of public control until its activities became so menacing and the conditions and temper of the nation so changed that the gap was finally closed.

B. 1939 AND AFTER

(a) The Barlow Report

In July 1937, the Prime Minister, Neville Chamberlain, appointed a commission under the chairmanship of Sir Montague Barlow 'to inquire into the causes which have influenced the present geographical distribution of the industrial population of Great Britain and the probable direction of any change in that distribution in the future; to consider what social, economic or strategical disadvantages arise from the concentration of industries or of the industrial population in large towns or in particular areas of the country; and to report what remedial measures if any should be taken in the national interest . . .'.[2] The commission's report, issued December 1939[3] with twenty-six volumes of testimony, was a major Governmental and social document.

The commission declared, 'The concentration of population in the great towns, especially since the Industrial Revolution . . . has been marked by a disastrous harvest of slums, sickness, stunted population and human misery', and asked, 'Are these vast concentrations a necessary feature of our commercial and industrial life from the point of view of economic prosperity?' The answer was 'No'. Industrial concentration generally yielded '(a) proximity to market, (b) reduction of transport costs, (c) availability of a supply of suitable labour'. But these advantages were increasingly accompanied by '(a) heavy charges on account mainly of high site values, (b) loss of time through street traffic congestion in the very large towns . . .

---

[1] *Speakers' Handbook*, 1949–50, p. 377.

[2] Royal Commission on the Distribution of the Industrial Population, *Report*, Cmd. 6153 (London, 1940), pp. vii–viii.

[3] The report was completed in August 1939, but the outbreak of war delayed publication until December 1939.

(c) the risk of adverse effects on efficiency and output on account of the fatigue incurred by workpeople through having to make long daily journeys between home and workplace. . . .' The disadvantages 'may become so serious as to make it economical for some firms to seek new sites at a distance from the centre. That stage has been reached in London and in some other large towns. . . .'[1]

'It is no part of statutory planning, as at present existing, to check or to encourage a local or regional growth of population. Planning is essentially on a local basis; it does not, and was not intended to, influence the geographical distribution of the population as between one locality and another.' To remedy this deficiency, a national planning authority was proposed, to redevelop congested urban areas, disperse industries and population from such areas, and encourage a reasonable balance and diversification of industrial development throughout Britain.[2]

The commission recommended that 'by the well considered development of garden cities, satellite towns and trading estates a useful contribution can be made towards the solution of the problem of relieving overcrowded and congested urban areas . . . .'

'(i) The communities should be as far as possible complete units and placed well outside the existing town so as to enjoy advantages of air and space not possible at the centre or in the immediate suburbs, and they should be protected by a belt of open country so as to avoid eventual coalescence with the existing town.'

'(ii) They should be off the main arterial roads of traffic, but have good access to them, and should be near enough to the big centre to enjoy its advantageous marketing facilities.'

'(iii) They should provide industrial and other occupational opportunities, preferably with reasonable diversification, for a large, if not the greater, proportion of the inhabitants.'

'. . . such development', it noted, 'is not likely to proceed successfully if left entirely to private enterprise, on account, mainly, of the magnitude of the financial commitments involved'; financial assistance by the Government to local authorities was proposed, to encourage them to undertake the job. The minority report recommended formation of a new planning ministry empowered 'to promote, assist or encourage the building of satellite towns . . . by local authorities, public utility companies or other bodies: and to make grants and raise loans for the purpose of acquiring land and building-development values'.[3]

Following this report, the Coalition Government passed the Minister of Town and Country Planning Act, 1943, which trans-

[1] Cmd. 6153, pp. 8, 97, 49.
[2] Cmd. 6153, pp. 104, 201–2.
[3] Cmd. 6153, pp. 136, 133, 136, 223.

THE NEW TOWN IDEA

ferred the planning powers of the Ministries of Health and Works[1]
to a new Ministry 'charged with the duty of securing consistency
and continuity in the framing and execution of a national policy with
respect to the use and development of land . . .'.[2] This constituted,
however, only a fraction of the Barlow Commission's recommendations for a central planning authority with strong powers. For a while
it seemed that, under the pressure of wartime conditions, the
Government would accede to the full demand, but, as it developed,
a National Government with a Conservative preponderancy was unwilling to legislate permanent compulsion on the location of industry
and the use of land. No immediate measures were taken to implement
the commission's recommendations on satellite towns. However, the
Town and Country (Interim Development) Act, 1943, extended
planning control to the whole of England and Wales,[3] and the Town
and Country Planning Act, 1944, conferred upon local planning
authorities 'new and positive powers for the re-development of towns
by means of large-scale public acquisition of land and by securing
that land so acquired is brought into use for its appropriate purpose,
including power for the authority, if need be, *themselves to carry out
any necessary development*'.[4]

(b) The Problems of London

Nowhere in Britain were the problems accompanying urbanization more pronounced than in London. In Whitehall, the City,
Bloomsbury, and the West End the heart of a nation and an empire
beat; in the East End, south of the Thames, in the sooty brick
suburbs that stretched in every conceivable direction to incon-
ceivable distances, its entrails coiled. Speaking in 1891, Lord Rose-
bery, Chairman of the London County Council, had said, 'There is

[1] A new Ministry of Works and Buildings, headed by Lord Reith, was set up
in 1940. In February 1942, under the Minister of Works Act, the Minister of
Works and Building became the Minister of Works and Planning, and inherited
all the functions of the Commissioner of Works, and all those of the Minister
of Health under the Town and Country Planning Act, 1932 (except those exer-
cisable under section 32 of that Act). The Minister of Works and Planning (still
Lord Reith) was instructed by the Government to execute the main recommendations of the Barlow Report.
[2] The Minister of Town and Country Planning Act, 1943, 6 & 7 Geo. VI,
ch. v, 1.
[3] By providing that 'all land not already the subject of a [planning] scheme or
of a resolution to prepare or adopt a scheme would be subject to a resolution
to prepare such a scheme, deemed to have been duly passed by the local
authority' (Beattie, op. cit., p. 550).
[4] Ibid., our italics. More specifically, the act authorized local authorities to
acquire compulsorily and redevelop land in war-damaged areas or land characterized by bad layout and obsolete development, as well as land in adjacent or
'overspill' areas required for use as open spaces or to relocate population and
industry.

no thought of pride associated in my mind with the idea of London. I am always haunted by the awfulness of London: by the great appalling fact of these millions cast down, as it would appear by hazard, on the banks of this noble stream. . . . Sixty years ago . . . Cobbett called it a wen. If it was a wen then, what is it now? A tumour, an elephantiasis sucking into its gorged system half the life and the blood and the bone of the rural districts.'[1] The words reflect the rural leanings of the aristocracy, but are not without truth therefore. Sixty years later again, the coming of motor traffic and a great expansion of the built-up area had made London's problems increasingly intractable.

In the twentieth century, the decline of old heavy industries in northern areas (following Britain's decline from the eminence of world trade with the growth of American, German, and other foreign competition) and the corresponding rise of mobile light industries and corporate and Governmental bureaucracy (that turned an increasing proportion of the nation's manpower into professional and white-collar workers) led to a pronounced shift of population into the London region.[2] The Barlow Commission called attention to 'the vast—and many would add alarming—growth of population in London and South-Eastern England, largely at the expense of the rest of the country'.[3] From 1919 to 1939 'the population of the area covered by the Greater London Plan [a doughnut-shaped area with an outer diameter of 60–70 and an inner diameter of 11–16 miles surrounding the County and City of London] increased by 2,032,400 from 4,084,900 to 6,117,300';[4] since 1921, Greater London was absorbing, on an average, one-third the total increase of national population. The results were 'overcrowding; . . . an increase in land values; the absorption of open spaces; smoke and noise and desola-

[1] Quoted from Howard, op. cit., p. 42.
[2] 'The effect of synthetic developments and of hydro-electric power was to free industry from its old dependence on iron and coal. Industry no longer needed to be strongly localized in areas where natural products occurred, nor to rely wholly on imported raw materials. . . . One result was that new "light industries" were set up in the pleasanter Home Counties, with easy access to the gigantic London market, instead of in the gloomy districts of the industrial north. This drained away population and money from the north, as was sadly apparent in the number of shops to let in the main streets of its big cities' (Robert Graves and Alan Hodge, The Long Week-End (London, 1940), pp. 394–5). '. . . two main groups have taken part in this movement [of population to Greater London]. . . . One, precipitated by the dislocation of the national economic life in the heavy industries of South Wales, the North and North-West, is composed of skilled and unskilled industrial workers. The other, to a smaller extent, is composed of the white-collar workers, clerks, assistants and scientific workers required to conduct the business of commerce and bureaucracy. This last group is increasing at a faster rate than the other' (Patrick Abercrombie, Greater London Plan 1944 (London, 1945), p. 28).
[3] Cmd. 6153, p. 16.　　　　　[4] Abercrombie, p. 27.

tion; traffic congestion and long daily journeys; damage to health and national income from loss of vitality and waste of working hours in sickness and travelling; the burdens of administering palliative services'.[1]

The attempt to control the development of London has a long and dismal history. Already in 1580, 'conditions being such as her Majestie cannot neglect to remedie', Queen Elizabeth had ordered 'all manners of Persons, of what qualities soever they be, to desist and forbeare from any new buildings of any house or tenement within three miles of any of the gates of the said cittie of London'.[2] But, throughout following centuries, little effective control was realized—except by fire and bomb—for what harassed the traveller, distressed the housewife, and injured the child, profited the landowner and admirably suited leaders and followers in Government, industry, and society.

(c) *Abercrombie's* Greater London Plan, *the Reith Committee Reports, and the New Towns Act*

We have already mentioned the failure of several inter-war Government efforts to deal with the London problem. How much greater success will be afforded the *Greater London Plan 1944*, which Professor Patrick Abercrombie prepared for the Minister of Town and Country Planning to guide the future development of the metropolis and its environs, remains to be seen. Abercrombie divided Greater London into four rings—Inner Urban, Suburban, Green Belt, and Outer Country—within which additional industry was to be banned. The Green Belt of open spaces and parks would surround the inner zones, from which 1,033,000 persons were to be dispersed mainly into the Outer Country Ring or beyond. Some 383,250 of this number, together with relocated industry sufficient to employ them, were to be housed in eight new 'satellite towns' to be built in the Outer Ring. Modern standards for the allocation of land, schools, community, and commercial facilities in these towns were outlined; ten possible sites were designated, and a sample plan was presented for a satellite town of 60,000. (See map, p. x.)

The new Labour Minister of Town and Country Planning, Lewis Silkin, appointed on 19th October 1945 a New Towns Committee whose terms of reference were 'To consider the general questions of the establishment, development, organisation and administration that will arise in the promotion of New Towns in furtherance of a

[1] Abercrombie, p. 28. For a gory but well documented account of the economic, social, human and inhuman ills, ailments, and maladies of London, see Robert Sinclair, *Metropolitan Man* (London, 1937).

[2] Quoted in Abercrombie, p. 29. A review of similar futile attempts in subsequent centuries can be found in S. E. Rasmussen, *London: The Unique City* (London, 1937), pp. 63–75.

policy of planned decentralization from congested urban areas; and in accordance therewith to suggest guiding principles on which such Towns should be established and developed as self-contained and balanced communities for work and living'.[1] The committee, headed by Lord Reith, set to work energetically in an effort to influence the course of legislation then being drawn up by a triumphant Labour Party, and presented reports in January, April, and July 1946.[2] Public corporations with powers of compulsory purchase and financed by the Exchequer were proposed as, in general, the most suitable agency for planning and building New Towns,[3] all of whose lands they would eventually own. Industry and population from congested areas would be systematically decamped to these towns, sited at least twenty-five miles from the centre of London (ten or fifteen miles from other cities) to ensure that they became self-contained, yet near enough to induce industrialists and workers to move. A maximum population of 30,000 to 60,000 was set, and each town would be surrounded by a protective belt of agricultural land in which further construction would be prohibited. The goal was a balanced community enjoying the latest architectural and engineering standards of layout, landscaping, communications, utilities, industry, shops, schools, and housing. 'Our responsibility', the committee stated, 'is . . . to conduct an essay in civilisation, by seizing an opportunity to design, evolve and carry into execution for the benefit of coming generations the means for a happy and gracious way of life.'[4]

On 5th March 1946, the Minister of Town and Country Planning, in a statement to the House of Commons, indicated the Government's formal acceptance of 'the main principles underlying the Greater London Plan'—the division of Greater London into four Rings and the planned decentralization of 'a million persons and . . . a related quota of industrial firms . . . mainly in a few new towns and in selected existing towns within 20 to 50 miles of London's centre'.[5] And, on March 12th, he announced that

'the Government propose that an immediate start should be made with the development of a satellite town at Stevenage. To this end my Department, in collaboration with other Departments and the local authorities affected, are already taking the necessary preparatory steps under my existing powers for the acquisition of the land required, the provision of

---

[1] New Towns Committee, *Final Report*, Cmd. 6876 (London, 1946), p. 2.

[2] Published as *Interim Report of the New Towns Committee*, Cmd. 6759; *Second Interim Report*, Cmd. 6794; and *Final Report*, Cmd. 6876.

[3] In particular cases the Committee felt that provision should be made for local authorities and authorized associations to build new towns, but it opposed the employment of private enterprise or housing associations (Cmd. 6759, pp. 9–10).

[4] Cmd. 6759, p. 4.   [5] *Hansard*, 5th March 1946, vol. 420, cols. 189–92.

public services and the preparation of layout plans. . . . For the full development of the town, further powers are needed and the necessary legislation will be introduced as soon as possible.'[1]

The New Towns Act (1st August 1946) provided most of the machinery that the Reith Committee deemed necessary for the implementation of its proposals. (The most significant omission, to which some later difficulties may perhaps be attributed, was the failure to create a Central Advisory Commission to supervise and co-ordinate the work of New Town Corporations.) It authorized the Minister of Town and Country Planning to establish development corporations to plan and build New Towns in designated areas. '. . . every such corporation shall have power to acquire, hold, manage and dispose of land and other property, to carry out building and other operations, to provide water, electricity, gas, sewerage and other services, to carry on any business or undertaking in or for the purposes of the new town, and generally to do anything necessary or expedient for the purposes of the new town. . . .'[2]

The first New Town Designation Order, for Stevenage, Hertfordshire, was issued by the Minister of Town and Country Planning on 11th November 1946, and by December 1949 eight New Towns had been designated and Development Corporations established in the Greater London area (Basildon, Bracknell, Crawley, Harlow, Hemel Hempstead, Stevenage, Welwyn Garden City, and Hatfield), six in other parts of Britain (Peterlee and Newton Aycliffe in Durham, Corby in Northamptonshire, Cwmbran in Wales, and East Kilbride and Glenrothes in Scotland) and additional sites had been proposed. By April 1950, all New Town Corporations in the London region had drawn up development plans and construction had begun on some sites, but progress had been delayed by a number of causes, chiefly the capital restrictions imposed by the Government in consequence of the country's economic crisis.

C. WHY THE GOVERNMENT ENDORSED DECENTRALIZATION

Clearly, the years of the Second World War brought a marked change in the Government's determination to deal with the problems of urban planning, with which the building of garden cities had become associated. In part, this was a natural consequence of pre-war developments and, in part, of circumstances created by the war. The prolonged depression of the 1930's, particularly acute in the mining and industrial sections of the North and Midlands, necessitated some Government action. 'It never occurred seriously to

[1] *Hansard*, 12th March 1946, vol. 420, col. 198 (written answers).
[2] New Towns Act, 1946, 9 & 10 Geo. VI, ch. 68, 2 (2)

anyone that there should be national control of the location of industry till the inter-war years. Then the continuing serious unemployment and distress to the depressed areas became a matter of public concern.'[1] The corresponding development of 'foot-loose' light industries both facilitated the possibility of industrial relocation and aggravated the problems of established urban areas. However, the Conservative Party, which dominated Parliament,[2] was unwilling to exercise compulsion upon the location of industry,[3] or to take radical planning measures whose effect would be to depreciate the value of urban real estate.

(a) The Impact of the War

In 1939, war brought first the threat and then the reality of German aerial bombing, and urban decentralization became an urgent military necessity. The Barlow Report, prepared just before the outbreak of war, contained a chapter on 'The Nature and Extent of the Air Risk' in which it was noted that

'London, by reason of its size and accessibility from the Continent, is an immense liability from the defence point of view. . . . The disadvantages of the density of the population in the East End . . . would diminish if the population were dispersed into properly planned smaller centres separated from one another by belts of open country. . . . A policy of decentralisation or dispersal of industry from overcrowded areas is definitely to be recommended on strategical grounds: of this there can be no question. . . .'[4]

But, Osborn contends, the Barlow and previous Government reports 'might as well have been written in Sanskrit for all their effect on the minds of the public or the sectional planners. What made this country planning-conscious was the bombing of our cities in 1940–1. This let in daylight in a double sense.'[5] Purdom goes so far as to maintain that the policy of building New Towns 'was accepted by Parliament (though nothing was said to admit it) because it was a necessary preparation for the coming [third] war. Only by spreading

[1] E. D. Simon, Rebuilding Britain (London, 1945), p. 180.

[2] Coalitions of various parties held office throughout most of the inter-war period, but, except for 1929–31, when they yielded first place to Labour, the Conservatives were the strongest party and generally held a decisive majority of seats in Parliament.

[3] E.g., on 18th November 1936, Runciman, President of the Board of Trade, told Commons that the Government sympathized with efforts to prevent further industrial concentration around London, but could not accept the principle of compulsory location. 'I do not think we can consent to any proposal which would mean that you were to take a factory owner or a works manager and compel him to put down his industry in such area as we like' (Hansard, vol. 317 col. 1859).

[4] Cmd. 6153, pp. 99, 103.   [5] Osborn, Green-Belt Cities, p. 47.

people and industry could there be the slightest chance of this country surviving under attack by the new forms of aerial warfare.'[1]

The truth was probably less foresighted. In his *Greater London Plan*, Abercrombie stated that 'strategic considerations related to national defence will not be dominant factors in the post-war planning of the Region, either as regards types of industry, the size of industrial concentrations, their relationships to industrial populations, or the use and development of London as a great port'.[2] And we have heard two well-informed officials independently argue that defence had less influence upon the passage of the New Towns Act than might be supposed. One declared that the Act was adopted by the Labour Party mainly for political reasons, during the post-war flush of social change. The other said this was untrue—the Government's wish to implement the Greater London Plan 'was much more responsible and Abercrombie is a Tory'—but agreed that military considerations had little to do with the matter: Abercrombie's plan 'was for the 20th century not the 21st and you can't change London overmuch in 20–50 years or move the port'.

To the extent that the war resulted in the extensive destruction of urban areas; the extensive evacuation of persons, industries, banks, Government departments, valuables, etc. from these areas;[3] and the establishment of a Government apparatus to control these movements; it obviously created physical conditions favourable to a national planning programme. But beyond these physical factors lay a less tangible factor of incalculable importance—'the moral and psychological need for something to which the nation can look forward, an ideal to sustain it through the days of privation, endurance, sacrifice and suffering', was how William Robson put it in 1941. 'Hitler's bombers have transformed [planning] . . . from a Utopian dream to a necessity.'[4]

(b) The Labour Victory

The building of satellite towns in the London region had been a Labour Party policy since 1918, but, although Labour held a clear majority on the London County Council after 1934, 'it was impossible to get the . . . Council to take action'.[5] This failure has been ascribed to the division of planning powers 'between the L.C.C., the City of London and 77 separate town planning authorities, who agreed on only one thing: that nothing should be done to plan the

---

[1] Purdom, op. cit., pp. 377–8.   [2] Abercrombie, p. 38.
[3] At the outbreak of war several hundred organizations with at least 200,000 employees were removed from London (The National Council of Social Service, *Dispersal* (London, 1944), p. 12).
[4] William Robson, *The War and the Planning Outlook* (London, 1941), pp. 7, 12.
[5] Purdom, p. 47.

metropolis either as a whole or even piecemeal. . . .'[1] The gulf between local and national power was bridged by the Labour Government which took office in July 1945 with an overwhelming parliamentary majority, opened the first session of the House of Commons by singing 'The Red Flag', and proceeded to nationalize the Bank of England, coal, gas, and electricity, airlines, railways, and medical services. This Government had little (initial) hesitancy about offending private interests, and it had the strength and the will to effect (or, at least, inaugurate) its programme. It was aided by lingering war-time controls on manpower and materials, as Abercrombie noted:

'The present is a unique time for a bold [planning] policy to be initiated by Parliament. Never before has industry experienced a control so far-reaching over place and methods of work. Never before has there been direction of labour on a comparable scale. Never before has the possi-bility of choosing a new location been denied to management and to operatives alike. At the present moment the building industry acts only under direct Governmental licence; there is no room for individual choice in the erection of factories or of new housing accommodation. The machinery, therefore, is created; it has in fact functioned over a period of years.'[2]

For years planners had preached their gospel to a few converts, with limited political effectiveness; after the Labour victory of 1945, planners and politicians were temporarily united.

Finally, Labour enacted the Town and Country Planning Act (August 1947) to climax a century of planning legislation. We can-not discuss fully this highly important but complex and difficult measure. ('It's a complicated Act,' said one Stevenage informant required to be familiar with its provisions, 'and it's not understood by people who should know about it, like myself, much less by others.' The difficulties 'arise because of our complicated system of land tenure', the Minister of Town and Country Planning explained. '. . . superimposing this Act on our existing system of land tenure involved a good deal of complicated and technical provisions in the Act which are essential and which I very much regret . . . but which I cannot help'.)[3] Its most important provisions were undoubtedly the attempt to solve the problems of compensation (by providing that a sum of £300,000,000 be apportioned to landowners adversely affected by planning prohibitions against the development of their land) and betterment (by imposing upon owners changing the use of their land a charge, payable to the State, equalling the amount by

[1] William Robson, in Ian McCallum (ed.), *Physical Planning* (London, 1945), p. 51.
[2] Abercrombie, p. 187.
[3] Lewis Silkin, address reported in Town and Country Planning Summer School 1949, *Report of Proceedings* (London, 1949), p. 11.

which the value of the land would be increased by development). Local authorities were required to prepare overall plans (reviewable by the Ministry of Town and Country Planning) and revise them every five years, in accordance with which all development was to be licensed. The Conservative Party opposed the Act at every stage of its passage through Parliament, objecting to the 'manifest inadequacy' of the sum provided for compensation; and claimed subsequently that the Act was 'a serious hindrance to housing and all development'.[1] The Act has by no means proved popular among all sections of the Labour Party. It did, however, at last grapple with, if it did not overcome, the basic problem of compensation and betterment that previous planning statutes had, to varying degrees, evaded and which had, in turn, frustrated them:[2]

'town planning had almost broken down before the Act because of the detrimental effect of having to pay compensation whenever an application for permission to develop was refused: and . . . it was becoming increasingly difficult for local authorities to refuse applications for development, even when they were quite satisfied that it was against the public interest, because by so refusing they might have become involved in exceedingly heavy claims for compensation on the part of the owner. . . . The purpose of the 1947 Act . . . was to remove these . . . detriments to good planning so that local planning authorities could consider the development of their areas free from the bogy of having to pay compensation.'[3]

(For an additional discussion of this Act, see Chapter V, pp. 143 ff.)

(c) The Sociology and Economics of Government Housing

Finally, some comments on the recent housing situation in Britain may make the New Towns Act more intelligible. Before the First World War, almost all housing had been provided by private enterprise,[4] but building virtually ceased during that war, precipitating a severe shortage that Lloyd George's Government, which blithely

---

[1] The Campaign Guide General Election 1950, p. 491; and The Conservative Party, The Right Road for Britain (London, 1949), p. 38.

[2] Previous Acts had paid increasing attention to the problem, attempting to reduce the frequency and amount of claims for compensation against a local authority for loss of value, and to increase the amount of betterment which a local authority could claim from an owner, as a result of a planning scheme. But their provisions had not been sufficiently comprehensive or successful (Cmd. 6386, pp. 93 ff. and 106 ff.).

[3] Lewis Silkin, address reported in Town and Country Planning Summer School 1949, op. cit., pp. 12–13.

[4] Although local authorities had been empowered to build working-class houses since 1851, only 11,000 or 5½ per cent of the 200,000 houses built in England and Wales from 1909 to 1915 were built by local authorities (Report of the Private Enterprise Sub-Committee of the Central Housing Advisory Committee of the Ministry of Health, Private Enterprise Housing (London, 1944), p. 5).

promised returning soldiers 'homes fit for heroes', vainly sought to remedy. Costs soared so high that the bulk of the public was priced out of the market,[1] and speculative builders would not risk building.[2] The situation was especially serious in regard to working-class accommodations, whose minimum standards had been raised by law and which had to let at small weekly rentals. The Government's only recourse was to subsidize the building of houses by local authorities. As costs declined in ensuing years, private builders recommenced operations, but never again did they satisfy the bulk of the working-class demand. Table I tells the story.

TABLE I[3]

HOUSES BUILT IN BRITAIN, JANUARY 1919–1937

Type*	Number	Built by Private Enterprise	Built by Local Government
Middle-class houses	1,800,000	1,800,000	—
Working-class houses	1,500,000	550,000	950,000

* A working-class house is 'a house with a rateable value up to £13 in the provinces and up to £20 in the Administrative County of London'.[4]

From 1919 to 1937, almost two-thirds of working-class houses were built by local authorities subsidized by the Government; to new housing for the poorest classes, speculative builders no longer made the major contribution.[5]

These trends were accentuated by the Second World War and the return of Labour to power in 1945. Again war brought cessation of

[1] 'In July 1919, building costs were practically 200 per cent above pre-war costs (as compared with an increase of 110 per cent in the general cost of living) and they continued to rise' (*The Campaign Guide General Election* 1950, p. 452).

[2] 'The speculative builder can only build . . . where he is confident that he will be able to sell his houses at a profit . . . . in the boom of 1920 there was no speculative building because the cost of building was so high the builder had no confidence in finding purchasers at a profit. Conditions gradually improved, but it was not till about 1930 that they became really stable, so that the builder felt confident that he could invest money on a substantial scale in house-building and that there would be a reliable market for the houses at a reasonable profit' (E. D. Simon, *Rebuilding Britain* (London, 1945), p. 77).

[3] Reproduced from Simon, op. cit., p. 86.   [4] Simon, op. cit., p. 235.

[5] The total number of houses built by private enterprise between the two wars was still, however, greater than the number built by local authorities. From 1st January 1919 to 30th September 1939, of some 4,105,139 houses built in England and Wales 1,137,036 or 27·7 per cent were built by local authorities, 431,678 or 10·5 per cent were built by private enterprise with State financial aid, and 2,536,425 or 61·8 per cent by unaided private enterprise (F. J. Osborn (ed.), *Planning and Construction* (London, 1948)).

normal building;[1] again a serious shortage developed, aggravated now by extensive destruction from enemy action;[2] and again prices soared.[3] In the post-war period, housing was probably the single most urgent domestic question facing political parties and the nation.[4] Labour policy catered primarily to the working and lower-middle classes, glad to be housed in flats and houses owned and rented by local authorities. From August 1947 to June 1948, all private house construction was stopped, and subsequently the proportion of one private enterprise house to every four local authority houses was set. From 1st April 1945 to 31st December 1950, local authorities built 635,095 new permanent houses and flats in Britain, and private builders only 125,372.[5]

The New Towns Act, then, fitted into a strong tradition of Government-aided housing. During the First World War, a Liberal Government introduced rent controls that endured, in diminishing measure, through two decades of peace, and were reimposed with full stringency in 1939.[6] The Government also regulated the building industry after 1939 by means of licences required for all construction and repairs, price control and priority distribution of materials, and control over the wages and mobility of labour.

The participation of Government in housing was, of course, a political question—in general, Conservatives encouraged private

---

[1] 'Only 200,000 new houses were completed between 1939 and 1945' (*Speakers' Handbook* 1949–50, p. 357).

[2] Some 225,000 houses were destroyed, another 250,000 rendered uninhabitable, and 775,000 damaged by enemy action in Great Britain during World War II (*The Campaign Guide General Election* 1950, p. 463).

[3] 'Whereas the tax-free income per head of the average British citizen increased by 66 per cent between 1938 and 1947, building costs increased by 140 per cent in the same period, thus far outpacing the rise in family income' (*The Campaign Guide General Election* 1950, p. 475).

[4] An analysis of the 1945 General Election showed that 97 per cent of Labour and 94 per cent of Conservative candidates raised the housing question in their election addresses. 'Throughout the country no other question, not even the Japanese War . . . nor foreign policy . . . is treated so generally' (R. B. McCallum and Alison Readman, *The British General Election of 1945* (London, 1947), p. 96). In 1949, housing remained the principal problem which inquiring citizens brought to the 540 Citizens' Advice Bureaux throughout the nation ('Citizens' Advice Bureaux', *The Times*, 14th November 1949).

[5] To the total of 821,518 new permanent houses and flats built in this period in England, Wales, and Scotland, may be added 157,146 temporary houses provided almost exclusively by local authorities. Conversions, repairs to war damaged buildings, etc., brought the total number of dwelling units provided to 1,312,660 (Ministry of Local Government and Planning, *Housing Return for England and Wales, 31st December* 1950, Cmd. 8138 (London, 1951), p. 3).

[6] 'In 1923, 98 per cent of the country's houses were controlled; in 1931, 70 per cent; in 1937, 44 per cent; and in 1938, 25 per cent. In 1939, the outbreak of . . . war brought practically all decontrolled houses back into the net of control' (*The Campaign Guide General Election* 1950, p. 480).

building and ownership while Socialists preferred local government ownership. But it was also a social and economic question. Unlike the middle classes, the working classes had no capital to invest in the purchase of a home, and their wages did not suffice to pay the instalments on a home-purchase scheme (or they were not sufficiently enthusiastic about home ownership to dispose of their wages in this way). Either they had to be housed in sub-standard slums, which public morality and social (and political) expediency would no longer approve, or the Government must finance at least the difference between an economic rental and the rent a worker could afford. In effect, twentieth-century housing was becoming another service, like free education, unemployment benefits, or old age pensions, which society provided its workers the better to ensure its own stability.[1]

As the Government subsidized housing, the burden upon the Treasury grew. The Barlow Report noted that 'rehousing in flats on central sites imposed a much higher charge on public funds than rehousing in cottages on suburban sites'. In 1939, the Exchequer subsidy on inexpensive sites amounted to £5 10s. per dwelling per annum for forty years, compared to £26 per flat for an equivalent period on central urban sites.[2] The cost of land in central urban areas was, of course, much higher than in suburban areas, and higher in suburbs than in the open country.

'For instance, the cost of the land at Stevenage [New Town] may be of the order of £500,000, whereas if the proposed population were housed on the outskirts of London, the land might cost £2 million to £3 million, or if in the centre of London, in flats, many times that figure. . . .'[3]

Although the New Towns policy, therefore, combined idealism with practical long-range economics, its short-range economics were not so favourable, because of the large initial outlay required for the preparation of roads and basic services in a rural area—a factor which was to operate against New Towns when the Treasury curtailed capital investments in 1947. All in all, the cost of rehousing the same population in an established urban area or a New Town was probably roughly equivalent.

[1] Cf. Catherine Bauer, 'The right to live in a decent dwelling has taken its place among the "national minima"—the right to good and abundant water, to sanitation, to adequate fire and police protection, to the use of paved and lighted roads, to education, to a certain amount of medical care, and . . . to various forms of social insurance'. She estimates that 70 per cent of the housing built in ten European nations (excluding Russia) from 1919 to 1932 was built with some form of State financial aid (*Modern Housing* (London, 1935), pp. 129, 126–7).

[2] Cmd. 6153, pp. 85, 72.

[3] The Minister of Town and Country Planning, *Hansard*, 8th May 1946, vol. 422, col. 1083.

'The investment in the new towns must not be regarded as an addition to the aggregate of national expenditure on rebuilding, but as an alternative distribution of part of it. A variety of agencies, public, public utility, and private, would in either case be spending money on new development and rebuilding on a commensurate scale. To a large extent the nation will be spending [on New Towns] outside congested areas money otherwise spent, possibly to less good purpose, within them. The task is to allocate in the most efficient and socially useful manner an investment which is, in one way or another, inevitable.'[1]

(d) Opposition to Decentralization

The New Towns Act was not adopted without serious opposition from both urban and agricultural interests who may yet force substantial changes in the programme. Urban landowners, industrialists, and others who stood to gain by preservation of existing urban concentrations were joined by architects, planners, and intellectuals of diverse social origin and politics who may be called 'ideologists of the city'. In their minds, the giant city was the natural and vital expression of twentieth-century life and economy:

'It [is] . . . high time someone . . . pointed out to "decanters" and "decentralisers" that they are "doing a Canute", and a tide of human determination may soon drown them. . . . Planners have, since Ebenezer Howard's day, tended to assume that both the demand for city life and the form it has taken are "menaces". . . . Now the demand for city life is reasonable: a great city like London offers a thousand attractions quite unobtainable elsewhere, and by no means all pernicious. Large numbers of people have shown that they will not be satisfied with anything else, and any attempt to foist them off with life in a town relatively inaccessible to the larger cities will inevitably dissatisfy them and is therefore foredoomed to failure.'[2]

'. . . The world-wide trend towards . . . urban as opposed to rural life [is] . . . not due to whim or perversity, but to the shift of occupations that goes with a rising standard of living. A majority of services are most efficiently rendered in centres where there are a very large number of clients: the demand that industry makes for services, especially for first-class transport as well as for numberless grades of labour, is also most easily met in the great cities. For the young, in fact, who are seeking a career, it is in the great cities that most frequently "opportunity knocks".'[3]

[1] Cmd. 6794, p. 13. Cf. T. H. Sheepshanks and G. H. Henderson (Accounting Officers, Ministry of Town and Country Planning), 'If the development were not undertaken in new towns it would have to be undertaken elsewhere and accordingly there will normally, although not always, be no substantial increase in cost as a result of concentrating the development in new towns: and there will be cases where the new town method of providing what is needed will in the long run be demonstrably the cheapest' (New Towns Act, 1946, *Accounts* 1949–50 (London, 1951), p. 6).

[2] Peter Peck, letter in *The Listener*, 4th May 1950, p. 789.

[3] E. G. R. Taylor, 'The Menace of Monstrous Cities', *The Listener*, 20th April 1950, p. 695.

Planners of this persuasion, who wanted to build flats and improve communications and other services in urban areas, regarded the garden city movement as a retrograde and futile effort to restore a vanished era or, with sardonic tolerance, as a luxury the nation could afford only on a small scale. The *status quo* was on their side, and they won victory after victory as hundreds of houses and factories went up in established urban centres throughout Britain to every one in a New Town.

The ideologists of the city were supported by ideologists of the countryside who, for all the indignant disclaimers of garden city enthusiasts, viewed New Towns as merely another form of urban sprawl. In Great Britain between 1927 and 1939, 'about 60,000 acres of agricultural land were lost each year to buildings and other developments',[1] and the number of persons engaged in agriculture declined from 1,949,000 in 1861 to 1,091,000 in 1948.[2] Rural interests protested that New Towns consumed more land than rehousing an equivalent population in urban areas and, by making higher paying jobs available nearby, would drain labour from the farms. At both Welwyn Garden City and Letchworth, farmers had opposed the garden city; and the Barlow Commission reported that

'the Ministry of Agriculture express a preference for the fringe extension of existing industrial towns on the ground that the building of satellite towns would probably take more good ground from agriculture and would absorb into industry existing agricultural labour over a wide radius instead of taking the existing unemployed from the towns.'[3]

The Barlow Commission had focused attention upon industrial and urban concentrations. To counterbalance this, the Committee on Land Utilisation in Rural Areas, headed by Lord Justice Scott, was appointed in October 1941 by Lord Reith, then Minister of Works and Building, to consider 'the effects upon agriculture of the de-centralisation and dispersal of industry and population' recom-mended by the Commission, and 'the conditions to be enforced for the protection of agriculture'.[4] In its report issued in 1942, the com-mittee blew hot about preserving agricultural land and improving rural amenities and cold about relocating industry in the countryside.

These arguments and forces persisted after the war, and proved particularly embarrassing to planners who cherished the countryside in true English fashion, and a Government which curried favour from farmers—indeed, all parties now felt that the national welfare necessitated cultivation of the maximum possible acreage. L. Dudley

---

[1] *Speakers' Handbook* 1949–50, p. 379. L. Dudley Stamp estimated that 50,000 acres of agricultural land were lost to development in 1946–8 (letter, *The Times*, 3rd May 1949).
[2] Cmd. 6153, p. 96, and *The Campaign Guide General Election* 1950, p. 207.
[3] Cmd. 6153, p. 14.   [4] Cmd. 6378, p. iv.

Stamp, Director of the Land Utilisation Survey of Britain and prominent exponent of agricultural interests, protested that

'In present town-planning policy I sense an obsession with space. Spacious living is not necessarily gracious living. . . . Not a single one of the proposed new towns ventures away from a lowland agricultural site. . . . I am not convinced that our descendants will appreciate having been provided with "new towns to starve in".'[1]

Gordon Stephenson replied 'we should all be pressing for intense building activity in carefully selected new towns and for less in suburbs—this, more than anything else . . . will give the greatest protection to the agricultural interest';[2] while the Minister of Town and Country Planning remarked that critics of New Towns 'had not yet discovered how, with 1,500,000 more people to provide for in the increase of population in the last 10 years, they could give people more room in which to live, and more convenient and comfortable places, without using up more land'.[3]

These continuing disputes would be settled not in the ideological, but in the political—or, more likely, the economic—arena.

[1] Letter to *The Times*, 3rd May 1949.   [2] Ibid., 24th May 1949.
[3] Address to Town Planning Institute reported in *The Times*, 3rd November 1949.

CHAPTER TWO

Stevenage
A Backward Glance

A. PRE-NINETEENTH CENTURY

H ISTORY is a bottomless sea, and sea upon sea has welled
over Stevenage.
Paleolithic flake implements are sparsely distributed
throughout Hertfordshire and an important find has been made a
few miles north of town. The open downs to the north are presumed
to have been more suited to the agriculture and pasturage of neo-
lithic man than the wooded southerly lowlands; and again in the
Iron Age, the former sites show full indications of occupation—at
Hitchin and Letchworth, for instance—while Stevenage apparently
remained fairly densely wooded and uninhabited till Saxon times.
The most notable local antiquity, six barrows which line the road at
its southern exit from town, have been broken into so often that
they are now more useful to the children who play King of the Castle
upon them than to the serious archaeologist; they are taken to be
Roman or possibly Danish burial mounds. If Roman, the present
Great North Road may lie on the line of a secondary Roman road,
but the main Roman route linking St. Albans with York ran to the
west of Stevenage (parts showed up in aerial photos taken for the
Development Corporation).[1] Twelve miles to the south-west, Verulam, near the modern St. Albans, was the chief Roman town in
Herts; receiving municipal status in A.D. 62 and still inhabited in the
fifth century, its buildings, Roman theatre, and forum, surrounded

---

[1] According to the Stevenage Development Corporation, *Stevenage New Town
Technical Report*, July 1949, the route from St. Albans to York passed through
Graveley, a mile and a half north of Stevenage.

by town walls, covered two miles in circumference. At this period, 'The influence of London has not yet begun. The forests which lay round the north of London have not yet been pierced. Verulam is an independent town, not . . . an annexe of the capital, and the country houses and farms around it are rural dwellings.'[1]

In the sixth century, a few thatched huts probably stood near the present church; in the eighth, Stevenage came temporarily under Danish control. About 1060, Edward the Confessor gave a large plot of land in the region of the church to the monastery of St. Peter at Westminster, and 'a small establishment of monks was kept there, who saw to the production and dispatch of vegetables to the parent institutions'.[2] The monastery retained possession until the Dissolution, when the land came to the Crown which soon transferred it to the Bishops of London; in 1868, the Ecclesiastical Commissioners, present Lords of the Manor, received possession.

The oldest stones in the parish church, which stands on high ground half a mile north-east of the town, belong to the early twelfth century. 'The church used to be in the town,' an eleven-year-old boy writes in a school essay, 'but somehow or other it has got away from Stevenage.' Considerable speculation attaches to how the feat was accomplished. Legend says that when the church stood in the village, 'it there attracted so many worshippers that the devil, in a pet, snatched it from its foundations, and poised it on an inconvenient knoll. . . .'[3] Saxon settlements kept off the road for protection and it is not uncommon for Hertfordshire churches to lie a short distance from the village—'This arrangement originated probably at the time when the Lord of the settlement built the church on the demesne land which surrounded his dwelling. . . .'[4] In 1281, the Abbot of Westminster was granted a licence to establish a market on the fork of the main road, and by the fourteenth century London merchants with money to invest had already begun to buy property in Stevenage. 'As the traffic through the main roads increased, inns and houses sprang up along the road frontage. . . .'[5] Fire and plague have also been adduced as motives for the town's move from the old site by the church and, at the New Town inquiry of October 1946, a farmer pointed out that the development of Stevenage 'had mainly taken place in the lower ground sheltered from the north and north-east winds' which blow in winter and early spring across the flat country from the North Sea to the high land by the church.

At least from the medieval period, the economy of Stevenage was

---

[1] Royal Commission on Historical Monuments (England), *An Inventory of the Historical Monuments in Hertfordshire* (London, 1910), pp. 3–5.
[2] *Stevenage New Town Technical Report*, op. cit., p. 5.
[3] E. M. Forster, *Howard's End* (London, 1945), p. 265.
[4] Royal Commission on Historical Monuments, op. cit., p. 7.   [5] Ibid.

evidently bound to that of London, which provided a market for its cash crops, a clientele of travellers for its shops and services, and a steady stream of settlers. These features have remained basically unaltered unto the present day, although the extent and nature of the trade and the type of migrant have, of course, constantly changed.

The fine Roman roads fell into such disrepair in subsequent centuries that wheeled traffic became almost impossible. A presentment of 1658 declares that the highway from Stevenage to Baldock is in 'great decay.... the inhabitants of Baldock ought to repair the same'.[1] The state of the roads and the absence of a national police force encouraged highwaymen, and it is at this period that a Stevenage native enjoyed his notorious but brief career, ended on the gallows in December 1694. The Turnpike Act of 1663 required large landowners to provide tools and the labour of two men six days a year for the upkeep of the roads. As commerce revived and fast stage-coaches replaced the earlier heavy wagons with broad-rimmed wheels, Stevenage became an accepted stop on the London route—between 1820 and 1840, twenty coaches daily ran through town. The High Street still gives evidence of this traffic in the large number of inns where victuals and rest were available to travellers and where fresh horses were provided for the coaches which parked along its great breadth.

B. NINETEENTH CENTURY

By 1801 the village had assumed the proportions of its modern shopping centre, stretching half a mile along both sides of the highway from the fork at the north. It had a population of 1,254 (607 males, 647 females, 285 families) and 258 houses—'by far the greater part . . . were covered with thatch and received their light through small leaden casements'.[2] Fires in 1807 and 1829 destroyed much of this housing, so that few older buildings survive.

A considerable middle class of innkeepers and traders had already developed. The 1801 census lists 229 persons as 'maintained chiefly by agriculture' as against 101 'tradesmen, artizans, etc.' and the latter figure rises steadily thereafter while the proportion of the former declines. Even before the railway came in the middle of the century, professional and business people were commuting to London several days a week by coach or trap. But leaders of local society persisted in thinking of the village as almost exclusively agricultural, and throughout the nineteenth century the rector's memorandum book measures the town's prosperity in such terms:

[1] Hertford County Records, *Notes and Extracts from the Sessions Rolls 1581 to 1698* (Hertford, 1905), vol. i, p. 126.
[2] E. V. Methold, *Notes on Stevenage and Baldock* (St. Albans, 1884?).

'1853. The harvest of this year was deficient. . . . The winter of 53 & 4 was very severe & provisions being at a high price much suffering was caused to the poor.

'1854. The price of corn in the first half of this year rose to 76s. per quarter. . . . The harvest of this year was one of extraordinary abundance. A great part of the wheat land of the Parish was said to produce from 35 to 45 bushels per acre, and other cereal crops were equally large.

'1865. In the Autumn of this year the Cattle Plague appeared & spread gradually thro the kingdom. . . . A day of humiliation and prayer tho not ordered by the Queen was generally observed. . . . In this Parish . . . on Sunday Mar. 16. Churches crowded with attentive congregations.'

To the native agricultural stock was added the London business man who sought, in proportion to his means, to emulate the life of the landed gentry. E. R. Roper-Power writes of the county seat, Hertford, that 'The gently undulating character of the surrounding countryside, together with its proximity to London, have made it a favourite site for the parks and estates of successful merchants for more than three centuries. Its somewhat studied rustic appearance has appealed to sophisticate Londoners who, lacking the deep roots of traditional contact with the soil, have sought a compromise in their desire for manorial status.'[1] Much the same is true of the Stevenage environs, except that fewer large holdings developed and no single landowner held sway, as happened elsewhere in Herts (Power suggests that the competition of the London *nouveaux-riches* for land prevented its gradual monopolization). The nearest large estate, in the parish to the south, belonged in the nineteenth and twentieth centuries to the line of a prominent novelist, knighted in 1838 and created a Baron in 1866. The descendants of Lord L. rose to the first eminence in national and empire affairs, and contributed frequent benefactions to Stevenage causes, but were too far removed to exercise that constant tutelage which is the mark and burden of a local Lord of the Manor. Dickens was a good friend of this novelist and visited Stevenage often in connection with an ill-fated project to establish there almshouses for impoverished writers. A neighbouring pub still preserves in its name, Our Mutual Friend, associations with this venture, and in *Tom Tiddler's Ground* Dickens gives us a picture of Stevenage in 1861:

'The village street was like most other village streets: wide for its height, silent for its size, and drowsy in the dullest degree. The quietest little dwellings with the largest of window-shutters (to shut up Nothing as carefully as if it were the Mint, or the Bank of England). . . . a score of weak little lath-and-plaster cabins clung in confusion about the Attorney's red-brick house. . . . Some of the small tradesmen's houses, such as the crockery-shop and the harness-makers, had a Cyclops window in the

[1] E. R. Roper-Power, *The Social Structure of an English County Town* (Hertford, 1937) (Typescript, doctoral dissertation, London University), p. 57.

middle of the gable, within an inch or two of its apex, suggesting that some forlorn rural Prentice must wriggle himself into that apartment horizontally when he retired to rest, after the manner of the worm. So bountiful in its abundance was the surrounding country, and so lean and scant the village, that one might have thought the village had sown and planted everything it once possessed, to convert the same into crops.'[1]

The railway ended the coaching days and put several Stevenage innkeepers out of business. The opposition of local landowners to the railway's coming recalls in many ways the New Town dispute. Engineers and surveyors setting out the lines were often protected by guards, and navvies invaded the village to the dismay of gentlemen and ladies. A prominent squire, a tall, white-haired man of seventy described as 'an eccentric of the old school', was convicted by the Stevenage Bench—of which he was chairman—of assaulting and beating engineers and smashing their instruments. After the railway opened in 1848, the Company brought action against the parish to reduce assessments of £750 per mile, but the case was settled out of court upon the parish's agreement not to increase the rating for three years.

A more amusing but equally instructive episode of a similar nature occurred at the turn of the century when the Urban District Council opposed the setting up of a telephone exchange in Stevenage, prevailing upon twenty of twenty-seven persons who had petitioned for the installation to withdraw their application. A stout-hearted councillor asserted 'it was a great pity to stop business by refusing to have the telephone service. Baldock and Hitchin had it and plenty of places were anxious to get these business connexions.' Opponents countered, 'The majority of the town are against it . . . our beautiful little town is to be spoilt for the benefit of a few subscribers'. At a meeting in June 1905, the Council resolved to inform the Postmaster-General that, as 'no public demand for the service existed in Stevenage', the scheme should be abandoned. One councillor opined that if the matter were postponed long enough the Council might at least succeed in getting the wires put underground. However, when a court notice was served 'to show cause against an order being made enabling the Postmaster-General to instal the telephone along various streets of the town', the Council abruptly acquiesced, asking only that the superintendent engineer 'paint the [telephone] poles . . . white at the bottom and the tops green', a style one councillor had noticed somewhere in his travels and which all agreed would least injure their aesthetic sensibilities.

In 1851, the population had risen to 2,118, although the town remained a compact mass restricted to the High Street except for

[1] 'Tom Tiddler's Ground', in *Christmas Stories* (*The Nonesuch Dickens*, London, 1937, pp. 500–1).

some houses grouped about the church and a few neighbourhood greens. There were still ponds in the High Street and many present-day streets were then open meadow. The town was, however, now in the throes of urban development stimulated by London capital, whose effects were recorded by the rector in his notebook:

'1851. A New Street was partly formed, called Albert Street, & opened this year. It was planned by Mr. [F] who sold the land on each [side] of it in small plots of building purposes.

'1853. . . . A new road or Street was opened leading from the main Street to the Railway. It had been laid out & formed by Mr. [D] at his own cost & was given by him to the Parish as a public road.

'1858. The British Land Co. purchased some fields between Letchmore Green & the Street & laid out a New Street called Albert Street, selling small plots of ground on each side of it to house builders.'

In 1884 a district building society was formed to finance private house construction and provide a profitable outlet for local capital.

By 1901, the population had risen to 3,958 (1,812 males, 2,146 females, 919 houses) and, ten years later, 4,856 or almost four times the 1801 figure. The town had doubled its frontage on the Great North Road, built out into the open country on the east and up to the railway on the west. Despite this boom, a housing shortage prevailed. The parish magazine carried an appeal by the rector. 'I have an excellent and experienced Clergyman ready to come as Curate . . . but I cannot anywhere find a suitable house for a married man with three children."[1] While the Medical Officer reported in 1901:

'The house accommodation for the working classes is below the demand. Working men have either to take a house at a rental they can ill afford or else they have to occupy the older cottages, which though not bad enough to condemn, are both inconvenient and insanitary. . . . The old cottages are not white-washed or cleaned down often enough; there are some which have not had the walls or ceilings white-washed for years. The tenants cannot afford to do it, and are reluctant to put pressure on the landlords as they are afraid that they may be turned out or the rent raised if these necessary repairs are done. Some of the landlords seem to consider their duties begin and end in taking their rent.'[2]

Matters were little changed in 1916, when the surveyor informed the Council 'that 270 houses were provided with dustbins and 830 were without'.[3] The congested living conditions, poor sanitary arrangements, and frequent pollution of water led to outbreaks of typhoid and other preventible diseases. Many older inhabitants remember these days well and mix romance with fact in fond reminiscences. 'It was a lovely little town then,' recalled a retired merchant who came to Stevenage early in 1900. 'Everyone knew everyone. There was an open drain on the High Street; the culvert

[1] *Stevenage Church Magazine*, February 1882.
[2] *Hertfordshire Express*, 8th March 1902.   [3] Ibid., 3rd June 1916.

was bricked over by one merchant and others followed suit, but wagons were always breaking through into the drain and there was no end of trouble. We had policemen, of course, one or two bobbies, water, but nothing like a town hall: we've always been short of public buildings. The roads and footpaths weren't up to the level of a big town.' (He was wrong about the town hall, built in 1872.)

In 1873, the landowners and ratepayers constituted the parish an Urban Sanitary District, the first step in municipal organization under the Local Government Act, 1858; in 1894, the present Urban District Council was formed. The Acts under which these measures were authorized were designed to transfer power in local government from the old Conservative Anglican landowning class, which had formerly dominated the parish councils and judicial benches, to the newly risen bourgeoisie, many of whom were Liberal nonconformists.[1] The Local Board replaced the unsatisfactory wells with a new system of waterworks in 1887, planted trees to beautify the town, and, with county and national help, other improvements were gradually effected—between 1909 and 1916, for instance, a new post office, fire and police stations were built.

These measures were not taken, however, without a bitter political battle between landowners, farmers and their entourage on one side, and merchants, business and professional men on the other. By the 1870s, the latter had grown sufficiently strong to contest the leadership of the landed classes, but were still too weak to unseat them. Battle was joined over the Local Board's sewerage scheme. The leader of the opposition, Mr. D, an engineer of national repute, contended that this scheme (about which he had been pointedly not consulted, despite his offer of free services) was mere windowdressing and quite inadequate to the needs of Stevenage. At a June 1876 inquiry, he charged that

'much the greater majority of the twenty-four members constituting the [Stevenage] Board have a greater interest in land than they have in houses, while some of them live out of the parish though farming land in it, and the effect of this preponderating influence has been an utter absence of any works of sanitary improvement, while the repair of the highways from which the occupiers of land derive benefit have been charged upon the occupiers of houses to the full extent of their rateable value, at the same time that the occupiers of land have been relieved of three-fourths their previous contribution.'

[1] Cf. R. C. K. Ensor's comment about the Local Government Act, 1894, which created urban district councils, following the Local Government Act, 1888, which created the county councils. 'Upon bodies administering so large an area as a county poor men could seldom afford to sit, and the new councils tended to be manned by almost the same class as the old quarter sessions. So there arose . . . a renewed liberal demand for elective parish councils . . .' (*England 1870–1914* (Oxford, 1936), p. 213).

41

(the Local Board consisted of twenty-four members during the first few years of its existence and was thereafter reduced to twelve—the present number on the Urban District Council—at the recommendation of the Local Government Board). When the inquiry went against them, the opposition submitted a memorial to the Local Government Board in London demanding an investigation. A local newspaper editorialized:

'The opponents of the Stevenage Local Board, as it is at present constituted, show a wonderful amount of ingenuity and perseverance in placing obstacles in its path, in perplexing its movements and in bringing it into general disrepute amongst the inhabitants of the town. They impugn its honesty, disparage its officers, dispute its rate, defy the Bench and bring down Government Inspectors in order to compass their ends. In short, their will clearly is to quash the present Board and to re-constitute the Sanitary Authority of the district. . . .

'The residents in the town, it is alleged, wish for a complete system of sewerage and water supply, whilst the inhabitants of the rural portions of the district prefer the *status quo* with shallow and polluted wells and leaky drains. . . . with regard to the . . . Board . . . it will be found . . . that of the twenty-four sixteen actually live in the town, nearly the whole of whom are principally engaged in business distinct from farming. . . . it may be stated that the householders have more than 500 votes, whilst the farmers and occupiers of land in the rural parts of the parish have not more than a hundred.'

The latter argument discounted the great influence which farmers and landowners wielded over the non-agricultural section of the community. A spokesman for the memorialists replied, also, that ' A large proportion of the ratepayers are farm labourers occupying cottages in the town although in the employ of the county farmers. . . . The large majority of voters are farm labourers who are under the influence of their employers the farmers.' This view was supported by the results of the next local election, in April 1877, reported as follows by the rival newspaper:

'. . . it was . . . hoped that instead of continuing so many farmers on the Board . . . the ratepayers would select the practical men of the parish—men who by their education are best fitted for the important work. . . . The result of the election has not verified these hopes, for out of the four candidates elected no less than three are farmers. . . . when we come to dissect the votes we find that the majority are not returned by the "initials" of the inhabitants, but by the extraordinary number of crosses, which in reality means that the uneducated portion of the community [i.e., illiterate farm labourers] have ruled the election.'

The political situation at this time, with the local middle classes in the minority despite their national ascendance, offers parallels with the situation after the Second World War, when the same forces were now in power in Stevenage, with the working classes in the minority despite Labour's national triumph.

C. TWENTIETH CENTURY

It is not, of course, possible to point to any one moment when the Liberal middle classes suddenly triumphed and the gentry acknowledged defeat. But the shift of power from the latter to the former can be detected in a series of gradual developments—the steady rise in value of the built-up part of town while agricultural values fell, the opening of Baptist and Methodist churches in 1857 and 1876, the rise in importance of the Urban District Council and the decline of the Parish Council and, generally, the increased influence of secular bodies in Government, education, and most areas of social life, and the substitution of the legal and economic sanctions which define relations between equals in modern capitalist society for the religious and personal bonds which defined human relations in medieval society and which lingered—and linger—on to a surprising degree in rural England (especially in relations between farmer and labourer, master and servant).[1] For the purpose of this brief history, it may be said that the transition was substantially complete by the end of the First World War, which provided an added leaven to the normal slow ferment of classes. Yet, having said this, it might with equal truth be unsaid, for there are those who argue that economic and political facts do not take adequate count of the measureless grip which the landed aristocracy exerts over English minds and that this grip is never stronger than in defeat, when the erstwhile victors (be they business or labour leaders) don the Nessus shirt of the aristocracy and, try as they may, cannot remove it without mortal cost. So, though by no stretch of the imagination can one find representatives of the landed gentry in Stevenage today and all positions of importance are held by business or professional men, an occasional officer retired from the armed services, farmers, a representative of church or chapel, and, in recent years, men risen from the working classes, the code of the gentleman governs all these men (all do not succeed in emulating it), all honour the King, and His Majesty's peerage is their highest common goal.

[1] 'In many respects . . . [England] is still thoroughly mediaeval. The modern idea that the relations of the millions of human beings must be regulated by law, that there is a communal life above the individual life, that the State has paramount rights over the individual, is much less developed in England than in Germany, France, or any other modern community. The relations between Englishmen are governed, not by written law, not by a constitution or a civil code, but by unwritten tradition. . . . Right down into the nineteenth century, the State was, like the mediaeval State, a mere bundle of private rights and duties' (Wilhelm Dibelius, *England* (London, 1930), p. 487).

In 1919, the rector still spoke of 'the village', an uncertain term for a population of 5,000, but the church, which always represented the 'best' elements of society, naturally preferred to err on the side of caution. The rector discussed the question of mortuary fees thus in the church magazine:

'Personally, I dislike these fees for more reasons than one; they are not understood by people, and they seem to me to be somewhat invidious, and I have been considering how they can be abolished. But I recognise that I am not quite a free agent in the matter. I have no business to give away the rights of my successors. I therefore propose in all cases to return mortuary fees—as a matter of fact they are very few—to those who pay them. I must ask that they should be paid in the first instance. . . .'[1]

E. M. Forster's novel *Howard's End*, first published in 1910, provides an impression of Stevenage during the first decade of the century, as well as a prophecy of its future. 'It's not really the country, and it's not the town,' one character says; and another, '. . . "London's creeping." She pointed over the meadow—over eight or nine meadows—but at the end of them was a red rust.'[2] The roofs of town were stretching out over adjacent farmland: it was a process that could not be stayed, and London was the distant motor. Despite the efforts of its strongest citizens, Stevenage was succumbing to Progress—although Progress came first to London, and then to neighbouring towns (usually Hitchin, three miles north). The newspaper announced in 1910:

'Some excellent animated photographs have been exhibited at the Town Hall [Hitchin] this week by Dr. —— and have given pleasure to large audiences. The pictures are particularly clear and free from flicker, and the subjects varied and up-to-date. . . . The exhibition will be continued throughout next week. . . .'[3]

In 1923, a Hitchin hotel had installed a 'First-class wireless station . . . . the proprietors extend a hearty invitation to all to come and hear the latest news, Bulletins and Concerts broadcasted from Stations hundreds of miles away'.[4] And in 1927 electricity was still a novelty:

SMILES AT BREAKFAST!

'Of course, dozens of them in homes where breakfast is cooked electrically. You can't help being good tempered when you've nothing to grumble about. You sit down in the comforting heat of an electric fire to a meal quickly and efficiently prepared—there are none of those iritating delays that gradually steal the time before the train goes—everything is so

[1] *Stevenage Church Magazine*, January 1917.
[2] Forster, op. cit., pp. 341, 340.
[3] *Hertfordshire Express*, 12th February 1910.   [4] Ibid., 6th January 1923.

very satisfactory. In fact, everything is always just what you want it to be in an electrified home.'[1]

(In 1948, some 32 per cent of Stevenage homes still had no electricity laid on, while scarcely 13 per cent cooked by electricity—most people preferred gas.)[2]

One hundred and twenty-four Stevenage men were killed in the First World War. War brought a small evacuation of Londoners as a result of the Zeppelin raids, and many persons stayed on. 'They thought it was a nice little town, and the rates were low,' the retired merchant said. 'But then they wanted amenities, and they still wanted low rates.' 'In the early twenties,' another resident recounted, 'when there was so much unemployment, the Council got a grant from the Government to put up an avenue west of the railway. The landowners made a neat profit on the deal, as the price of land per foot of frontage went up from thirty shillings to four pounds a foot. They cashed in and got a lot of money.' This was the beginning of Fairview Road, later marked for destruction on the New Town plan. About a hundred semi-detached houses were built here, and perhaps as many elsewhere in town, by private contractors between the wars. Before the First World War there was only one sizable factory in Stevenage. A number of factories now opened, and the Council began building a working-class housing estate on the eastern out-skirts with the aid of Government subsidies. The Housing Act, 1933, cancelled these subsidies, so that, after 330 houses had been completed, the Council stopped construction, although additional roads had been laid.

Throughout the inter-war period (as after), the Council was dominated by Independents who scrutinized all expenditure to ensure that it led to no avoidable increase in rates. E. D. Simon's analysis of the Manchester city council in 1926 would be equally true of Stevenage after a lapse of years:

'Hitherto the councils have been largely dominated by the richer suburban voter, for whom the corporation provides very fully all the services he needs, and whose main interest in the work of the council is therefore to see that the rates are kept low. Power is gradually being transferred to the poorer classes . . . who need all kinds of services they do not now get.'[3]

Before the First World War there was no Labour Party in Stevenage, although trade unions occasionally backed a Council

[1] Advertisement in *Stevenage Church Magazine*, December 1927.
[2] According to a survey of 961 houses in Stevenage conducted by the Development Corporation in the summer of 1948. 'The survey . . . is believed to have included all non-municipal working-class housing and a proportion of middle-class housing.'
[3] E. D. Simon, *A City Council From Within* (London, 1926), p. 104.

candidate and succeeded in having him elected. As a representative
of the working classes the member might be respected and influential, but his influence derived more from the tolerance of other
councillors than from Labour's own power. During the war, local
unions dwindled almost to extinction—in one important union, for
instance, only three members remained as others left for the army or
munitions work. Labour's post-war upsurge was not viewed
favourably by many sections of the community, who felt their
security endangered; students at the Stevenage grammar school
debating, in November 1920, the motion that 'Strikes are justifiable',
rejected it by 28 votes to 8. The Diocese bulletin stated:

'One prophecy may be made for January, 1921, with absolute safety,
that it will be a month of labour unrest. If there are no big strikes actually
in progress they will be threatened. How sick we all get of these endless
labour troubles! . . . [but] what is the Labour Movement? It is the pressing forward of those classes which in the past have had little or no voice
in deciding the affairs of the nation, determined now to have their "place
in the sun". When it was decided to give education to all, and later a vote
to all, the principle of equality was conceded. What is happening now is
a natural consequence of those great decisions.'

Howard's first garden city, Letchworth, five miles to the north,
had long been a strong Labour centre. With the help of supporters
from Letchworth, a branch of the party with about twenty members
was formed in Stevenage in 1922. Between elections, political interest ebbed—upon one occasion, only three persons turned out to
hear a national Labour leader (he was taken on to Hitchin, where he
addressed a crowd of ten). The party had somewhat greater success
at elections, however, and managed to elect a few councillors. The
first Labour councillor won his seat about 1924 or 1925; in 1929, there
were two, and by 1938 four Labour councillors. This ratio of four
Labour to eight Independent councillors was preserved by agreement throughout the Second World War, when elections were
suspended.

'Independents' were mainly Conservatives (that party's policy
being opposed to 'politics' in local government) and usually included a few Liberals as well; but if they voted together it was
generally due to self-interest, the influence of particular members,
and such personal and social pressures as operate in any small town,
more than to a political organization which co-ordinated action and
furnished a common programme. There were always strong-minded
Independents who stuck to their opinions with special relish if these
antagonized the Church, the Conservative Party, or the ratepayers.
Upon occasion a union of such councillors with the Labour opposition achieved a slim majority and the Council might, in the view of
sober business men, get a bit out of hand.

Something of the sort happened in the '30s when the Council decided to build a swimming pool and went so far as to invite tenders for the work. A Ratepayers' Association was formed to combat the proposal. 'People should pay for what they get,' said a Conservative informant reviewing the event.

'I don't like the tendency which is growing of people getting something for nothing. If you belong to a tennis club, you pay a fee to be allowed to use the court, but you don't expect the racket and equipment to be provided free—you provide that yourself. Well, we said Stevenage was too small a town to support a pool—there's one at Hitchin, which the boys and girls use—and it shouldn't add to the rate. Have a pool, all right, if you want one—but make those who want to use it pay for it.'

A Labour informant had a different opinion:

'The Ratepayers' Association was really the Conservative Party in disguise. They called a meeting in the Town Hall once, got all their officers appointed, and then found they didn't have a working man with them. They got in touch with a friend of mine and got him to sit on the platform—wanted to co-opt him chairman. I went to see him afterwards, and told him they were just the Conservative Party, everyone of them belonged to the Party, and he checked up and saw it was so, and I got him to quit. That was the last worker they had with them.'

The Association defeated Labour candidates, electing four of their own who quashed the scheme (and Stevenage has no pool today). A former councillor sighed, 'It became very quarrelsome on the Council then'.

The Second World War had, of course, effects upon many aspects of life in Stevenage, as in every British town, which will endure for generations. Thirty-nine Stevenage men died in the war, but the town itself was spared, although enemy planes sometimes flew over, at least one 'buzz bomb' landed in a nearby field, and 654 air-raid warnings were sounded.[1] A grammar school boy writes, 'The most damage, I believe, was done by the allied troops or rather their vehicles which they parked on the Avenue where they were hidden under the trees, for the surface was not meant for vehicles and consequently deep ruts were made, the grass on either side was torn up and a considerable number of the younger trees broken down'. The Avenue having since been repaired, the sawn-off stumps of iron and steel railings, gates, chains, etc., requisitioned by the Council on behalf of the Minister of Supply, remain the most noticeable scars of war.

While the armed services drained off local manpower, thousands

[1] The air raid count was made in Hitchin (*Hertfordshire Express*, 12th May 1945). Throughout Hertfordshire, some 4,421 bombs from 100 to 4,000 lb., 85 parachute mines, and 30,500 incendiaries fell during the war. There were 2,086 casualties, including 256 deaths (*Hertfordshire Express*, 19th May 1945).

of London evacuees jammed into the town. In 1939 the population was 5,670; December 1940, the number of *civilians* stood at 7,873. A factory bombed out of London moved to Stevenage; a local firm built a new plant in a few weeks; all factories produced at capacity and labour was commandeered to man them. 'As the tempo of the war increased . . . [the town] began to resemble a modern Tower of Babel, with a floating population of soldiers, sailors, airmen, industrial workers, Indian trainees, land girls, Jewish evacuees, refugees from the Continent, American soldiers, girl factory workers from East Anglia, and civil defence workers. . . .'[1] Hospitality committees and social clubs formed to ease the problem were not equal to the task, and the forced reception of workers and slum-dwellers in middle-class homes produced many difficult situations here as elsewhere in Britain, which were eased only by the gradual return of migrants to their homes and the war's end. 'The return of London evacuees is leaving Stevenage quiet at the moment,' noted the *Hertfordshire Express* in May 1945, 'but it will not be quiet for long if Prof. Abercrombie gets his way.'[2]

The local result of the July 1945 General Election came as a surprise. Three majors contested the (Hitchin) constituency and the Labour candidate won by a margin of 346 votes, polling 20,779 to his Conservative opponent's 20,433. The Liberal was a poor third with 7,515. Not since the Liberal landslide of 1906 had the Conservatives lost the constituency. 'In the years to come 1945 will be remembered, just as 1906 is remembered as the year of Liberal triumph, as the date of the great swing in Britain to the Left', said the victorious Labour M.P. '. . . they [the voters] had broken down the last vestiges of feudalism that had still existed in many parts of the constituency.'[3] 'For the first time in history we have a representative in Westminster who we can really say is "Our M.P.",' said the chairman of the Stevenage Trades Council.[4]

Stevenage in 1945 was, then, no longer a village nor yet a full-fledged town; greatly influenced by London, it nevertheless retained significant native traditions and prized its agricultural components above their strict rank in the local economy; more conservative than the industrial North or most metropolitan boroughs but lacking the true squirearchy of rural counties, its sympathies were with the old England but it was being engulfed by the new. Industry employing substantial labour had developed hand in hand with a class of clerks and business men who commuted to work in London. Morning and evening the great ebb and flow of cycle, bus, car, and train was

---

[1] *Hertfordshire Express*, 5th January 1946. The town referred to was actually Letchworth, but the experience of Stevenage was similar.

[2] Ibid., 19th May 1945.   [3] Ibid., 4th August 1945.

[4] Ibid., 11th August 1945.

visible throughout Hertfordshire as workers journeyed considerable distances across the countryside between homes and jobs that had got distressingly separated.

It would be foolish to claim that Stevenage was a typical English town, whatever that might be. The last available census (for 1931) showed, however, that the distribution of the county's working population was surprisingly representative of the average for England and Wales, with a somewhat larger proportion engaged in agriculture, building, the professions, and personal services, and a smaller proportion in manufacturing, and, of course, mining. Hertfordshire has benefited in recent decades both from the southward movement of industry and population from the depressed Midlands and North, and the suburban movement outward from London. The town shared in the benefits to business, but increased population also brought increased demands upon the rates, and the growing working class, heartened by Labour's national victory, threatened to disturb the repose of the local middle classes.

It is perhaps futile to speculate what would have been Stevenage's fate had it not been chosen as the site of a New Town; but it could hardly have achieved an isolation it never had, or won exemption from the political and economic forces of the times. The middle and upper classes do not, for the most part, welcome the enfolding arms of Government, but have lost the power to resist, and done much to provoke, the embrace which the working classes either enjoy or are more able to endure.

CHAPTER THREE

The Stevenage Project

THE story of Stevenage New Town is dual. At Whitehall, elected M.P.s, ministers, and appointed civil servants initiated the enterprise and made all major decisions. The Ministry of Town and Country Planning was new, hopeful, idealistic, and no doubt wished to introduce as much democracy as possible into planning procedure. But it was a national agency, the staff thought in national terms, and their duty was to implement Government policy: this New Town was merely one of many problems to them; their jobs and security were not dependent upon Stevenage citizens, whose opinions and actions had, therefore, to be considered only in so far as law, expedience, and conscience prescribed. At Stevenage, of course, decisions made in Whitehall were of vital importance to many families; but the channels by which opinion could normally be conveyed to Whitehall were slow and ineffective —and, indeed, from sad experience with the administrative machinery of democracy, some persons despaired of ever influencing events. The Stevenage Urban District Council of twelve elected councillors was the principal vehicle for communications up and down and legally recognized spokesman for local opinion in official discussions. To an extent, the Council *was* representative of a majority of electors; but it also represented the voices of its dominant members, who were inevitably isolated from important sections of the community.

The resultant sequence of events reproduced in miniature the cosmos of a modern democracy's relations with its citizens.

A. ABERCROMBIE PROPOSES

Abercrombie's *Greater London Plan*, published for official use in December 1944, set forth criteria for a satisfactory New Town site:

good road and rail services; land suitable for industry; gas, water, electricity, sewerage, and drainage services must be readily availlabe; development should not adversely affect agriculture, the beauty of the landscape, wireless transmission and reception, neighbouring airports, or the prosperity and economic balance of neighbouring towns; the site should exploit normal trends of outward population movement and also serve to retain industrial connections with the Midlands and North (for these reasons, only one site south of London was suggested); 'good accessibility to the metropolis is abso- lutely essential; but [sites] . . . should be sufficiently far out to deter people permanently from travelling backwards and forwards. . . .' With all these and other factors to consider, it is not surprising that Abercrombie experienced 'some considerable difficulty . . . in sug- gesting satisfactory sites for the necessary number of new towns in the country belt and within a reasonable distance of London'.[1] One of the sites selected was Stevenage, a Hertfordshire town thirty miles north of London, with a population of about 6,000:

'As a nucleus for expansion to satellite town size this site makes use of a small old-established agricultural and residential town on the Great North Road at its junction with the Hitchin Road. Stevenage is excel- lently located for transport, served as it is by the main London and New- castle line of the L.N.E. Railway, . . . by the Great North Road, for which a diversion is proposed skirting the site on the west, and by a projected east and west road linking the Midlands with Colchester. The town is tending to develop industrially and has a few modern factories on the west side of the main L.N.E. Railway dealing in engineering and school equipment, etc. Ample land is available for industry on the west side of the railway, from which it is possible to provide siding connections. The main street of Stevenage is a fine wide shopping street, possessing distinct character, and would form a good shopping centre for a much bigger town. The present shopping facilities are not good, and a cinema, faced with badly designed sham half-timber work, terminates the main street vista on the north. Most of the modern housing is rather drab. Expansion should take place mainly on the east of the present town, leaving an area on the west of the railway for industry, where it is undesirable to have residential development. Though industry would be located on the west side, this should be no disadvantage to the town in view of the smokeless nature of modern industry. Sewage would have to be dealt with independently of any centralised disposal works, but there is no special difficulty on this site.'[2]

On 12th December 1944, the Minister of Town and Country Planning forwarded advance copies of the Abercrombie plan to the 143 local authorities and county councils in the Greater London area

[1] Patrick Abercrombie, *Greater London Plan* 1944 (London, 1945), pp. 160–1.
[2] Ibid., p. 161.

for their consideration.[1] The Town Planning and Development Committee of the Stevenage Urban District Council discussed the plan on 17th January 1945 and recommended 'That the proposal to site a satellite town at Stevenage be approved in principle subject to reservations with regard to financial provisions and any necessary boundary revisions'. The Council adopted this recommendation and, in March, the Council chairman, addressing the annual meeting of the local Chamber of Trade on 'The Future Development of Stevenage', contrasted a town of 30,000 having a rural complexion and lined with broad avenues, with the congested growth that might otherwise have been expected.

At the Ministry's suggestion, a delegation of the mayor and five members of the Tottenham (London) Borough Council came to Stevenage on April 25th and discussed with the Town Planning Committee the building of a garden city of 30,000, to house excess population from Tottenham, Edmonton, and Wood Green on two thousand acres of residential and four hundred acres of industrial land. The Stevenage Council agreed to the proposal a few days later after a debate in which one councillor suggested that 'before negotiations go too far we [should] call a public meeting, ask the Tottenham people down to explain their scheme and take a public referendum', and the (Labour) chairman of the Town Planning Committee replied that whatever the Council might decide, when the Abercrombie Plan was officially adopted a scheme such as this would probably be foisted on them anyway and it was better to go into a scheme under the auspices of a local authority than one in the hands of private developers.[2] However, two months later it was learned that the Tottenham Council had shifted its attention to another site. The local newspaper noted that,

'Although the Stevenage Urban Council welcomed the scheme in principle, because it appeared to simplify development on the lines of the Abercrombie Report, there were some misgivings over its eventual effect.

'It is felt that the town may have a chance of more varied development by slower and more evolutionary means.'[3]

On June 12th, the Town Planning Committee visited the Ministry's offices in London where, among other matters, the question of the satellite project was discussed.

These preliminary approaches were often forgotten in later months, and many Stevenage residents were hardly aware that they had taken place. Perhaps there was little reason to give them much attention since, at the time, no irrevocable action was—or could be—

[1] Ministry of Town and Country Planning, *Greater London Plan, Memorandum by the Ministry of Town and Country Planning on the Report of the Advisory Committee for London Regional Planning* (London, 1947), p. 13.
[2] *Hertfordshire Express*, 5th May 1945.   [3] Ibid., 7th July 1945.

undertaken. It should be remembered that the war in Europe was not over until May and, in Asia, August 1945, and the result of the first General Election in ten years, which replaced Churchill's National by Attlee's Labour Government, was not known until July 26th. Plans, expectations, and uncertainty abounded. The nation did not yet know upon what political and economic course it was heading.

At the Ministry of Town and Country Planning, preparations had been under way for some time to make Stevenage the prototype and model of future New Towns. 'The initiative and drive to get things under way came from [Mr. K], an architect, who was at that time an administrator charged with responsibility for the Greater London Plan.'[1] As early as October 1944, after he had had a survey of the area conducted, this Ministry official had suggested that a garden city be built at Stevenage. In ensuing months, technical and legal information was gathered for a draft plan from other Government departments, county agencies, and officers of the Stevenage Council. From these inquiries and hints dropped in the course of routine conferences, Council members gained some idea of what was afoot. (For example, at a morning conference at the Ministry on 30th August 1945, representatives of the Council and Ministry agreed to bar surface mineral workings east of the railway, the proposed residential section of the New Town.)

In October 1945 things really began to happen. Three representatives of the Ministry twice visited the Council offices (on October 5th and 16th) and confided that the Ministry intended to start work immediately on a master plan, while other bodies would examine problems of finance and administration (the Reith Committee was appointed for this purpose on October 19th). It should be noted that this activity was in advance of specific enabling legislation—the New Towns Bill was published 24th April 1946 and the New Towns Act did not become law until 1st August 1946.

The day after the second visit, Council representatives attending a conference at the County Hall in Hertford heard a county officer say that the Ministry intended to set up Government-sponsored corporations to acquire the land for and develop such of the New Towns mentioned in the Greater London Plan as would be approved; because this step would require legislation and the Ministry wished to make an early start at Stevenage, the Minister had decided to make use of a provision of the Town and Country Planning Act, 1932, under the terms of which he had requested the county, as agents for the Ministry, to purchase immediately and, if necessary, compulsorily,

[1] Gordon Stephenson, 'The Place of the Architect in the Building of a New Town and in Redevelopment', *Journal Royal Institute British Architects*, June 1948, p. 334.

5,500 acres of land including the whole of the Stevenage Urban District except for the built-up area.[1] (The officer was later reprimanded for disclosing confidential information.) This was far more decisive, and in some ways alarming, information than had yet been communicated to the Council. That night the Town Planning Committee remained in session until 11.30 discussing the advisability of holding a public meeting or referendum on the New Town issue; finally it resolved 'to recommend that the Minister of Town and Country Planning should be asked to send representatives to meet the whole of the Council on this question . . . and that the Ministry be informed that the Council wish in future to be informed directly of developments in this scheme'.

The highlights of the officer's statement (which, considering that the Reith Committee did not deliver its first report to this effect until 21st January 1946, constituted an unusually early and accurate local revelation of national policy), appearing in the *Hertfordshire Express* of 20th October, evoked a rumble of public protest in the form of two letters to the *Express* from prominent citizens. The first came from Mr. Z, Lord of the Manor of Aston, a village three miles from Stevenage:

'It is exceedingly disquieting to read in the Press that the development of a "Satellite" town at Stevenage has been decided upon. I cannot think that this statement is correct. . . .

'The development of a "Satellite" town at Stevenage would have a devastating affect on the neighbourhood and would convert a pleasant market town into a dormitory for workers in London, as has been the case at Welwyn Garden City, bringing with it an urban population with entirely a different outlook, habits and behaviour to that to which the residents of Stevenage have been accustomed.'[2]

The second was from Mrs. N, wife of Mr. N, a leader in Stevenage church and cultural activities, who occupied what was perhaps the single most valuable residential property in town:

'Ever since the proposal was made that Stevenage should be turned into a satellite town I have been waiting for some expression of local opinion in your columns. But with the exception of Mr. [Z']s letter . . . there has been none.

'Does this mean that nobody objects, or merely that everyone is waiting for someone else to begin the discussion? The lead should of course come from the Urban District Council, but so far as one can judge . . . their attitude to the proposal is that of a rabbit confronted by a boa-constrictor. The situation may be equally hopeless, but it seems a pity to die without fighting. . . .'[3]

[1] *Hertfordshire Express*, 20th October 1945.
[2] Ibid., 27th October 1945. For subsequent correspondence involving Mr. Z see Chapter V, pp. 139–41.
[3] Ibid., 10th November 1945.

But back to the Council, whose aforementioned resolution elicited an invitation to visit the Ministry on 16th November, when Mr. K and other Ministry officers told the six Council delegates that Cabinet approval of the project was confidently awaited. No definite plan was yet available, but work was proceeding to devise one. The county should purchase the necessary land by 1st October 1946; building should start in eighteen months, enabling the town to reach a population of 45,000 in five years; some 250 factories had indicated willingness to transfer to Stevenage. The Council pointed out the importance of knowing the layout (especially the limits of the industrial zone) and of the railway's conversion to electricity. According to one informant, the Council left this meeting with the impression that 'we were told almost everything there is to be told at present'. If so, this was less than councillors wanted to know. When, early in December, a ratepayer inquired at the Council for information, he received a letter saying, 'The Satellite Town proposals are still in a very nebulous state. No exact information is available as to the area to be covered by the new town. . . . Any definite developments must await the report of Lord Reith's Committee which is unlikely . . . until next June.'

The inquiry resulted from a report of the London visit that a councillor had given in public at the regular end-of-the-month Council meeting, whence it got into the local Press.[1] A Ministry officer strongly protested against this disclosure. Ministry officials were involved in negotiations and consultations with the Ordnance Survey, the Ministry of Transport, the Ministry of Agriculture and Fisheries, and some twenty other Government departments; they were preoccupied with decisions of the Cabinet, the Reith Committee, the London County Council, the Advisory Committee for London Regional Planning,[2] various other bodies, and the Minister; and, naturally, did not wish to be embarrassed by premature revelations to a small local council that had little experience or authority in either town planning or Government diplomacy. It was equally natural, of course, for the Council to become disturbed and affronted by the increasing suspicion that important measures were being taken behind its back. Nevertheless, the Council continued to support the

---

[1] *Hertfordshire Express*, 1st December 1945.

[2] At a conference of representatives of regional planning bodies and county councils in the Greater London area convened by the Minister of Town and Country Planning, 26th October 1945, this committee, with the Liberal leader Clement Davies as chairman, was appointed to re-examine Abercrombie's proposed New Towns. In its report dated 17th July 1946, the committee reduced the number of New Town sites in the vicinity of London to four, but agreed that Stevenage should be developed to an ultimate population of 60,000 (Advisory Committee for London Regional Planning, *Report to the Minister of Town and Country Planning* (London, 1946), pp. 12–13).

project. To dispel public apprehension, it decided unanimously that the time had come 'to call a public meeting to explain the principles underlying Sir Patrick Abercrombie's plan for the future of Stevenage'[1] and, on 8th December, released a public statement approving 'the general principles and conclusions' of the Abercrombie plan, but advancing various suggestions for industrial, residential, and commercial zoning in the New Town.

By December, the Lord President's Committee had approved the Stevenage project. The first interim report of the Reith Committee, presented on 21st January 1946, stated:

'Stevenage is suggested in the Greater London Plan, 1944, as one of the new towns in the outer ring round London. We are informed that the development of this town is a matter of urgency, and that the agency must be chosen before legislation can be obtained.

'It is possible that by a special arrangement with the Hertfordshire County Council, at the request of the Minister of Town and Country Planning, the necessary land may be acquired for the County Council under Section 35 of the Town and Country Planning Act, 1932, the Exchequer providing the necessary finance. We recommend that there shall be an arrangement between the County Council and a government sponsored corporation established by Royal Charter, which will enable the latter to proceed in advance of legislation.'[2]

A draft charter for the proposed New Town corporation, drawn up at the committee's request by the Treasury Solicitor, was presented in the report.

Why was the Stevenage project 'a matter of urgency'?

The Ministry stated that it was pushed ahead 'to provide valuable guidance in the framing and administration of the new legislation which, it was foreseen, would be necessary . . .'[3] (i.e., in advance of the New Towns Bill, introduced in the House of Commons 17th April 1946). Speed was obviously essential if the New Towns programme was to realize its bold vision, help rehouse London's surplus population, and restrain the ceaseless growth of the metropolis— Abercrombie had calculated that the programme should be completed within ten years. Already the London County Council's and other authorities' inroads into the Green Belt Ring threatened the success of the Greater London Plan.

But why *Stevenage* and not another site? Of course, judged from the map and such data as could be obtained by preliminary surveys, the site appeared to Ministry planners 'ripe' for development and for

---

[1] *Hertfordshire Express*, 1st December 1945.

[2] *Interim Report of the New Towns Committee*, Cmd. 6759 (London, 1946), p. 15.

[3] Ministry of Town and Country Planning, mimeographed Press notice *Development of Stevenage as a 'New Town'*, 6th May 1946.

many bombed-out London industries seeking new locations. But so were other sites subsequently chosen for New Towns. In the last analysis it can be said that Stevenage came first simply because *it happened to come first*; because at an indeterminate moment Abercrombie, K, or somebody else lit upon it, the wheels of the Ministry then began to turn in that direction and had not yet met a sizable obstacle. It is neither a criticism of nor a compliment to the highly competent Ministry officers to observe that they were driving at speed along an unmapped road.

There is a story of how Stevenage came to be chosen which illustrates this rather well. It was told at the 5th November 1945 meeting of the Hertfordshire County Council by Mr. W. H. Gaunt, chairman of the Council's Town Planning Committee and a member of the Reith Committee.

'A few months before the [Reith] . . . committee came into being he (Mr.' Gaunt) was asked to assist the [Ministry] . . . with his views as to how the new towns should come into being, and he expressed certain views as to the control of the land which would be required. A few weeks ago he was told the Minister approved his advice and asked whether they could be put into effect on some site.

'The suggestion was made that Hertfordshire, because of its progressive outlook, might provide such a site, and the experiment might begin in the area of Stevenage, about which there had been little controversy. . . .

'Maj. Gen. —— [Stevenage representative on the county council] said there had been no controversy or opposition to the satellite town at Stevenage simply because no-one knew anything about it.'[1]

Partly as a result of the disclosures that the Council had made in October, Ministry officials became more cautious about confiding in the Council. On 10th January 1946, two Council representatives visiting the Ministry were shown confidential plans for the layout of the proposed New Town, the situation of neighbourhood units, and the line of major roads. And on 8th March, the Ministry forwarded a plan showing the approximate area to be purchased. But most news came *ex post facto* or from private sources, and even staunch Labour councillors began to complain about the Ministry's lack of co-operation: the Council was often asked for information and was sometimes retrospectively advised of developments, but it was seldom consulted as an equal partner in the course of planning. A Council representative recorded his observations of a meeting at the Ministry convened on 9th April to discuss problems of sewage disposal and water supply in the New Town. 'It is obvious that it is the Government's intention to proceed with the development of Stevenage at the greatest possible speed. Nothing the people of Stevenage say, or might have said in the past, will make any difference to the

[1] *Hertfordshire Express*, 10th November 1945.

development taking place here, we were told.' At this meeting, the chairman of the Town Planning Committee expressed to the Ministry 'the Council's complete dissatisfaction with the measure of co-operation which had been shown up to the present. . . .'[1]

That respectable Stevenage citizens were becoming increasingly annoyed at the distinction being thrust upon them was demonstrated at the educational meeting which the Urban District Council staged on 6th February in the Town Hall. After F. J. Osborn, chairman of the Town and Country Planning Association and a member of the Reith Committee, addressed the 'large gathering' on New Towns, he was asked many questions. 'Most of them', an informant reported, 'pursued the question as to why the people of Stevenage had not been asked before the Satellite scheme had been supported.' (The support referred to was the resolution of 'agreement in principle' passed by the Urban District Council in January 1945.)

'Several questioners asked if the plan was purely mythical, or if it was actually on the drawing board, and who was actually responsible for the scheme.

'Mr. Osborn said he was not in a position to disclose what was going on between the County Council and the Ministry, . . . but he believed there was a very real proposition. . . .

'Mr. —— asked if the present population of Stevenage did view the plan with disfavour, what action would the Ministry take.

'Mr. Osborn's answer was that this was a democratic country, and their views would have weight if there was sound reason behind them, but, if it were in the interests of Greater London, the town could be built in Stevenage whether they wanted it or not.'[2]

Each announcement in the Press increased the tension and the Council offices were visited by unusual numbers of inquiring citizens. All sorts of rumours began to circulate, including one (early in April) 'that a man, named, had actually received notice and an offer to lease his land back to him'. By this time, an observer noted, there was 'a state of affairs approaching panic in the town'.

Special interest attached to the 30th March Council election when nine vacancies were to be filled, because, owing to the war, the customary yearly elections had been suspended since 1939. The Council's political composition remained unchanged as a result of the election —8 Independents (or Conservatives, as opponents called them) to 4 Labour—and the three highest candidates on the poll endorsed the New Town (although their popularity was probably not due to this fact, since they were well known locally and two had had previous Council experience). But seven new Councillors were inexperienced, and among them were forceful business men who had little use for Government planning and had pledged to oppose the New Town.

[1] *Hertfordshire Express*, 4th May 1946.   [2] Ibid., 9th February 1946.

B. THE MINISTRY DISCLOSES

In response to the 9th April protest, three senior Ministry officers attended a session of the Stevenage Council on 25th April, which, despite all expectations, proved rather peaceful. A draft plan was produced and the siting of industrial and shopping areas discussed, councillors requesting certain changes to avoid demolitions. The Ministry promised to consult the Council more frequently in the future.

Simultaneously, the axe fell. At the homes of 178 property owners, the postman delivered envelopes 15 by 10 inches, marked O.H.M.S., and rubber-stamped THE MINISTRY OF TOWN AND COUNTRY PLANNING. Inside, accompanied by a form of agreement for completion, was the following letter, dated 24th April:

'Sir,
> 'Town and Country Planning Act, 1932 (Section 35)
> 'Acquisition of land for a garden city

'I am directed to inform you that the Minister of Town and Country Planning has under consideration the acquisition, on behalf of the Hertfordshire County Council, of land in the neighbourhood of Stevenage with a view to development of the area as a garden city.

'Under the powers conferred upon him by Section 35 of the Town and Country Planning Act, 1932, the Minister may acquire land for such a purpose either by agreement or compulsorily, and he is prepared to consider purchasing by agreement the land . . . shown . . . on the plan annexed to . . . this letter, of which it is understood you are the freehold owner.

'Accordingly, I am to inquire whether you are prepared to sell by agreement to the Minister your interest in the said land. . . .

'Should you state terms which prove acceptable to the Minister, the memorandum of agreement will be signed on the Minister's behalf and one copy will be returned to you.

'In conclusion, I am to request that you will communicate your decision to the Minister in writing before the expiration of twenty-eight days from the date of this letter.

'I am, Sir,
'Your obedient Servant,
'_____
'For Treasury Solicitor.'

The area covered by these notices amounted to some 5,000 acres including 3,600 acres of farmland, or all the land within the proposed New Town except for the main built-up part of Stevenage and some large factories (excluded because it was doubted that the Ministry had power to acquire them under the 1932 Act). By concluding agreement the owner was liable to eviction upon three months' notice.[1]

Although old members might have deduced that some such action impended, the Council had received no prior notification and most councillors felt betrayed. The affected public, without even the Council's preparation, was outraged. The Ministry plan required some demolition, but as these sites had never been precisely specified (partly because the plan was not final, and partly because the Ministry wished to minimize this matter) many persons feared the worst. It was almost impossible to get alternative accommodation, and the housing shortage had raised the value of real estate far above the legal level of compensation then prevailing for compulsory purchase (1939 valuation, plus 30 per cent in the case of owner-occupiers). Landowners were naturally among the most influential families in town, and circles of sympathetic friends quickly formed round them. One business man, who had been writing letters of protest to the Press, asked twelve friends to his house to organize an opposition group: the Stevenage Residents' Protection Association was formed on 1st May, and grew rapidly until it claimed some 1,200 members.

On Monday, 6th May, the Minister paid a visit to Stevenage which we shall describe in some detail, because it serves so well to indicate the temper of those days, the difference between the worlds in which officials and citizens moved, and the strained and artificial circumstances under which they sometimes met.

Councillors had known the date of the visit for a month, and one Labour councillor had been instrumental in persuading the Minister to acquaint himself personally with Stevenage, meet the Council, and perhaps address a public gathering. On Wednesday morning, 1st May, the Council clerk and surveyor (acting on the Council's instructions and in order to inform citizens about the Ministry proposals) posted a five-foot coloured New Town plan in the window of a High Street store. A crowd collected almost immediately, and

---

[1] With one exception, where a two-year period was mentioned, no owner was informed that his property would not be required within a period exceeding one year, and in only a few cases 'where this seemed to be safe' was one year mentioned (Ministry of Town and Country Planning, *Stevenage New Town. Report on Planning and Development Proposals*, 55 pp. mimeographed, 31st July 1946, pp. 35–6). Notices went to 178 or 179 (several excellent sources disagree) individuals or groups, inviting them to treat in respect of:

> 160 houses or cottages
> 26 farms
> 60 units of land apart from farms
> 4 licensed houses
> 10 allotments
> 4 building sites
> 2 playing fields.

throughout that day and late into the evening clusters of people examined the map, their eyes moving uncertainly from the legend to the whereabouts of their homes and other landmarks. Reporters and photographers from the local and national Press (the Conservative anti-Government Press had been beating loudly on the Stevenage drum for some time) added to the commotion of the scene and pestered Council officers so that they could hardly work. Preparations were made to ensure that adequate numbers of police would be on hand to shepherd the crowds and protect the Minister, and every detail of the itinerary was carefully planned.

An informant who was a participant in the proceedings recorded his impression of the Minister's arrival:

'[The Minister] came in a large car with —— a few minutes before 1.0. The newsreel men had the camera working as he got out in front of the hotel and walked with the [Council] clerk up the path to the entrance. Inside, the clerk introduced the Chairman and the other councillors. [The Minister] was immediately caught by reporters and was unable to get in to lunch for some minutes. We went across to the Council Chamber under another battery of cameras. In the Council Chamber there was a crowd of reporters with and without camera. One of the newsreel men climbed on top of the safe to get a good shot of the head of the table just before the meeting commenced. The proceedings were fairly satisfactory although [the Minister] was quite adamant about the decision to put a New Town at Stevenage.

'The meeting finished about 4.30 and we set off on the tour of the district. A police car led, followed by [the Minister's], and about twenty cars full of camera men and reporters. We went out to Coreys Mill, and stopped while the position of the A1 bypass flyover was explained to [the Minister]. The reporters and camera men ran up expecting [the Minister] to get out of his car and look at maps, to be shown positions of future building, etc. We went on by Todds Green and Fishers Green and into the fiercely disputed region of Fairview Road. We stopped halfway down Fairview Road. An elderly man and woman came to the gate, and then the man came to the car window. In a moment the camera men and reporters were out streaking down the road, the newsreel man had his camera turning, everything was being taken down in shorthand. [The Minister] got out of his car to talk to the two old people and to go into their garden. In a moment the camera men were jumping over the garden fence, one went upstairs to take some shots out of the bedroom window. A crowd of newspapermen surged up the narrow garden path between the apple trees at the back of the house. One reporter said to me "and this is the nationalised strawberry bed".'

On their drive, the Ministerial party was greeted with many posters and chalked inscriptions like 'Hands off Our Homes' and 'NO! NO! Mr. Minister'. When the Minister alighted from his car on Fairview Road (according to newspaper accounts) he said to Mr. T, the elderly, bare-headed man who had approached, 'Is there anything you want to ask me?' Mr. T invited the Minister to inspect his garden and a conversation something like this ensued at the gate:

'Mr. T. When have we got to move . . . are you going to turn us out?
'Minister. You are not going to be turned out. You will never be asked to move until there is somewhere for you to go. We shall build you another home.
'Mr. T. But we have lived here twenty years. Save this road.
'Minister. You won't be asked to go until you get another house as good as you have here, if not better.
'Mrs. X (a grey-haired woman, alternately described as Mr. T's wife or neighbour). It won't be prefabs?
'Minister. No, it won't be prefabs.
'Mrs. X. But we may run on for years worrying whether we shall be turned out or not. We don't want another house. We want this one.
'Mr. T (putting a hand on the Minister's shoulder and pointing to an apple tree laden with blossom). Can you put in a tree like that? It is twenty years old. You can't give me back my fruit trees!
'Minister. No, that is true.
'Mrs. X. Why can't you build your factories somewhere else?
'Mr. T. This is freehold property. Can you take it from us?
'Minister. We will carry out this very unpleasant operation in a way which will make it the least inconvenient for you.
'Mrs. X. We are too late in life to start a new home.'

Mr. T escorted the Minister through the garden with its pear trees, raspberry canes, ripening gooseberries and rhubarb, and implored him to build factories further down the road. The Minister was kind but firm; they shook hands upon parting, and the remainder of the tour passed without notable incident.

Four hours before the public evening meeting was to begin a queue formed outside the small town hall and soon stretched round the corner and down the High Street—some persons brought folding chairs, stools, sandwiches, and containers of tea. The streets were full of cars; music came over loudspeakers installed to carry the Minister's speech to the crowds (estimated variously as 1,000–3,000 strong) who could not cram into the hall which, on this occasion, held 300–400 persons.

Cheers and boos greeted the Minister as he made his way from his car through the crowd to the platform, upon which sat local and county dignitaries. As the Council Chairman (a stalwart New Town supporter) opened the meeting, 'This is a great day for Stevenage, . . .' hoots of laughter, catcalls, and a general uproar drowned the rest of his sentence. He proceeded to review the Council's planning record, shouting louder and louder as the audience grew noisier and ruder. The 1937 scheme, he said, interrupted by war and revived in 1943, had envisaged an ultimate population of 30,000 for Stevenage. 'Nobody that I know of objected to that. Every organisation in the town was circularised. Not one of them objected. Every organisation was consulted and no one replied. In that plan there would have been a certain amount of redevelopment and there would have been demolition of houses . . . but . . . in the older part of the town.'

When the Minister rose the hubbub revived. (A pro-Minister informant ascribed it to 'organized rowdies, including anti-Semites'.) The Minister said he would not speak unless people would listen, and he did not intend to shout, and sat down again. This had a salutary effect upon the audience, which remained surprisingly quiet thereafter except for a few interruptions mainly from two bitter opponents. The speech that he gave is so central to our story that it is printed below almost in its entirety. After referring to the recommendations of the Barlow Report and the *Greater London Plan*, the Minister spoke of his appointment of the Reith Committee:[1]

'I have now had the advantage of two interim reports—both unanimous —from this Committee, and based upon these reports the Government has decided to introduce legislation to facilitate the creation of these new towns.

'The New Towns Bill, published twelve days ago, will receive its Second Reading on Wednesday, and I am here today—(*Voice*: You are leaving it a bit late). In anticipation of the passage of the Bill—and I have no doubt that it will go through—certain preliminary steps have been taken regarding Stevenage by way of discussion with some of the local authorities concerned—(*Voice*: There has been no discussion with the Stevenage Local Authority)—and the preparation of a plan, and the giving of notices for the acquisition of land, under powers which I already have in pursuance of the Town and Country Planning Act, 1932.

'This brings my story up to date.

'Now I propose to tell you in some detail why Stevenage was recommended by Sir Patrick Abercrombie and approved by the Government. I will then deal with objections which have been brought to my notice, and finally I will tell you a little about the plans and proposals we have in mind for Stevenage, the kind of town we want to build, and what it will mean to Stevenage.

'Why was Stevenage chosen? Well, it is in a convenient situation to attract industry. It has direct and easy road and rail communications with the industrial North. It is on the side of London where the greatest amount of overcrowding exists. The railway can be extended and electrified here, and provision made for a new railway station with sidings for factories. It is indeed admirably situated for expansion as a self-contained community with a proper balance of industry and population.

'From a housing point of view the land is good, its slope is largely south-west and west. It is of some advantage that it has already a number of established industries, some of which are growing and desire to expand.

---

[1] This text is reproduced mainly from the Ministry's advance Press notice interleaved with interpolations many of which are recorded in *Law Reports Appeal Cases*, 1948, p. 90. We were unable to consult a verbatim transcript; it is possible that slight changes were made in the course of delivery.

From enquiries we have made there is no doubt at all that there will be no dearth of light industries which would otherwise have settled in London, or which are already in London and desirous of expansion, ready to come to Stevenage.

'I think you will agree that if we are to carry out our policy of creating a number of new towns to relieve congestion in London we could hardly have chosen for the site of one of them a better place than Stevenage.

'Now I know that many objections have been raised by the inhabitants of Stevenage, perhaps not unnaturally.

'Some say we are a nice quiet small town or large village which has a charm of its own, and we want to continue to enjoy all the advantages of a small town; quick access to the countryside, the village atmosphere, and so on. We don't want to become urbanised, with the noise and bustle of a town with a population of 50,000 like Watford or St. Albans.

'Others complain of being disturbed or dispossessed, and a number of you have already received notices enquiring whether you are prepared to sell your land by agreement.

'A special complaint is about the proposed demolition of about 150 modern houses, built between the wars, for the purpose of creating sites for industry.

'I cannot, of course, deny that the character of Stevenage will be changed when it becomes a town with a population of 50,000, as compared with its existing character. I believe on the whole it will be an even better place to live in than it is today.

'Change is inevitable—nothing stands still—and Stevenage, even if it was not to become the site of a new town, would not have remained unchanged for long.

'Between the wars there was considerable development. Before the first world war the built-up area of Stevenage was mainly confined to the region of the High Street, with a number of roads running off it; today it straggles and sprawls over a mile or more in many directions, providing one of the very bad examples of ribbon development.

'Your own Council has been considering the future of Stevenage. It had recognised, as I do, that Stevenage cannot stand still. Its very attractiveness for the purpose of a new town would in any case have brought about large scale development. Your Council themselves, therefore, prepared a plan, under which an expansion of population to 30,000 with the appropriate industry is provided for. That is not so very different after all from my proposal of an ultimate population, possibly in ten years, of 50,000.

'Let me show you your Council's plan. Here it is. If this is the alternative to the creation of a new town, then whatever my views about new towns might be, if I were an inhabitant of Stevenage I would prefer the new town. This plan, which I recognise is only in its preliminary form, and would no doubt have been improved upon if it had been proceeded with, offends against many of the canons of good planning. For instance, it divides the residential population into two, by means of the railway, which many of you will no doubt know is one of the main defects of Welwyn Garden City. In order to preserve a number of small houses, factories are to be built on both sides of the row of houses when clearly the most convenient place for industry is the whole of the area between the main road and the railway.

'Moreover, it is clearly more satisfactory to group your industry altogether rather than to separate it with a row of houses in between.

'I do not want to stress that there is no substantial difference in character between a plan which provides for an expansion of population to 30,000 as against one to 50,000. In both cases a large amount of land has to be acquired, and people in due course dispossessed. The Council's plan would in fact necessitate the dispossession of nearly as many people as the New Town's Plan.

'The carrying out of the plan will involve, as I recognise, the acquisition of some thousands of acres of agricultural land—either plan does. The Ministry of Agriculture has been consulted about it, and they recognise the paramount needs of providing additional land for housing, and they have agreed. Not all the land will be needed at once, and I am prepared to give an undertaking that every consideration will be shown, both to owners of land and of houses. Possession will not be taken until it is absolutely essential for the purpose of carrying out the scheme, and the longest possible notice will be given.

'I have heard complaints about the amount of compensation that will be given. That is not a matter over which I have any control; the basis of compensation to be paid over the next $3\frac{1}{2}$ years is laid down in the Town and Country Planning Act, 1944. This is the basis upon which compensation is paid for all land required for public purposes. It is the basis settled by the late Coalition Government and it is not for me to question it, even if I could.

'And now I come to the final part of my speech. What kind of a town are we going to make of Stevenage?

'I do not think you will wish or expect me to deal in detail with the proposed development. An outline plan, showing our broad proposals, is exhibited in a shop in the High Street, which you can look at and study for yourselves. As you will see, the industry is grouped on the western side of the town, the Great North Road which at present runs through your High Street will be diverted to the west, and the industrial zone will be between this new diverted Great North Road and the railway, the place where I submit it should be. The station itself will be moved about a mile or so to the south, so that it may be more conveniently situated for the centre of the new town, and give the most convenient access to the commercial and business areas. The main business and shopping centre is proposed in the plan to be created about a mile to the south of the present centre. The town will be divided into neighbourhood units, each of about 10,000 population. Each neighbourhood unit will contain its own subsidiary shopping centre, open space, schools and other community facilities, so as to make them as self contained as possible. One of the advantages of building a new town as we are doing is that it enables the County Council to provide schools of the best and most modern character, according to the very highest standards of education as laid down in the Education Act of 1944. I want to carry out in Stevenage a daring exercise in town planning. (*Jeers.*) It is no good your jeering: it is going to be done. (*Applause and boos. Cries of "Dictator".*)

F

'After all, this new town is to be built in order to provide for the happiness and welfare of some 50,000 men, women and children. One of the things which is most lacking in our present day towns, but which is still retained in the villages, is the spirit of friendliness and neighbourliness, the sense of belonging to a large family, a community. In the towns there is an almost complete sense of isolation. I should like somehow so to build our new town that this neighbourly, friendly, social spirit is not lost. I believe that the principle of the neighbourhood unit goes some way towards securing this, perhaps not all the way. Some of you may have read about the "Reilly Plan" for the development of Birkenhead. It is a proposal for breaking up the neighbourhood unit into smaller units of about 40 or 50 families living in houses round a green, each unit containing perhaps a nursery school, a communal kitchen and restaurant, and a small community centre. In the communal kitchen food would be prepared in turn by a rota of women living in the unit and either delivered to the homes or consumed at the restaurant. That is one idea which may be found to be worth trying out. There are others. I am sure the last word has not been said in working out a way of life.

'I want the new towns to be beautiful. I am a firm believer in the cultural and spiritual influence of beauty.

'New towns, where the opportunity [exists] of starting afresh without the handicap of existing bad development, give us the opportunity of making these experiments.

'I know that I am calling upon many of you to make some sacrifice for the attainment of these ideals; and sacrifice is not pleasant or easy. Selfishness is, I am afraid, much easier.

'For a number of years we in this country stood together and suffered together, whilst fighting for an ideal, for a democracy in which we believed. I am sure that this spirit is not dead in Stevenage, and, if you are satisfied that this project is worth while, and for the benefit of large numbers of your fellow human beings, you will be prepared to play your part to make it a success.

'The project will go forward, because it must go forward. It will do so more surely and more smoothly, and more successfully with your help and co-operation. Stevenage will in a short time become world-famous. (*Laughter.*) People from all over the world will come to Stevenage to see how we here in this country are building for the new way of life.

'I am convinced that you will allow our task to proceed with your good-will, your co-operation, and your blessing. You are at the parting of the ways. I know that future generations will look back with pride at what we are doing tonight—at the new Stevenage which will arise. Let them be able to say "Those who came before us helped to achieve this —they had vision—they did not stand in the way".'

During the question period, the Minister said, 'Local authorities will be consulted all the way through. But we have a duty to perform, and I am not going to be deterred from that duty. While I will consult as far as possible all the local authorities, at the end, if people become fractious and unreasonable, I shall have to carry out my duty.' Applause, boos, and cries of 'Gestapo!' and 'Dictator!' came from the audience. The Minister left the meeting to discover his 25 h.p. Wolseley had been tampered with (by 'boys' one informant said), the tyres deflated and sand put into the petrol tank. Behind, in the town hall, £40 was collected towards a fighting fund for the Residents' Protection Association.

C. STEVENAGE OPPOSES

The previous month, the Council had requested the Ministry of Health's sanction to spend £60 on a referendum to ascertain the will of the electors on the New Town issue. The referendum was held 18th May although consent for the expenditure had not been granted. ('The Minister [of Town and Country Planning] didn't want us to hold a referendum,' a prominent citizen asserted. 'I paid the cheque out of my own pocket—£65 it was.') Voters were offered three alternatives:

'1. I am in favour of the scheme for a satellite town at Stevenage as outlined by the Ministry of Town and Country Planning.

'2. I am in favour of the scheme as outlined by the Ministry subject to a substantial reduction in the number of houses to be demolished and other modifications to be submitted by the Council. Also subject to compensation being paid to all owners of land and property upon the basis of the market value at the date of the acquisition by the Ministry, and comparable accommodation, with payment of removal and incidental expenses, being offered to all displaced families.

'3. I am entirely against the siting of a satellite town at Stevenage.'

Three days after the Minister's speech, the Residents' Protection Association held its first public meeting in the town hall at which the packed audience of about 400 passed, with six or seven dissenting votes, a motion demanding a public inquiry into the New Town. 'We imagined that tyranny was dead,' said the chairman of the meeting, 'but now I feel that a different sort of tyranny is still abroad —the tyranny of the acquisition of houses and lands, and the tyranny of control from Whitehall over homes.' The Assistant Secretary of the National Federation of Property Owners pledged the Federation's support to the Protection Association.[1] During the following week the Association conducted a vigorous campaign; it held another meeting in the town hall at which about 250 people endorsed a resolution supporting proposal 3; on the day of the referendum (a Saturday), it employed cars to take electors to the poll, and two loudspeaker cars toured the town urging everyone to vote for proposal 3 and have nothing to do with proposal 2, which was termed

[1] *Hertfordshire Express*, 11th May 1946.

'a trap'. No propaganda was conducted in favour of the New Town. The results surprised many persons who had expected the opposition to win an overwhelming victory:[1] proposal 1 received 913 votes or 36·4 per cent of the valid number of votes; proposal 2 only 282 votes or 11·2 per cent; and proposal 3, 1,316 votes or 52·4 per cent.

As Independent councillors had pledged to support the policy endorsed by a majority of the electorate, the Council now informed the Ministry that it objected to the siting of the New Town at Stevenage and asked for a full inquiry. The Minister replied on 14th June that, while due weight was certainly attached to the views of the electors of Stevenage, a referendum which reflected their views alone must necessarily be of limited significance in relation to such a matter as the siting of the proposed New Town. The New Towns Bill had passed its Second Reading on 8th May, and the Council made representations to Members of Parliament during the Committee Stage for the inclusion of an amendment rendering compulsory upon the Minister the holding of a public inquiry to hear any objection made to a proposed New Town designation order; this amendment was accepted by the Minister at the Third Reading and incorporated into the Bill,[2] which received the Royal Assent on 1st August. Five days later, the Minister published a draft order designating Stevenage as the site of a New Town and appointed an Advisory Committee to lay the groundwork for its subsequent development.

October 7th and 8th, a Ministry inspector held a public inquiry at the Stevenage town hall at which the Residents' Protection Association, the local branch of the National Farmers' Union, the Urban District Council, the Metropolitan Water Board, the Lee Conservancy and Lee Catchment Boards (who were concerned that the New Town not diminish the supply of, and its sewerage not pollute, London's water), and fifteen individuals entered objections. As no witnesses appeared for the Ministry, opponents' hopes were high that the scheme might be abandoned, but on 11th November the Minister confirmed the Stevenage New Town (Designation) Order and, on 5th December, transformed the Advisory Committee into the Stevenage Development Corporation with powers under the New Towns Act to carry the project to completion.

The Council now wavered in its resolution to oppose the New Town. When the Designation Order was issued, a Labour councillor

[1] Others, like many councillors (who favoured it) and *The Times'* correspondent, thought proposal 2 would obtain a majority (*The Times*, 14th May 1946).
[2] According to G. V. Berry, 'New Towns—the Particular Case of Stevenage', Society of Clerks of Urban District Councils, (report of) *Annual Meeting and Conference on 16th and 17th May 1947* (Barnet, Herts).

moved that the Council 'co-operate conscientiously in the successful building of the New Town', provided the Minister reconsider the demolition of houses; he believed most citizens would agree with such a decision, despite the results of the referendum 'decided by the loudspeaker vans and motor-cars of the opposition'. Four Labour and two Independent members voted for the motion and six Independents against; it was carried 7 to 6 on the chairman's casting vote (the chairman having thus voted twice, the Council was actually divided evenly on the matter). The best intentions of the Council, however, had no discernible effect upon the Minister, who refused a request to receive a Council delegation, leading the chairman (a Labour man) to say, 'I voted for the new town and I am still voting for it, but the way in which we have been treated is abominable'.

One day, the national Press carried pictures of the Stevenage railway platform, where STEVENAGE signs had been replaced by hanging boards marked SILKINGRAD. And three residents jointly representing the Residents' Protection Association and the local branch of the National Farmers' Union brought action in the High Court to have the Designation Order annulled on grounds that the Minister, having shown himself biased (notably in his town hall address of May) had not fairly considered objections entered at the public inquiry.

The case was heard 10th and 11th February 1947 in the King's Bench Division by Justice Henn Collins, J., and on the 20th judgment was issued quashing the Order. 'I am convinced', the judge ruled, 'that he [the Minister] did not consider the question: "Aye or No should the Order be confirmed?" with an open mind, but that he meant to confirm it whatever the force of the objections might be. . . . This, in my judgment, involves a denial of natural justice. . . .' However, on 24th March, Lords Oaksey, Morton, and Tucker, L.JJ., of the Court of Appeal, reversed this decision, holding that even if the Minister were biased in May, before passage of the New Towns Act, it had not been proved that he remained biased afterwards, while fulfilling his duties in regard to the inquiry. The cases hinged upon the problem of water supply and sewage disposal in the New Town, raised at the inquiry, about which the Minister had appointed a consultant to advise him. Justice Collins reasoned, 'It is obvious that those difficulties must be met before the scheme can go through. The Minister acknowledges that they have not been met, and that he is taking advice as to how it can be done. . . . How can it be said that he weighed the objection with an open mind when he acknowledges that he did not, and does not, know the force of it?' The Court of Appeal, however, noted (partly because of some evidence which had not been before the trial judge) that objectors had not held the sewage and water problems to be insoluble, but only that their solution would be expensive.[1]

The expense of litigation had now exhausted the funds but not the determination of the Protection Association, which launched a campaign in April to raise £3,000 needed to carry the case to the House of Lords. 'Surely you cannot have failed to remember the little man who was here that night and said "You are going to have the scheme whether you like it or not",' an Association leader told a town hall gathering. 'In England, people will not tolerate such dictation . . . and it filled us with a sense of burning injustice, which has not become cooler.' A leaflet 'The Battle of Stevenage' carried the appeal to many parts of the nation. It spoke of 'the inevitable chaos which must result if Stevenage, this gracious old Market Town with roots in the fifteenth century, is crucified on the cross of progress' and described the opposition's fight as 'the story of David and Goliath all over again: the small men against the powerful bureaucratic machine'.

Meanwhile the work of the Development Corporation of nine members which the Minister had established was being hampered by the continuing court action. On 2nd July, the Minister authorized the Corporation to proceed with work 'to a reasonable extent without reservation'. The Corporation agreed that this authorization included the signing of engineering contracts, but, in practice, work was largely confined to preliminary consultations and engineering surveys. On the Ministry side there was no inclination to admit defeat even if the House of Lords decision went against the Government, since the future of the entire New Towns programme might thus be endangered. The Minister would, of course, comply with such conditions as the Lords might impose, but there was nothing to keep him from using his powers under the New Towns Act to issue another Designation Order and hold a fresh inquiry.

The need for such action was obviated, however, when the House of Lords upheld the Minister's Order on 24th July 1947. It was the unanimous opinion of Lords Thankerton, Porter, Uthwatt, Du Parcq, and Norman that the questions of justice and Ministerial bias with which the two lower courts had been concerned—i.e., the right of local citizens, under the basic principle of English natural justice, to a hearing before an impartial judge (the Minister)—was completely irrelevant to the case, because the Minister was acting throughout in an administrative and not a judicial or quasi-judicial capacity.[2]

[1] We have consulted transcripts of the proceedings and judgment in the High Court, but the most accessible sources for these cases are 'Franklin and Others *v.* Minister of Town and Country Planning', *All England Law Reports*, 1947, vol. 1, pp. 396–9, pp. 612–20, and *The Times Law Reports*, 1947, vol. 63, pp. 143–5, 185–91.

[2] 'Franklin and Other . . . Appellants; and Minister of Town and Country Planning . . . Respondent', *Law Reports Appeal Cases* (1948), pp. 87–106.

D. GOD DISPOSES

Hardly was the Lords' decision announced when, in August, because of the national economic crisis, the Treasury forbade the Corporation to enter into any contracts. The Chancellor of the Exchequer, Sir Stafford Cripps, told Parliament on 23rd October that 'Work on the new towns during the coming year will, in general, be limited to the provision of basic services. . . .'[1]

For its office space, the Corporation had taken possession of a mansion and seventy-five accompanying acres together with some army huts erected during the war at Aston, in the countryside south-east of Stevenage just inside the border of the designated area. A reporter visiting Aston that week 'found the Corporation living a somewhat worried existence . . . with a sword of Damocles in the form of an imminent Government "axe" hanging over their heads. Everyone expects that within the next ten days a ministerial announcement will decide the future fate of the new Stevenage—whether it will go forward according to plan . . . or . . . be relegated to the limbo of . . . increasingly forgotten projects.'[2] A poem by Sagittarius, patterned after Oliver Goldsmith, appeared in the *New Statesman and Nation*:[3]

THE DESERTED SATELLITE

Sweet Stevenage! loveliest township ever plann'd,
Before the dollar crisis stripp'd the land,
Who could, unmov'd, trace thy forsaken sites,
Fairest of London's stillborn satellites?

O thou, the city planner's lawful pride,
With industry and housing side by side,
Abandon'd ere thy ground-plan was unroll'd,
Farewell, sweet Stevenage! thou art pigeon-hol'd.

· · · · ·

And residents who curs'd thy smiling birth,
Thy blighted bowers taunt with vindictive mirth.

· · · · ·

More weed-grown, more forsaken year by year,
Farewell, thy landscap'd plots that never were!
Thy visionary vistas fade and wilt,
Sweet Stevenage! loveliest town they never built.

The Minister of Town and Country Planning told the House on

[1] *Hansard*, 23rd October 1947, vol. 443, col. 280.
[2] *Hertfordshire Mercury*, 1st November 1947.
[3] *New Statesman and Nation*, 18th October, 1947.

THE NEW TOWN IDEA

6th November 1947 that 'while the development of Stevenage as a New Town will continue, constructional work will in general be limited to the provision of water and sewerage services and of roads' during the coming year.[1] This was a direct consequence of the Government's decision to redress the adverse national balance of trade with dollar countries by redirecting internal capital investments towards those industries exporting to dollar areas. '. . . in order rapidly to increase the volume of exports in the near future, labour, coal, steel and other materials must be switched from manufacture for the home market to manufacture for export', the Chancellor of the Exchequer reported to Parliament in December 1947. New Towns in the London area would be most affected by this directive, the Chancellor explained:

'There are so far two types of New Towns: towns intended to take industry and population from overcrowded large cities as an alternative to their continuous unplanned expansion outward which is regarded as uneconomic, and towns intended to provide for immediate industrial needs or for mining. . . . Stevenage, Crawley, Hemel Hempstead and Harlow fall into the first category; Aycliffe and Easington [later named Peterlee] into the second; in Scotland East Kilbride is designed to meet immediate industrial needs. . . .

'. . . the Government have . . . decided:—

'(1) New Towns designed to serve immediate industrial needs or mining areas should go ahead within the limits of the housing programme.

'(2) Work on New Towns designed to provide for industry and population decentralised from overcrowded cities should in general be limited during 1948 to starting the provision of water and sewerage and roads and should use not more than an average of 300 workers.'[2]

This effective limitation of the Stevenage New Town labour force to seventy-five men may be contrasted with the Reith Committee's estimate that a peak force of 5,000 men was required to complete a New Town of 60,000 within fifteen to twenty years.[3]

The original Ministry programme, which had prompted the dispatch of acquisition notices in April 1946, had called for the construction of 1,000 houses in the first two years (January 1947–December 1948), bringing the total Stevenage population to 10,000. Henceforth, the timetable had been:

[1] *Hansard*, 6th November 1947. vol. 443, col. 259 (written answer).

[2] *Capital Investment in* 1948, Cmd. 7268, presented by the Chancellor of the Exchequer to Parliament, December 1947 (London, 1947), pp. 4, 10.

[3] '. . . It will build up to this figure in the first three years, and will fall off off after the peak of construction is passed, which, however, will probably not be until the eighth or ninth year' (*Final Report of the New Towns Committee*, Cmd. 6876 (London, 1946), p. 60).

Years	Houses to be Built	Total Population
1949–1950	3,000	22,000
1951–1952	4,000	38,000
1953–1954	3,500	52,000
1955–1956	2,000	60,000

This programme was now patently unrealizable and, as in following months the delays of bureaucracy and local opposition were added to continued national economic difficulties and growing pains natural to any new corporation, revised programmes fell equally behind schedule. There is reason to believe that Stevenage New Town and, to varying extents, other New Towns, fell so far behind their initial schedule that some ground lost by the *Greater London Plan* can never be recovered. 'We have assumed that if the creation of the [Stevenage] new town is to make an effective contribution to the solution of London's housing and decentralization problem it must be substantially complete by 1957', said the Ministry in July 1946.[1] In September 1950, the *Architects' Journal* noted that 'at the present general rate of progress *fifty years* or more are going to be required to build all the new towns'.[2] From the end of the war to 31st December 1950, the London County Council had completed 30,033 permanent new houses and flats; at that date *all* New Towns had completed 583.[3] Industry was going to 'development' areas designated by the Board of Trade and to existing urban centres, housing was going into existing urban centres—and into Abercrombie's Green Belt; neither industry nor housing was going in sizable numbers to the New Towns.

Development Corporations and Ministry spoke hopefully of the benefits to be derived from a slow start—careful planning, integration of the new community with the old, a solid foundation for the future superstructure. But such hopes were born of necessity not preference. It is neither a criticism of nor a compliment to the highly competent planners to observe that now they were hardly driving at all, or were forced to drive at an excruciatingly slow speed.

The first annual report of the Stevenage Development Corporation was acidly (but accurately) reviewed in a local paper:[4]

[1] Ministry of Town and Country Planning, *Stevenage New Town . . .*, op. cit., p. 37.

[2] Editorial, 'New Towns', *Architects' Journal*, 7th September 1950, p. 229.

[3] Ministry of Local Government and Planning, *Housing Return for England and Wales 31st December 1950*, Cmd. 8138 (London, 1951), pp. 7, 30–1.

[4] *Letchworth Citizen*, 20th May 1949. The report summarized was published as New Towns Act, 1946, *Reports of the . . . Development Corporations for the period ending 31st March 1948* (London, 1949), pp. 73–86.

'TWENTY HOMES IN TWO YEARS'

'Stevenage Development Corporation spent £205,534 from the date it was set up—November 11, 1946—to March 31, 1948. During that time 20 prefabricated aluminium bungalows were erected near the headquarters at Aston.'

The prefabs were erected in March 1948 for the Corporation's staff; not a single house had yet been built for Londoners. The second report, covering the period to 31st March 1949, had little more to boast of: 'Progress has again been slow and no major work of construction has been accomplished. . . .'[1] At this date, virtually none of the 6,070 acres in the designated area had been acquired by the Corporation.[2] The preparation of a revised Master Plan drawn to the scale of six inches to one mile had, however, been completed; a one-acre tree nursery with about 2,000 trees and shrubs had been established; soil surveys and a topographical survey at a scale of 1:500 and a vertical interval of one foot were well under way; and records of rainfall, wind velocity, barometric pressure, and stream-flow were being kept. The main signs of Corporation activity visible at Stevenage were an information office that had opened on the High Street and the ubiquitous surveyors who scurried about in jeeps and popped up everywhere with rods and transepts.

Corporation members and their staff were frankly unhappy about the state of affairs. An officer who addressed the Stevenage Chamber of Trade dinner on 17th November 1949 expressed gratitude at having been asked to speak on the 'activities' instead of the 'progress' of the Corporation; he did not know how the Corporation could go any slower than it had been going; there was 'so much to do: so little done'. The following verses by a local wit were sung at a Stevenage variety show (to the tune of Much-Binding-in-the-Marsh):[3]

> At Still Waiting For A Town
>   The Corporation now has been elected
>   The site for building also is selected
> At information centre you can gather all the gen
> Mathematical, geographical, statistical but then
> The only question they can't answer if you ask is when
> At Still Waiting For A Town.

[1] New Towns Act, 1946, *Reports of the . . . Development Corporations for the period ending 31st March* 1949 (London, 1949), p. 129.

[2] During the first year, the Corporation bought for office space two country mansions with 201 acres of accompanying land (one mansion proved to be a white elephant and went unused). As of 31st March 1949, only eighteen more acres had been acquired by purchase or lease; these were mainly scattered plots and cottages to house the Corporation's staff.

[3] Courtesy of the author, Mr. Stanley Bunting. The song was first performed 7th November 1949.

74

At Still Waiting For A Town
  Surveyors now for months have been surveying
  The pros and cons and hows they have been weighing
They've taken samples of the earth to tell the sand from clay
They've dug the holes and filled them in and hid them so that they
Can come and dig them up again some other sunny day
At Still Waiting For A Town.

. . . . .

At Still Waiting For A Town
  The fourteenth master plan is put on show now
  With speed phenomenal the town will grow now
Delays are nearly over, we soon shall clap our hands
At twenty thousand pre-fabs upon our fertile lands
For soon they'll *need* a new town just to house the master plans
At Still Waiting For A Town.

Towards the end of the year there were definite signs of improvement in the Corporation's situation. Four years after Ministry
officials had broached the project to the Council and three years after
the issuance of the Designation Order, the first substantial engineering work was finally begun in October 1949, bulldozers levelling a stretch of field south of town for a two-mile road to open up
land for a housing development. The Master Plan for the New Town
was approved by the Minister 22nd February 1950, after interminable delays for revisions and a public inquiry (on 18–19th October
1949) at which objections had been voiced by the Council and the
Residents' Protection Association. As of July 1950, about 1,000
acres or 16 per cent of the designated area had been acquired by the
Corporation.[1] Best of all, some houses were actually being built: at
31st December 1950, 28 permanent new dwellings had been completed and 306 were under construction.[2]

The first London family to move to Stevenage New Town occupied their home on 2nd February 1951.[3]

Relations with the Council had also improved. The Corporation
took over the town's waterworks by voluntary agreement 1st April
1950 at terms financially favourable to the Council; and the Council,
by a vote of 6 to 2, obligingly relaxed their byelaws to allow the
Corporation to build 250 houses with reduced room height (in keeping with the latest minimal architectural standards for health and

[1] D. Rigby Childs, 'Progress Report on Stevenage', *Architects' Journal*,
31st August 1950, p. 213.
[2] Ministry of Local Government and Planning, *Housing Return for England
and Wales 31st December 1950*, Cmd. 8138 (London, 1951), Appendix B, pp. 24–5.
The completed buildings were mainly in-fillings on scattered lots in Stevenage
for which main services were already present.
[3] *Hertfordshire Mercury*, 9th February 1951. Houses completed before this date
had been occupied by employees of the Corporation.

safety and effecting a saving of time and money during construction).[1] The plan for the redevelopment of old Stevenage would be prepared jointly by the Council and the Corporation, and agreement was also reached upon the Corporation's financial contribution towards the cost of extending the Council's sewage works to a capacity adequate for 18,000 people (a necessary interim measure while negotiations proceeded for the construction of a long-term regional works at Rye Meads to service the Stevenage New Town of 60,000, the Harlow New Town, and other centres draining into the middle reaches of the River Lee).

Despite its legal defeat, the Protection Association remained in being, having resolved in April 1948 'that its purposes be extended to include the protection of the interests of Stevenage in relation to any proposals of the Stevenage Development Corporation or the Minister of Town and Country Planning'; in effect, this meant the exploitation of opportunities to obstruct the progress of the New Town and to secure all possible concessions for property owners and ratepayers.

Ministry and Corporation officials had started work on the New Town with high ideals, great ambition, and no experience. By 1950, they had gained a good deal of frustrating experience which must have served to moderate their ambition and ideals. The New Towns programme was a bold venture for a young Ministry and, if it could not resolve in a score of years problems created by over a century of urbanization, it could still hope to achieve standards utopian for previous generations. In the move from planning to practice, the planners experienced the recalcitrance of many people to being planned, the compulsion of economic factors, the power of the *status quo*, the conflict of interests between rival individuals and groups within and without the Government; the importance of 'connections' and of personalities; of patience; of power; and of chance. In short, they experienced something of the world.

[1] A Ministry of Health committee had just recommended that local authorities consider reducing the minimum room height in new housing from 8 ft. to 7 ft. 6 in. as a means of economy (Ministry of Health, *The Cost of Home Building* London, 1950), pp. 22, 28).

Part Two
The New Town Plan

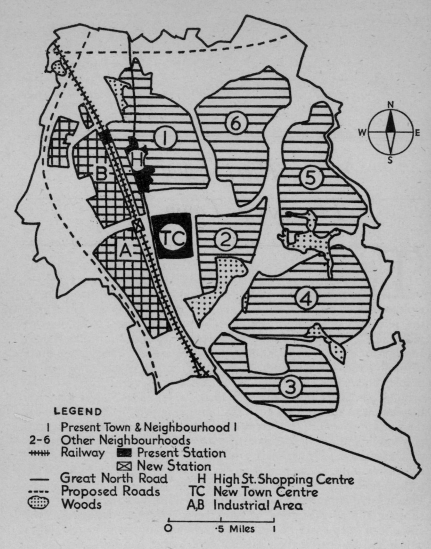

LEGEND

| | Present Town & Neighbourhood I
2-6 | Other Neighbourhoods
╫╫╫╫ Railway   ■ Present Station
          ⊠ New Station
—— Great North Road   H High St. Shopping Centre
---- Proposed Roads   TC New Town Centre
⊞⊞ Woods   A,B Industrial Area

O   ·5 Miles   I

STEVENAGE NEW TOWN MASTER PLAN, 1950

CHAPTER FOUR

Sociological Components

Technicians at the Ministry of Town and Country Planning prepared in 1945 and 1946 a draft plan for Stevenage New Town modelled upon and developing standards and principles outlined in the *Greater London Plan*.[1] It had been hoped that the responsible architect would subsequently accept employment with the Development Corporation, but, as this did not materialize, another architect was appointed in October 1947. His views, quite naturally, did not coincide with those of his predecessor on all points, and some delay inevitably resulted in the revision of the original plan and preparation of a final version. The Master Plan was forwarded to the Stevenage and County Councils in April 1949 for their comments and, in October, a Ministry inspector held a voluntary public inquiry in the Stevenage town hall at which the Corporation explained its proposals and representatives of the Stevenage Council and the Residents' Protection Association voiced objections (other bodies submitted their views to the Ministry privately). Finally, in February 1950, the Minister approved the Master Plan substantially as submitted, except for a recommendation that the amount of open space be reduced, thus removing many uncertainties which had hampered the Corporation's work.

The initial plan has been characterized as 'skilful, expensive, unimaginative, and somewhat rigid'.[2] It was, of course, a preliminary draft, prepared in a short time at little expense, whose chief purpose was 'to show that a town of requisite size could be built within certain boundaries and would satisfy the conditions and standards laid

[1] Patrick Abercrombie, *Greater London Plan* 1944 (London, 1945), pp. 110–21, 169–71.
[2] C. B. Purdom, *The Building of Satellite Towns* (London, 1949), p. 422.

79

down'.[1] The overall composition—the siting of the industrial zone west and six residential neighbourhoods east of the railway, a central shopping centre, highway by-pass, belt of surrounding farmland, etc.—was retained by the Corporation, but modifications and refinements were introduced in the size of the town centre and industrial area, railway bridges and other features, and the design of the road network.

The outline of the Master Plan and something of the spirit behind it is suggested in the following passage from a booklet issued by the Corporation:

'The new Stevenage will comprise an area of about six thousand acres. The existing town of about 6,500 people covers only a fraction of it, the rest being farmland and woodland. By no means all of this will be built over. The woods and copses will be preserved, so will the vast majority of single trees and many of the existing hedgelines. Fairlands Valley, which runs from north to south through the middle of the site, will remain open space. Other green spaces will be retained as town parks, while there will be a broad belt of farmland separating Stevenage from any other village or town. . . .

'The present town of Stevenage is itself to be the nucleus of the first neighbourhood of the New Town. There will be added in due course . . . five other neighbourhoods [each with an average population of 10,000]. . . . Each will have its own local shops and schools and playgrounds, there will be houses and flats of different types and sizes to suit differing families, and the gardens will vary in size to cater for different tastes. Arid stretches of brick and asphalt will be avoided. There will be trees to punctuate the buildings, grass commons between houses, views of open country at the turn of the road.

'The big shops, and those to meet other than daily needs, will be in the new Town Centre, planned as a focus, quickly reached by bus from the furthest parts of the town. Here also will be cinemas and theatres, the new Town Hall and other public and cultural buildings, including the principal Anglican church. . . .

'The Great North Road will no longer run through the heart of the town, but will by-pass it on the west. Between this new by-pass and the railway there is relatively flat ground which the Plan reserves for industry, and in which there are already several large factory buildings.'[2]

The proposed land use is given in Table II. (The open space and possibly also road reservations indicated there, as of July 1949, will presumably be reduced in the light of the Minister's recommenda-

[1] Gordon Stephenson, talk on 'New Towns' printed in *The Architects' Journal*, 3rd October 1946, p. 251. The Ministry plan is briefly described in 'Stevenage. A Plan for a New Town', *The Architects' Journal*, 12th September 1946, pp. 187–90.

[2] *The New Town of Stevenage* (Stevenage Development Corporation, 1949), pp. 8, 17.

tion.) It is not our intention, nor are we qualified, to discuss technical features of the plan, but only some of its social implications.

TABLE II[1]

MASTER PLAN—LAND USE (*July* 1949)

Land Use	Acres	per cent
Residential	1,753	28·7
Farmland	1,544	25·3
Open spaces	672	11·0
Woods	252	4·1
Allotments*	135	2·2
Industrial	448	7·3
Schools and college	334	5·5
Neighbourhood centres	164	2·7
Town centre	100	1·6
Road reservations	387	6·3
Railway land	146	2·4
Roads not included above	90	1·5
Miscellaneous†	75	1·2
TOTAL	6,100	99·8‡

* American readers may need to be told that allotments are small plots, generally leased by people with insufficient garden space, upon which vegetables for home consumption are grown.
† Including helicopter field, cemeteries, sewage and water works.
‡ Percentages refuse to add up to 100.

A. THE 'BALANCED' COMMUNITY

The concept of the 'balanced' neighbourhood and community is one of the outstanding social features of the plan. This idea was advanced in the report of the New Towns Committee—indeed, was part of its terms of reference, which required the Committee 'to suggest guiding principles on which such Towns should be established and developed as self-contained and balanced communities for work and living'.[2] The Minister of Town and Country Planning not only adopted but perhaps extended this policy, stating,

[1] From *Stevenage New Town Technical Report* (mimeographed report accompanying the Master Plan), (Stevenage Development Corporation, July 1949). Referred to henceforth as *Corporation Master Plan 1949*.
[2] *Final Report of the New Towns Committee*, Cmd. 6876 (London, July 1946), p. 2.

'I am very concerned indeed not merely to get different classes . . . living together in a community, but to get them actually mixing together. . . . Unless they do mix, and mix freely, in their leisure and recreation, the whole purpose of . . . a mixed community disappears. There is no value in having different strata of society in different streets if they do not mix; the whole purpose is to ensure that they do mix.'

—and then added hopefully that sociological research was necessary to determine what housing arrangements were best suited to achieve this goal.[1] The chairman of the Stevenage Development Corporation declared, 'We want to revive that social structure which existed in the old English villages, where the rich lived next door to the not so rich, and everyone knew everybody. . . . The man who wants a bigger house will be able to have it, but he will not be able to have it apart from the smaller houses.'[2] And a Corporation officer said, 'We want to contrive it so that none of the residential neighbourhoods, not even a large area within a neighbourhood, should be dominated by a single class or group.'[3]

Ministry and Corporation policies were designed to further this goal in a number of ways. A Harlow Corporation memorandum on the selection of industry advised:

'To obtain the mixed community we are aiming at, preference should be given to industries employing a high proportion of skilled workers, of technicians, and of administrative grades. . . . The Corporation will, as far as possible, avoid taking firms from industries likely to decline in prosperity or subject to heavy cyclical unemployment. . . . It would be an advantage if it were possible to have some firms whose heaviest demand for labour was in the winter months in order to take up some of the "slack" in the building trades. Trades subject to seasonal winter unemployment should be avoided.'[4]

The Lord President of the Council announced in January 1948 that 'The Government have decided that the new town at Stevenage will be given preference in considering the sites of new scientific establishments in the London region. . . . Stevenage will be one of the important scientific centres of the future.'[5] Two sites totalling eighty-two acres have already been reserved by the Corporation for branches of the Department of Scientific and Industrial Research—a Corporation report noted, 'They will be highly acceptable as incomers, particu-

[1] Lewis Silkin, 'Housing Layout in Theory and Practice', *Architects' Journal*, 8th July 1948, p. 45.

[2] As reported in the *Letchworth Citizen*, 1st August 1947.

[3] From a B.B.C. talk, *The Social Pattern of a New Town*, February 1949.

[4] *Industrial Structure of the Town—the Social Factors to be Taken into Account in the Selection of Industry* (mimeographed report), (Harlow Corporation, February 1949).

[5] Report of speech by Herbert Morrison at Letchworth, *Hertfordshire Express*, 12th January 1948.

larly because of their social structure which is something out of
the ordinary, including . . . an unusually high proportion of professional and technical men and women'.[1]

It was hoped to obtain a majority of small firms in the New Town,
with only a few employing 1,000–2,000 workers, so that the local
economy would not be dominated by any one industry and a wide
range of employment would be available. A solid representation of
independent professional persons and members of distributive and
service trades was also to be encouraged to a total of perhaps 13,000
or more—equal to or greater than the number of industrial workers.
'We have to see that there are no less people employed in services at
Stevenage than in an average town of the same size. For an under-
serviced town will not attract residents of higher incomes and then
it will lose in prosperity.'[2]

A complementary housing policy was to be pursued. In May 1946,
the Minister told the Association of London Property Owners that
he had 'not the slightest objection to individuals building their
houses under lease' in New Towns;[3] and the Reith Committee soon
recommended that New Town Corporations

'should see that larger as well as smaller houses are built and houses for
sale as well as for letting, and encouragement should be given to private
builders and housing associations. In all neighbourhoods sites should be
made available for houses to be built to owners' requirements, and . . .
building licences, contracts, and loans from local authorities or building
societies [should be facilitated].'[4]

The Stevenage Corporation proposed, in July 1949, that each
neighbourhood 'will contain approximately 80 per cent housing of
the type subsidized by the Government, 15 per cent of a rather higher
standard and 5 per cent of what might be termed houses for the
managerial classes. . . .'[5] 'It is not the intention of the Corporation to
do all the house-erecting themselves,' an officer explained. 'Sites will
be available for persons who wish to build their own houses. They
will be able to employ their own architects, engage their own
builders, and the only requirement will be that the plans should be
subject to the approval of the Corporation . . . in order that there

[1] Corporation report, 30th June 1948.
[2] From a Corporation officer's B.B.C. talk *The Social Pattern of a New Town*,
February 1949.
[3] Statement by the Minister at the Association luncheon, 1st May 1946,
quoted by Purdom, op. cit., p. 410.
[4] Cmd. 6876, July 1946, p. 30.
[5] '. . . these proportions . . . will be constantly under review in the light of
experience gained as the town is built' (*Corporation Master Plan* 1949). The
four-to-one ratio between houses of low and high space standards was that prevailing at the time in the Government's allocation of housing licences between
local authorities and private builders.

should be no disharmony in the development of the new town.'[1] Housing priority would be given to school teachers, nurses, and professional persons whose presence was deemed desirable as much as to construction workers and others actively engaged in building the New Town.

Ministry and Corporation members and staff were no more naïve about the English class structure than any similar assemblage of managerial, professional, and white-collar workers. The policies they sought to implement were, it is true, partially a product of a Labour Government newly come to power and a long succession of idealists aspiring to it; but they were equally a product of Conservative and Liberal Governments and ideologies—of eminently practical capitalists, politicians, peers, and men whose business had always been to rule efficiently and who, while not immune from ideals of their own, had no intention of liquidating the existing order of society. The notion of a 'balanced' community, of course, posited the existence of social classes, and set forth a basis on which they should live together. The Reith Committee recognized this in forthright fashion:

'There may ... be some doubt as to the full significance of a "balanced" community, and still more as to how it is to be achieved. So far as the issue is an economic one, balance can be attained by giving opportunity for many sorts of employment which will attract men and women up to a high economic level. Beyond that point the problem is not economic at all nor even a vaguely social one; it is, to be frank, one of class distinction. ... If the community is to be truly balanced, so long as social classes exist, all must be represented in it.'[2]

What, then, were the motives behind the policy of a 'balanced' community?

(a) Economic Motives

As pointed out in Chapter I, the insistence upon higher standards for working-class housing led to the introduction of Government subsidies to meet the deficit between the rental which workers could pay and the cost of construction. Hence, the greater the proportion of working-class housing in a New Town, the greater the cost to the Treasury. But even with the Government subsidy, it was difficult for local authorities to make council houses an economic proposition, because the cost of services and maintenance generally exceeded their yield in rates (local taxes).[3] Under Labour control, the tendency

[1] Statement by Corporation officer at the Master Plan inquiry, 18th October 1949.
[2] Cmd. 6876, p. 10.
[3] As a county officer explained in a memorandum on New Town finance dated July 1947, 'Working-class houses are by themselves the most "uneco-

was for a local authority to shift the burden from council house rents to the general rate—i.e., from the working-class tenant to the independent middle-class ratepayer; under Conservative control, to raise rents and protect the ratepayer.[1]

Because of increased prices it was impossible for the Corporation to build in 1949 working-class houses similar to the Stevenage Council's pre-war houses to let at comparable rents, and, as it was not a rating authority, the Corporation could not—even if it wished —throw the burden directly upon the local ratepayer. To increase further rents which promised, in any case, to be higher than Council house rents would be embarrassing, if not suicidal, for both the Corporation and the Government. The cost would, probably, eventually fall upon the London boroughs exporting population to the New Town and upon the Treasury.[2] But the problem would be eased by building more houses for the middle classes, which were not subsidized by the Government (capital coming from private individuals or building societies) and could be let economically on a ninety-nine-year lease. In other words, the more 'balanced' the community, the better would be the chance of a balanced budget for Corporation and Treasury and the smaller the Government capital investment required to complete the New Town.[3] The economics of this situation had been clearly stated by Lewis Mumford:

'Without doubt the prime obstacle to urban decentralization is that a unit that consists of workers, without the middle class and rich groups that exist in a big city, is unable to support even the elementary civic equipment, of roads, sewers, fire department, police service, and schools. At present it is only by remaining in metropolitan areas, where the taxes derived from the well-to-

nomic" of rated subjects; they create the largest demand for the local authority services, and are unprofitable in the sense that the rate income from them falls short of the rate-expenditure on those services'. For a definition of rates, see p. 157, note 1.

[1] Thus the official local government journal of the Conservative Party stated, 'It is . . . just that the [council] rents which should be charged should cover all outgoings, after allowance has been made for the [Government] subsidy. It is obviously unfair for the extra burden to be repeatedly thrust upon the ratepayers . . .' (*The Councillor*, April 1949, p. 8). Labour authorities, of course, have also often raised the rents of council houses.

[2] The Minister of Town and Country Planning stated on 8th May 1946 that he contemplated 'an agreement between the exporting authority and the corporation, under which the exporting authority will pay to the corporation the whole or part of the rate subsidy [usually paid by the local council]. . . . But where a corporation is not able to secure a rate contribution from any local authority, that rate contribution will have to be made good by the Exchequer' (*Hansard*, vol. 422, cols. 1082–3).

[3] In May 1946, the Minister estimated the capital cost to public funds of the development of a New Town at about £19 million 'on the assumption that most of the middle-class houses, the shops and the factories will be built by private enterprise' (*Hansard*, vol. 422, col. 1083).

do districts can be partly applied to the working class quarters, that the worker can obtain even a modicum of the facilities for a good life.'[1]

Another presumptive virtue of the balanced community, of course, was the greater stability of its industry and business. The disastrous effects of a trade slump in a one-industry town (with the wrong industry) were obvious. The effort to achieve immunity from the economic ills of the times was understandable and commendable; its realism, however, depended upon the degree of immunity it was hoped to attain. In the imagination of some New Town planners— or, to be more accurate, New Town propagandists and publicists— one detected a static world in which capitalism (free, State, or international) and economics (variations in productivity, supply and demand, wages and prices) never were. They regarded London as a monstrous agglomeration which lived by draining goods and wealth from the whole of Britain, and hoped to redress the balance, at least slightly, in favour of the countryside. But New Towns, by definition, were 'satellite' to London's sun, and it was difficult to see how the parasite of a parasite could become much healthier than its host or less dependent upon the mother nation (or the nation, at its most insular, independent of the world). S. R. Dennison properly cautioned that

'The idea of "balance" of industries should not be pressed too far. The unfortunate consequences of the dependence of communities on a single major industry have often been painfully manifest, and the encouragement of some diversification is a means of counteracting this. But once we go beyond this generalisation, the ground becomes less sure; certainly it is not possible to delineate, as some have tried to do, an "optimum" scheme of balanced industries for any particular size of community—still less would it be possible to "plan" communities accordingly.'[2]

It need hardly be added that such economic 'balance' as any New Town may achieve can only be at the sufferance of other communities which must specialize economically (because of immobile mines, seas, and heavy industries or the almost equally immobile capital and cultural accumulations of the past).

The enthusiasm of New Towns for light industry was also influenced by physical considerations. 'We are very anxious that our industries shall be a model of its kind, with sports grounds, open spaces, parks and gardens,' said one chairman of the Stevenage Corporation. '. . . factory buildings . . . have to be adapted for their purpose . . . but also gracious in appearance and pleasant to work in,

[1] Lewis Mumford, *The Culture of Cities* (London, 1940), p. 459; italics in original.
[2] In the *Report of the Committee on Land Utilisation in Rural Areas*, Cmd. 6378 (London 1942), p. 116.

not "dark satanic mills".[1] A member of the Hemel Hempstead Corporation observed that 'physical planners have a weakness for light industry. It tends to be cleaner and to lend itself more easily to modern architecture. . . . it is not every site, superficially attractive, which will carry the foundations of a factory containing heavy machinery. Again, the transport demands of light industry are less exacting. . . .'[2] It was easier to accommodate and to prettify a research laboratory or a dress factory than coke ovens or a hot steel mill.

In the idea of 'balance' one could detect also the age-long search for the economic and social 'norm', the golden mean in which all the parts of a community and all citizens would work together harmoniously and without friction and enjoy a blessed and lasting state of 'health'.[3] In practice, this 'norm' often meant the national industrial, social, and demographic *average*, as determined by the Registrar-General's 1931 census.[4] The ideal was so lofty and the practice so mundane that it seems kindest to omit all criticism beyond the comment of the Hemel Hempstead Corporation that 'It is doubtful whether, in a period of social and economic transition, the term [balanced community] can be more than an elusive but inspiring concept. . . .'[5]

[1] *Municipal Journal*, 25th July 1947.
[2] J. E. MacColl, 'The social implications of the new town', *Fortnightly*, December 1947, p. 430.
[3] Cf. Lewis Mumford, 'The ideal of balance is very close to the Greek ideal of the Golden Mean in conduct; and even of the Renaissance ideal of the gentleman. . . . To achieve balance, a variety of occupations, a variety of environments, a variety of social groupings must be open to the individual . . . to permit a periodical shaking up of routines. . . . In the interests of balance, we must look forward, as Sir Thomas More did in his Utopia, to an alternation of rural and urban occupations. . . . We must expect more manual work from the intellectual . . . and . . . more intelligence and intellectual effort from the rank and file of humanity. . . . This effort to achieve balance . . . is essential to the creation of a common world, more orderly, more harmonious than was Western society' (op. cit., pp. 152–3).
[4] Arthur Smailes, for example, defines a 'balanced' community as one with a 'representative' or 'normal' economic and social structure, i.e., 'one which conforms to that of the country as a whole' ('Balanced Towns', *Journal Town Planning Institute* (1945), vol. 32, p. 30. Cf. also his article 'Balance and Planning', *Sociological Review* (1944), vol. 36, pp. 18–23). R. K. Kelsall, a research officer at the Ministry of Town and Country Planning, notes that 'the tendency has been for some planners to seek to apply the idea of a balanced community in an unduly rigid and unrealistic way. . . . they have occasionally sought to reproduce [in New Towns] the national pattern of industry, of age and sex distribution, of social groups and so on' (*Citizens' Guide to the New Town and Country Planning* (Oxford 1949), p. 64).
[5] Report of the Hemel Hempstead Corporation, in New Towns Act, 1946, *Reports of the . . . Development Corporations for the period ending 31st March 1948* (London, 1949), p. 65.

(b) Social Motives

By comparison with economic motives, the social motives for the balanced community were ambiguous. Indeed, they sometimes seemed to represent opposing goals and forces—the classless and class societies, the Socialist and Conservative Parties and ideologies.

A high degree of class segregation in housing and social intercourse almost invariably characterizes contemporary urban society (the lower degree of segregation often prevailing in rural areas does not contradict this fact, but suggests something of the world and the century from which many planners drew inspiration). Different patterns of segregation obtain, however, in different urban areas, which influence the nature of community life and inter-class relations. The middle-class suburbs and working-class slums of metropolitan areas exemplify the one-class neighbourhood which may extend over a large area, while in districts like London's Chelsea or Bloomsbury or almost any small town various social classes live together in closer proximity. A modern version of the latter type of environment was what Ministry and Corporation planners hoped to achieve in the New Towns, since they believed this induced social consequences—greater political and social stability and a broader range of social and cultural activity—preferable to those of one-class neighbourhoods.

Planners often try to repair with one hand what they have damaged with the other—that is, they try to remedy conditions which are themselves (in part) a consequence of previous remedies. And so, to a considerable extent, the 'mixed class' neighbourhood and town was advocated now as a reaction against the one-class neighbourhoods which had developed partly as a consequence of the zoning regulations of inter-war planning legislation, under which vast districts were 'developed at the scale of one house to the acre, eight to the acre, or twelve to the acre, thus inevitably segregating families according to their incomes',[1] and partly as a consequence of previous (and continuing) housing policy which produced segregated working-class council estates in every urban area:

'Historically, large-scale class segregation . . . is a comparatively recent thing. It did not occur in the medieval city, and such segregation as there was in pre-Industrial Revolution towns was on a small scale. Even then it occurred only in the planned streets and squares of London, Bath and similar places: and it was a segregation by *streets* rather than by quarters or whole towns: there were streets of big houses and streets of little ones, but generally they were near to each other and closely associated. In the naturally growing towns larger houses and cottages stood . . . side by side in exactly the same way as they do in villages to-day. The split came with the rapid development of the new 19th-century industrial towns, and as the housing conditions of the workers became more and more debased

[1] Robert Graves and Alan Hodge, *The Long Week-end* (London, 1941), p. 175.

88

the split widened, till the middle classes began to live in special places of their own. . . .

'The recent and present segregation . . . has arisen . . . from activity by government itself. . . . As a result of governmental activity in the housing of the working classes, we have now in every town or city in the country whole estates devoted entirely to the housing of one particular wage-earning group. . . .'[1]

The experience of Letchworth and Welwyn Garden City did not suggest that the New Towns would have an easy time realizing their goal of mixing classes. Both garden cities had

'sought to minimize the segregation of houses of different sizes or for people of different incomes. The placing of the larger owner-occupied houses cheek by jowl with the smaller weekly-rented houses was not found popular; but groups of varying sizes of houses have been successfully placed in the same road or neighbourhood. There is less segregation of the classes than in other towns. It has been found, however, that whatever the town planner may desire, people have a marked tendency to segregate themselves by class or income. An area in which there are some noticeably large and poor families comes to be regarded as lacking in "social tone". The better-off tenants (whether they are clerical workers or the more highly-paid factory workers) spontaneously move to streets in which, even if the houses are no larger, the social atmosphere is regarded as superior. In the less favoured parts, rents fall, and in the more favoured parts rents rise, and this intensifies the distinction. . . . once an area loses prestige it is extremely difficult to prevent the movement from it of the better-off people to an area they like better. . . .'[2]

In the early days at Welwyn and Letchworth, it was noted, class distinctions were at a minimum:

'Everybody without exception went to the same meetings and functions, to the same religious meetings, political discussions, dances, social gatherings, tennis parties. . . . The first wedding, the first christening, the first funeral, the first event organized by some new society . . . were matters of at least curious interest to all. There was no established social hierarchy . . . nobody who by traditional right must be asked to be chairman or secretary of anything.'[3]

Apparently this was due to the pioneer environment, which has had similar consequences elsewhere.[4] In any event, the relatively classless period soon ended, and when F. J. Osborn arrived at Letchworth in its eighth year earlier residents pitied him 'for having missed the golden age'. As both towns grew, 'ring-fenced social groups tended

[1] Thomas Sharp, *Town Planning* (Harmondsworth, Middlesex, 1940), pp. 85-6.
[2] F. J. Osborn, *Green-Belt Cities* (London, 1946), pp. 92-3.
[3] Ibid., p. 116.
[4] For example, much the same change from an initial 'classless' to a class-organized community is reported for the London County Council's housing estate at Watling (Ruth Durant, *Watling* (London, 1939)).

to appear',[1] and, it will be recalled, the Minister of Town and Country Planning, in the course of his Stevenage speech, referred to Welwyn as a town cut in two by the railway—which meant (as is widely known) cut into two social classes.

There was little reason to believe that the situation at Stevenage New Town would be significantly different, or even as favourable during the early years, since different social classes were already entrenched in the town and the incoming population, coming mainly from London boroughs where severe overcrowding existed,[2] would be largely working class. 'We are hoping to avoid "one-class" neighbourhoods without putting various different sorts of people bang next door to one another', a Corporation officer said,[3] suggesting that the Corporation intended to follow a policy of moderate dispersal of housing, along the lines that met with limited success at Welwyn. Another alternative was the policy adopted by the Glenrothes Development Corporation of leaving an ' "adjustment area" . . . unbuilt upon in each residential precinct so that an opportunity will remain for correction of initial faults of balance'.[4] However, on any estimate, the vast bulk of housing would be Government-subsidized working-class houses, and it remained to be seen how much a few larger houses interspersed amongst this mass could change the general character of a neighbourhood.

The County Council was sceptical of the Corporation's chances of achieving a balanced neighbourhood structure in the New Town, observing that

'a high proportion of small houses is to be erected. Experience in other parts of the country in population movement of this type has shown that the difficulty of introducing houses for the higher income groups is so great as to be well-nigh insuperable. If this difficulty, which strikes at the root of the problem of creating a balanced community, is to be overcome, more effective steps than mere reservation are necessary.'[5]

A 1942 Mass-Observation working-class housing survey (100 cases of which were selected from a working-class area in Letchworth), concluded,

'People like sociable, but not inquisitive, neighbours of the same "class" as themselves. This last point was one of the sorest in the whole

[1] Osborn, op. cit., pp. 116–17.
[2] According to a Ministry memorandum of 3rd December 1949, Stevenage New Town was to draw its population mainly from Enfield Urban District and the boroughs of Edmonton, Hendon, Hornsey, Tottenham, and Wood Green.
[3] *Hertfordshire Express*, 27th August 1949.
[4] New Towns Act, 1946, *Reports of the East Kilbride and Glenrothes Development Corporations for the period ending 31st March 1950* (Edinburgh 1950), p. 35.
[5] Hertfordshire County Council, Appendix 'B' to the Report of the County Planning Committee dated 4th November 1949. 'Stevenage Development Corporation—Outline Plan. Observations of the Hertfordshire County Council.'

social set-up, and there were two sharply contrasted viewpoints. Some people considered that their neighbours belonged to a lower social grade than themselves and were dragging the neighbourhood down; while others disliked what they alleged to be the "snobbishness" of their neighbours.'[1]

Even more pertinent were the findings of a survey conducted by a Government research agency for the Ministry of Town and Country Planning in the winter of 1946–7. At the time it was anticipated that a large portion of the New Town's population would come from the London borough of Willesden, and the Social Survey was requested to obtain data on those elements of the population willing to migrate. Some 1,448 Willesden housewives were questioned.

'Rather more than half (54 %) the informants said that they were living in a street of mixed social classes; and the higher the economic group, the greater was the proportion saying this. Almost two-thirds (62 %) of the informants, however, said that they would prefer the single-class street, and it was noticeable that the higher economic groups preferred this rather more frequently. It was clear that most Willesden people preferred to have as neighbours others of their own social status. It thus seems contrary to the wishes of the majority of the Willesden people that the planning of a new town should result in the close inter-mixture of classes in the same street.'[2]

Largely for financial reasons, the County Council, after an initial period of benevolence, grew more critical of the Corporation's policy, and its astringent remarks about the balanced community were part of a larger campaign to reduce the New Town to a population of 18,000. The meaningfulness of abstract questions pertaining to such complex matters as social class is dubious, and the simple quantification of answers by Mass-Observation and the Social Survey undoubtedly left deeper truths obscure. Yet planners (if not discomforted by these) would doubtless be comforted by contrary findings, so that if these (and many similar) data were to enter the scales at all, their weight fell against the feasibility of a balanced community.

All planners, of course, were by no means in agreement on the possibility or desirability (the two are more closely related than 'objective' sociologists recognize) of mixing social classes. For example, one authority argues:

'There are many places in which all classes are already trained to mix without prejudice; the only thing is that the home neighbourhood is not one of these places. Like attracts like, and there's no harm in this. So let us have our precincts of professional men, our closes of clerks and our

[1] Mass-Observation, *An Enquiry into People's Homes* (London, 1943), p. 207.
[2] Bertram Hutchinson, *Willesden and the New Towns* (The Social Survey, London, December 1947), p. 2.

avenues of navvies, and let us so arrange them that no one is ashamed of his neighbours, and we shall have peace over the garden wall.'[1]

Another maintains that one of the surest ways of *hampering* the development of 'the spirit of neighbourliness' would be 'to enforce, by planning, a mixture of social strata . . . .'

'Though social stratification has led to geographic separation . . . it is unrealistic to assume that . . . class divisions can be overcome merely by reducing the physical distance between them. . . . all that would be achieved by "social mixing" is the present pattern of social and geographic differentiation on a smaller scale. It is therefore better that the neighbourhood should be populated by people of an approximately similar background and tastes, and thus provide a sound basis for the neighbourhood spirit.'[2]

Another reasoned, 'As long as social distinctions are so marked and living standards vary widely, like will continue to live with like because it is convenient and satisfactory to do so'.[3] And many upheld a middle position. 'It is not segregation into individual streets that matters. It is segregation into quarters, into whole towns and suburbs, that is bad.'[4] 'Some segregation of classes is inevitable and not to be deprecated; what is to be deplored is such massed segregation as to create different world.'[5]

The advantages of class *segregation* can readily be imagined and are, indeed, the social part and psychological parcel of a class system of society: in its relative isolation from others, each class can freely enjoy the material, social, and psychological rewards which its station in life permits. The men who can be seen lying drunk in the Skid Row of any large American city enjoy the rewards of their status much as do their opulent brethren who sprawl over the tables of fashionable clubs, although it is not customary for the two classes to enjoy themselves together. Custom implies general, not invariant, practice; what a man elects to do one way he can also elect to do another, and no sociological or psychological law prevents a rich man from associating with a poor man if he chooses to—of course, he often does. But more often he does not; indeed, one contemporary school of sociology[6] both defines and determines social class by the

---

[1] John Madge, 'Human Factors in Housing', *Current Affairs*, No. 50 (London, 20th March 1948), p. 14.

[2] Gordon Campleman, 'Mixed-Class Neighbourhoods: Some Sociological Aspects', *Town and Country Planning*, August 1950, pp. 330–1.

[3] Ruth Glass, 'Social Aspects of Town Planning', *Town and Country Planning Textbook* (London, 1950), p. 216.

[4] Thomas Sharp, *Town Planning*, p. 89.

[5] Gwilym Gibbon, *Problems of Town and Country Planning* (London, 1937), p. 113.

[6] That of W. L. Warner, Allison Davis, and their many associates, who define a social class as 'the largest group of people whose members have intimate access to one another. A class is composed of families and social cliques. The inter-

frequency and intimacy with which individuals associate together, and, in this view, a degree of contact between members of different classes as high as that between members of the same class is anomalous. It does not follow that each—or any—social class need be *content* with its lot; if it were, there would be no revolutions or pressure for social change. But each class must live its own life and not that of another, and nature readily conspires to make that life liveable.

In favour of encouraging social intercourse between different classes is, of course, the tradition that all men are equal before God and the gravedigger in their quantum of humanity. The opposite proposition, however, that (through birth or chance) all men are unequal, can lead to the same conclusion: charity and effective social control both require the upper and middle classes to retain contact with the lower classes. It is interesting to recall that Ebenezer Howard adduced for his balanced garden cities the same arguments that were used against the early exclusively lower-class colonization of Australia:

'We send out colonies of the limbs, without the belly and the head, of needy persons, many of them mere paupers, or even criminals; colonies made up of *a single class of persons* in the community, and that the most helpless and the most unfit to perpetuate our national character. . . . The ancients began by nominating to the honourable office of captain or leader of the colony one of the chief men . . . of the State, like the queen bee leading the workers. Monarchies provided a prince of the royal blood; an aristocracy its choicest nobleman; a democracy its most influential citizen. These naturally carried along with them some of their own station in life—their companions and friends; some of their immediate dependants also—of those between themselves and the lowest class; and were encouraged in various ways to do so. The lowest class again followed with alacrity, because they found themselves moving *with* and not *away from* the state of society in which they had been living. . . . They carried with them their gods, their festivals, their games—all, in short, that held together and kept entire the fabric of society as it existed in the parent state.'[1]

This was the opposite of a revolutionary creed, as a Stevenage Communist perceived when he dismissed the theory of a balanced community as 'not in line with the Socialist theory of a classless society', adding scornfully, 'I can't imagine people of the retired

relationships between these families and cliques, in such informal activities as visiting, dances, receptions, teas, and larger informal affairs, constitute the structure of a social class. A person is a member of that social class with which most of his participations, of this intimate kind, occur' (Allison Davis, Burleigh B. Gardner, and Mary Gardner, *Deep South* (Chicago, 1941), p. 59).

[1] This passage is quoted by Ebenezer Howard in *Garden Cities of To-morrow* (London, 1941), pp. 119–20. It is ascribed to Dr. Hind's *Thoughts on Secondary Punishment* (1832).

class settling down here among the working-class people of Stevenage. I'm afraid they will regard the working-class woman as very convenient labour for dinner parties and so forth'. That Ministry and Corporation officials conceived their task in benevolent and not repressive terms, and were as likely to suggest that the upper classes would benefit from contact with the lower classes as vice versa,[1] did not contradict the conservative function of the concept. The chairman told the Press that the Corporation hoped to persuade 'some retired, fairly wealthy people' to come to the New Town 'because they are so invaluable at organizing clubs and activities'.[2] In the same manner, the National Council of Social Service complained that because of workers' segregation on new council estates, little 'community activity' occurred there; residents had 'a large store of latent talent in the social and creative sense. This talent, however, needs some preliminary leadership to unlock it and make it available. . . .'[3] Which class would provide, or design, the key to the strangely impounded and misdirected talents of the working classes was not difficult to imagine. 'Community activity', of course, was a euphemism (and none the less a euphemism for being sincerely espoused) for 'activity congenial to the middle classes'. Boumphrey has observed that

'The whole essence of Howard's idea was that by rehousing the working-class man in a garden city, he would be transported into a clean atmosphere and healthy surroundings . . . and instead of wasting his spare time in the gin palace, to the detriment of his health, pocket, and home life, he could spend it in the healthy and fascinating pursuit of gardening.'[4]

We conclude, then, that many garden city and New Town planners

[1] As did a Corporation officer in February 1949: '. . . it is not going too far to say that the presence of better-off people in a town benefits the rest of the population because it means that the community as a whole can afford a wider and more interesting range of services and amusements. Then we have to think of the effect on each other of different social groups. There is reason to think that a community is more stimulating, and its members are more likely to stimulate one another, when you get a variety of occupations and of social groups' (B.B.C. talk, *The Social Pattern of a New Town*).

[2] *Letchworth Citizen*, 1st August 1947.

[3] *The Size and Social Structure of a Town*, A Report by a Survey Group of the National Council of Social Service, 1943, p. 3.

[4] Geoffrey Boumphrey, *Town and Country Tomorrow* (London, 1940), pp. 46–7. Cf. the propaganda of an early garden city society which complained that in towns 'the healthful influence of the garden has been shut out. . . . "Of all the flowers the human flower has the greatest need of the sun." . . . Give workmen little front gardens . . . and set neighbour competing with neighbour, and in a few years these front gardens will become pictures of floral neatness' (National Housing and Town Planning Council, *How to Town-Plan, The Building and Equipment of Cottages in Garden Suburbs* (1910), pp. 3, 15). Evidence presented later in this chapter (p. 113) suggests that, on the whole, workmen's gardens are still not as neat as those of the middle classes.

merely translated into sociological terms and architectural forms middle- and upper-class ideologies of a conservative or liberal-reformist nature, and that the 'balanced community' concept thus served the forces of law and order, middle-class morality, and the social and political *status quo*.

That, for other planners (and, formally, for the Socialist Government), the 'balanced community' concept was part of a utopian Socialist creed, is too evident to require emphasis. Indeed, this was often all that the Conservative Stevenage home-owner saw.

B. THE REILLY GREEN

The 'Reilly Green' or garden common was an example of how many planners hoped to foster the ideals of community 'balance' and 'neighbourliness'. The Corporation was noticeably reticent in its public declarations concerning this proposal, but the Minister cited the Reilly Plan in the course of his Stevenage speech as 'one idea which may be found to be worth trying out'. In May 1949, a Corporation spokesman suggested that these commons 'are still at the study stage and have not yet been approved. . . .'[1] The fullest official statement by the Corporation, as of July 1949, was that

'The neighbourhood will itself be sub-divided into smaller units likely to encourage social relations between families by grouping round commons and greens, in enclosed streets or culs-de-sac, so that people have the chance to meet and come to know each other. . . . [Garden commons] are spaces behind the private gardens which will be used communally, where children may play in safety, away from traffic, and yet beside their homes, and where people may sit and meet. These commons, being linked, will form a pleasant means for pedestrians to move about the district.'[2]

Lawrence Wolfe has glorified the Reilly Plan as 'a new way of life' capable of remedying such defects of the present 'isolationist' urban life as loneliness, juvenile delinquency, parental cruelty, poor health, declining birth-rate, late marriage, ignorance, property-possessiveness, narrow-mindedness, etc.[3] Its originator, the late Sir Charles Reilly, had no such pretensions about his scheme.[4] The essence of the plan, Sir Charles noted, was 'houses round greens, as in pre-Industrial Revolution England, and the greens themselves

[1] 'Living space in a new town—garden commons as an experiment', *Labour Councillor*, May 1949, pp. 36–7.
[2] *Corporation Master Plan* 1949, pp. 21, 23.
[3] Lawrence Wolfe, *The Reilly Plan* (London, 1945).
[4] 'I cannot attempt to explain', he writes, '. . . the enthusiasm of Lawrence Wolfe for the many implications he has found in the plan which, I confess, I did not fully see when I drew it. . . . It is rather like being told one is really an angel when one thinks of oneself as a very ordinary, sinful human being' (Sir Charles Reilly, Introduction to Lawrence Wolfe, op. cit., p. 9).

arranged like the petals of a flower round a community building, the modern equivalent of the village inn. . . .' Drafted originally in February 1944 for the Birkenhead City Council, the scheme rapidly became the subject of local and then national controversy. Birkenhead Communists and the Labour Party endorsed it, and Conservatives therefore opposed it 'even if', Sir Charles remarked, 'in their hearts they liked the idea of the revival of the village green and village inn'; in December 1944, the National Labour Party passed a resolution approving 'the ideas for community planning shown in Professor Sir Charles Reilly's plan. . . .'[1]

To attribute Reilly's and, especially, Wolfe's planning proposals to the Stevenage Development Corporation or the Ministry of Town and Country Planning, down to the last detail of a communal catering service for delivering food in thermos containers to each house, eliminating 'the muddlesome, costly and wasteful apparatus of the kitchen' and enabling the housewife to subsist on 'only a small electric cooker somewhere in a cupboard for such emergencies as the brewing of a pot of tea in the middle of the night', would be preposterous.[2] What they have more or less in common is the goal of human happiness, or the utopian design of improving the human condition by architectural—or, more broadly conceived, by human —means. Many sociologists, psychologists, physicians, politicians, artists, folk-dancers, priests, pacifists, and generals have shared this ambition, which each would further by means peculiar to his profession. The goal is probably as old as man, although in recent centuries it has assumed characteristically political forms: '*Any character, from the best to the worst, from the most ignorant to the most enlightened, may be given to any community, even to the world at large, by applying certain means; which are to a great extent at the command and under the controul, or easily made so, of those who possess the government of nations.*' This statement on the title page of Robert Owen's *A New View of Society* (1813) was matched by the more modest outlook of Ministry architects:

'We do not claim that a sensible physical arrangement of houses and other buildings normal to a good residential neighbourhood will auto-

---

[1] Sir Charles Reilly, ibid, pp. 9–11.
[2] Wolfe, p. 102. During the second reading of the New Towns Bill, however, the Minister did refer favourably to the communal kitchen scheme: 'I think it is an idea worth trying out. Obviously it depends on whether the women in the various households can co-operate to make it a success. . . . I believe they can, but one can only make sure by trying' (*Hansard*, 8th May 1946, vol. 422, col. 1090). Cf. a similar passage in his Stevenage speech, Chapter III, p. 66. It is interesting to note that communal kitchens and dining halls 'to prevent the loss and waste, as well as the discomfort, which arises from each individual or family cooking their own food' were also a part of James Silk Buckingham's harsh utopia (James S. Buckingham, *National Evils and Practical Remedies* (London, 1849), p. 146).

matically produce a friendly and neighbourly spirit. But we do claim that it will give considerable initial advantage to the development of a healthy social life'.[1]

While the Corporation simply declared, 'Above all the town should be planned so as to lighten the burdens and increase the happiness of family life'.[2] The goal was surely worthy; if it stemmed from conviction and not mere sentiment, it was an article of faith which upheld, if it could not quite transform, the spirit. Like other religions, its validity was not amenable to proof.

C. THE 'NEIGHBOURHOOD'

While the Reilly Green was a somewhat controversial proposal, the 'neighbourhood unit' was accepted by Abercrombie, the Reith Committee, the Ministry, and the Development Corporations as the basic principle upon which New Towns should be planned. True, the 'optimum' size was debated. Abercrombie had derived a unit of from 5,000 to 10,000 population (he preferred the latter figure) from the Ministry of Education's calculation that

'if the planning of a neighbourhood unit could be based upon a population constituted so as to be an exact reproduction, according to social class and income, of the population as a whole, the best size would be either 5,000 to contain one school for children aged 5–7 and one for children aged 8–11, or alternatively a population of 10,000 containing two of each such schools.'[3]

There were not lacking critics who objected that 'this number of people constitutes a town and not a neighbourhood at all'[4] and preferred a smaller unit. At Aycliffe New Town, for instance, it was discovered (not surprisingly, as the New Town was restricted to a total population of 10,000) 'that 2,000 people form a natural social unit . . . they provide just enough infants to support one nursery school; and, at approved housing densities, occupy an area such that no one need be more than a quarter of a mile from the nearest shops. They even make a neat round for a milkman.'[5] The Reilly Green was, essentially, another proposal to break up the larger 'neighbourhood' into smaller—and, its advocates believed, more 'viable', 'natural', or 'healthy'—units. But, while the recommended size

[1] *Stevenage New Town. Report on Planning and Development Proposals* (mimeographed report accompanying the preliminary Ministry plan), (Ministry of Town and Country Planning, 31st July 1946), p. 27. Referred to henceforth as *Ministry Plan 1946*.
[2] *The New Town of Stevenage*, p. 17.   [3] Abercrombie, op. cit., p. 114.
[4] Gordon Rattray Taylor, 'New Towns', *New Statesman and Nation*, 21st May 1949, pp. 521–2.
[5] Ibid.

varied with local conditions and the factor emphasized—the administrative convenience or financial economy of the authorities, the moral or aesthetic satisfaction of New Town planners, or the convenience of hypothetical New Town residents (generally measured by the distance or travel time which some people elsewhere lived, or said they wished to live, from their work, shops, pubs, friends, church, or cinema; each measure giving somewhat different results) —there was almost universal agreement upon subdividing the New Town into some smaller units.

Each of the six neighbourhoods at Stevenage New Town was to have, in addition to nursery schools and at least two combined junior and infant schools,

'shops for everyday needs within walking distance for the housewife. . . . In each neighbourhood sites will be reserved for places of worship. Each neighbourhood will have a maternity and infant welfare clinic; in some cases this will be combined with doctors' and dentists' consulting rooms, and with recreational club-rooms for family needs. Some public-houses will also be sited in the neighbourhoods, also some of those semi-industrial services which are needed to meet a local demand.

'For each neighbourhood playgrounds will be planned. These playgrounds will be rather different from the normal, since they will range from small enclosures for kindergarten age children, to the larger playgrounds for adolescents. Playgrounds for older children will be sited round natural hollows (with which the site abounds), by small copses or wherever the lie of the ground will encourage the children to invent their own games and entertainment. There will also be tennis courts, bowling greens, and football and cricket grounds for adults, and for the elderly or contemplative a public garden with trees and flower-edged walks.'[1]

The genesis of this 'neighbourhood' idea, as Abercrombie pointed out,[2] was (like that of the 'balanced community') the attempt to remedy the physical and social problems of the middle-class suburbs and working-class estates built between the two wars, which were characterized by extensive areas of uniform housing and of similar income and age groups, inadequately provided with educational, commercial, and recreational facilities.

That it is possible and desirable to locate and build schools, shops, pubs, playgrounds, etc., in a New Town so as to serve the physical needs of children and adults more conveniently than they are served in many existing areas we do not for a moment dispute. Physical standards of housing are generally (but not invariably) rising, and it would be strange indeed if a modern town could not improve upon an old one in these respects. It is against the social engineering of the 'neighbourhood' that criticism must be directed—or, rather, not against social engineering itself as the open political activity of various planners and social groups, but against the pretence that their

---

[1] *The New Town of Stevenage*, pp. 24–5. [2] Abercrombie, pp. 111 ff.

social policy is determined objectively, that it is not merely historically useful but also scientifically valid.

Different planners had different conceptions of the 'neighbourhood'; the broad social objective, however, was to improve the general welfare and create a beneficent and stable environment in which the needs of all ages, classes, and interests would be met, all would live together on friendly terms, and those vague but good things, 'neighbourliness', 'community activity', or simply a '*community*', would grow and prosper.

The utopian aspect of this goal, which assumes that human action can effect a net increase in human happiness, has already been noted in our discussion of the Reilly Green; and the ideological aspect, which seeks to impose upon the mass of the people standards of conduct and a physical and social environment which only certain people (in this case, New Town planners and supporters) admire or profit from, in our discussion of the 'balanced' community. Both aspects stand out clearly when one marshals the contradictory views of different planners on the same policy (which it is easy enough to do)—for can it have been scientifically established that the 'neighbourhood unit' will increase human happiness or neighbourliness when some planners (to whom one must also allow an honest search for human happiness and the truth) believe the opposite?

So, most New Town planners regarded community centres and 'neighbourhood units' as means of integrating the diverse activities of individuals and families into an organic social whole of progressively larger dimensions—the community, town, region, and nation—and rationalized this goal in terms of a structural-functional or organic sociology (or social philosophy), often that of Geddes and Mumford,[1] in which individuals and groups in a society are likened to the parts of a mechanical system or the organs of an organism, whose specialization contributes to the harmonious functioning of the whole. But their critics, seeing the reverse side of the coin, argued that 'self-contained' community centres, neighbourhoods, and towns tended to *break up*, and not unite, the community, town, and region.[2] So, New Town planners believed that sociability and

[1] The Greeks were also consulted, as by Ministry architects: 'There is nothing new or magical in the idea of the living quarters of the new town being a series of organised parts within the whole structure. Aristotle and other Greek philosophers who might well be quoted and Howard . . . clearly developed the idea that the individual home is only the basic unit in a neighbourhood. In the plan for Stevenage we do no more than translate this very sound, time-honoured concept into a pattern in accordance with the standards and requirements of modern life' (*Ministry Plan* 1946, p. 27).

[2] Thus Gordon Rattray Taylor suggested that 'Community spirit is built out of a vast number of face-to-face groups; and, by drawing people out of such local groupings, a civic community centre may actually reduce cohesion, not increase it' (op. cit., p. 522).

99

community activity could be organized or, at least, encouraged by a congenial physical environment and genuine social reform which would counteract the consequences of industrialism, occupational specialization, and class segregation and conflict.[1] But their critics believed that the historical process which had produced these effects would continue and could not be overcome by the efforts of a few planners and reformers.[2]

Is there no way of reconciling such divergent convictions or of choosing between them on objective grounds? Is it not possible to say that houses, shops, and community centres of type A and arrangement B are better calculated to promote the happiness and welfare of a neighbourhood than are type A' and B'?

In our opinion the answer must be 'No'. Sometimes it is easy to specify what immediate measure will promote the happiness of a man or a group—a larger house and garden, for instance, or cheaper beer. To know the subsequent effect of this measure, however, requires the gift of prophecy. Some people are so bold or simple as to supply permanent specifications for human happiness: love, security, productive work, a high standard of living, the acceptance (or renunciation) of the world. But they have not indicated (to the satisfaction of others) either what immediate measures will secure this goal or, else, what action can free man from nature and history, which have previously forestalled the reign of happiness. Among these people are the great saints and philosophers (not to mention economists, psychoanalysts, housewives, and planners), but we do not observe that their teaching has been consistent or that they have been notably happier than other men. Certainly it is not clear from their teaching if houses are to be preferred to flats, communal gardens to private gardens, or a 'neighbourhood unit' of 10,000 to one of 2,000.

'The real trouble', it is often said, 'is lack of adequate basic research and, above all, research into the kind of life people want to lead and the kind of life which fosters happiness.'[3] But there are not one but many different kinds of people who want to lead different kinds of lives at different times. It is doubtful if any team of planners,

[1] 'It has not been thought necessary until quite recent times to organize sociability in a deliberate way. . . . It was only the atomisation of social life in suburbs and housing estates that led to the use of terms like "neighbourhood" and "community" to represent entities which had not arisen spontaneously but were deliberately planned and fostered' (Charles Madge, *Communal Facilities for Housing in the United Kingdom*, mimeographed paper, January 1950, p. 13).

[2] '. . . the return to the small self-contained urban [neighbourhood] unit appears to be a forlorn hope. The existing trend is for a progressive division of labour and of interests. . . . This trend can be controlled but it cannot be cancelled' (Ruth Glass, 'Social Aspects of Town Planning', *Town and Country Planning Textbook* (London, 1950), p. 216).

[3] Taylor, op. cit., p. 522.

assisted by no matter how many experts (nurses, sociologists, psychologists, historians, politicians, and priests) and data (social surveys and social statistics, public meetings and discussions and the honest solicitation of popular opinion) can foretell and reconcile the needs of all groups (young and old, sociable and solitary, inebriate and puritanical, proletarian and bourgeois, conformist and nonconformist) or even of one group in one plan.

It may be concluded, therefore, that there are no universally acceptable architectural or sociological principles for engineering the happiness and success of a neighbourhood or community, but only different principles catering to the needs of different social groups and planners. Many New Town planners try to understand and cater to the needs of industrial workers, but, as no full-time planner is himself an industrial worker, it is more than likely that mistakes will be made. Again, most key planners are salaried intellectuals whose outlook differs in certain respects from that of the commercial and white-collar middle classes for whom the New Town will cater, so that here, too, mistakes are likely. Fortunately, many planning decisions are unlikely to affect the happiness of New Town residents one way or the other, for the residents will probably be less concerned about them than are the planners and, being ordinary people and not abstractions, will be able to adjust satisfactorily to a variety of physical and social environments.

D. THE PLANNERS' MENTALITY

Much might be written about 'planners' mentality', that state of mind apt to be induced by a drawing board and pencil and the power, with a few strokes of the hand, to materialize a vision. One informant told of two Corporation planners who 'when gazing into a shop full of china rabbits, were appalled by the standard of public taste, and want to evolve some scheme for improving it'. Another related how, at a meeting between Corporation and Council on the location of the New Town centre, a Corporation representative said it was important that the centre have 'a sense of drama'. 'Not the best way of impressing businessmen,' he added. After this citizen emerged from a discussion at the Corporation offices on planning proposals for 'neighbourhood unit I'—i.e., the existing town of Stevenage—he observed, 'Their ideas seem so theoretical and so far off, their approach is so academic, as if they are dealing with a virgin site in public ownership and as if the people are counters in a game'.

The planners were aware of this danger. A chairman of the Development Corporation noted:

'The planner's language, which abounds with such words and phrases as compensation and betterment, residential density, neighbourhood unit, overspill, decant and zoning has deteriorated into a jargon which is designed to save or prevent thought on the part of those who use it and to discourage the interests of people accustomed to the straightforward vocabulary of everyday life. . . . almost all recent plans suffer not only from the fact that they remain, very largely, plans but also, . . . because they were offered to the broad mass of the people immediately concerned ready-made and with room for relatively minor amendments and adjustments.'[1]

The all too common (and all too human) truth was that the planner scented a promising track and made off it, barking as he went; he was seldom really perturbed to find himself alone, because he considered himself a pioneer or explorer and, besides, could always count on the company of some other pioneers.

Some planners would hit, e.g., upon the idea of the cul-de-sac, and for decades fellow planners would incorporate culs-de-sac in their plans. It seemed so transparent that these broke up 'ribbon development', encouraged 'neighbourliness', prevented traffic accidents, and ensured peace and quiet. It might come as a surprise to discover that these virtues were sometimes foisted upon a recalcitrant public which was not eager to buy houses on culs-de-sac (as did at least one builder who found that housewives 'wanted to be on a road with through traffic so as to have something to watch and to be interested in')[2] or that other planners regarded culs-de-sac as the essence of bad design.[3]

Or a planner took it as 'a principle of architectural manners that structures for private and commercial use should by their very form and layout defer to the church building' and envisaged a hundred New Towns, in all of which 'the focus of interest is the church. . . . This central shrine can be seen from every main street, and is the spiritual and cultural hub of everything that is finest in the common life of the people.'[4] (This particular proposal was sponsored by the Industrial Christian Fellowship which may be forgiven for sentiments that, voiced by a sectarian group, might be considered presumptuous.)

[1] Monica Felton, 'Democracy in Town and Country Planning', *Political Quarterly*, Jan.–March 1949, vol. 20, pp. 78–9.
[2] E. D. Simon, *Rebuilding Britain* (London, 1945), p. 75.
[3] Thus R. K. Kelsall gives as one rule for a good housing layout, 'Don't have culs-de-sac; these merely involve people in longer journeys, and can easily be avoided' (op. cit., p. 70), and Thomas Sharp takes detailed and violent exception to Welwyn Garden City culs-de-sac on the grounds that they violate privacy by permitting neighbours and passers-by to view back-garden activities. 'Is this amenity? Is it even common decency?' (*Town and Countryside* (London, 1932), p. 151).
[4] A. Trystan Edwards, *A Hundred New Towns for Britain*, p. 8; and P. T. R. Kirk, *New Towns for Old*, p. 9 (pamphlets published by the Industrial Christian Fellowship, London, no dates).

Finally, the case may be instanced of a Corporation officer who, in the course of a radio talk on the Stevenage New Town, found himself discussing 'the wearability of grass. Grass in an estate must stand being walked on, played on, kicked over. So research is being done on the kind of grass to be grown and how to keep down maintenance cost by, for example, using a rotor-scythe instead of a lawn-mower.' Distressingly, a county newspaper chose just this passage to editorialize upon:

'They are deciding, believe it or not, what type of grass is to be sown in the New Town of Stevenage. "The wearability of grass", Mr. —— . . . pointed out in a recent . . . broadcast, is an "important practical problem". . . .
'This is, no doubt, all very useful, but the thousands of people on local council's waiting lists, for whom Stevenage New Town is partly designed, will no doubt be interested primarily in the fact that not one brick has yet been laid. That the work of Mr. —— and his colleagues is important we are quite prepared to agree, but it is surely tactless to spend so much time talking about the minor problems of social amenities when people are living a whole family in one room. . . .
'Perhaps 1949 will see a real beginning to the work of Stevenage, and if so, many local families will be made happy. . . .
'In the meantime, with the best goodwill in the world, we would advise Mr. —— and his fellow planners to "Cut the cackle and get to the houses".'[1]

The fault was not the officer's, since his statement was undoubtedly true and, to many listeners, interesting; had he not made it, it was likely under the circumstances that another passage would have been singled out for criticism. The episode does point up, however, the inevitably different preoccupations of planners and other citizens, which verged upon the humorous, the commonplace, and the tragic.
The saving feature was that there were almost as many sects among planners as there were planners. The proponents of New Towns found strong opposition among those in favour of concentrated urban development; battle was joined on the number of bedrooms to be built in a house, on the number of houses to be built in an acre, terraced v. non-terraced houses, the size and height of windows, central heating v. the open fire, etc. One school

'found its flag in the aristocratic planning of the eighteenth century, a period when the dominant class lived in detached country palaces and grand squares, but housed their retainers in tidy mews and rows of cottages—just as they dressed them in respectful uniforms. This school detested the informal layouts of a democracy which, having only one dwelling per family, wanted it to be their country house and town house as well. . . . Enthusiasts for the street were offset by Le Corbusier, who

[1] *Letchworth Citizen*, 1st April 1949.

called it a "gloomy canyon" and proposed to house the townsfolk all gloriously in towers of steel and glass. Space-cutting English architects who showed how you could crowd houses together at forty to sixty per acre were countered by the generous American, Frank Lloyd Wright, who showed how you could spread them out at one per acre. And these conflicting principles were exploited journalistically by the Sad Fog-Blowers and the Merry Dust-Throwers.'[1]

It was understandable that a young architect rose at a conference of planners to ask innocently:

'How was it that so many speakers could put forward such different and conflicting ideas on the same subjects? Did it mean that their ideals were different too? How was it that to-day in the twentieth century, architects were still designing in styles ranging from Lutyens to Le Corbusier? . . . How was it that so many separate and rival societies existed for architects, surveyors, engineers and the like?'[2]

The young man called the distinguished assemblage 'a medley of squabbling dictators', but the remedy he suggested—welding planners together 'in one corporate body—*a National Planning Front*'[3]—was surely worse than the disease.

E. FLATS *v.* HOUSES

It struck a layman sometimes that planners' feuds were about as significant as the dispute between Lilliputians who opened their eggs at one end and those who opened them at the other, but wars have been fought over lesser issues, which can reflect the serious conflicting interests of social groups. An important instance was the dispute over 'flats' *v.* 'houses' or, more broadly, high *v.* low density development, that has continued for many years and has had repercussions at all New Towns.

Perorations on the subject of high and low density development presented a delicious example of adjectival fever or rationalization run wild—that ineradicable malady in which the wish is father to a fact and fancy gives it free expression. Proponents of high density urban development declared:

'There seems to have got about an idea that there is virtue in mere space as such. . . . But . . . there is a great deal to be said for maintaining a sense of enclosure in a town, a sense of compactness and intimacy. Most of our recent building estates are far too wide open. They are loose, draughty, somehow "uncontained" places. They lack snugness and a sense of intimacy.'[4]

[1] Osborn, *Green-Belt Cities*, p.44
[2] In H. B. Newbold (ed.), *Industry and Rural Life* (London, 1942), p. 141.
[3] Ibid; italics in the original.
[4] Thomas Sharp in Newbold, op. cit., p. 118.

SOCIOLOGICAL COMPONENTS

'If the houses are aligned in friendly streets where the neighbours help one another in their domestic difficulties, people of the lower income groups find it much easier to bring up children than in the frigid social atmosphere of the typical garden suburb.'[1]

'This "Garden City" [12-houses-per-acre] convention, which is surely unchristian, has done much to disrupt the social life of the English people in recent years.'[2]

Supporters of garden city space standards, on the other hand, termed high density housing 'the slums of tomorrow',[3] and flats 'birth-control barracks'.[4] Sooner or later the discussion invariably got down to the subject of the family, which no one was ever against:

'I do not myself think that at present levels of amenity and convenience the flat can compete with the house for the purposes of bringing up a family. Human ecology would seem to demand that the family with young children should have space at the door, space for wheeling out the pram and hanging out the washing, space for children to play and for a garden. In asserting this demand, F. J. Osborn has done a great service to the family. . . .'[5]

Having, in common with other New Yorkers, Pueblo cliff-dwellers, and urban Europeans (including some with phenomenally large families) survived a childhood in flats, we hope to be excused for offering ourselves and our friends as evidence that 'human ecology' does not 'demand' a house (detached, semi-detached, or terraced) and garden (large, middle-sized, or small) in which to rear young. That most Englishmen demand it is undeniable, but this is not the first time that a line has been drawn between Englishmen and the rest of humanity.

Garden city propagandists usually concede that a few flats are permissible for old and newly-married—i.e., childless—couples. '. . . alas! that these dwellings are not designed solely for bachelors and the childless', editorialized *Town and Country Planning* about the flats which were to be erected at Stevenage and Harlow New Towns. 'Can it be that the natural activities of children in new towns are to be cramped in order that they and their parents may be used, at

[1] A. T. Edwards, letter, *The Times*, 25th June 1949.
[2] A. T. Edwards, *A Hundred New Towns for Britain*, p. 7.
[3] Eric Macfadyen, letter, *The Times*, 9th June 1949.
[4] 'The editor of *Town and Country Planning*, during the first session of the present Parliament [1945], attacked the Minister of Health in the House for his desire to set up "birth-control barracks" all over the country . . .' (Roy Lewis and Angus Maude, *The English Middle Classes* (London, 1949), p. 255).
[5] Charles Madge, 'Better Living Space', in *Better Living, Contact* 15, July 1949, p. 6. But cf. Le Corbusier, 'This so-called family house will never merit its title, but will drag society into the universal wasteland of garden cities' (*Concerning Town Planning* (London, 1947), p. 68).

greater public cost, to "diversify the skyline"?'[1] We have seen no statistics on the subject, but hazard the guess that there are more children per room in working-class flats (and most flat-dwellers are working-class people) than in middle-class houses. It does not follow that these children are any the worse for having been reared in flats, but only that they are different, in some ways, for being working-class, from middle-class children. The implication that their life would be improved if they lived in houses (i.e., if they lived more as their middle-class critics live) indicates again the bond between the garden city idea and the regnant, puritanical middle-class ideology.

The adulation of the family is almost in inverse proportion to its size, now at its lowest ebb since census data have been kept. In 1811 there was an average of 4·74 persons in each family in England and Wales and 5·65 persons in each inhabited house; by 1931 these averages had fallen to 3·72 and 4·38 respectively.[2] It was estimated in 1947 that the size of the average British household was 3·67 persons and 56 per cent of all households contained no children under fifteen years of age.[3] A detailed study of the Manchester population concluded, '*approximately 66 per cent of all dwellings should be designed for families with no young children, while only 34 per cent of all dwellings would be designed for families with children.* . . . few housing programmes have yet taken account of the actual structure of population, supplemented by a survey of what the *voluntary* structure of families would be like, given adequate provision of dwellings in the right places'.[4] Of course, there is no such thing as a completely 'voluntary' family structure, and pro-house planners argued that this was a policy of defeatism, whereas the provision of a house and garden for every family would encourage an increase of the birth-rate.

Asked if he prefers a house or a flat, most Englishmen in recent years have answered 'a house'. Thus a Mass-Observation 1941–2 survey of 1,100 people, mainly working-class housewives (160 of whom lived in London flats, 500 in London houses, and 440 in houses in five other English cities) found that

'for every one person who said that she would like to live in a flat, ten said that they would like to live in a small house or bungalow. Even among

---

[1] *Town and Country Planning*, June 1950, p. 223.

[2] *Whittaker's Almanack* 1949, p. 634.

[3] P. G. Gray, *The British Household* (The Social Survey, London, 1949), pp. 5–6. The Stevenage Corporation's 1948 survey of every fourth house in Stevenage found that 'The average family, excluding lodgers . . . consisted of almost exactly 3 persons'.

[4] Marianne Walter, 'Flats', *Architects' Journal*, 6th February 1947, p. 146. Italics in original.

those actually living in flats, more than twice as many people said they preferred a small house or bungalow as said they would like to stay in their present or move to another flat.'[1]

In replies by 1,056 (mainly working-class) Stevenage New Town housing applicants in Nov.–Dec. 1949 to the question 'Would you prefer a house or a flat?' 66 or 6 per cent said they preferred flats, another 85 or 8 per cent preferred flats to nothing, while the remaining 86 per cent unequivocally preferred houses.[2]

There is little reason to doubt that such polls accurately represent the general feeling on the subject. But they also reflect the prevailing distribution of housing accommodations in Britain. According to a survey of 13,000 people representative of the adult civilian population of Britain, in the first quarter of 1949 82·2 per cent of British families lived in houses and 17·8 per cent in flats. A larger proportion of lower-income than of higher-income groups lived in flats and, of course, in absolute numbers, the great majority of flats was occupied by lower-income groups—according to this survey, 75 per cent of the flats in Britain are occupied by households whose chief earner earns £399 or less a year.[3]

A survey conducted by the Government Social Survey in March–April 1947 of a national random sample of 5,997 households drawn from electoral registers gives the following regional distribution for various types of housing:

[1] Mass-Observation, *An Enquiry into People's Homes*, p. 46.

[2] The *Daily Mirror* of 16th November 1949 contained an article on the Stevenage New Town which mentioned that building operatives and 'key workers' would be granted housing priority, gave the Corporation's address, and reported that forms would be sent to housing applicants. In response to requests, the Corporation mailed out some 1,450 forms during the next four weeks; of the 1,056 persons who returned completed forms by 19th December 1949, 369 or 35 per cent were building operatives.

[3] Hulton Press, *Patterns of British Life* (London, 1950), pp. 8, 101. Dividing the sample into three groups in accordance with the yearly income of the head of the household (AB, £650 and over, comprising 11 per cent of the sample; C, £400–649, 17 per cent of the sample; and DE, £399 or less, 72 per cent of the sample) the following breakdown is obtained:

Class	per cent in houses	per cent in flats
AB	86·9	13·1
C	82·3	17·7
DE	81·5	18·5

	Great Britain %	Scot-land %	North %	Mid-lands and Wales %	South and East %	London %
Detached house ..	13	18	8	13	21	7
Semi-detached house	30	14	26	34	37	30
Terraced house ..	45	8	60	52	39	46
Flat	12	60	6	1	3	17
	100	100	100	100	100	100

The high proportion of flats in Scotland and their virtual absence from all other regions except London is noteworthy. This survey also confirms the disproportionate concentration of the poorer classes in flats.[1]

Among persons living in flats, there is a noticeable increase in the proportion preferring flats to houses. Two-fifths of the housewives in Mass-Observation's sample of 160 London flats did not want to live in a small house.[2] 'At a . . . discussion amongst young people living in Quarry Hill Flats [Leeds, the largest and most modern block of working-class flats that had been built in Britain] . . . on whether they would prefer to set up home in a similar block or in a cottage dwelling, the voting was 50–50.'[3]

Pro-house planners pointed to the opinion polls among the population at large and to the actual distribution of housing accommodations in the nation as evidence of the overwhelming desire of 'the people' for houses. Pro-flat planners replied that:

(a) As most people had no personal experience of flats, expressions of opinion about them were meaningless. 'The classic example of a fruitless inquiry into matters unknown by those interviewed is the frequent flat versus house questionnaire.'[4]

(b) As most flats were built for the working-classes, 'the people' did not disapprove of flats per se but only of working-class flats. Flats 'have . . . come to be associated with the smell of petrol and overcrowding of people, with dark and noisy ground floor rooms, with washing hanging out in dim wells, and children on paved grey

[1] P. G. Gray, The British Household (The Social Survey, February 1949), p. 17. According to this survey, the proportion of households living in flats ranged from 17 per cent for those households whose chief wage earner earned less than £156 a year to 8 per cent for those households whose chief earner earned over £520 (ibid).

[2] Mass-Observation, op. cit., p. 221.

[3] Charles Jenkinson, Our Housing Objective (London, 1943), p. 20.

[4] Ruth Glass, 'Social Aspects of Town Planning', Town and Country Planning Textbook (London, 1950), p. 219.

yards many stairs away from their mothers.'[1] '. . . the bitterest criticisms of flat life from those who have experienced it, come from people who occupy . . . "working-class" flats. In so-called "luxury" flats, standards are very much higher and criticism is very much less.'[2]

(c) No matter what they might *say*, the occupants of urban flats found them so convenient that very few could, in fact, be enticed into houses. 'In the experience of the . . . [London County Council], 95 per cent of people preferred to live in flats, providing they were near their work, and only 5 per cent wanted houses.'[3] '. . . Less than 10 per cent of the families in the first slum clearance area which the L.C.C. tackled after the war were on the waiting lists for a new house. They prefer the London they know, and the higher post-war rents for new houses are a deterrent to their readily moving out.'[4]

As the last consideration struck directly at the feasibility of New Towns, let us stop for a moment to examine it. Already in the spring of 1945, the Tottenham Borough Council (which, it will be recalled, was then investigating the possibility of relocating its surplus population at Stevenage) had been worried about the problem.

'It seems that the most difficult hurdle to surmount will be the wishes of the people of Tottenham. It is in the national interest, and it is also the wish of the Council that people living in bad conditions, together with a number of factories, move to a garden city, but however attractively the garden city is designed and developed, there is the probability that only a small proportion of the displaced people will wish to leave the Borough. We will therefore have to construct blocks of flats for those who cannot be persuaded that a cottage and garden outside Tottenham provides opportunities for a better life than a block of flats within the Borough. . . . The advantages of life in a garden city are more intangible than are the disadvantages, and it is hard to persuade the people immediately affected of the national, regional, local and personal advantages of dispersal.'[5]

The results of an inquiry at the end of 1946 into the willingness of housing applicants in the Tottenham, Edmonton, and West Ham Boroughs to move to Stevenage or Harlow New Town were more optimistic:[6]

[1] Marianne Walter, op. cit., p. 145.
[2] The Association of Building Technicians, *Homes for the People* (London, 1946), p. 20.
[3] Lewis Silkin (formerly chairman of the London County Council Housing Committee), in F. E. Towndrow (ed.), *Replanning Britain* (London, 1941), p. 110.
[4] C. W. Gibson (chairman of the London County Council Housing Committee), letter to *The Times*, 14th August 1950.
[5] Rees J. Williams (Tottenham Borough Surveyor), in Barbara Bliss (ed.), *The New Planning* (London, 1945), pp. 34–5.
[6] From C. B. Purdom, *The Building of Satellite Towns* (London, 1949), p. 435.

	Tottenham	Edmonton	West Ham
Letters dispatched	7,775	2,500	16,000
Replies received	4,669	1,438	9,360
favouring Stevenage	1,311	438	
„ Harlow	2,862	685	6,440
„ either	120	305	
favouring neither	376	10	2,920

The survey is unsatisfactory for several reasons: 40–42 per cent of
the persons canvassed did not reply, and without knowing how they
felt and the exact phrasing of the question one cannot make a
reliable interpretation of the findings. The remarkably low proportion of 8 per cent of those replying in Tottenham and 1 per cent in
Edmonton (compared with 31 per cent in West Ham) who did not
wish to move to either New Town makes one suspect that the free
expression of opinion was somehow inhibited. Nevertheless, one
would judge from these figures that the proportion of the
population in these boroughs willing to move to a New Town
would then have been sufficient to ensure its success. The Social
Survey's poll of a sample of 1,448 Willesden housewives, in the
winter of 1946–7, confirms this impression. 'Of the whole Willesden population of all ages, 49 % were willing to move to a new
town. More were prepared to go if they were assured of a house and
their present employer in the town, than would go if a new job were
offered, or if the working members of the household had to travel
from the town daily to their present workplace.'[1]

Evidently the desperate housing shortage prevailing immediately
after the war and the personal mobility which the war had promoted
made large numbers of people willing to move from London to New
Towns if houses and jobs were provided for them there. Circumstances may, of course, change. As of 1950, increasing numbers of
houses and flats had been built in or near London, the rents of New
Town houses threatened to be very high, and difficulties had been
experienced in getting Board of Trade sanction for the transfer of
industries to New Towns. The influence of these factors upon the
growth of the New Towns remains to be seen.

It is important to note that people willing to move to a New Town
were apt to differ significantly from those who remained behind.
The indications of the Willesden survey were that a high proportion
would be industrial workers and 'there would be some under-
representation of Willesden people from the professional, technical
and, especially, self-employed groups'.[2] The latter, as has been

[1] Bertram Hutchinson, *Willesden and the New Towns*, p. 3.   [2] Ibid., p. 4.

observed, were precisely those groups which the Corporations wished to attract in order to 'balance' the New Towns economically and socially. The Willesden survey also suggested that migrants would be younger than the average of the population,[1] which was also the experience at Letchworth and Welwyn Garden City. This meant that the excess of births over deaths would be proportionately higher in New Towns than in the nation at large and that

'some 10 to 20 per cent of the population at the end of twenty years will represent natural growth of the migrant population. . . . In fact a new town of 60,000 is perhaps most realistically to be regarded as capable of relieving an overspill of about 45,000. . . . But . . . [the existing Stevenage population] must be subtracted from the above figure . . . to give 38,000 as the possible upper limit for population to be brought in from London. . . .'[2]

The large numbers of children which could be expected in New Towns in early years would also make for heavy expenses for school construction.[3]

But let us return to the house–flat controversy and examine some of the contentions of those who oppose flats: that they are noisy, and lack privacy and garden space which houses provide.

The argument that flats are noisier than houses is common. But a national survey of noise in working- and middle-class homes concludes that 'In the case of house dwellers about four-fifths noticed noise from their neighbours, about a quarter were troubled by the sounds and about one-fifth complained that their sleep was disturbed'. True, the report proceeds, 'The proportions for flat dwellers in general were higher, being 95 per cent, 41 per cent and 34 per cent compared with 78 per cent, 26 per cent and 19 per cent for those in houses', but special afflictions assail each type of house. Thus, 18 per cent of persons living in terraced houses found their

[1] '. . . while 45 % of the whole Willesden population was under 30 years of age, this age-group constituted 52 % of those prepared to move, and only 32 % of those who would remain behind. Similarly, while 21 % of those who said they did not wish to move were 60 or more, only 4 % of the moving group were as old as this' (ibid., p. 3).

[2] *Population Forecast for Stevenage* (mimeographed report), (Stevenage Development Corporation, 18th March 1949).

[3] After one Stevenage Corporation member presented a statement of the need for schools in the New Town at a 5th April 1949 meeting, another member 'suggested that the Corporation should endeavour, as far as possible, to attract a well-balanced community to Stevenage in the first place. It would help considerably if a normal proportion of older people could be moved to Stevenage as well as young people with children.' The financial roots of the 'balanced' community are evident! J. E. MacColl, a member of the Hemel Hempstead Corporation, remarked wryly that 'If we continue to build new towns at the present rate it will not matter if we receive only young families because by the time the last families have arrived the first ones will be old age pensioners' (at a London planning discussion, 14th October 1948).

sleep disturbed by the sound of road traffic, compared to only 7 per
cent of persons in flats; noise from domestic animals and poultry
was high in semi-detached houses; framed flats were noisier than
masonry and brick flats, etc.[1]

As for the matter of privacy, one pro-flat planner observes that

'The space between the fronts of two rows of houses facing each other
in twelve to the acre development is usually about twenty-three yards, of
which approximately half is public highway. This means that passersby
on the footpaths can look straight into the front windows from a distance
of little more than five yards. The only remedies are to cut out much of
the light from the rooms by hanging net curtains over the windows, or to
do the same, so far as the ground floor is concerned, by growing a hedge
six feet high . . .'[2]

Another feels that, in 12-to-the-acre house development such as that
at Welwyn Garden City, which was the most widespread standard
in housing developments between the two wars,

'one's eyes are everywhere shocked by the views through yawning gaps
between the houses—by the indecency of back elevations, by bare and
untidy gardens divided by post and wire fences in various stages of dilapi-
dation, . . . by spasmodic jumbles of irregular out-buildings, by the
intimacy of underclothes on washing lines, and by all the forms of indecent
exposure habitually practised by garden-city developers.'[3]

And a third, that 'There is actually less chance of keeping a prying
eye fixed on an internal family flat entrance than on the front door of
a cottage facing a street of cottages. . . . It is no accident that the flat
dweller, contrary to the street dweller, does not know his neighbours.'[4] A Corporation survey of some 500 council *houses* in Stevenage and vicinity, conducted in the summer of 1948, found that 59
per cent of those interviewed 'felt the lack of privacy in their gardens
as against 40 per cent who did not have this feeling'.[5]

[1] Dennis Chapman, *A Survey of Noise in British Homes* (National Building
Studies Technical Paper No. 2, London, 1948). 'Interviews were conducted
with persons living in 2,017 small and medium-size dwellings . . . where persons
earning up to £10 a week were likely to be found. . . . There were 537 small or
medium-size flats and 1,480 houses' (p. 2). Principal noises singled out were the
radio, 'people moving', doors banging, 'cistern', and 'children'.

[2] Boumphrey, *Town and Country Tomorrow*, p. 53.

[3] Thomas Sharp, *Town and Countryside*, p. 152.

[4] Hugh S. Phillips, *Housing and Town Planning* (mimeographed), (Guildford,
1944), p. 8.

[5] The survey, conducted by five students under the direction of Corporation
officers, covered 506 households (504 answered the questions) in and around
Stevenage, principally houses belonging to the Stevenage Urban District
Council and also some council houses in Knebworth and aluminium bungalows
in Knebworth and Woolmer Green. While the standard of accommodation and
privacy of new council houses was roughly comparable to that of working-class
houses which the Development Corporation would build, the standard of the
aluminium bungalows was distinctly lower.

Other common objections to flats are that they afford no garden space, or that residents, especially of top floors, have too far to go to their allotments. Mass-Observation noted that 'The desire for a garden was an important factor in deciding whether or not people wanted to live in a flat. Only 5 % of those who wanted gardens wanted to live in flats, whereas 46 % of those who did not want gardens preferred a flat to a small house.'[1] There can be few more fervent passions in modern England than gardening. But fully half the men and women in Britain do not garden at all, and only 31 per cent garden regularly.[2] And, in Stevenage and throughout the country, allegations are common about the indifference displayed by many council tenants to their gardens. One 1948 report states:

'It is a general experience that the standards of gardening on municipal estates deteriorated considerably during the war, principally because of the absence of men in the forces, and recovery seems to be slow. . . . the problem remains primarily one of interesting and encouraging the reluctant gardener.'[3]

The Development Corporation's survey of 500 council house gardens classified 29 per cent as in 'good', 63 per cent in 'indifferent', and 8 per cent in 'bad' cultivation; a 1937–8 Birmingham survey of 7,023 working-class people found that among those who *liked* gardens 41 per cent of gardens were in 'good', 44 per cent in 'fair', and 15 per cent in 'bad' condition;[4] and Mass-Observation's wider survey judged only 39 per cent of working-class gardens 'well kept' and 25 per cent 'neglected', compared to 73 per cent and 7 per cent respectively, for middle-class gardens.[5] These figures suggest that when F. J. Osborn writes that 'two-thirds of the gardens [in 12-to-the-acre development] are well cultivated; one-third partially cultivated; and only about 7 per cent neglected'[6] he is, in common with other advocates of the small house and the garden city, either indulging in wishful thinking or thinking of the gardens of middle-class and not working-class people.

[1] Mass-Observation, *An Enquiry into People's Homes*, p. 222.

[2] According to their 1949 survey of a national sample of 13,000 persons, 41·6 per cent of men and 21·8 per cent of women, or 30·9 per cent of both sexes over sixteen years, gardened regularly; 41·6 per cent of men and 57·1 per cent of women, or 50 per cent of both sexes never gardened (*The Hulton Readership Survey* 1949 (London, 1949), p. 42).

[3] Central Housing Advisory Committee, *The Appearance of Housing Estates* (London, 1948), p. 7.

[4] In this survey 'working-class' was defined as 'those living at that economic level—labourers, artisans, craftsmen, warehousemen and clerks, and unskilled labourers' (Bournville Village Trust, *When We Build Again* (London, 1941), pp. 44, 84).

[5] Mass-Observation, op. cit., p. 168.

[6] F. J. Osborn, in Gilbert and Elizabeth McAllister (eds.), *Home, Towns and Countryside* (London, 1945), p. 113.

On the matter of the distance people are prepared to travel to allotments we have little evidence, aside from the obvious fact that many cycle considerable distances already. An analysis of the 59 allotment-holders in a West London area in 1940 showed that 12 lived within a quarter of a mile, 21 between a quarter and half a mile, 19 between half and one mile, and 7 over a mile from the allotments park;[1] and of 42 council tenants in the Stevenage area wanting allotments in 1948, 17 expressed a willingness to travel a quarter of a mile, 19 half a mile, and 6 a mile or more to reach their allotments.[2]

Accordingly, we find it difficult to establish the superior virtue of houses to flats objectively on grounds of the greater degree of quiet and privacy and the greater opportunity for gardening that they afford. On the contrary, words like 'privacy' and 'gardening' are used with an evident emotional connotation by adherents of both schools and refer not merely to the actual feelings and behaviour of residents in houses and flats but also to the bias of the planner (which is reflected in their different usages of these words, and their different conceptions about what residents feel and do).[3] Perhaps there is more agreement about the meaning and measurement of 'noise', which, it is generally admitted, is greater in flats; but the advocates of flats suggest that this can be reduced by proper design and construction.

Such considerations, and the purely mechanical differences between the two kinds of accommodation, do not seem sufficient to account for the popular prejudice in favour of houses and against flats, which, in the last analysis, is inexplicable on wholly rational grounds and attributable instead to complex historical causes. It has been noted that

[1] US (Mass-Observation Bulletin), 17th May 1940, p. 161.

[2] The forty-two tenants belonged to the sample of 506 council households in Stevenage and vicinity surveyed by the Corporation in the summer of 1948.

[3] Thorstein Veblen's analysis of the class significance of privacy may be borne in mind. 'Through . . . discrimination in favour of visible consumption it has come about that the domestic life of most classes is relatively shabby, as compared with the éclat of that overt portion of their life that is carried on before the eyes of observers. As a . . . consequence, . . . people habitually screen their private life from observation. So far as concerns that portion of their consumption that may without blame be carried on in secret, they withdraw from all contact with their neighbours. Hence the exclusiveness of people as regards their domestic life, in most of the industrially developed communities; and hence, by remoter derivation, the habit of privacy and reserve that is so large a feature in the code of proprieties of the better classes in all communities' (The Theory of the Leisure Class (London, 1924 [first published 1899]), pp. 112–13). It may be suggested that those planners who wish to impose this essentially middle-class value upon the working classes are generally in favour of building houses instead of flats for them; proponents of flats need not oppose this value, but merely rank some other value above it.

'The origin of flats on the Continent was the need for a large number of people to crowd together for safety within the walls of a city. As there was no serious warfare in England after the seventeenth century, English towns were able to spread themselves during the great period of population increase between 1760 and 1900, and flats were only built in a few of the very largest cities.'[1]

Like any other historical phenomenon, the factor adduced is unlikely to be sole or universal cause (it does not, for instance, explain the American experience), although it should offer one realistic direction for investigation. Another is suggested by Dibelius, who sees in the English house and garden—especially the front garden, 'a ridiculous little strip of ground, useless in itself'—a 'pathetic survival of the ideal to have a park surrounding the mansion as the nobleman had. Similarly, the "hall", even if it had room for coats and umbrellas only, pays tribute, at least in name, to the hall of the baronial castle.'[2] And, as the most obvious facts are often those most readily overlooked, we may be forgiven for observing that England, the home of the Industrial Revolution and the greatest capitalist Power of the nineteenth century, had a fondness for petty, as well as massive, private property.

Whatever the original causes, they have clearly lost much of their force today (or one school of British planners who, to a disinterested observer, appear as competent and logical as their rivals, would not be championing flats with such vigour and conviction) and the small house has simply been established, like tea, the peerage, chimney pots, pounds-shillings-pence, judicial wigs, and the left-hand rule of the road as a part of English culture that most natives consider indispensable but for which foreigners manage readily enough to find alternatives.

English flats, as we have noted, are inhabited mainly by workers —in many cases, because of high ground rents, they were built by municipalities with Government aid as part of slum clearance projects in congested urban areas. Inhabitants usually have little capital or property, earn not a yearly salary but a weekly wage, and pay weekly rents to the municipality. It is understandable if the middle-class mind, which no longer monopolizes politics but still dominates most vehicles of culture and remains the mainstay of conservative morality, dislikes flats and considers the life that is led in them undesirable. For it is conventional bourgeois doctrine that home owners make the best citizens. Privacy and quiet may be little greater in most houses than in flats, and the house bear little more resemblance to a country manor. But at least the house resident is *trying*: he is playing

---

[1] Mass-Observation, *An Enquiry into People's Homes*, p. 46.
[2] Wilhelm Dibelius, *England* (London, 1930), p. 156. Cf. the title of J. M. Richards's book on the suburban house, *The Castles on the Ground* (London, 1946).

the social game as well as his income allows. And, instead of living in collective flats where the very breath of life stales, boxes that rest upon other boxes and not on the good (private) earth, he would like to see everyone (and especially council tenants) made in his (is it manorial, rural, feudal, romantic, bourgeois, or merely suburban?) image, patiently cultivating his *own* garden.

We have referred to the arbitrary cultural or historical factor in the flat–house controversy but rational factors cannot be minimized, because they assert themselves inexorably whilst emotions ebb and flow and often find alternate outlets. Perhaps the most important factor is the relative cost of each mode of development. Lack of a comparable basis of computation makes it by no means an easy matter to determine. The English experience

'has generally shown that in blocks above the height of two storeys, the building cost per dwelling begins to rise above what can be achieved for cottages. Tenement buildings beyond four or five storeys, moreover, generally carry increased running costs in the shape of provision and maintenance of lifts, lighting of corridors, etc. The choice of the block type of dwelling is, therefore, governed by land values. Where these are extremely high, as in many slum clearance areas, it is usually the most economic method of housing owing to the greater density per acre of dwellings provided.'[1]

Against the greater cost of flats and urban land must be reckoned the cost of providing basic services in rural areas. A vast capital outlay is required to instal roads, sewers, water, gas, electricity, etc., in a New Town, and it is invariably more expensive per dwelling unit to service low than high density development on a given site. A Development Corporation engineer estimated the cost (in December 1949) of supplying the same services to a new flat at Stevenage as roughly £150 as against £200 per house; the cost of construction would be roughly £2,000 per flat and £1,500 per house. 'It all comes to pretty much the same thing in the end,' was his opinion. Detailed cost comparisons prepared by the Corporation in autumn, 1949, showed an overall cost of £588 more per flat than per house. (The estimate assumed 221 flats at 15·1 flats per acre on a 14·6-acre site, housing 773 persons at an average cost of £2,300 per flat or £657 per person; and 160 houses at 10·95 per acre on the same site, housing 560 persons at an average cost of £1,712 per house or £491 per person.) However, central heating and hot water at an estimated cost of £150 per flat were not installed in the houses, nor were such services as laundries, central garbage disposal, and elevators, so that, the report concluded, 'it was difficult to draw an accurate comparison between two such widely differing schemes'.

The other major desideratum is the desirable maximum density of

[1] Political and Economic Planning, *Housing England* (London, 1934), p. 65.

development—low in England compared to most European and American cities.[1] Garden city enthusiasts set twelve houses per acre in urban and eight in rural areas as the maximum density, complaining that even this figure 'allows each house a garden less than a third the size of a lawn tennis court'.[2] This was the basic standard governing houses construction between the wars, as 'established by the Tudor-Walters Committee (1918), whose report set the character of the housing effort of 1919 onwards. . . . The Housing Acts prescribe maximum densities only for those houses which rank for public loans or subsidies. Two-storey houses may not be built, without Ministerial consent, at more than twelve per acre . . . in urban, and eight per acre in rural, areas.'[3]

Planners who did not share the garden city movement's antipathy to the city rebelled against this 'suburban' space standard which they deemed incompatible with the continued existence of great cities, blamed for its wastage of agricultural land, and deplored on aesthetic grounds. '. . . to attempt to re-house all the inhabitants in single-family houses, particularly of the detached or semi-detached types, would be impracticable in the central and sub-central parts of London. It would mean that only a quarter or a third of the present population could be re-housed there.'[4] Thomas Sharp believed that

'If we abandoned the twelve-to-the-acre dogma and worked on the rational planning that would permit thirty and more houses to the acre (with proper orientation), then we could provide reasonable living conditions for all . . . under far better hygienic conditions than those that exist in our present space-squandering, aesthetically-barren, socially-empty suburbs.'[5]

A. Trystan Edwards, who admired Georgian terraced houses and squares, reckoned that 'A rigid enforcement of these [post-1919

[1] *Report of the Committee on Land Utilisation in Rural Areas*, Cmd. 6378 (London, 1942), p. 71. Although the overall density of population in the United Kingdom is fifteen to twenty times that of the United States, the maximum urban densities are far below; the density of New York City, for example, is twice, and that of Manhattan eight times, that of London (H. Kamenka, *Flats* (London, 1947), pp. 33, 35).

[2] Report of a conference of horticulturists, representatives of national gardening societies, and officials of the Town and Country Planning Association, *The Times*, 8th August 1949. The conference agreed to 'oppose attempts to induce planning authorities to permit greater housing densities in new towns and rebuilding programmes'.

[3] F. J. Osborn, in G. and E. McAllister (eds.), *Homes, Towns and Countryside*, p. 106. Cf. the Local Government Board, *Manual on the Preparation of State-aided Housing Schemes* (London, 1919), 'The number of houses to be built on a site should not, save in exceptional circumstances, exceed 12 to the acre in urban areas and 8 to the acre in rural areas' (p. 6). These standards applied only to houses; no maximum density was fixed for flats.

[4] Catherine Bauer, *Modern Housing* (London, 1935), p. 77.

[5] Sharp, *Town Planning*, p. 83.

117

12-to-the-acre] regulations would result in the sacrifice of nine-tenths of our national heritage of noble building'.[1] He advocated a density, similar to Sharp's, of 100 persons to the acre in New Towns.[2] 'This permits of plenty of light and ventilation in the rooms, a wide range of internal accommodation and private gardens for all, supplemented, of course, by "major open space" which could be readily accessible.'[3]

The Reith Committee proposed for New Towns an average net density of 25–30 persons per residential acre which, added to the acreage for open space, industry, trade, schools, etc., gave an overall density of 12–15 persons for the entire town, a liberal garden city space provision which may be compared on the one hand with the residential density of 136 persons per acre which the County of London plan set for rehousing the population of central London and, on the other, the figure of about fifteen persons per acre in the built-up part of old Stevenage.[4] The Stevenage Master Plan of July 1949 provided for a net density of 34·2 persons per residential acre and a gross overall density for the whole New Town of 9·8 persons per acre (or 13·2, discounting 1,544 acres of farmland included within the designated area).[5] Or, 60,000 persons were to be housed on the 1,753 residential acres of a New Town whose total acreage was 6,100. To take an extreme contrast, 35,000 people are housed on 35·5 acres of built-up land within the 130-acre tenement town of Parkchester, New York City.

Low densities were attacked by farmers as consuming land the nation could not afford to lose at a time when all parties agreed upon the need to encourage the maximum possible agricultural production. During the wartime emergency some 52,000 acres of grassland had been ploughed up in Hertfordshire to raise the tilled acreage to a peak of 171,000 in 1944. The Ministry of Agriculture set this figure as its target for 1950 (in 1949 155,000 acres were cultivated), but county farmers doubted that it could be reached, largely because 5,000 acres had been lost to agriculture in the five years after 1944, and the four

---

[1] A. Trystan Edwards, *Modern Terrace Houses* (London, 1946), p. 23.
[2] The translation from houses-per-acre to persons-per-acre may be made at 3·5–4·5 persons per house.
[3] Letter, *The Times*, 25th June 1949.
[4] Cmd. 6876, p. 15; Abercrombie, p. 31; the Stevenage estimate is based upon a built-up area of 411 acres and a population of 6,500.
[5] 'Net residential acreage comprises all residential areas including all internal roads plus 20 feet of any road bounding the area', but excluding primary schools and neighbourhood shopping centres. Net residential densities varied from a low of 19 persons over the 344·5 acres of neighbourhood 1 (comprising most of the present town of Stevenage), to a high of 80 persons in 50 acres of neighbourhood 2. A density of 40 was planned for the remaining 115 acres of the latter neighbourhood, and net densities of the other four neighbourhoods were 35, 40, 33·5, and 35 respectively (*Corporation Master Plan* 1949).

New Towns and other construction projects in Hertfordshire promised to consume another 10,000 acres by 1952.[1] Advocates of 12-houses-to-the-acre development replied unconvincingly that intensive cultivation of gardens and allotments in residential areas yielded more produce than did normal agricultural use of the land saved by higher density development.[2]

The Hertfordshire Planning Committee criticized the Stevenage Corporation's Master Plan on the grounds that

'The area of public open space is nearly four times the minimum standard of six acres per thousand laid down by the Greater London Plan. ... Such liberal facilities for recreation are highly desirable in themselves, but one cannot help wondering whether the pendulum has not swung a little too wide—having in mind the overriding need to conserve agricultural land and the fact that some 26 per cent of the designated area is being allocated for what may be described as recreational open space.'[3]

The Minister of Town and Country Planning's recommendation, in February 1950, that the open space allocation of the Stevenage Master Plan be reduced indicated the Government's sensitivity to rural interests, inevitably disturbed by the New Town programme. While that programme as a whole represented a triumph for the garden city movement, it was a tenuous triumph which political and economic developments might upset, and both Ministry and Development Corporations were anxious to mollify agricultural interests to

[1] *Hertfordshire Mercury*, 9th December 1949.

[2] F. J. Osborn argued that 'The value of the output of food in domestic gardens . . . is for every acre occupied four or five times that of farmland' (in H. B. Newbold (ed.), *Industry and Rural Life* (London, 1942), p. 122) and, therefore, that to increase the density of development from twelve to eighteen houses per acre 'would not increase food production; it would reduce it. Although, for each 36 houses one acre would be "saved" the area of the back garden would be reduced from 200 square yards to less than half. In a garden of 200 square yards some vegetables could be grown, but this could hardly be done in a garden half the size' (letter, *The Times*, 9th March 1950).

This view rested upon the problematical assumptions that everyone with a certain amount of, and no one with less, land cultivates a garden, and everyone with a garden plants it full of vegetables. The Committee on Land Utilisation in Rural Areas reported unelegantly, 'We have examined carefully the view that the gardens, being intensively cultivated, of a garden suburb, provide more produce than if the whole area were farmed, but we are unable to accept this view. The comparison in the case of good land should be between the proportion of the gardens which is used in the growing of fruit and vegetables and the whole area if it were under intensive market gardening. Reliable figures of the proportion after due allowance has been made for roads, footpaths, actual house area, garden paths, lawns, flower beds, etc., of the total area used productively are not available, but in cases examined it is not above 25 per cent, and we take the view that once good agricultural land is taken for housing, it is of necessity lost to agriculture for ever, no matter how desperately it may be needed in the future for food production' (Cmd. 6378, p. 72).

[3] County Planning Committee report, 15th June 1949.

any extent compatible with the basic principles of New Towns. Hence, on the issue of flats *v.* houses, they generally tried to steer a middle course between the warring factions, although the predilection of each Corporation clearly influenced the outcome and some were noticeably reluctant to yield to Ministry pressure for an increase in New Town densities (a problem which was aggravated on some sites by the existence of large areas already developed at low densities).

Judging from such construction programmes as had been announced by March 1950, from 15 to 20 per cent of the dwellings which most New Town Corporations in the Greater London area intended to erect would be flats—a proportion which, perpetrating the prevailing national proportion, the urban school of planners considered too low and the garden city school too high. '. . . the first plans for these new towns are still clouded with garden-city suburbanism', said Thomas Sharp, 'and future building . . . will need to be more compact and more truly urban.'[1] Robert Lutyens hailed a ten-storey block of flats designed for the Harlow New Town as a 'triumph of common sense and propriety. . . . In Le Corbusier's phrase, instead of parks in cities, let us have more cities in parks to demonstrate our national renaissance.'[2] To which F. J. Osborn retorted that flats were 'imaginative luxuries' which only a few persons wanted or could afford; the bulk of the nation must be housed in 'functional earth-bound houses'.[3] One of our informants commented about the flats which the Harlow and Stevenage Corporations proposed to build, 'Someone unkindly said that, now there were no cathedrals to build and indeed practically nothing but dwellings, the architects turned to flats because they gave large, high buildings as monuments to their own skill!'

The Hemel Hempstead Corporation dropped a proposal for ten-storey flats, their doubts having been confirmed by Ministerial and local criticism. But the first housing project of the Stevenage Corporation, on which construction started in April 1950, called for the erection of 112 flats, fifty-four in one seven-story block and the rest in three- and four-storey blocks, on a site adjoining the present town. The Corporation backed this project despite objections from the local Council, whose chairman publicly[4] termed the flats 'barracks' and said that they would not be at all in keeping with the neighbourhood. The then Corporation chairman had once written:

'I think it very probable that as time goes on a higher percentage than at present of families of certain kinds and tastes—principally where there are no children—will deliberately choose to live in flats: and I can see no

[1] Thomas Sharp, *English Panorama* (London 1950), p. 109.
[2] Letter, *The Times*, 7th February 1950.   [3] Ibid., 13th February 1950.
[4] At the 27th June 1949 Stevenage Council meeting.

reason why for such people blocks of flats should not sometimes be erected in semi-rural or rural surroundings. . . . But all evidence shows that the overwhelming majority of families with children prefer houses, and I believe experience shows that houses are far more desirable for them than block flats situated in towns.'[1]

Inevitably, the Corporation pursued a similar compromise policy, and a subsequent announcement emphasized that these would be 'middle-class' flats renting at higher rates than Council houses.[2] 'A start on other similar schemes depends largely on the popularity of these dwellings.'[3]

F. STEVENAGE COUNCIL PROPOSALS

The Stevenage Council and local opponents voiced three main objections to the New Town plan. First, of course, they wanted the New Town sited elsewhere. But if it were to be at Stevenage, they thought certain changes should be made in the location of the New Town centre and industrial area; over these features of the Master Plan, the Corporation exhibited little inclination to conciliate local interests.

(a) Siting

New Town opponents contended that:

1. Development of a New Town at Stevenage in such proximity to other towns would ultimately result in an urban coalescence along the Great North Road from Hitchin to Welwyn Garden City. To this objection, the Minister countered that 'planning powers already

---

[1] Charles Jenkinson, *Our Housing Objective* (London, 1943), p. 20.
[2] The *Hertfordshire Express*, 13th May 1950.
[3] A reader of this section comments, 'The author in stressing throughout sociological and ideological matters (including political) shows a virtually complete neglect of economics. It is a fact that at the present time a flat costs *very much* more than a house of equivalent size, takes longer to build (being more costly in labour and materials) and, in the general economic sense, is harder to run by a woman with children. The only reason that flats are built in reconstruction schemes is that the land is very costly and for some most odd reason it is generally assumed that the most economic way to redevelop it is with buildings costing more per unit!' The author agrees about the importance of economic factors but the calculation can be made in different ways—for example, the greater cost (to both the nation and the resident) of coal in the open house fire than in centrally-heated flats, and of transportation from suburban houses than from more central urban flats, might be included. The cost of the lower agricultural production resulting from suburban expansion cannot simply be calculated in sterling (it is often cheaper to import foreign than to produce native food); during a war it may be calculated in blood. And a smaller centrally-heated flat can yield a net living space equal to or greater than the average English house in which only one or two rooms are actually heated and inhabited throughout the day.

available to local Planning Authorities are sufficient to prevent such coalescence'.[1]

The Minister was undoubtedly better able than local citizens or the Council to judge the regional consequences of disparate urban development. Indeed, continuous urban development had been threatened by pre-war plans of local authorities in the region, which the *Greater London Plan* and the Stevenage New Town were designed to prevent. Summarizing existing local plans in 1946, Ministry officers had warned that 'drastic revision of these Planning Schemes will be required immediately if Stevenage New Town is to be safe-guarded from straggling development which might otherwise tend to link it with Hitchin on the North-West and Knebworth on the South, with only a thin separation on the North between it and Letchworth'.[2] Only time could tell if the Ministry's measures would prevent this happening.

2. Stevenage was too close to London to become self-contained. As an Independent councillor stated,[3] 'The Real Question is whether these new towns, if sited within a radius of 30 miles of London, will achieve the object in view, namely to become self-contained and not dormitory towns. It is my view that any New Town built within a radius of 30 to 40 miles of London will, with improved means of transport, become in a matter of 10 or 20 years, another London suburb straggling still further into the countryside.' To this objection, the Minister replied that the provision of local industry and employment would counterbalance the pull of London; and 'it is proposed to take positive action to prevent the new town from becoming a dormitory by providing accommodation predominantly for those who wish to live and work in the new town. We will not take people to Stevenage who continue to work in London, and we hope the cases will be few of people leaving Stevenage to return to London.'[4]

The Barlow Report suggested that 'possibly places like . . . Stevenage while . . . outside Greater London should also for some purposes be regarded as falling within the London conurbation'.[5]

[1] 8th November 1946 statement.
[2] *Ministry Plan* 1946. Even after the Development Corporation was established, the Council tended to sanction the spread of commercial development along the Great North Road. At its November 1948 meeting, for instance, the Council approved the Town Planning Committee's recommendation permitting the branch of a national bank to take over a residence on the London Road beyond the point where the Council had previously resolved to stop commercial development. A councillor warned that 'it was the "thin end of the wedge". Commercial development on the London Road must be stopped somewhere' (*Hertfordshire Express*, 3rd December 1948).
[3] In his election leaflet, 29th March 1947.
[4] 8th November 1946 statement and Stevenage speech, 6th May 1946.
[5] Cmd. 6153, p. 7.

In December 1949, 224 local residents—mainly salaried or self-employed persons in white-collar, professional, or commercial occupations—held railway season tickets for the trip from Stevenage (21 tickets were first and 203 third class); the average number of reduced-rate daily workman tickets was 175, making a total commuting population which can be variously estimated at from 9 to 12 per cent of the total employed population.[1] At Welwyn Garden City eight miles to the south, some 15 per cent of employed residents commuted to work in London offices, leading the subsequent Minister of Town and Country Planning to call it 'really a dormitory town that was started for the middle classes';[2] whereas only a 'negligible' number commuted from Letchworth, five miles north.[3] Stevenage was thus already on the borderline between 'dormitory' suburb and self-contained town, and the New Town might be pushed in one direction or the other by the improvement of transportation or the development of local industry. It was the Government's hope that the effect of the latter would outweigh the former, but, as there was little prior experience to go on when the New Towns programme was adopted, this could remain only a hope.

Abercrombie had recommended electrification of the railway from London to Hitchin, an improvement long overdue since service on this line was no better in 1950 than it had been in 1884.[4] Purdom

---

[1] The difficulties of obtaining a reliable estimate of the total number of employed persons in Stevenage are compounded by the uncertain match between the geographical areas and the dates upon which the respective calculations of employment and railway tickets are based. An employed population of 2,368 for the Stevenage Urban District was secured by a 1:4 survey of electoral register households conducted by the Corporation in March 1948, but we have based our minimum and maximum estimates upon the Ministry of Labour's figure of 3,409 persons in the broader area of the Stevenage Employment Exchange insured against unemployment in 1947 (before the legislation of July 1948 broadened the range of insurance), and 4,670 persons in 1948 (after the legislation came into force).

[2] Lewis Silkin, in F. E. Towndrow, *Replanning Britain* (London, 1941), p. 110.

[3] The figures for Welwyn Garden City and Letchworth are from F. J. Osborn, *Green-Belt Cities*, p. 115, and also letters by Malcolmson and Osborn in the *Hertfordshire Express*, 2nd and 16th March 1946, in which it is stated that for the past fifteen years an average of 1,200 persons daily have travelled from Welwyn Garden City to work in London.

[4] In June 1884 there were eleven trains daily from Stevenage to King's Cross, London, the slowest of which took seventy-five and the fastest fifty minutes for the thirty-mile journey. By January 1950 the number of trains had increased to twenty-three, but the slowest now took ninety-two minutes, the fastest forty-nine, and the average sixty-two minutes. Deterioration in rail service was widespread throughout Britain. In the summer of 1949, the best services from London to Scotland and West England 'were in every case inferior to those of 1906, and most of them were slower than in 1900' ('Slower British Trains', *The Times*, 9th January 1950).

argued that the Stevenage New Town 'will not progress without fundamental improvements in transport to London; for the present railway service will not be able to serve an additional population of 60,000 people'. He believed 'the regular movement of population from the new towns to London and vice versa is an advantage rather than not. . . . for the resources of the metropolis should be made available to them'.[1] This, however, meant the open espousal of a dormitory town, at least for a sizable proportion of the New Town's middle classes, which the *Greater London Plan* was designed to forestall.

Indeed, the Government's logic and goal were ambiguous. If the New Towns were to be 'self-contained', clearly they should be moved as far as possible from the orbit of London. Already in 1949, a Ministry officer noted, 'Stevenage . . . is now felt by some people to have been rather too near London to form an ideal New Town; and if the choice of this and its counterparts were being made again, settlements at a greater distance might possibly be chosen'.[2] But the New Towns could not move too far if they were to attract industry and population from London, a consideration which apparently predominated in the initial choice of Stevenage and other sites in the Greater London area.[3] We concur in the opinion of an informant that 'If adequate industry is provided, the working-class will be self-contained with negligible exceptions. The doubt is whether enough middle-class employment can be found. If not, the alternatives are—sacrifice balance and be self-contained, or be balanced at the expense of a commuting middle-class.'

3. A virgin site should be chosen. To this, the Minister replied, 'It will be apparent that in a largely populated area such as the Greater London Region undeveloped sites suitable for large-scale urban development are now practically non-existent . . . . many sites have been examined from this point of view, and the Minister is satisfied that no equally suitable alternative sites are available for early large-scale development'.[4] After looking at thirty sites, Abercrombie had put forward ten, of which several were subsequently rejected by the Inter-Departmental Committee which carefully examined their suitability. Obviously the Ministry staff chose Stevenage over other urban

---

[1] Purdom, op. cit., pp. 430, 385.

[2] R. K. Kelsall, *Citizen's Guide to the New Town and Country Planning* (Oxford, 1949), p. 56.

[3] The Minister noted, 'it is essential that we should not only provide housing accommodation for overcrowded London, but that we should also take industry out of London. . . . The industries already in London are dependent on London for their materials, and they have a direct tie with London in other ways. There is a limit, therefore, to the distance to which they are prepared to go' (reply to a question in the Stevenage town hall, 6th May 1946).

[4] Statement, 8th November 1946.

or rural sites on the basis of the best information available to them, and factors which might subsequently emerge were irrelevant to that initial judgment. In the Ministry's opinion, local opposition was not a sufficient reason to change a site that otherwise suited the national interest.

4. Sewage disposal for a town of 60,000 would contaminate the water supply to London. It was the feeling that the Minister had not adequately reckoned with this difficulty that largely led the High Court to nullify the Designation Order and the County Council to recommend, later, that the New Town be restricted to a population of 18,000. It was (and, in June 1950, remains) a serious difficulty (though more for financial than engineering reasons) which, until resolved, endangers the entire Stevenage New Town project, but the details are so technical that discussion of the matter has been relegated to Appendix A.

(b) New Town Centre

The New Towns Committee advised that 'The industrial zones and the central business zone should be convenient of access from all parts of the town. They should, if practicable, be near each other and near the main railway and bus stations.'[1] This reasonable general policy was applied to the Stevenage site by Ministry architects in their 1946 plan:

'We have tried several different sites for the town centre, and, in our opinion, one is by far the most suitable. This site lies immediately South of the old town and adjacent to the new railway station. It is in the centre of gravity of the whole town and between the two central roads leading from the residential to the industrial area. The site is level, over 50 acres in extent, and within easy walking distance of the bulk of the industrial estate. It is adjacent to the 'bus station, the railway goods yards, the telephone exchange . . . and the Post Office Parcels Office . . . [and has] direct approaches from the London and Northern entries to the town.'[2]

Against this disposition, retained in the Corporation's Master Plan, the Stevenage Council (and the Residents' Protection Association) asked that the New Town centre be moved further east, on higher ground in the geographic centre of the residential area. At the Master Plan inquiry of October 1949, a good deal of mock argument was entered by both sides on this question. The Council surveyor suggested that a more prominent location was preferable to the low-lying position desired by the Corporation and, balancing a cardboard cut-out of the designated area on a metal point, demonstrated that the Council's site lay at the New Town's 'centre of gravity'. On the Corporation's side, it was soberly contended that executives from the industrial area would find it advantageous to have banks, labour

[1] Cmd. 6876, p. 14.   [2] *Ministry Plan* 1946, p. 25.

exchange, insurance companies, and post office close at hand. To which the Council replied that the Corporation was sacrificing the welfare of thousands of housewives, who would be compelled to undertake long shopping trips daily, for the benefit of a few business men: of 700 persons then employed in the largest Stevenage factory, the surveyor stated, only three had any occasion to visit the town centre regularly during working hours; on the Corporation's plan, 33,000 persons would live outside a $1\frac{1}{4}$ mile, and 10,000 outside a $1\frac{3}{4}$ mile, radius from the town centre, as against 14,000 and 500 persons, respectively, on the Council's proposal.

These arguments were incidental to the main issues. Aside from planning aesthetics, financial and engineering considerations dominated the Corporation's choice. Their site was the natural place for the centre in terms of land values and traffic routes; to force development eastward would complicate the projected road network, risk a dispersal of land values, and yield small return on capital investments in roads and shops until the New Town was completed, for the Council's site would be marginal during early stages of construction; and there was danger that the Corporation might subsequently be forced to permit shops to migrate back to the area initially proposed, with disadvantageous consequences.

On the Council's part, the wish was expressed 'to maintain the residential character' of the district slated by the Corporation for commercial use, and to minimize competition with local traders. A Council spokesman stated at the inquiry that 'The proximity of the New Town centre to the shopping centre of old Stevenage will result in the steady decline of the existing shopping centre'. (To this, a Labour councillor representing the local Trades Council, countered, 'the workers of Stevenage . . . will be the main users of the New Town centre, and the chance of having a new shopping centre attached to the old one does appeal to them. It gives them more shops and, what is more, it gives them a sort of competition. There should be no objection because we have been told that competition is the lifeblood of industry. . . . We, the workers, look forward to it.') We were inclined to accept this as an important motive underlying the Council's proposal; however, informants who helped shape that proposal (independently and, we are convinced, both honestly and truthfully) privately denied it. In their opinion, they and others were primarily concerned to preserve some sixty-eight houses whose demolition was necessary under the Corporation's scheme. No representations had been received from local traders, and the public reference to avoiding competition was a conscious rationalization rather than a primary objective of Council policy. At the October 1949 inquiry, the Corporation solicitor, cross-examining a Council witness, charged that the Council's plan was devised solely to obviate demolitions. 'Now, have you not in fact started your plan from one known factor: You have said, "We must avoid the demolition. Let us see what we can do." Is that a fair suggestion to put to you?' No direct answer was given, but *qui ne dit mot consent*.

(c) The Industrial Area

Demolitions certainly accounted for the Council's opposition to the location of the northern part of the industrial zone which, on the Master Plan, encompassed a road along which one hundred semi-detached houses had been built after the First World War. No other Corporation proposal roused such intense and protracted opposition.

Abercrombie's *Greater London Plan* recommended that industry be located west of the railway 'where it is undesirable to have residential development'.[1] Unfortunately, some residential development had already taken place there. Commenting on Abercrombie's plan in December 1945, the Council said:

'industrial development in this district should be confined to an area of about 500 acres alongside and west of the railway, south of the termination of the residential property in Fairview Road. . . . In order to avoid a long narrow industrial area it is suggested that land east of the railway and south of the Urban District boundary should also be zoned for industrial development. . . . There should . . . be a break between the residential property in Fairview Road and the industrial zone by the suitable planting of the narrow strip of land. . . . It is realised that this strip is a totally insufficient screen but is the only land left available for that purpose. . . .

On the Council plan for Stevenage, drafted in October 1937 for submission to the Minister of Health under the Town and Country Planning Act, 1932, and intended to provide for an ultimate population of 34,000, industry had been zoned west of the railway but south of Fairview Road which, together with adjacent land west and north, had been reserved for residential development.

Architects of the Ministry of Town and Country Planning reported in 1946:

'At an early stage we came to the conclusion that the only reasonable place for the industrial estate was between the main railway line and the new Great North Road. Here the land is relatively flat and industries would be most directly connected to road and rail transport facilities. With the industrial zone in this position no major industrial traffic need cross the railway into the residential areas of the town. . . .
'We have carefully considered the proposals of the Stevenage Urban District Council . . . that the industrial area should be south of [Fairview Road]. . . . If the industrial area (of at least 500 acres) were in this position it would entail: (a) a more costly Trunk Road which would run, in part, through Knebworth Park; (b) about 200 acres of the Park being brought

[1] Abercrombie, p. 161.

into industrial use; (c) costly levelling as the land to the S.W. is very un-
even; (d) confused zoning in the North-West unless the —— and ——
factories are demolished.

'It is unfortunate that the best site for larger industries . . . has been
partly developed for residential purposes along Fairview Road. . . . At
either end of this road lie the two largest industrial establishments. . . .
Taking all factors into account it seems essential, if the town is to be built
on a good plan, that the houses on Fairview Road should eventually give
way to industrial development, and that there should be no residential
area west of the railway.'[1]

The 1949 Master Plan zoned for industry 440 acres west of the
railway. Area 'A,' over half this total, lying south of Fairview Road,
was not in dispute. In place of the northern area 'B', the Council
proposed an alternate 130-acre site in the north-east corner of the
New Town, to be serviced by road: 'This proposal would mean
that further residential development would take place to the west
of Fairview Road, to provide for, in all, in this area, a population of
about 3,000. The people here would use as their neighbourhood
shopping centre the one already existing in Stevenage.'[2] Corporation
experts testified it would be more expensive to develop this site,
which lacked road or rail communications, water, gas, or electricity
services. This was doubtless true, and the Council suggestion that
light industries not requiring rail facilities be located there ignored
the national interest as Abercrombie had seen it:

'It is . . . desirable that industrial estates should be planned with direct
rail facilities. If such facilities are not provided this can only mean, in the
long run, that more and more long-distance heavy goods traffic is thrown
on the roads. Even if factories at first make no use of sidings they may
eventually expand to such a size that the volume of goods dealt with will
justify rail facilities. . . . It is accordingly recommended that industrial
estates should not be planned in areas where estate sidings cannot, where
the necessity arises, be provided. . . .'[3]

In addition to the north-east site, the Council, at various times,
proposed alternate locations south of area 'A' and along a little-
used railway line on the southern fringe of the New Town. These
were also dismissed by the Corporation as inadequate on technical
grounds. Through more than three years' discussions, the Corporation held firmly to its choice of the Fairview Road section for industry, and its only concession to local feeling was an agreement to
delay this development until a later stage of the programme.

Initially, the Council's policy aimed not only to avoid demolition

[1] *Ministry Plan* 1946, p. 24.
[2] Statement by the Council surveyor at the Master Plan inquiry, 18th October
1949.
[3] Abercrombie, p. 61.

but also to make old Stevenage a more important centre of the New Town (whereas the Corporation merely wished to preserve it more or less intact as the smallest of six neighbourhood units). Thus the Council suggested in December 1945 that by moving the by-pass road further west, it might be possible to site a neighbourhood unit west of the railway and 'the present town might be then used as the central unit'.[1] Subsequently, however, the Council discarded this proposal as practical objections to it became clear.

Ministry and Corporation technicians were not blind to the Council's proposals, but their main obligation was to prepare as excellent a plan as they could devise in the light of geographic, economic, architectural, and engineering considerations. They would not sanction a proposal which, they felt, might produce the same undesirable consequences as at Welwyn Garden City, where the railway bisected the town into two residential (and class) areas. Indeed, in 1946, the Minister had asked his staff if it would not be possible to plan the New Town on the basis of the Council's 1937 planning proposals. In April 1946 he was advised:

'If we attempted to retain the present High Street in an enlarged form as the central shopping area of a town of 60,000, it would mean extending the town further to the north and we should then commit a similar fault to the Council because it would have to extend to the further side of a main east-to-west arterial road which has already been pushed as far north as possible. Thus to provide for a population of 60,000 any balanced plan must provide for expansion eastwards and southwards. . . . The layout for a town of 60,000 is, therefore, very largely dictated by certain fixed features and a mere expansion of the Council's own planning proposals for a larger population would not meet the case.'

Professionally, the Ministry staff outranked the Council in numbers, experience, resources, and professional status, so that even their preliminary plan must be rated technically superior to the Council's. The Council's 1937 plan, drawn up rapidly (by a native of Stevenage, a Labour supporter who subsequently became chairman of the London County Council for one year, and was town planning consultant for the Hitchin and Stevenage Urban District Councils) to satisfy local needs, mainly perpetuated existing land use; it could not possibly have served as the basis for a model New Town—a Council informant privately acknowledged that 'It wasn't a scheme, really, just a few sketchy plans. It was so bad, it wasn't worth their [the Ministry 1946 technical staff's] while.'

The position adopted by Corporation and Ministry at the many local inquiries and conferences was that only those proposals merited acceptance which were at least as good, on planning grounds, as their own. The Minister said exactly this in his May 1946 speech in

[1] From the Council's December 1945 statement on the *Greater London Plan*.

the town hall: 'I am perfectly ready, as I said to your Council, to discuss any alternative proposals which will produce an equally good result. That must be a condition; any alternative plan put forward must be as good as the plan I have submitted to you.' But the Urban District Council and other local bodies did not have a large budget and staff available for no other purpose than the preparation of plans and, under the circumstances, could never speak as authoritatively on planning matters as either the Corporation or the Ministry. It was not surprising, therefore, that the Minister held the Council's (1937) plan 'offends against many of the canons of good planning' and the Corporation considered the Council's subsequent criticisms 'neither valid nor substantial'.[1] A division of opinion was always possible in planning questions, and the planners naturally preferred their own opinions to those of local citizens, who spoke with authority only on local interest and sentiment, which could not invariably be reconciled with the best principles of town and country planning.

That these principles might occasionally be compromised for the gain of goodwill did not seem to occur to many planners. The Corporation favourably received Council suggestions for the creation of an artificial lake, lorry parks, and details of some railway crossings; religious care was taken to preserve the cricket ground, the avenue of lime and chestnut trees and, indeed, every possible tree, spring, pond, and hedge; the most maniacal planner did not dream of levelling a foot off any of Stevenage's six Roman barrows, and the Ministry had issued an order scheduling some 90 buildings in the designated area as of special architectural or historic interest—a step preliminary to their immortalization. But the 111-odd houses on Fairview Road and 68 on the projected site of the New Town centre would suffer for being ordinary; the only concession made to local opinion was a promise to delay demolitions as long as possible.[2]

[1] The Minister's remark was made in the course of his 6th May 1946 speech at Stevenage; the Corporation's comment was contained in a 1948 report to the Minister reviewing discussions with the Council on the Master Plan.

[2] While the Ministry approved the Corporation Master Plan in February 1950, including the necessary demolitions in both the industrial and town centre areas, Ministry technicians observed, 'The location of factories in the industrial area should be so arranged that the residential character of Fairview Road is preserved as long as possible. We note that the Corporation share this view and intend that Fairview Road and the area immediately adjacent should be the last part of the industrial area to be developed. . . . We agree that this is most desirable and that the strength of the Development Corporation's case for acquiring the Fairview Road properties for industrial development can only be decided when they can prove that they are an essential part of the development of the whole industrial area.' In regard to the town centre, they said, 'we are satisfied that by careful phasing of the opening up of the area, all but a very few of the existing houses could if necessary remain until a late stage in the development of the town centre'.

The cost of demolition and erecting equivalent accommodations elsewhere (which the Corporation was bound by law to provide before evicting tenants) would make these areas expensive to develop, but did not deter the planners from their goal. A Corporation official declared publicly that the houses in Fairview Road were not houses 'to perpetuate as monuments'. 'Of course they are not', a resident of the road retorted. 'Who wants to live in a monument? They are, however, the homes of hundreds of decent and respectable home-loving human beings.' The official immediately apologized for the statement, and the resident accepted his apology, which was, of course, the diplomatic thing to do on both sides; but no amount of diplomacy could disguise the difference of outlook.[1]

The seventy-year-old Earl L (descendant of the novelist mentioned in Chapter II), large local landowner, lifelong proponent of town and country planning, and president of the Garden Cities and Town Planning Association, felt it his duty to appear at the Ministry inquiry of October 1946 and tell the inspector that 'it is carrying principle to the point of madness to insist that people who already live on the other side of the railway and who are prepared to live there must vacate their houses and live on the other side whether they like it or not'. But he was an old man and died shortly thereafter. Younger men at the Corporation and Ministry had fastened on an ideal which they meant to realize and, for them, present pain was a necessary part of future achievement or, as they often put it, personal sacrifice was necessary for the general welfare. The doctrine was easy to uphold because the sacrifice was not theirs.

[1] This exchange took place in the correspondence columns of the *Hertfordshire Express*, October 1949. The Corporation officer wrote, 'While it is, I think, true that most of the houses in Fairview Road are of no outstanding architectural merit, yet my remark, made impromptu in answer to a question, was a clumsy and unfortunate one, and might well be taken to imply a lack of sympathy with those householders who will be displaced by the building of the New Town. This is far from being the case, and I hope that . . . residents in Fairview Road will accept my apologies.'

CHAPTER FIVE

Local Interests

W E will discuss only a few rational interests (causes, motives, or arguments—the concepts are here inter-linked), for the most part publicly expressed, which led local citizens to oppose or support the New Town.

A. NEW TOWN OPPONENTS

(a) The Agricultural Interest

As has been observed, the New Towns programme ran counter to rural interests because of its demands upon agricultural land. This was protested again and again at Stevenage, as by one councillor: 'This is not the time to take valuable agricultural land to build houses. A house is no good if your belly is empty. Most people would rather have a full belly in a crowded house than an empty belly in a mansion.'

The farmers immediately affected had little chance, under prevail-ing conditions, to obtain land elsewhere. The demand for Hertford-shire farms in 1947 'far exceeds the supply. Business men are taking up farming [as landowners, for an investment]. Small farmers who did well during the war are looking for larger farms, and with the security which will be provided under the new Agricultural Bill the difficulty of finding a vacant farm will be even greater.'[1] The situa-tion had not altered by January 1950, when an estate agent reported:

'very few agricultural properties in this district have been available for sale or to let, and if vacant possession is offered, the price is about four

[1] Wilfrid Roberts, 'Farmers and the New Towns', *Hertfordshire Countryside*, Autumn 1947, p. 42.

times the pre-war figure. Very few farmers, who have to make their living from the land, can compete, knowing that, in addition, they will have to find capital to run, at least, a partially mechanised farm. The advent of the Agriculture Act of 1947 gives such security to the sitting tenant that rank bad farming, or death, seem to be the only chances by which a landlord can regain possession!'[1]

Before passage of the Town and Country Planning Act, 1947, legal compensation by the Corporation was based upon 1939 values, grossly under prevailing market value or the cost of obtaining equivalent alternative property outside the New Town. Understandably, the chairman of the Residents' Protection Association complained on behalf of local property-owners, 'we feel that we are labouring under deep injustice; we have had no consideration, and we are being hurt apparently without a cause'.[2]

The Minister promised that 'Whilst . . . ultimate displacement from farms . . . is inevitable, full regard will be had to the need for giving adequate notice'.[3] But Stevenage farmers were advised that

'at any rate until 18th April 1951, the development corporation would have power to use the speedy procedure conferred by the Acquisition of Land . . . Act, 1946, which would enable the corporation to enter on and take possession of land within less than a month from service of notice on the farmer of their intention to do so. No farmer can be expected to conduct his farm on sound lines with the threat of this possibility.[4]

It will be recalled that the terms of acquisition which the Ministry served upon local property-owners in April 1946 rendered them liable to eviction upon three months' notice and, at that time, the Ministry planned to proceed so rapidly that only one owner was informed his property would not be required within a year. Later, Government capital restrictions frustrated the Corporation's intention to acquire land at least two years before possession was needed.

[1] Report on Hertfordshire in *The Estates Gazette*, 14th January 1950. The county situation was typical of that prevailing throughout Britain. 'In their annual review of transactions in real property a firm which manages a large area of agricultural land in various 'parts of the country says: "There has been no falling off in the demand for farms with vacant possession, while the supply has been even smaller than last year. Previously unheard-of prices per acre have been paid, particularly for comparatively small farms with possession, and in a number of cases the buyers are newcomers to farming with little or no previous experience' " (*The Times*, 28th December 1949).
[2] Statement at the October 1946 Ministry inquiry.
[3] Reply dated 8th November 1946, issued to objections raised at the October 1946 inquiry.
[4] From the mimeographed brief (Appendix Part II), submitted by the Residents' Protection Association to the House of Lords, *On Appeal from His Majesty's Court of Appeals in the Matter of the New Towns Act*, 1946 *and in the Matter of the Stevenage New Town* (*Designation*) *Order*, 1946.

'Not only would this two year period have given to the Corporation sufficient time within which to serve the statutory one year's notice to quit on any tenant farmer and to make satisfactory arrangements with him and with the Ministry of Agriculture and Fisheries for continued occupation, under short tenancy or licence, of those parts of the holdings which will not be required for development at the outset, but it would have enabled the farmer properly to arrange not only the immediate planning of his holding but also his impending move from it. It is feared that, as a result of the delay in authorising the acquisition of the land, entry may have to be effected at shorter notice than is desirable in the interests of food production, of the farmer personally and consequently of local public relations.'[1]

The Corporation planned to retain for agricultural purposes a valley running through the centre of town, although the County Council viewed this proposal as 'impracticable'.[2] L. Dudley Stamp has observed that

'An efficient farm is a neatly balanced factory in which the loss of one field in 12 completely upsets a three-, four-, or six-course rotation. Efficient farming is obviously impossible on land designated for a new town even when building is not to begin at once. Similarly, though some use may be made of land which the town-planner for his own purposes desires to leave open, the standard of farming cannot be high or efficient.'[3]

In his comments on the Master Plan in February 1950, the Minister stated that, while retaining an open mind on the subject, he believed an attempt should be made to farm this valley as the Corporation proposed and the resident farmers were prepared to do.[4]

Planners reasoned that the garden city would ultimately benefit agriculture by restricting urban encroachment and providing a nearby market for vegetables and dairy products. However, these long-term considerations could benefit only those farmers who survived and, under the Agriculture Act of 1947, farmers already enjoyed a guaranteed market for almost everything they produced. The

[1] Stevenage Corporation report, in New Towns Act, 1946, *Reports of the . . . Development Corporations for the period ending 31st March, 1948* (London, 1949), p. 80.
[2] Hertfordshire County Council, *Report of the County Planning Committee,* 4th November 1949, Appendix B.
[3] Letter, *The Times,* 3rd May 1949.
[4] The Minister had been informed by his technical staff that 'The Ministry of Agriculture and Fisheries have expressed great doubts about the practicability of carrying on farming in this wedge which they do not think would be possible to do economically because of the difficulties of trespass and expensive fencing. We appreciate that the upper end of the wedge is somewhat steep for development and it is generally accepted that it forms a pleasant amenity feature. We understand that the present farmer is willing and desirous of carrying on in the restricted area which will be left in the valley and we think that the Corporation should be permitted to try this out, but they should be prepared to develop the lower part of the valley . . . should this become necessary.'

immediate threat to the livelihood of local farmers was unmistakable,
as the Corporation was the first to recognize. Some would lose 'such
a large part of their holdings that they will no longer be able to farm
the remainder. There is, unfortunately, no other farmland in our
possession which we could offer them in return.'[1] Other farms would
be drastically slashed. 'Take ——' (head of a family who had farmed
in Stevenage for many generations), the rector said. 'He owns 800
acres—like Job he is, farms *for* the land, not for what he can take
from it. He'll be left with two allotments, 200 acres. He's insulted if
they want to *pay* him for the land. They *can't* pay him; his life is
ruined.'

Most farmers in the district were tenants: these were hardest hit,
as they received only minor compensation upon removal. 'The programme of land acquisition which has now been approved entails
very real hardship to several of the tenant farmers, and it seemed possible that there might be something in the nature of a public outcry',
the Corporation observed in October 1948.[2] The feared protest did
not materialize, but individual farmers played an important part in
organizing opposition to the New Town: the district branch of the
National Farmers' Union early decided to co-operate with the Residents' Protection Association and the two groups jointly contested
the Designation Order in the courts.

Many opponents of the New Town found it more convenient to
question the suitability of the site than to attack the entire programme and much of the debate at Ministry inquiries, therefore, was
concerned with the quality of local soil. Although one might think
that here, if anywhere, was an objectively ascertainable fact, expert
opinion managed to coincide with the expert's attitude towards the
New Town. Thus, Abercrombie wrote:

'good agricultural land, though not of the highest class, occurs in north
Hertfordshire. . . . This land . . . should be avoided where possible in
selecting building sites, but because it occurs in greater quantity than the
land of the highest class, its loss would not be felt so severely.'[3]

In 1944, when New Towns were just an idea, L. Dudley Stamp,
director of the Land Utilisation Survey of Britain, said:

'it is to be hoped that these good lands on the Chalky Boulder Clay will
remain predominantly agricultural and rural. Where, however, there is a
marked through line of communication . . . there is every justification for
the siting of such a satellite as is proposed at Harlow . . . just as one
would not discourage the growth of . . . Stevenage.'[4]

In 1949, however, he objected that 'Not a single one of the proposed

[1] Corporation report to Minister, October 1948. [2] Ibid.
[3] Patrick Abercrombie, *Greater London Plan* 1944 (London, 1945), p. 26.
[4] L. Dudley Stamp, in Abercrombie, p. 93.

new towns ventures away from a lowland agricultural site'.[1] The Development Corporation held that the Stevenage site 'consists almost entirely of mixed farmland graded by the Ministry of Agriculture and Fisheries as of not more than second quality'.[2] It was presumably the Ministry of Agriculture rating that the Minister of Town and Country Planning had in mind when, answering a question at the Stevenage town hall, he stated, 'this is not regarded as the best type of agricultural land'. Whereupon a farmer rose from the audience and declared:

'The land the Minister proposes to take is some of the best land in this district. I have acted as Crop Reporter for the Minister of Agriculture for the past fifty years, and I have been sending in cropping returns for this district. The land you are taking is first-class for Hertfordshire. . . . The wheat yield for this district over a period of seven years has been 21 cwts. to the acre, and . . . the average for the whole country is 18 cwts. to the acre.'

The Residents' Protection Association stated, 'The land affected is mainly good loam, above the average in natural fertility and is intensely farmed. . . . holdings are among the best-farmed land in the country'.[3]

There was a similar delightful dispute about the effect of prevailing winds. The Protection Association objected that, as the industrial area was in the west, prevailing westerly winds would blanket the town with smoke and smells. The Ministry technical staff admitted,

'Theoretically, industries should not be placed on the West of the town (prevailing winds being from the South-West), but we do not consider it a disadvantage where the control of location will ensure that those causing smells will be on the outer edge of the zone and the emission of black smoke would be forbidden. Special (or noxious) industries should not in any case be allowed in Stevenage.'[4]

The opposition also contended, 'a considerable part of the area selected for urban development is situate on high ground which is exposed to the winds which blow from the North Sea across the flat country to the east and north-east' at certain seasons, notably spring.[5]

[1] Letter, *The Times*, 3rd May 1949.
[2] *Reports of the Development Corporations for the period ending 31st March*, 1948, p. 75. After a two-year geological survey, the Corporation reported, 'Basically the area is formed by a main valley and its tributary valleys formed in chalk. These have been filled in with glacial deposits of sand, gravel, clay with flints and brickearth, which are as deep as 120 feet in places. In course of time the steep sides of the chalk valleys have become exposed, leaving layers of clay with flints on the high ground and the unconformed glacial deposits in the valleys. Thus the surface soil varies considerably and there are sudden local changes, even within the area of a field or garden' (*Corporation Master Plan* 1949, p. 4).
[3] See note 4, p. 133.   [4] *Ministry Plan* 1946.
[5] Statement by local farmer at the Designation Order inquiry, October 1946.

The Minister countered drily that 'In selecting the area for the new town, the Minister consulted the appropriate meteorological authority and he is satisfied that climatic conditions are not such as to prevent the successful development of a new town'.[1]

The truth was that relatively good farmland was also apt to be good land for building purposes—well drained, relatively level, with a good bearing capacity, and near to transportation facilities and other services—and something was gained and something was lost by each mode of use. The choice rested not simply upon objective determination of what was best for 'the nation', but also upon the relative power of rival social groups and Ministries, and a political decision by the Cabinet. Although the struggle was generally couched in reasonable terms (reason was more efficacious than passion, moderating the intensity of the opposition and placating a neutral section of the community which might otherwise join the fray), this could not entirely cloak the naked facts of power. The Ministry of Agriculture had been consulted, of course, by the Ministry of Town and Country Planning,[2] and formally, if unenthusiastically, agreed to the decision to site the New Town at Stevenage. The Minister of Town and Country Planning cheerfully told his Stevenage audience, 'Everyone has reason to hope that our food difficulties will be over in one or two harvests, and I do not contemplate that this land will be required for the next two years'. The years belied the Minister's hope; but agriculture was never more than one of many factors he had to consider.

'In siting [a] . . . new town, the value of lost farm produce must be weighed against the cost of building, of services, possibly of railways, for the alternative sites, as well as many other factors. The Ministry of Town and Country Planning is not likely to make a wise decision if the spotlights are focused solely on local agricultural production.'[3]

One cannot yet say how well or ill advised was his decision in the use of Stevenage.

(b) The Rural Cult

The handbook of the Stevenage Urban District Council states:

'Stevenage is in the midst of unspoilt rural countryside, well wooded, of gentle slopes giving at points extensive views over the flatter country-

[1] 8th November 1946 reply to objections.

[2] Such consultation was standard Government practice. 'Shortly before the outbreak of war [1939] an arrangement was made between the Ministry of Agriculture and the Service Departments under which no agricultural land was to be taken without prior consultation with the Ministry of Agriculture. During the war this arrangement has been extended to all other Government Departments interested in the taking of land' (Report of the Committee on Land Utilisation in Rural Areas, Cmd. 6378 (London, 1942), p. 35).

[3] F. J. Osborn, letter, The Times, 26th May 1949.

side to the north. . . . Walking the pleasant footpaths which radiate in every direction from the town a visitor will find it hard to believe he is only thirty miles from London. The paths wind by hedgerows full of wild flowers, through tangled woodlands to picturesque little hamlets and to scatterings of ancient cottages about expansive greens.'[1]

The colouring of these lines is as informative as their content, for there is little the English middle classes love more passionately and, as it becomes rarer, guard more assiduously, than the countryside. Upon at least three occasions in recent years, students at the Stevenage grammar school debated the proposition that 'Town life is better than country life' (heated discussion arose as to whether Stevenage was 'town' or 'country') and upon each occasion the motion was defeated by an overwhelming majority.[2] These are but local symptoms of a disease—the-exaltation-of-animals-and-nature —which has ravaged England more remorselessly than other nations. The aphorism, 'God made the country, man made the Town', conveys, one imagines, more about the Englishman's mentality than it does about God's. Nigel Harvey fruitlessly protests that Cowper's line is 'fatuous', for the domesticated crops and animals and laboriously tended fields and hedges of the 'natural' countryside are as artificial as the factory or the street; modern farmers are not simple rustics but shrewd business men with a sizable capital investment, and the urban folklore of the countryside reflects not facts but 'vague memories, superficial observation and sentimental dreams'.[3] His voice is unheard because people do not wish to hear it.

Many organizations such as the Council for the Preservation of Rural England, the Society for the Protection of Ancient Buildings, and the Association of Parish Councils, voice rural interests amidst the loud urban world, and not a week goes by but the decay of a Norman church, the erection of a power station in 'unspoilt' country, or the pollution of a stream becomes the subject of nation-wide interest. In Hertfordshire, the Hertfordshire Society

'endeavours unceasingly to stimulate interest in rural areas, and to see that the materialistic aims of "planners" do not conflict with the claims of agriculture, or our rural heritage. . . . Nobody can deny that the past thirty years have witnessed appalling and unnecessary desecration of many areas of the English countryside, and . . . development of mechanized agriculture, requirements of modern transport facilities, open-cast mineral excavations, etc., all constitute grave changes to rural areas, which demand an ever-watchful eye. . . . Protection of the Hertfordshire countryside

[1] Stevenage Urban District, *Official Handbook* (London, 1947?), p. 7.
[2] In March 1919, the motion was lost by 32 votes to 5; in March 1930, by 10 to 2; of the spring 1936 debate no record is available beyond the notation, 'The motion . . . was defeated by an overwhelming majority'.
[3] Nigel Harvey, 'The Unnatural Countryside', *New Statesman and Nation*, 8th October 1949, pp. 378–80.

against the inroads of new town planning schemes can be achieved only
by dovetailing modern development with historic tradition.'[1]

The New Town was regarded by many influential Stevenage
citizens as part of the urban onslaught upon rural life which must be
resisted. Many had themselves moved from London to escape the
city; now it was thrust upon them. 'I came here to be out of the dirt
and din', said a business man who continued to commute to work in
London. 'Now look what's happening. I'm going to be right in the
middle of it.' Like him, many of the most active leaders of the Residents' Protection Association were not natives but London business
men. 'It wasn't the natives of Stevenage who made the most noise
over the New Town,' said one (native) informant. They were joined,
of course, and stoutly supported by natives who, like a sixty-year-old
labourer, considered it sacrilege to disturb scenes familiar since
childhood:

'I don't like to see the beauty spots being violated. My great grandfather was here, and his father before him. We belong here, and I shouldn't
like to see the beauty taken away. If they are going to put factories up our
countryside is going to be polluted, especially the air, and people come
here specially for that. I suffer from lung trouble, and the air at present is
grand for that. Have you seen the beauty of the place? That avenue of
chestnuts, up by the school, and the parish church?'

For many months, the local and national Press carried letters on
the threatened 'spoliation' of Stevenage and the neighbouring
countryside. One particularly interesting series concerned Aston, the
village on the outskirts of the designated area where the Development Corporation established its offices. A septuagenarian Justice of
the Peace, graduate of Eton and Trinity College, Cambridge, member of the Stock Exchange for fifty years, founder of a host of national
and empire associations, and an original member of the Garden City
and Town Planning Association, and Lord of the Manor in this
village, Mr. Z, wrote as follows in March 1946:

'There are those who seek happiness in life in the peace and beauty of
rural surroundings and their recreation in country sports, natural history
and rambles, and who derive inspiration from poetry, art and literature of
an elevating and instructing character; on the other hand there are those,
mainly newcomers, . . . who seek their pleasures in cinemas, dance halls,
night clubs and public houses, but little weight need be attached to their
views.
'It is impossible to reconcile these two outlooks on life. . . . I can see
no good reason why the old residents of Stevenage should have a population of this class thrust upon them, completely re-moulding their mode of

[1] Report of address by the secretary of the Hertfordshire Society, *Hertfordshire Mercury*, 2nd June 1950.

life and aspirations, and bringing in its wake the strain and unrest of a dominating industrial city.'[1]

(Addressing the House of Commons two months later during the second reading of the New Towns Bill, the Minister of Town and Country Planning insidiously remarked, 'I want to see the new towns gay and bright, with plenty of theatres, concert halls, and meeting places'.)[2]

By September 1947, the matter was being pursued in the correspondence columns of *The Times*, where Mr. Z stated, 'My home was built by an ancestor in 1540, and I have visions of fried-fish shops and cinemas at my garden gate, while the peaceful rural village of Aston is being rapidly converted into an industrial slum'. When a Corporation officer replied that the Corporation 'hopes to be a good neighbour to Mr. [Z] and to others whose ancestors have lived for many generations in rural Hertfordshire', but resolutely affirmed that 'cinemas and fish and chips shops will undoubtedly have their place' in the New Town, Mr. Z retorted:

'I regret that I can see little prospect of "good neighbour" relations being established between the Corporation and the parish of Aston for the following reasons: Possession has been taken of the village green and cricket ground; Army huts erected for war purposes in the very centre of the village, under a verbal promise of removal on the termination of hostilities, have been requisitioned for the purpose of billeting navvies and other workers in the new town; . . . an old Queen Anne residence, immediately opposite the church and rectory, has been purchased at the expense of the State and the land is being actively prepared for an industrial settlement, to the dismay of the parishioners.'

A special correspondent thereupon investigated these charges for *The Times* and reported from Aston:

'Fears expressed recently that this little village near Stevenage will be overwhelmed by the building of the new satellite town would appear, upon examination of the present plans, to be premature. . . . [The army huts] will later disappear. . . . Aston and the sixteenth-century manor house will be in the green belt surrounding the town, whose outer buildings will be over half a mile away. This does not appear to be clearly understood or believed as yet in the village, and there is still a feeling of uncertainty. There are, however, a number of inhabitants who regard with favour the nearness of a large town.'

Which elicited from Mr. Z the response that

'The message addressed to you by your special correspondent from Aston indicates a lack of appreciation of the mentality of country folk. . . . While it is no doubt true that rural scenery is appreciated by those who

[1] Letter, *Hertfordshire Express*, 2nd March 1946.
[2] *Hansard*, 8th May 1946, vol. 422, col. 1090.

pass it by in a car or charabanc, their El Dorado is not weeding or pruning in a cottage garden but rather the cinema or the dancehall. A distance of half a mile from the centre of infection cannot inoculate against the latter mentality, which, it is true, may have an attraction for a small proportion of the "bright young things" in a country parish. It is, however, an influence baneful in the eyes of country folk. . . .'[1]

The Ministry and local rural councils took precautions to prevent villages just outside the New Town boundaries being subjected to a sudden rush of building, exercising surveillance over new development to ensure that it 'fell within the natural and proper growth of those villages as agricultural villages'.[2] But it was futile to maintain that the New Town would not effect almost as radical changes in the life of these villages as it would in Stevenage. 'I cannot, of course, deny that the character of Stevenage will be changed when it becomes a town with a population of 50,000, as compared with its existing character', the Minister told his Stevenage audience. 'I believe on the whole it will be an even better place to live in than it is today. Change is inevitable—nothing stands still—and Stevenage, even if it was not to become the site of a new town would not have remained unchanged for long.'

But listeners had their own visions of the future, and derived little consolation from the Minister's philosophy. All did not have the opportunity or the ability to adequately voice their feelings. The novelist E. M. Forster, who had lived in the district, spoke for many in a national radio broadcast:

'I was brought up as a boy in one of the home counties, in a district which I still think the loveliest in England. There is nothing special about it: it is agricultural land, and could not be described in terms of beauty spots. It must always have looked much the same. I have kept in touch with it, going back to it as to an abiding city and still visiting the house which was my home, for it is occupied by old friends. A farmer is through the hedge and when the farmer there was eight years old and I was nine we used to jump up and down on his grandfather's straw ricks and spoil them. Today he is a grandfather himself, so that I have the sense of five generations continuing in one place. Life went on there as usual until this spring. Then someone who was applying for a permit to lay a waterpipe was casually informed that it would not be granted since the whole area had been commandeered. Commandeered for what? Hadn't the war ended? Appropriate officials now arrived from London and announced that a satellite town for sixty thousand people is to be built there. The people now living and working there are doomed; it is death for them and they move in a nightmare. . . . Anyhow the satellite town has pushed them off as completely as it will obliterate the ancient and delicate scenery.

[1] *The Times*, 20th, 25th, September, 3rd, 7th October 1947.
[2] Testimony of clerk of Hertford Rural District Council at the October 1946 inquiry.

Meteorite town would be the better name, for it has fallen on them out of a blue sky.

' "Well," says the voice of planning and progress, "why this sentimentality? People must have houses." They must, and I think of working-class friends in London who have to bring up four children in two rooms, and many are even worse off. But I cannot equate the problem. It is a collision of loyalties. I cannot free myself from the conviction that something irreplaceable has been destroyed, and that a little piece of England has died as surely as if a bomb had hit it.'[1]

(c) Property Interests

'. . . if it should become necessary to seek the death of someone . . . [the prince], should find a proper justification and a public cause, and above all he should keep his hands off another's property, for men forget more readily the death of their father than the loss of their patrimony.'—Machiavelli.

1. Values and Compensation

Stevenage was named in the *Greater London Plan*, which was privately available towards the end of 1944[2] and published early in 1945; in April 1946 the Ministry showed its hand openly with notices to local property-owners; and the New Town Designation Order was issued in November 1946. Anything from fifteen to twenty-four months was therefore available for speculation in Stevenage property; and several banks, stores, and other national organizations succeeded in getting a commercial foot in the New Town (but 'No more than in any other place, extraordinary as it may seem', commented one well-placed informant) by buying property on the High Street. Speculators risked a great deal, however, until the Corporation made some declaration of its land policy, since the Corporation had powers of compulsory purchase at rates below open market value, and it was uncertain when (if at all) it would purchase the built-up part of Stevenage, or, until the Master Plan was finalized, what use was intended for other areas. At the 29th October 1945 Stevenage Council meeting, the chairman of the Town Planning Committee warned speculators in land that the price paid by the Corporation would be on the basis of 1939 values.[3]

Even before the issuance of the Designation Order, this situation led to a decline in the value of those residential properties which changed hands. The chairman of the Residents' Protection Associa-

[1] E. M. Forster, 'The Challenge of Our Time', BBC broadcast of 7th April 1946, printed in *The Listener*, 11th April 1946, p. 452.
[2] A limited number of copies for the use of officials and the Press was published in December 1944 and the plan was then put on show at the Ministry of Town and Country Planning. On 12th December, the Ministry dispatched copies to local authorities in the Greater London area, including the Stevenage Urban District Council.
[3] *Hertfordshire Express*, 3rd November 1945.

tion complained at the October 1946 inquiry, 'There has been a general sterilization; and at the moment it means that everyone within the area is punished; their property is reduced in value; they are anchored and they cannot go without a certain loss, knowing that if they go out they get a comparatively small price and they have to buy at 1946 prices elsewhere'.

If it was changed at all, the situation was aggravated by the Designation Order, which made it a foregone conclusion that the Corporation would ultimately acquire the freehold of most or all the land in the area. The same experience was repeated in other New Towns, where the value of property declined as a result of the Designation Order.

To complete the picture, something more must be said about the Town and Country Planning Act, 1947, which put a damper upon land speculation throughout Britain that the American reader may find it difficult to grasp. Indeed, it is among the most disputed and least understood of recent laws. The general intention was that the State and not the private individual should control all development, or change in the mode of use, of land, and reap whatever profit derived from development by levying a 'development charge' upon the developer equalling the difference between the former (or 'existing use') value and the new value after permission to develop had been granted by the Government. 'The broad effect is that the value of land in the market should in future be its existing use value, and owners lose their "development values".'[1] To compensate owners for this loss, a global sum of £300,000,000 (which the Conservatives claimed was far too small) was set aside for the whole of Great Britain, out of which payments were to be made. Theoretically, a purchaser wishing to develop land should pay, all told, no more than in a free market, but, in fact, he has at times had to pay twice over—a bonus above the 'existing use value' to the landowner to induce him to sell, and then the national 'development charge' for permission to develop. It has been charged that strict enforcement of the law leaves the owner no incentive to sell and the purchaser no incentive to develop.[2] The Act posits a free market as the basis for

[1] Ministry of Town and Country Planning, *Town and Country Planning Act, 1947, Explanatory Memorandum*, Part I (London, 1947), p. 15.

[2] The Minister of Town and Country Planning denied this. 'Possibly the most persistent criticism of the Act is that it has held up development because of the provisions relating to the development charge. That is not true; development has been held up because of the general economic situation. . . . There is a shortage of labour and materials . . . and houses are only built today under special licence. . . . It is not true that there is little or no available land on which to build' (Lewis Silkin, in Town and Country Planning Summer School 1949, *Report of Proceedings* (London, 1949), p. 12). However, the Central Land Board which he appointed to collect development charges and apportion the £300,000,000 compensation, in its first report for the period up to March 1949, 'records its

computing values, but this has become a rather mythical abstraction due, in part, to the operation of the Act itself. The 'free market' in real estate, as in raw materials, manufactured commodities, labour, rents, etc., has of course taken devious turns in recent years round stringent Government controls, but still finds means of manifesting itself.

The prevailing basis of compensation for compulsory purchase of property by public bodies when the Stevenage Development Corporation was established in December 1946 was the level of prices current at 31st March 1939, plus a maximum supplement of 60 per cent in the case of owner-occupiers. The 1939 line was recommended in the report of the wartime Coalition Government's Expert Committee on Compensation and Betterment, headed by Mr. Justice Uthwatt;[1] a maximum supplement of 30 per cent to owner-occupiers was added by the Town and Country Planning Act, 1944 and incorporated into the New Towns Act 1st August 1946.[2] As real estate prices had risen above this level by 1946, Stevenage property-owners loudly condemned the compensation rate as 'outrageous' and 'confiscatory'. One trader protested that 'what might have been bare justice in 1944 is grossly unfair today', and a New Town supporter contended, in June 1947, that he would receive only £910 for a house which would cost at least £1,500 to duplicate elsewhere. (The *elsewhere* was significant, because if owners were willing to remain in the New Town they would suffer no financial injury beyond that involved in the shift from freehold to leasehold, as the New Towns Act required the Corporation to offer them equivalent accommodation 'on terms settled with due regard to the price at which any . . . land has been acquired from them'.)

In July 1947, a month before the new basis of compensation pro-

concern that, in spite of the liability for development charge, land was still being widely offered and taken after the Acts came into operation at prices that included the full development value, and it emphasizes that buyers should not have to pay twice over for development value—once in the price of land and again in the development charge. The board reports that few transactions took place at existing use value in the early part of the period under review, but latterly there has been some improvement. . . . The board reports that at present much building land has been taken off the market or is available only to purchasers who will pay the full development value' (*The Times*, 9th August 1949).

[1] The Committee recommended that 'the compensation payable on public acquisition (or control) of land should not exceed sums based on the standard of values at 31st March, 1939'. On 17th July 1941, Lord Reith announced the Government's acceptance of this recommendation (Expert Committee on Compensation and Betterment, *Final Report*, Cmd. 6386 (London, 1942), p. 79).

[2] Initially the 1944 bill had set 1939 values for the compulsory purchase of land. 'The hullabaloo over this . . . item began at once, and finally—the Prime Minister intervening—was settled with an up-to-30 per cent concession . . . only to owner-occupiers' (Astragal, in Ian McCallum (ed.), *Physical Planning* (London, 1945), p. 15).

vided by the Town and Country Planning Act, 1947, came into force
the Corporation chairman acknowledged that the former compensation was 'a bit stingy'.[1] In his May 1946 Stevenage speech, the
Minister stated that it would be calamitous to pay out public money
at exploitative prices and, besides, 'That is not a matter over which I
have any control. . . . It is the basis settled by the late Coalition
Government and it is not for me to question it, even if I could.'
However, on 22nd July 1946 he issued an order increasing the maximum supplement for owner-occupiers from 30 per cent to 60 per
cent where the notice to treat was served on or after that date. The
Town and Country Planning Act, 1947, further placated property-
owners by replacing the 1939 standard of valuation by a new basis
of valuation after 6th August 1947, which was higher than the previous but slightly less than the free market rate until 1st January
1954, when parity would be reached.[2] If these terms did not delight,
at least they somewhat mollified property-owners. After the defeat
of the House of Lords appeal in July 1947, a leaders of the Residents'
Protection Association went so far as to credit the Association with
the change, stating that the court action

'has been worth while, if only for the better rates of compensation for
property-owners which we have got, not only for people of this district,
but for everyone throughout the country where these new towns are
built. Your Association has put into the pocket of every freeholder in
Great Britain hundreds and, in some cases, thousands of pounds.'[3]

Development Corporations could still purchase property compulsorily below the free market price, but capital restrictions prevented
them from immediately buying up all the land within the designated
areas of New Towns, as they would have liked to do; and although
they wished to avoid piecemeal acquisition for fear of the adverse
effect upon public opinion, they were driven to this measure by the
natural reluctance of owners to sell voluntarily at a loss. The Hemel
Hempstead Corporation complained that it had

'expected to be able to buy suitable properties which came into the market, but the question of price has presented almost insuperable difficulties.
The Corporation is limited to paying no more than the compensation pay-

[1] *Hertfordshire Express*, 25th July 1947.
[2] Under the terms of the 1947 Act, compensation was based upon existing use
value calculated on current prices, except for property sold with the right to
immediate or early vacant possession. The Act attempted to eliminate the special
scarcity value which the post-war housing shortage attached to this class of
property by valuing it 'as if a lease terminating on the 1st January 1954, were
interposed between the owner and the right of vacant possession'. In these
cases, therefore, compulsory purchase prices will reach the market price in 1954,
when the 'notional lease' runs out (*Town and Country Planning Act, 1947, Explanatory Memorandum*, pp. 14–15).
[3] *Hertfordshire Express*, 25th July 1947.

able on a compulsory purchase . . . which excludes some part of the current premium commanded for houses with vacant possession. Save in quite exceptional circumstances, therefore, the Corporation cannot buy by agreement houses so offered. No acceptable method of overcoming this difficulty has been found. The Corporation hesitates to resort to compulsory acquisition to provide houses for its staff, particularly as, in the absence of a policy of comprehensive land acquisition, it would cause arbitrary discriminations between property owners.'[1]

The Stevenage Corporation faced identical difficulties and, in May 1949, finally undertook the compulsory purchase of five sites scattered throughout the built-up portion of Stevenage, upon which to erect thirty-six houses for staff accommodation. When the Corporation offered one owner £60 for the present (agricultural) use value of his plot, he said he would gladly pay them £120 to tear up their offer. (Presumably, however, he could enter a claim at the Central Land Board for compensation from the £300,000,000 sum allotted under the 1947 Act for such cases.)

The cries of 'robbery' and 'sterilization' which went up from Stevenage property-owners in 1946 were raised by property-owners throughout Britain after the passage of the Town and Country Planning Act, 1947. 'New Towns were the forerunners of the 1947 Act,' remarked one informant. 'This has made universal sterilization, but the New Town residents still think they are different from the rest of the country—which is partially true as the threat is more nearly present over the whole designated area.'

2. Freehold and Leasehold

'The unitary ownership of land is the real key to good town planning.'—The Economist.
'In any community where goods are held in severalty it is necessary . . . to his own peace of mind, that an individual should possess as large a portion of goods as others with whom he is accustomed to class himself; and it is extremely gratifying to possess something more than others.'—Veblen.[2]

The Reith Committee recommended that Development Corporations own the freehold of all New Town property. Such ownership, it reported, 'is essential . . . to secure complete control over redevelopment . . . to guide, in the interests of the public and traders in general, the shopping and other business development of the town . . . [and] to prevent a serious leakage of values created by the expenditure of the agency'.[3] The Minister told his Stevenage

[1] New Towns Act, 1946, *Reports of the . . . Development Corporations for the period ending 31st March*, 1948 (London, 1949), p. 64.
[2] Editorial, 'New Towns', *Economist*, 6th April 1946, p. 525; and Thorstein Veblen, *The Theory of the Leisure Class* (London, 1924), p. 31.
[3] *Second Interim Report of the New Towns Committee*, Cmd. 6794, April 1946, p. 4.

audience, 'It is the intention of the Government's proposals that the whole of the town shall be owned by the Corporation and leases will be offered to existing occupiers'; and the New Towns Act made this possible but not necessary. So far as a property-owner was concerned, this meant that his freehold could be bought at a loss, if he wished to acquire an equivalent freehold outside the New Town; alternatively, he would be offered a 99-year lease on equivalent property in the New Town planning on terms satisfactory to the Corporation.

During its second reading, Viscount Hinchingbrooke had objected to this provision of the New Towns Bill which 'ensures that no one . . . in new towns shall own his own house or plot of land. What is the intention here? Clearly it is to proliferate the creatures of the Minister and assure him of a goodly supply of Socialist tenants in the national interest.'[1] On 15th Mary 1950, Conservative M.P. Bernard Braine raised the question of freehold rights in the New Town of Basildon, asking the Minister of Town and Country Planning to

'give a categoric assurance that freeholders whose properties are left unaffected by the master plan will be left in possession of their freehold rights. . . . He could also give to those who are dispossessed the opportunity, if they wish to take it, to acquire freehold land elsewhere in the area at an equivalent valuation.'

To this, the Parliamentary Secretary of the Ministry, George Lindgren, replied:

'which is the proper body to hold the freeholds of land within a [new] town—the individuals, or the community as a whole? There may be a cleavage between the two sides of the House upon this, but I hold the view, as do the Government, that the land belongs to the people. . . . It would be impossible to create the new town and allow the freeholders to remain.'[2]

It was not for nothing that, in his inaugural ceremony, as the Stevenage rector rang the church bell, the Bishop of the diocese took his hand and announced that he was now the *freehold* owner of all parish lands. 'An Englishman's home is his castle,' said a member of the Residents' Protection Association, 'which is what the Ministry doesn't understand. The dream of all Englishmen, including the artisan, is to save up till he can buy his own home and own the freehold on which it stands.' In June 1947 a hot interchange took place between members of an audience which packed the town hall to protest 'The Curse of the State Plan', and the Labour M.P. who was heckled and told to 'sit down!' after asserting 'there is no difference between freeholds and leaseholds for 999 years. In all

[1] *Hansard*, 8th May 1946, vol. 422, col. 1155.
[2] Ibid., 15th May 1950, vol. 475, cols. 963–8.

modern freeholds there are restrictive covenants.' Someone rose from the audience to say, 'Land bought freehold may cost £200 an acre, but with it the purchaser can do expressly as he likes, and has no further charges to meet. For that same acre, bought leasehold, the purchase price will be perhaps £80 or £85, but there will be innumerable charges to be paid during the lease period.' Amid applause, a leader of the Protection Association then came to the platform. 'The meaning of the word "freehold" is that it is free. (Hear, hear.) When you have land with freehold, as we have it here, it is free of everything, except loyalty to the Crown. Leasehold land has a limited life; it is a wasting asset, a dying thing.'[1]

Later in this chapter we shall discuss some of the specific disabilities which leasehold entails, but it is evident that the difference between freehold and leasehold is more than a difference in property rights. Above all, it signifies a difference in social status, as Mark Benny observed: 'the change of tenure [Stevenage owners] . . . are asked to accept . . . seems like social demotion, a wanton thrusting back to the class from which they have spent their best years in escaping'.[2] 'You are coolly asked', said a leader of the Protection Association, 'to barter your birthright for a mess of pottage.'[3]

The New Towns Act provided that 'a development corporation shall not have power, except with the consent of the Minister, to transfer the freehold in any land or to grant a lease of any land for a term of more than ninety-nine years, and the Minister shall not consent to any such disposal of land unless he is satisfied that there are exceptional circumstances which render the disposal of the land in that manner expedient'.[4] When the Stevenage Council asked the Corporation to grant leases of 999 years to all freehold owners, it was told:

'The Minister considers that the provisions limiting leases to 99 years should be relaxed only

[1] *Hertfordshire Express*, 7th June 1947.
[2] Mark Benny, 'Storm over Stevenage', *The Changing Nation*, Contact Books (London, 1947), p. 49.
[3] *Hertfordshire Express*, 11th May 1946.
[4] The principle that a 'local planning authority may not, in general, sell land which it acquires in connection with re-development schemes . . . or grant leases for longer than ninety-nine years' was introduced by the Town and Country Planning Act, 1944 (D. J. Beattie, *Hart's Introduction to the Law of Local Government and Administration* (London 1946), p. 551). During the third reading of the New Towns Bill on 30th May 1946, Asterley Jones, the Stevenage district's Labour M.P., moved an amendment to enable the Development Corporation to grant a lease of any length, which was withdrawn upon the Minister of Town and Country Planning's prophecy that long before the ninety-nine years had elapsed the law on landlords and tenants would be modified by the House. Both Socialists and Conservatives agreed upon the need for reforming the law of leasehold.

'(1) where land is held on charitable trusts or for ecclesiastical purposes
'(2) where sites are outside areas of development and where there is an overriding public advantage in the disposal of the freehold
'(3) where land comprises small unimportant parcels required by a developer to adjust his boundaries and where no planning advantage would result in the retention of freehold.'[1]

It is of interest to note that at Welwyn Garden City and Letchworth, although freeholds were retained by the Company, leases ran for 99, 990, or 999 years.[2] 'In the first thirty years', Purdom notes, 'there is hardly any difference to a lessee whether his lease is for 99 or 999 years, but after that period the term makes an increasing difference.'[3] The experience at Welwyn was that

'Most individual lessees accepted a 999 years' lease as virtually a freehold; the end of a 99 years' period seemed to some to loom too nearly ahead. . . . In the case of factory sites, industrialists building factories were found to be dynastic by instinct; they hated mere 99 years' leases. . . . In fact there were some applicants for sites who so strongly objected to anything but freehold property that they would not accept even a 999 years' lease.'[4]

Judging from such indications of their policy as have yet become available, the Ministry and New Town Corporations intend to impose 99-year leases upon both residential and industrial properties, with much shorter leases (probably 7, 14, or 21 years) for shops and commercial properties. An informant explained, '99 year *building* leases are common (and almost universal in some parts of the country); 7-14-21 year *occupation* leases are granted where the landlord builds and lets land and building'.

Aside from the obvious need of land for building and develop-

[1] Minutes, Urban District Council Town Planning Committee, 16th September 1948.
[2] At Letchworth, 'The land is let on lease for terms of 990 years for factory sites, 99 years for shops, and 99 or 990 years for residential sites. In the case of the 990 years leases, provision is made for a revision of the rent at the end of each period of 99 years, on the basis of the then value of the land, exclusive of the value of buildings on it' (Royal Commission on the Distribution of the Industrial Population, *Report*, Cmd. 6153 (London, 1940), p. 280).
[3] C. B. Purdom, *The Building of Satellite Towns* (London, 1949), p. 399.
[4] F. J. Osborn, *Green-Belt Cities* (London, 1946), p. 73. The Reith Committee observed, '. . . sometimes industrialists and others are chary of owning less than the fee simple. This objection is usually a financial one; factory owners, for example, may want to borrow money on the freehold, for the rate of interest on money secured on leaseholds is sometimes higher than on freeholds. . . . An option to renew at a valuation rental at the end of a ninety-nine years' lease would obviate some of these objections, but this is not possible under the existing English law of real property. To avoid any discouragement to industrialists settling in the new towns . . . it might be necessary, in exceptional circumstances, to offer leases for industrial buildings for a longer period than ninety-nine years . . .' (Cmd. 6794, pp. 6–7).

ment, which could have been satisfied for the most part from farmland without disturbing the built-up part of Stevenage, the Corporation desired to acquire all freeholds in the designated area for two
main reasons: to reap increases in value that would otherwise go to
existing owners, and to secure the landlord's large measure of control
over use.

The Town and Country Planning Act, 1947, levied a development
charge only on the increase in property value arising from a *change
in use*; where no change in use was involved, owners could still profit
from the enhanced values which the New Town produced. The
Government took the view that these values, deriving from Treasury
investments, belonged to the Government, or, more floridly, 'the
creation of a new town will make a very considerable addition to
the value of land in the area and, if the community itself creates the
value, the community surely has the right to take the results of the
increased value which it has itself created'.[1]

The case for the Corporation's acquiring the landlord's powers
was stated by the Reith Committee:

'Immediate purchase by the agency of the whole site would simplify
management and control. . . . The positive covenants in a lease are a far
more effective control over use than the negative covenants imposed on a
purchaser of the fee simple, and the arrangement of leases so that they fall
in at about the same time affords the only certain way of ensuring that any
given area can be redeveloped as a whole in due course. Control by virtue
of ownership is also more certain than control by byelaws or by the
Planning Acts.'[2]

More broadly, ownership bought out many vested interests that would
otherwise operate independently, and concentrated power in matters
large and small in the Corporation's hands. Sir Theodore Chambers,
the chairman of Welwyn Garden City, Ltd., has pointed out that

'vested interests are the true enemy of sound planning. This term "vested
interest" is sometimes used as a term of reproach, but "vested interests"
are simply something which exist and cannot be ignored. . . . They include
many other things than the mere ownership of the land. They include the
vital interest of the local authorities in their territorial boundaries and in
their rateable values. They include the assets of . . . institutions representing the investments of the capital of all sorts and conditions of people in
land and property. They include the interests of religious bodies and the
purveyors of entertainment and refreshment. They include the transport
authorities, water, gas and electricity undertakings and many other groups
who are vitally dependent upon the maintenance of the *status quo*. . . .
'It is far too little realized that it is not only land values which are
enhanced or reduced by changes in the density of population. It is to the

[1] George Lindgren, Parliamentary Secretary to the Ministry of Town and
Country Planning, *Hansard*, 15th May 1950, vol. 475, col. 968.
[2] Cmd. 6794, pp. 4, 6.

open and latent resistance of a host of these vested interests that one must attribute the fact that so little can be done to improve radically the living and working conditions of the mass of our population who live in our cities. . . .

'It is not surprising that a school of thought should have developed amongst those who appreciate these facts, in favour of designing and building new towns on unencumbered virgin areas—where the ownership of the land may be in the single hands of the entrepreneur, and where there are no vested interests to impede and restrict the scientific planning and building of the towns in their entirety.'[1]

So strongly did the Reith Committee feel about the need for New Town Corporations to own all the freehold if they were successfully and satisfactorily to conduct their programme, that it urged other public bodies with powers of compulsory purchase 'should be discouraged from exercising them, and should be persuaded to fall in with the general land policy of the corporation and accept leases'.[2]

One unpleasant discovery of the Corporations, as will be seen in Chapter VIII, was their relative lack of power *vis-à-vis* county councils, the Ministry, and other Government departments and agencies, which contributed to their slow progress. Possession of all New Town freeholds would not only ensure the Corporations supremacy over local interests, but strengthen them in relation with these agencies.

During the period under review, however, the outstanding feature of the Corporation's land policy was its indecisiveness, which kept owners in a permanent state of uncertainty. When the Corporation opened an information office on the Stevenage High Street in October 1948, 61 of the first 101 inquiries concerned individual holdings. 'What will be the fate of my property?' 'Are improvements worth while? Will they be compensated for?' 'Will my house [or land] be taken, and if so when?' For reasons outside the Corporation's control, few of those questions could be answered. The Reith Committee had warned, 'It is most important . . . that existing owners should know whether further land is liable to be purchased or not', and 'For the protection of owners, we think there should be a provision . . . to compel the agency to buy immediately any interest in land . . . where the owner is prejudiced by refusal of permission to develop'.[3] But the New Towns Act allowed seven years' grace before Corporations were required to purchase property upon an owner's request[4]—in the case of Stevenage, this meant November

[1] Quoted by E. D. Simon, *Rebuilding Britain* (London, 1945), pp. 185–6.
[2] Cmd. 6794, p. 6.   [3] Cmd. 6794, pp. 4–5.
[4] 'Where any land within the area designated by an order . . . as the site of a new town has not been acquired by the development corporation within the period of seven years from the date on which that order became operative, any owner of that land may by notice in writing served on the corporation require them to purchase his interest therein . . .' (*New Towns Act*, 1946, Section 6 (4)).

1953, and it appeared that the Corporation would use most or all of this time.

The main fault was not the Corporation's, for they wished to acquire all freeholds as soon as possible, and to make public declaration of their policy. Stevenage Corporation officers went to much trouble to ease the situation of particular individuals—urging, for instance, the purchase of two houses occupied by elderly couples anxious to move to avoid disturbance by impending construction, although neither property was required for early development and the Corporation could expect only a small return on the investment; and refraining from evicting persons in illegal occupation of two Corporation properties—but it was beyond their power to alleviate the difficulties of all owners. The relevant decisions were made at Ministerial and, ultimately, Cabinet level, and the Government, limiting Corporations to the barest necessities of existence, did not permit sorely needed national capital to be tied up in the purchase of New Town properties not required for immediate development.

Thus, in February 1948, the Minister was asked whether a Corporation might not issue a statement of land policy 'to allay the worst fears which inevitably attach to the absence of any information at all'. One Corporation chairman complained that inability to issue a statement 'had had the result that a section of the population, which they much desired to keep [i.e., middle-class property-owners] . . . had decided to go elsewhere'. The Minister replied that it would unfortunately not be possible for Corporations to issue public statements about their acquisition of land policy for some considerable time; with the exception of Aycliffe New Town, Corporations were only free to acquire, for the time being, such land as was needed for immediate development, with, perhaps, slight additions in those cases where the arrangement of ownerships rendered this desirable; objections had been raised to the proposition that residential property not needed for redevelopment should ever be acquired; the question whether commercial property in general should be acquired would be the subject of further examination.

A memorandum on land policy prepared by an officer in August 1947 for consideration by the Stevenage Corporation advised that all land in the designated area should be acquired, with the possible exception of churches, commons, and property belonging to local authorities and statutory undertakers; the acquisition of residential property in the built-up section of Stevenage was considered desirable to secure uniformity of control and treatment, and to avoid unfairness between owners. 'It is most desirable that all residents should become the direct tenants of the Corporation in some form or another.' In October 1947 and again in March 1948, drafts of public statements on land policy were prepared by Corporation officers, but so little could then be said with any certainty that it was deemed preferable to say nothing. Homilies such as 'The Development Corporation wishes to avoid disturbing existing occupiers wherever possible, and will in general be prepared to lease the properties back to them on terms which will permit their continued occupation for as long as practicable in the circumstances of each case' led one officer to comment that

'it is premature and perhaps even misleading to publish a statement upon acquisition of land policy at this stage. The paper . . . has no doubt been drafted in order to give the public a general and interim idea of what is likely to happen to their properties. It has of necessity to be vague because, in fact, Development Corporations have as yet no cut and dried policy. Its essential vagueness means not only that it tells the public practically nothing but in my opinion it definitely invites replies posing detailed questions, few of which we could answer.'

At this stage, most other Corporations apparently also concluded that it was best to suffer in silence. The Crawley Corporation, however, was bold enough to publish in November 1948 a 'Preliminary Statement of Land Policy', approved by the Ministry, which declared:

'Pending the publication of a further statement on their land policy, the Corporation will in general confine their acquisition of land and buildings to the following specific purposes:

'(a) *Land for Basic Services*—such as sewerage, water, roads.

'(b) *Land for Development*—such as factory and housing sites with allied services, required during, say, the next four years.

'(c) *Land and Buildings for the Corporation's own use*—such as hostels and labour camps, offices, stores and depots.

'(d) *Shop Properties.* . . .'[1]

The general outlines of this policy were paralleled at Stevenage and other New Towns, although other Corporations had, at this date, not yet persuaded the Ministry to sanction their acquisition of commercial properties.

3. *Demolition*

So inauspiciously was the news first broken to Stevenage citizens and so vague were subsequent Ministry and Corporation announcements that, in some quarters, the New Town was conceived more in terms of demolition than construction. Rumour outstripped the slow pace of events and materialized the worst fears. A Corporation officer reported in October 1947:

'people in the town expected a large proportion of the existing houses to be pulled down and they thought these demolitions were imminent. This belief was by no means confined to the more vocal opponents of the New

[1] New Towns Act, 1946, *Reports of the* . . . *Development Corporations for the period ending 31st March*, 1949 (London, 1949), pp. 59–60. Italics in original.

Town. It was found among doctors, ministers, works managers. The New Town was felt to be like a cloud hanging over Stevenage. (This image was frequently used to express the general sense of uncertainty and anxiety.) . . .

'Among properties said to be due for demolition were [two of the most stately houses in the area] . . . . well-known for their historic associations; neither is threatened. . . . [Both owners] are widely known as opponents of the New Town.

'It is also believed that the Avenue is to come down and that the Cricket Ground is to be built over. Both are strong focusing points of local sentiment.

'There is similar anxiety about the fate of Fairview Road. . . . Here there is a general fear that *all* the houses are due for *early* demolition, whereas only seven or eight houses are definitely to come down, and these within 5–10 years. It is also by no means established in people's minds that under the New Towns Act alternative accommodation must be found before anyone's home is taken.'[1]

The Minister was sensitive to the political discomfiture risked by the demolition of good houses during a national housing shortage— the Conservative Press (which meant most of the daily Press) could be expected to give loud publicity to the matter—and the Corporation wished to minimize a theme so bad for public relations. But the Labour Government had an overwhelming majority in the House of Commons and could mock at Conservative protests, while the planners' desire for a friendly local reception was apparently less strong than their ambition to build boldly and well; for they would ultimately be judged more on the plan's architectural merits and material success than on initial local sentiments submerged by subsequent events. Corporation officers hoped to conciliate the public with cautious statements:

'although their zoning proposals . . . would involve a certain amount of demolition, the Corporation were not vandals whose sole desire was to destroy, and, even if they were, the Ministry would see that they did not do so.

'in the next eight years the only houses to be pulled down were two pairs of semi-detached houses in Fairview Road. No building would be pulled down until it was absolutely necessary. It was quite possible that some of the houses in the Fairview Road area might remain indefinitely. . . .

'With regard to the Town Centre . . . 68 houses in all would have to be demolished, but not more than 10 of them during the next eight years.'[2]

But the efficacy of these remarks depended upon confidence in the Corporation's ability to carry out its intentions which, with the best will in the world, could not be shared by an independent observer

[1] 'Relations of the Corporation with Stevenage Residents' (mimeographed report), 9th October 1947.

[2] Statements of two Corporation officers at the Master Plan inquiry, October 1949.

(and, during the long periods of enforced idleness, could hardly have been held by the Corporation itself). For events demonstrated that the Cabinet, rival Ministries and Government agencies, the Ministry of Town and Country Planning, the Courts, and a host of ungovernable persons and unpredictable factors constantly jeopardized the Corporation's programme, and no one was in a position to guarantee that the best-laid plan would not be dropped or changed.

At different times, Corporation representatives gave different estimates of the projected number of demolitions. In the statement cited above, made in October 1949, the figure of 14 houses was given for the following eight years; two years before, it had been stated that 'about sixty houses' would be demolished 'within five to ten years from the beginning of active construction'.[1] According to the 1946 Ministry plan, 229 houses in the industrial area (including 113 erected after 1918, 96 pre-1914 or Victorian, and 20 older houses) and 137 east of the railway (comprising 19 post-1918, 90 Victorian, and 28 older houses)—a total of 366 or *some 21 per cent of the 1,767 residential houses then standing in Stevenage*[2]—'might ultimately require to be demolished'. The Corporation was most circumspect about announcing the number of demolitions required under its Master Plan, but it seemed that the final number would be little less than the Ministry figure, although the date of demolition would be somewhat postponed.[3]

Until the Master Plan was approved by the Minister in February 1950, the disposition of zones remained open; after this date, it was always possible that financial, legal, engineering, or other considerations would compel the realignment of a road or residential area, necessitating or obviating further demolitions. Thus, the report quoted above made light of a rumour that the lovely avenue of trees was to be destroyed, but, in the same breath that a Corporation expert denied this at the October 1949 Master Plan inquiry, he admitted that a major road would cross the newer part of this avenue, interrupting the pedestrian pathway to the parish church.[4]

[1] Private estimate by Corporation officer, 23rd October 1947.

[2] The figure of 1,767 houses includes 1,678 assessed dwelling houses plus 89 houses with shops in the Stevenage Urban District at 1st April 1947; 17 farm houses are excluded (County of Hertford, *Analysis of Rateable Value at 1st April*, 1947).

[3] All 229 houses west of the railway would be demolished, ultimately, on the Corporation's plan, except for an uncertain few which might have some use for industry. Extensive demolitions would also be necessary in the New Town centre.

[4] 'At the north end of the town, where the High Street merges into the Great North Road, is a pleasant avenue of lime and chestnut trees leading to the Parish Church. The first trees, those at the eastern end, were planted in 1756. In the year 1857 the avenue was continued to the gate in the High Street . . .

Nor, as often loudly proclaimed, did the New Towns Act guarantee alternative accommodations to *all* persons dispossessed by the Corporation, but only to those living in premises upon which redevelopment was to be carried out (comprising the majority of cases likely to be affected). Because of this loophole, for instance, the Corporation was not bound to find alternative accommodation for two persons whom it sought to dispossess early in 1948, or for others whose property would be adversely affected but not physically disturbed. The law read:

'The powers of a development corporation with respect to the disposal of land acquired by them under this Act shall be so exercised as to secure, *so far as practicable*, that persons who were living or carrying on business or other activities on land so acquired shall, if they desire to obtain accommodation on land belonging to the corporation, *and are willing to comply with any requirements of the corporation as to its development and use*, have an opportunity to obtain thereon accommodation suitable to their reasonable requirements on terms settled with due regard to the price at which any such land has been acquired from them.'

The italicized provisions undoubtedly seemed reasonable and even essential from the Corporation's point of view, but gave legitimate grounds for anxiety to local citizens.

Under these circumstances, the widespread fears of demolition and disruption must be considered as (if not exclusively, since fear is hardly the best soil for or fruit of reason, then), in good measure, rationally motivated. It was one thing for the Corporation staff to sit before their admirable maps and drawing boards and decide that a maximum of *n* houses need be destroyed; it was quite another thing to sit in a Stevenage house and not know exactly where the blow would fall. Each planner might feel certain of the cogent reasons for and the approximate scope of demolition; but Ministry and Corporation plans and planners came and went, and could not always agree among themselves.

One informant sympathetic to the Corporation pointed out, what was undoubtedly true, that

'The trouble with plans for new towns (and this is going to come out also in the town plans under the 1947 Act) is that they cannot clearly show to the ordinary resident the time factor. If you leave a developed area as it is, you are vulnerable for not having planned for its eventual redevelopment. If you show the proposed zoning for redevelopment when the present buildings are worn out, you alarm every resident who thinks he will be evicted tomorrow! Nor can he see the difference between pro-

and was finally completed by an extension, eastwards, to the Church in 1935–36 as a permanent memorial of the Jubilee and reign of King George the Fifth, the cost, amounting to £550, being raised by public subscription' (Stevenage Urban District, *Official Handbook*, p. 18).

posals that do involve demolition and those that merely imply development later.'

Another informant commented that 'A town growing to ten times its size has *always* changed, mutilated, and caused the destruction of many . . . houses and buildings. . . . The pre-war Local Authority plan for a town of 30,000 involved far more demolition than the New Town plan (including the whole of the High Street).' The Council plan, however, was contingent upon development taking place and did not, like the Corporation's, force development. Were development to have taken place under private auspices (unimpaired by the Town and Country Planning Act, 1947), owners would presumably have received the prevailing market rate for their property, although it was, of course, unlikely that the general public would have had the same opportunity to protest any demolitions.

The Council was certainly more sensitive to local feeling on the subject of demolition—and to local housing needs—than was the national Corporation. From 1926 to 1949, it had demolished only twenty-three dilapidated houses. 'I could have demolished fifty, which don't conform to the [health] standard, but until we overcome overcrowding, you can't do that,' said the Council's housing inspector in May 1949. 'I could demolish ten houses next week, but the [Housing] Committee of the Council wouldn't agree to it. People have been on the list for Council houses for ten years now.' The Corporation's proposal to tear down relatively new properties could not be cheered by its strongest local supporters.

(d) Ratepayer Interests[1]

There was a simple reason for ratepayer opposition to the New Town: development cost money. Although capital came from the Exchequer, this (plus 3 per cent interest) would eventually have to

[1] For the benefit of American readers, it may be explained that rates are local taxes levied to pay for the upkeep of county and town services such as sewage disposal, water supply, highways, street lighting, schools (the most expensive single item), police, etc. They are levied upon the *occupier*, not the *owner*, of real property other than agricultural land, and are calculated on the basis of the rent the tenant would pay for the property in a free market; 'but in practice, ever since 1918, rating authorities considered that the level of uncontrolled rents were so inflated by the scarcity of houses that severe hardship would have been caused to occupiers of small houses if gross values had been raised to the correct levels. The result has been that . . . small houses, particularly owner-occupied houses and council houses built since 1918, have been under-valued . . .' (R. Simon, *Local Councils and the Citizen* (London, 1948), p. 53). Dibelius pointed out that 'the antiquated rating system . . . sets the mass of middle-class voters against any municipal enterprise involving a rise in their rates. . . . This system suited the landowner, since it hit not the owner of the land and site but only the occupier, the man who paid rent. The landowner's assessment was fixed on the value of the house he inhabited himself, not on the income coming to him in

be repaid by the Corporations, whose success would, to a considerable extent, be judged by their ability to make the development profitable. Improved roads and services must sooner or later raise the level of local taxes. The Reith Committee had prophesied:

'Where the development of the new town is on a large scale relatively to the population and rateable capacity of the local authority . . . [any increase of rates] might be felt by existing ratepayers to be unfair, and in that case would be likely to encounter strong opposition. If the area of the district . . . were large, many of the ratepayers would derive no benefit from the services and would resent having to pay for them.'[1]

Within certain limits, the Corporation could write off early investments against the revenue that increased property values would eventually yield in rents, but beyond these limits (and beyond such equalization grants as the Government might award to ease the financial predicament of local authorities which had to provide in advance for the needs of an incoming population) ratepayers would have to foot the bill. The finance officers of four Corporations reported privately in June 1948:

'statements have been made suggesting that ratepayers will not have to pay more because of the coming of a new town and these are being loosely interpreted into meaning that there is some form of unwritten guarantee against rising rates. The basic assumption must surely be that eventually ratepayers of the developed new town must bear the cost of all their services. This may well mean rates reaching very high levels. In the interim stage, therefore, existing ratepayers must pay their share of new services and as new occupiers enter they must do the same. No opportunity should be lost of emphasizing the point that the citizens of any new town must ultimately accept the responsibility for their financial future and that the Development Corporations cannot for ever fill the role of financial backer. Subject to this, however, it is proper to make a contribution towards the cost of services provided in advance of requirement. . . .'

Hertfordshire was in a particularly difficult financial situation because of the siting of four New Towns within its borders (Welwyn Garden City, Hatfield, Hemel Hempstead, and Stevenage). The Chairman of the County Council Finance Committee pointed out that over £2 million in the 1950–1 budget would be spent preparing for the reception of the 192,500 persons the Ministry of Town and

rents of all sorts. His ally in the oligarchical period, the capitalist in the town, was equally benefited; he was rated on what he spent for his dwelling, not on the income coming to him from trade and industry. The full weight of the rate fell on the small middle-class man who spent a large proportion of his income on rent' (Wilhelm Dibelius, *England* (London, 1930), pp. 265–6).

The Local Government Act, 1948, introduced a revised system of rating valuation that came into force on 1st April 1952.

[1] Cmd. 6794, p. 17.

Country Planning intended to move from London to new and expanded towns in Herts, who would increase the county's population
by one-third. The County Council had resolved in February 1946
that every assistance be given to the Minister in the acquisition and
management of land for the purposes of the Greater Stevenage Town
on the understanding that costs and expenses incurred would be repaid by the Government. A memorandum prepared by a county
officer in July 1947 warned, 'It would be a matter of considerable
concern if the operations of a Development Corporation were to
result in a substantial increase in the rates in the pound which have
to be raised by the Local Authorities . . . it would create a great deal
of ill will . . . and . . . it would be unfair'.[1] However, despite many
representations by county officers and M.P.s to the Ministries of
Health and Town and Country Planning, satisfactory assurances
were not forthcoming from the Government of a special contribution to cover expenses entailed by the county in connection with the
New Towns, and the County Council was thereby led to change its
attitude and become increasingly hostile to the Stevenage New
Town. In November 1949, it recommended to the Minister that the
New Town be restricted to a population of 18,000, eliminating the
cost of a major sewerage works for a larger population.

As the law provided that, upon completion of the project, corporations would transfer their functions to the local authority (in
this case, the Stevenage Urban District Council), the County Council
wished to ensure that high operating expenses would not be transferred as well. (There was little danger of either a deficit or a surplus
being transferred, because the New Towns Act provided, 'Any surplus arising from the winding up of a development corporation . . .
shall be paid into the Exchequer; and any deficit shall be defrayed
out of moneys provided by Parliament'.) The County Planning
Committee complained to the Minister that the Stevenage Development Corporation's Master Plan

'has been accompanied by no statement of what are calculated to be its
financial implications. . . .

'The Minister will no doubt appreciate that it is of the first importance
to the County Council, whose own financial commitments in the provision
of services to new towns are extremely large, that they should have at the
earliest possible stage estimates of the ultimate total accretion of rateable
value, and the stages by which, and the extent to which, that rateable value
will become available to offset annual charges resulting from capital outlay upon services. . . .

'The County Council would be grateful for the Minister's assurance
that a sufficient measure of assistance will be available to local authorities

[1] *Memorandum on the financial relationship between Development Authorities and the
Local Authorities* (mimeographed), July 1947.

undertaking work . . . which may be left undone by the Development
Corporations to secure that no extra burden is thereby cast upon the
ratepayers.'[1]

The Minister replied that the New Towns Act gave Corporations
power to contribute to expenses incurred by local authorities in
connection with the development; the amount of contributions and
the terms on which Corporation assets and liabilities would be handed
over would be subject to negotiation. County officers were not
delighted with the results of ensuing talks with Ministry officials.
According to their version, the Ministry did not consider the question of cost when the Stevenage Master Plan was drawn up (this a
pro-Ministry informant denied) and suggested that the county had
no authority to intervene in this matter.[2] The County Council meeting of 19th October 1950 was told that the Ministers of Health and
Town and Country Planning had rejected the county's plea for special
financial aid. 'In the opinion of the ministries the burden placed upon
the ratepayers in Hertfordshire had not yet reached an unreasonable
level (members whistled) . . .'[3] In 1950 there were only two counties
where the average total rates levied was higher than in Hertfordshire.[4] The *Hertfordshire Mercury* editorialized:

'Are we to assume that this is an obligation which Hertfordshire owes
to posterity? . . .
'Rates in Hertfordshire have increased by leaps and bounds during the
last 20 years and whilst we would not deny that part of this expenditure
was probably due to past neglect, it does not alter the fact that the county
is now having to shoulder an extraordinary rate burden imposed by the
Government in pursuing what are, after all, experimental schemes of
planning. Even if these prove successful, they will not yield any return
for at least 20 years. . . .
'Schemes for new towns have been launched at a time when the old
towns are unable to satisfy their normal requirements and when rents are
high and the cost of living generally increasing. . . . We seem to be chasing
ideas while ignoring facts.'[5]

(e) Class Antagonism

During the war, Stevenage was host to some two thousand
evacuated Londoners and workers directed by the Government to
nearby factories or farms and billeted in local homes. Throughout

[1] Hertfordshire County Council, *Report of the County Planning Committee*,
4th November 1949, Appendix B.
[2] *Hertfordshire Mercury*, 3rd March 1950.
[3] Report by the County Council chairman of a meeting between county and
Ministry representatives (*Hertfordshire Mercury*, 20th October 1950).
[4] According to the Finance and General Purposes Committee's report
presented to the Hertfordshire County Council 1st March 1951 (*Hertfordshire
Mercury*, 2nd March 1951).
[5] *Hertfordshire Mercury*, 27th October 1950.

Britain, the enforced contact between lower-class visitors and middle-class natives led to unfortunate episodes and much ill-feeling on both sides.[1] A Labour councillor declared in 1941 that 'at the top end of the housing scale people with rooms to spare have shirked taking in evacuees, but are now taking in people able and willing to pay rents which are definitely exorbitant'. 'Where they'd [Londoners] move into a pub, the locals'd move out', one informant recalled. Some workers found themselves locked out if they got in late in the evening. Local citizens complained that lodgers were often dirty, smelly, noisy, troublesome, and dissatisfied with life in a small town; and the Londoners had complaints of their own. The simple truth was that class differences in attitudes and behaviour, in many cases, were too great to be ignored or peacefully overcome.

These wartime experiences were remembered a few years later when the New Town project was broached, and middle-class opposition was conditioned, in part, by the wish to avoid a new influx of working-class Londoners. When, on 8th December 1945, the Council stated its approval of the *Greater London Plan*, it added the significant proviso, 'It is hoped that there will be a wide variety of housing . . . combining harmony with individuality. . . . [and] that attention will be paid to the importance of obtaining a balanced population'. 'Balanced population', as has been pointed out, was often a euphemism for a high proportion of middle-class in relation to working-class residents and houses. 'The Council', commented one sophisticated informant, 'wanted Stevenage to be a restricted town, with land values high, select residents, and no large influx of industrial workers; but, in any case, Stevenage was becoming increasingly industrial, with the expansion of local factories.'

It was generally believed that New Town immigrants would come from East End slums and other overcrowded London quarters. At representative public meetings few opponents would repeat the words of one notable, 'We've had enough people from London here, and we don't want any more'. (On this occasion, one man replied, 'I'm from London, and I lost my home and wife there during the war'. 'If it hadn't been for the people of London, we might have lost the war', said another man, who demanded and obtained a retraction.) But, privately, many persons said, as did one merchant, that no one would want to live in a New Town 'filled with riff-raff from the slums'. At a Protection Association meeting in the town hall, 9th May 1946, a member of the audience said that 'as a former billeting officer he had had hundreds of evacuees through his hands, and had had twelve staying at his house, and he was sure the people

[1] Contact between lower-class visitors and lower-class natives was undoubtedly more numerous, but this does not concern us here since the dominant tone in Stevenage politics and society was set by the middle classes.

of Stevenage never wanted to see them again'.[1] 'The "upper-ten" are against the New Town purely for selfish and snobbish reasons', said a skilled worker. 'They just don't like the idea of crowds of ill-bred and noisy people.'

A few episodes in which prominent Conservatives and Independents figured illustrate the strong class factor in local opposition to the New Town:

At one meeting, a Labour speaker remarked about 'people who have come here from London and live in a house surrounded by a brick wall, because they want to keep themselves secluded'. This touched a sensitive spot in an influential member of the opposition, who dug his elbow into a friend's ribs, whispering 'He's having a dig at me'. 'Well,' the speaker recalled, 'I didn't even think about it, but unconsciously he may have been right. Because he was just then building a brick wall round his house.'

Driving through Welwyn Garden City, an opposition leader said scornfully, 'The whole idea of this place is they don't want people to have any privacy. No high hedges or any such thing.' It was easy to appreciate this attitude later, in the study of his home hidden behind high hedges off a secluded lane, and to sympathize when, over tea, he continued, 'Why, [the Minister's] idea of one of these "neighbourhood units" is they'd have all the houses built around a park, and two mothers would take turns minding the children, two in the laundry, and so on, every day. . . . We don't want people looking in our windows while we eat. I bought up this extra acre of land just to keep anyone from building on it.'

A representative of the Lord of the Manor at Aston strongly objected to the Hertford Rural District Council's proposal to erect houses on his land. 'The only things which have been built at the entrance to large country houses are lodges to house the people who work for the owner . . .' he said. 'Down through the years that has been the accepted ground of planning which one expects to see in country houses of historic interest. It would be fatal to build Council cottages up to the boundaries of this house which might well be scheduled as an ancient monument.'[2]

The wife of a company director inhabiting a fine Stevenage house said, 'It's certain that we shall be hemmed in by new houses and buildings of one sort and another—which is exactly what we moved here to avoid. This scheme is going to destroy the very things many of us came here for—quiet surroundings without a lot of people.'

Such attitudes reflected the generic desire of the middle classes to

[1] *Hertfordshire Express*, 18th May 1946.
[2] *Hertfordshire Mercury*, 10th March 1950. The rural council's proposal had no direct connection with the New Town, but the parallel is obvious. The Lord of the Manor was the heir of Mr. Z, referred to earlier.

keep their property from being depreciated, and their culture contaminated, by contact with the working classes. Respectable middle-class citizens and conservative agricultural labourers had greeted with similar antipathy and scorn the estate which the Stevenage Council built between the wars at the eastern edge of town to house workers employed in expanding local industries—'Chinatown' it was called. Ruth Durant suggests that 'the antagonism of the inhabitants of the district. . . . is typical of the early history of all Municipal Housing Estates which have been built on the fringes of urban areas'.[1]

(f) Planning v. Freedom

The Labour Party's 1949 policy statement asserted, '*There can be no advance without planning*. Economic planning is essential to ensure the public interest always comes first: that is a central principle of the Labour Party's policy.'[2] It was seldom a central principle of Stevenage Conservatives. 'I don't know if too much planning is a good thing,' one said, adding straightforwardly, 'I'm just dyed in the wool and I always will be.' A group of Young Conservatives agreed that 'the social structure of towns should not be created artificially but develop naturally'.[3] A local minister opposed large-scale planning and scheming because human nature could not be expected to conform to a pattern. A Welwyn industrialist observed:

'only dead things or things destined to die soon can be "capital P" planned. . . . The designers of Welwyn Garden City did not foresee the future (even the relatively near future)—who could? It's almost a natural law that the more specialized the design the swifter the obsolescence, the more organized the system the smaller is the defect of any function sufficient to cause death.'[4]

Over a pint of bitter in the working-men's club, a skilled craftsman criticized the orderliness of Letchworth. 'A town has to grow up, it can't be brought up. It takes time for traditions to grow.' A junior member of the Corporation staff, native of a nearby village, swore *he* would not live in the New Town. 'It's laid out too neat.' In different ways, these feelings struck a deep core in many persons (not by any means all Conservatives), to whom 'planning' meant the end of individual freedom, who disliked a completely modern, antiseptic, and—let the truth be said—moral town, without its quota of ill-lit narrow streets, cosy old pubs, pool rooms, and other dens of moderate iniquity.

[1] Ruth Durant, *Watling* (London, 1939), p. 21.
[2] Labour Party, *Labour Believes in Britain* (London, 1949), p. 6. Bold face in original.
[3] Report by a participant of a debate among Stevenage Young Conservatives, 7th October 1949, 'This House deplores the Minister's decision to establish New Towns at Stevenage and in other areas'.
[4] Quoted by Purdom, op. cit., p. 288. The statement was made in 1948.

THE NEW TOWN PLAN

Without question, planning *did* infringe the economic and social privileges of propertied classes. 'Why, there's a garden city—Hampstead, I think—where they made everyone paint their doors the same colour and have the same kind of curtain in their windows', a leader of the Residents' Protection Association expostulated. 'They tell you the size of hedge and the kind of flowers you're to plant in your garden and everyone has to plant the same flowers.' The strict leases of this middle-class housing estate, built by a private company after the First World War, obliged tenants to paint their house every three years and grow only a certain type of low, well-clipped hedge. At Welwyn Garden City and Letchworth

'The plans and external appearance and materials of all buildings, including extensions, are subject under the leases to the approval of the companies' architects. . . . This gives complete architectural control. . . . Guidance is given in the building regulations as to the standards used in approving designs, which cover such matters as the orientation of rooms for sun, the placing of outbuildings, the design of backs as well as fronts of buildings, and the character of fences and hedges. . . . And there are covenants requiring . . . the care of hedges and cultivation of gardens, and in some cases the retention of a layout of open forecourts and the prohibition of fences or hedges which would spoil such a layout. . . .
'Sheds, fowl houses, rabbit pens, amateur-designed porches, unauthorized trellises, etc., require the constant vigilance of the administration. They can spread like a rash, and once established are difficult to clean up. . . . It is important not to let any structure go unnoticed, but to insist on application for a permit in every case. Conditions can then be imposed. . . . In both towns, consents are necessarily often refused. . . .'[1]

It seemed certain that many of these precedents would be followed by the Development Corporations, for the New Towns Committee advised that:

'Leases should contain covenants that the placing, design, elevation and external materials of buildings should be approved by the agency. This should apply to extensions as well as new buildings and to outbuildings and fencing. . . . The overall height, fascia line, profile, building line and facing materials [of shops] should be subject to approval by the agency. Below the fascia line the shopkeeper should have more latitude, but the agency should nevertheless approve the designs of shop fronts, including awnings, lettering, and outside signs.'[2]

The power to impose such restrictions would stem from the Corporation's ownership of all the freehold in the area.

We come here to a crucial point which explained why so many people preferred to see the town's future development in the hands of the Stevenage Urban District Council. The difference was simply that the Council had less power than the Corporation and Ministry,

[1] Osborn, *Green-Belt Cities*, pp. 75, 102.   [2] Cmd. 6876, pp. 16, 34.

and such power as it had was locally controlled. The Labour Party asserted, 'we will have no truck with totalitarian or strait-waistcoat planning. Our aim is to lead the world in evolving democratic planning. By that we mean the continuing consent and co-option of the people in the objectives and methods of the plan.'[1] Yet in fact it gave control over the future development of Stevenage to a Corporation of eight or nine persons (only one of whom, during the first three years, was a resident of Stevenage), appointed by the Minister and responsible to no electorate. And beyond the Corporation, the final source of power at the Ministry lay accessible to Stevenage citizens only by entreaty.

The 'Council', on the other hand, was merely twelve local men and women approachable on the street or in a pub, elected by their neighbours, serving without pay—and, since its formation in 1894 —dominated by Independents (or, for the most part, Conservatives who did not stand as Conservatives). In 1948–9, the ten Independents consisted of two accountants, two merchants, a retired butcher, an estate agent, a builder, a farmer, a wealthy widow, and a housewife —in short, a representative group of middle-class ratepayers who owned their homes and, preferring private to public ownership, would have encouraged the Council's tenants to buy their houses had the Labour Government permitted this.[2] When the Council got out of hand as, from the ratepayer's standpoint it occasionally did, it was always possible to bring it back into line. (Indeed, until the Representation of the People Act, 1945, made the local franchise almost identical to the parliamentary one, only ratepayers could vote in local elections.) Thus, a decade earlier, after the Council voted to build an expensive swimming-pool, a ratepayers' association was organized which succeeded in electing councillors who reversed this decision (see Chapter II, p. 47). When, early in 1946, it dawned upon ratepayers that the Council had come out in favour of the New Town, they put pressure upon it to reverse its decision. A Conservative (who soon became an officer of the Residents' Protection Association) wrote a letter to the Press 'directing attention to the lassitude of the local councillors and the extent to which they were out of touch with the views of the electorate'; while another letter-writer stated directly that 'the Council has completely lost touch with the ratepayers'.[3] The referendum which they demanded was finally held in May 1946 and showed a slight majority of the elec-

[1] *Labour Believes in Britain*, p. 6.

[2] In 1948 the Council proposed to the Minister of Health that tenants be permitted to buy Council houses, arguing that this would provide the Council with money to build more houses, and make better citizens of the owners. The Minister replied that the proposal (frequently made by Conservative local authorities) was contrary to Government policy.

[3] Letters in *Hertfordshire Express*, 16th and 23rd February 1946.

torate opposed to the New Town, whereupon, as we have seen, the Council opposed the project for a time.

The Council exercised only statutory powers delegated by Parliament and, provided he conformed with the law, any owner was free to behave as he pleased on, and do what he wished with, his property. Once the Council acquired property, however, it acquired in turn all the powers comprising the traditional freedoms of propertied men in capitalist society, and was able, by voluntary contract, to deprive its tenants of many of these freedoms. 'The powers of the city as local authority are limited to such powers as are expressly given by statute. . . . But the powers as landlord are limited only where actions are expressly prohibited by statute; the landlord can lease land subject to any conditions he likes to impose.'[1] Stevenage Council tenants, accordingly (in common with council tenants throughout Britain and the tenants of most European and American municipalities) experienced disabilities and restrictions from which home owners were free. Among their conditions of tenancy were:

'The tenancy may be terminated by one week's notice in writing on either side. . . .

'The tenant will not be permitted to assign, underlet, or use the premises otherwise than as a private dwelling house, and may only take in lodgers with the written consent of the Council. . . .

'No animals other than dogs or cats shall be kept on the premises, without the consent of the Council. . . .

'No building, shed or other erection of any kind shall be built, placed or erected on any part of the premises without the consent of the Council.

'The dwelling house and the premises generally shall be kept by the tenant in a clean and orderly condition, and the front and back gardens shall be kept properly cultivated. . . .

'The tenant shall not do or permit anything to be done on the premises which shall be a nuisance or annoyance to the Council. . . .

'The Council shall be at liberty . . . to enter upon the premises at all reasonable hours of the day for the purpose of inspecting the condition thereof. . . .

'Any breach by the tenant of any of the foregoing conditions shall entitle the Council to determine the tenancy.'

Whether and how the Council enforced these provisions was not at issue, but rather that, because of its position as landlord, it was entitled to impose them. And so tenants had to request the Council for permission to erect a short length of boarded fence, install a wash basin in the bathroom, or keep a pig. Indeed, members of the Council staff complained that tenants, accustomed to applying for permission to do every little thing, constantly bothered them with trivial personal matters down to disputes over the neighbour's cat. That the terms of the Council's lease were common enough

[1] E. D. Simon, *Rebuilding Britain* (London, 1945), p. 202.

throughout Britain (and more lenient than the restrictions imposed in many private housing developments in the United States), and that the Welwyn Garden City leases and those recommended by the Reith Committee for New Towns derived directly from the practice of the better urban landlords of big private housing estates in Britain, was no consolation to the Stevenage property owner.

Undeniably, the trend in the modern state, and notably in Britain, has been to restrict the liberties of property owners, reducing their margin of privilege over municipal tenants.

'For the last hundred years owners of property have been compelled to an increasing extent, without compensation, to comply with certain requirements regarding their property such, for example, as maintaining or improving its sanitary equipment, observing certain standards of construction, providing adequate air space around buildings and streets of sufficient width. The underlying reason for such provisions is, obviously, that compliance with certain requirements is essential to the interests of the community and that accordingly the private owner should be compelled to comply with them even at cost to himself. . . . The view of the Legislature on these essential requirements for the well-being of the community has passed beyond the field of health and safety to that of convenience and amenity.'[1]

It is worth noting that the plan which the Council adopted in 1938 for the future development of Stevenage, and which aroused no local opposition, specified:

'The external appearance of any building intended to be erected on land in any use zone or in any private open space shall, if the Council so require, be subject to their approval, and a person intending to erect a building on such land . . . shall, if required by the Council so to do, apply to them for approval of the external appearance of the building, submitting for the purpose drawings and particulars. . . . The siting of any building. . . . shall be subject to the approval of the Council, and a person intending to erect a building on such land . . . shall before commencing the erection apply to the Council for approval.'[2]

After the war, three main controls over development were exercised in Britain: (1) control by *bye-law* (administered locally by the Stevenage Urban District Council); (2) by *planning permission* (administered ordinarily, in accordance with the Town and Country Planning Act, 1947, by the Hertfordshire County Council which delegated some powers to the Stevenage Council.[3] After 1st July

---

[1] Expert Committee on Compensation and Betterment, Cmd. 6386, p. 20.
[2] Stevenage Urban District Council, *Stevenage Planning Scheme*, October 1937.
[3] In August 1949 the situation was as follows: Applications for planning permission to develop Stevenage property were first submitted to the Stevenage Council, which sent them on to the County divisional planning officer at Baldock, who then tendered his advice to the Stevenage Council's town planning

1948, however, by directive of the Minister of Town and Country Planning the Stevenage Council was also obliged to submit planning proposals to the Corporation for its approval; the Corporation, in turn, had to submit its New Town proposals to the County Council until 1st March 1950 when this was obviated by another Ministerial order); (3) by *building licences* issued by the Ministry of Works; (1) and (2) were permanent controls, while (3) was a temporary measure deriving from wartime Defence Regulations. Planning permission theoretically extended to all construction and repair work down to the painting of a window frame or the repair of a garden shed,[1] although enforcement was seldom that strict. These controls were, of course, widely resented, and often deliberately or innocently ignored. Whether, under conditions then prevailing, they advanced or retarded the general welfare was a question that Socialists and Conservatives answered differently.

Nevertheless, significant privileges and rewards still attached to the ownership of property, and even in regard to restrictions applying equally to private owners and municipal tenants, the former were often in a stronger position. A private owner could be restrained by a court order from carrying out construction which the Urban District Council did not authorize, but for the same offence the court could evict a Council tenant for breaking the terms of his lease. The Council's Planning Committee, which issued planning permission for private development, was far less powerful than its Housing Committee, which administered the Council estate. Sheds, fences, and the like were always being built before permission was obtained, as people counted (usually correctly) on the Council's lenience to get permission *ex post facto*.[2] 'People in this town have got away with too much, building over the front line before submitting their plans, knowing they can get away with it that way,' Councillor X complained at one Council meeting. When the discussion turned to a Council tenant's request for permission to erect a shack and Councillor Y said, 'If you refuse, you'll get something erected *without* per-

committee. Thus, said a Stevenage Council informant, the town planning committee was 'only a rubber stamp'. Should it disagree with the planning officer, it could take the matter to a County sub-committee composed of three members each from the County and Stevenage Councils; but if this sub-committee disagreed, the matter was finally decided by the County Committee, which had no Stevenage representative.

[1] Until May 1950 when the Minister of Town and Country Planning issued an order eliminating the need for planning permission for minor repairs and construction (*The Times*, 11th May 1950).

[2] We once attended a large meeting of a Stevenage organization at which the chairman, a prominent, suave citizen with a fine sense of humour, asked 'Are any representatives of the Press here? They must be hushed up.' He then proceeded, 'We must get the hut up quickly, before the planning people find out about it. Because I understand you've got to get a licence for those things.'

mission', Councillor X retorted, 'We're not going to allow *that*, are we? We're the landlords—we're in a stronger position than just the Planning Committee'.

Whereas the planning powers of the Council were relatively weak and often circumvented by local residents, the planning powers of the Development Corporation and Ministry were strong and offered little prospect of circumvention, for the Corporation would be the monopolistic owner of all land and buildings. From the planners' viewpoint this was necessary and desirable. But as the Stevenage home owner saw it, he would be transformed from an independent citizen to a domesticated tenant in a glorified housing estate.

(g) The Residents' Protection Association

From its formation in May 1946, the Residents' Protection Association financed court action against the Minister's order and led the opposition to the New Town.

Members were enrolled upon a minimum subscription of 6d., 'To resist the proposal to establish a Satellite Town at Stevenage and to take such steps the Committee may think desirable to that end'. An officer swore an affidavit in December 1946 that the Association's membership was 'over 1,000 members who reside within the site of the proposed new town', and, at various other dates, figures of 1,100, 1,200, 1,224, and 1,300 members were given. These presumably represented the number of persons who had signed the above statement and/or contributed a donation towards the expenses of the Association; they could not be taken as a measure of the Association's active strength over any length of time, because periodic subscriptions were not required, nor was serious effort made to keep membership lists up to date. Thus, at an October 1949 Ministry inquiry, an Association officer gave the membership at 1,224 persons. Cross-examined by the Corporation solicitor, he asserted 'Nobody has resigned', but conceded that deceased persons—'perhaps five per cent'—were still registered as members.

The Association was most active in 1946 and 1947, when there was a chance of killing the New Town in the courts. In the spring 1946, it helped elect Independent councillors who swung the District Council from co-operation to opposition, duplicating, in this manner, the feat of the Ratepayers' Association which a decade earlier managed to gain control of the Council and defeat a proposal to build a swimming-pool in Stevenage. (On one occasion, an informant who had been active in both organizations made the significant slip of saying 'Ratepayers' Association' for 'Protection Association'.) Both organizations clearly represented the same conservative interests which dominated Stevenage politics for many years. Had the future of the New Town been entirely in local hands, there can be little doubt that the Protection Association would have defeated it.

After the appeal to the House of Lords was lost, a good deal of fire went out of the Association; some of its most active supporters lost heart and contemplated moving from Stevenage. On 5th April 1948, the secretary notified all members and subscribers:

'It may no longer be possible to resist the proposal to establish a new town at Stevenage but it will be possible to put forward the views of the members of the Association in connection with the various proposals of the Stevenage Development Corporation (e.g. the Development Plan) and to mitigate the effect of the order on the present residents of Stevenage.

'It is therefore essential that the Association should remain in being and that its purposes should be extended to include the protection of the interests of the residents of Stevenage and the taking of such action as the Committee may deem expedient in connection with any proposals of the Stevenage Development Corporation or the Ministry of Town and Country Planning.

'After meeting all their liabilities the Association have a small balance in hand. It has been suggested that this balance should be applied to the proposed extended purposes of the Association set out above but doubt is felt as to whether the balance may properly be so applied. If you wish to receive your share of the above-mentioned balance which would approximately be 7 to 8% of your Subscription the amount due to you . . . would be sent to you, but if I do not hear from you within fourteen days of the date of this letter I shall assume that you are agreeable that the above-mentioned balance should be made available for the proposed extended purposes of the Association. . . .'

Sixteen days later, a town hall meeting of 'perhaps 200 to 300 people' was told that not one request had been received for the return of money, and a resolution was unanimously adopted modelled on the second paragraph quoted above. According to the treasurer's report, the books showed a balance of £454: 1,397 residents had donated £2,607, and 844 persons from other parts of the country £1,711, towards the Association's fight. In all, £3,121 had been spent on inquiries and court actions.[1]

The executive committee elected at this meeting comprised eleven officers, mainly business men or farmers. When two Association officers appeared at the 11th October 1949 inquiry to protest a compulsory purchase order of the Development Corporation, they based their authority to speak for over a thousand residents upon this resolution. (The Association had not met once in the intervening eighteen months.) The Corporation solicitor charged that the officers actually represented only themselves and a few other persons. In fact, a week before, a Corporation employee delegated to discover whether the Protection Association had recently canvassed its members or if it even kept an up-to-date list of members, had interviewed

[1] *Hertfordshire Mercury*, 23rd April 1948.

more than twenty inhabitants with negative results. A Labour councillor publicly asserted:

'in the 1946 panic, when according to the tale of the day houses were going to be pulled down, tenants turned out and left high and dry, and various other horrible things were going to happen in Stevenage, this Association was formed. They just went round and collected sixpences everywhere, elected officers, and then suddenly it became more or less a secret association. I know of individuals who paid to that Association and who have never been notified of meetings nor asked their opinion in any shape or form; and yet they still claim them to be members of the Association. . . . It is such a democratic body that, as far as I can find out, there is no provision made for any meeting where the officers can give an account of their stewardship, or to have a re-election of officers, in any shape or form.'[1]

Of course, these were partisan statements, but no less partisan statements could be obtained from Association supporters. Undoubtedly, leaders of the Association expressed the feelings of very many residents. But, conducting their fight of 'the small men against the powerful bureaucratic machine', they created a small machine of their own which neglected some democratic forms which more experienced bureaucracies did not fail to observe.

Formally, the Association was not a political organization. 'We should like to make it clear', said the treasurer, 'that the Stevenage Residents' Protection Association is an entirely non-political organisation. . . . our membership includes support from members of Trade Unions and the Labour Party.'[2] 'In plain English, not one penny has been received from party funds. . . . we believe this matter to be above party considerations', said one officer; and another, 'Members of the Labour Party in this district, and high-up members at that, have come off their own bat and offered and given financial assistance to us'.

Yet the fact remained that most Association leaders were either members of the Conservative Party or sympathetic to its programme. 'Very few Labour people opposed the New Town—a few whose houses were to come down', stated one Labour informant, adding that perhaps half a dozen members broke with the Labour Party over the issue (some later rejoined) and sided with the Protection Association. Another (pro-New Town, Labour) informant estimated that less than 10 per cent of the 1,200-odd members of the Association were Labour supporters and the rest mainly Conservatives, with a minority of Liberals and non-partisans. The secretary of a local union declared, 'although the Stevenage Ratepayers' [sic] Protection Association may justly claim one or two Trade Unionists as mem-

---

[1] Statement at Master Plan inquiry, 19th October 1949.
[2] *Hertfordshire Express*, 15th June 1946.

bers, such members are wholly out of touch with the majority of the T.U. movement, and are therefore actively assisting a movement formed expressly to oppose working-class interests'.[1]

Stevenage delegates to the Conservative Conference at Brighton in the fall 1947, strongly criticized the Minister's powers of compulsory purchase, which the delegation chairman termed 'undemocratic, un-British and unconstitutional'; and Young Conservatives debating, in October 1949, the motion 'This House deplores the Minister's decision to establish New Towns at Stevenage and in other areas', expressed themselves as in favour of New Towns to take the overflow of population from London, but strongly against the methods the Government had used to implement the scheme—i.e., the setting up of Development Corporations out of touch (they believed) with local opinion, and the 'dictatorial powers' of the Minister. All Conservatives did not oppose the New Town: some supported it openly and others covertly. But, just as the merits of State planning outweighed its dangers in the minds of most (local and national) Labour leaders, so local Conservatives tended to adopt the opposite viewpoint. This had been a fundamental dividing line between the national parties in the 1945 General Election:

'The Labour party maintained that the real test of sincerity in this and every other domestic problem was whether or not the party had a *Plan*. They maintained that the Conservatives had no plan. . . .

'The Conservative party. . . . held that, in the interests of economic efficiency, the State should refrain wherever possible from such planning, in order to leave individual enterprises with the maximum freedom to make their own plans. . . .

'The Conservatives eschewed the long-term planning and the radical changes proposed by the Labour party. They tended to prefer expedient and opportunist remedies.'[2]

Pragmatically, the Protection Association had little chance of stopping the New Town so long as the Labour Government retained office. Although the broad outline of the New Towns programme had been supported by all parties, the Labour Government had been responsible for its administration and was not likely to reverse its own judgements. Accordingly, after the defeat in the House of Lords, the rationale of the Protection Association was to delay the Corporation and Ministry as much as possible by objections which involved time-consuming legal procedures, until a Conservative victory or economic vicissitudes led the Government to curtail or modify the programme.

During the 1945 Labour landslide a Labour M.P. was returned in

[1] Letter, *Hertfordshire Express*, 17th August 1946.
[2] R. B. McCallum and Alison Readman, *The British General Election of 1945* (London, 1947), pp. 52–3, 60–1.

this (the Hitchin) constituency for the first time, and he afforded the Protection Association small comfort. The prospective Conservative candidate, however (who won the seat in February 1950), promised, if the Conservatives took office, to arrange an interview at which Association representatives could put their case before the new Minister of Town and Country Planning.[1] At a Conservative town hall meeting on 4th February 1950, an Association officer asked if the candidate would vote for a revocation of the Designation Order; he replied there was a general consensus of opinion that New Towns were necessary, and could not hold out hope that Conservatives would revoke the scheme, but a Conservative Government would give property owners a fairer and squarer deal. (This implied a higher rate of compensation for compulsory purchase, and possibly, retention of some freeholds in private hands.) Apparently the answer did not satisfy, for another Association officer asked if the candidate would press for a new public inquiry into the Stevenage New Town, and he promised this would be his first duty. Addressing a crowded Stevenage audience the following week, the candidate got a big reception when, criticizing the Government's farm policy, he said, 'If they want to do right by agriculture, why should they take 6,000 acres of the best land in Hertfordshire for a satellite town?'[2]

The official Conservative policy on New Towns was stated as follows in 1951:

'During the debate on the New Towns Bill in 1946, Conservatives did not oppose the principle of the New Towns. But Conservatives are not committed to any existing site designated by the Socialists and reserve their judgment on this experiment in the light of the way it works out in practice. New Towns should not take away first-class agricultural land. . . .

'Conservative support for the New Town policy is conditional upon whether the nation can afford to pay for it. . . . Building costs in New Towns have so far been high. . . . It would defeat the whole purpose of the experiment if the New Towns were to become permanent high-cost areas.

'It has also been Conservative policy to press for justice for existing occupants. Development Corporations have a statutory obligation to offer those whom they displace alternative accommodation and also to compensate them. Conservatives wish to see that the compensation is

[1] A prominent Stevenage Independent was cynical about the candidate's move —'everyone makes promises at election time'—and the Association's prospects at such an interview, should it materialize. A knowledgeable Labour informant thought a Conservative Minister might hold a general inquiry into the lack of progress in New Towns, but doubted that special action would be taken in regard to Stevenage, or that a fledgeling M.P. could exert much influence over the Minister where local interests diverged from national policy.

[2] *Hertfordshire Express*, 11th and 18th February 1950; and *Hertfordshire Mercury*, 17th February 1950.

really adequate. The loss of a freehold is a serious matter. Conservatives have always opposed the Corporations undertaking anything more than strictly essential development activities. They do not wish Development Corporations to undertake trading operations in competition with local undertakings.

'Finally, there is no reason why the Development Corporations should themselves carry out all building and development. The Act specifically provides for building and development to be undertaken within the designated area by private enterprise but, owing to the way in which the Socialists have interpreted the Act, this has not yet been allowed to happen. Generally speaking, the Corporations should be wound up as quickly as possible and should give way to more democratic institutions. This is provided for by the Act, and Conservatives consider (a) that there should be greater liaison between Corporations and existing local authorities during the development of the New Towns, and (b) that the work of the Corporations should be handed over to a democratically elected body as soon as the town nears completion.'[1]

Leaders of the Protection Association took much the same line as the District Council on many questions, especially in the early days of the fight. The Council, as an elective body with important legal powers, rights, and duties, and ultimate heir to the Development Corporation, had a recognized status denied the Association; but these responsibilities inhibited councillors from adopting the Association's intransigence on some issues. It was important to both Association and Council leaders that they remain on friendly terms, because the Association was often in a position to embarrass and delay Council negotiations with Ministry or Corporation, while, without co-operation from some councillors, the Association's efforts would be weakened and misdirected. Formal or, more frequently, informal consultation often took place, therefore, at which information was exchanged and action co-ordinated.

There was, of course, nothing improper in such consultations, which left both parties free to act as their inclination and interests dictated. Direct negotiations between Association and Corporation were often impracticable, and Council representatives then served an important function as intermediaries between the opposing factions, each of whom, at certain times (notably in 1949, when the Council and Corporation had reached agreement on the transfer of the town's water works to the Corporation, which the Association's objection threatened to delay) exploited this means of sounding and exerting pressure upon the other.

We have dealt in this section primarily with the rational interests and motives of the opposition; implicit is an analysis of the social

[1] Conservative and Unionist Central Office, *The Campaign Guide* 1951 (London, 1951), p. 282.

composition of the opposition: not all, but many, and not solely, but mainly farmers, property owners, ratepayers, conservatives, members of the middle and upper classes, those who liked rural life. An opposition leader gave almost exactly this analysis when, at a meeting of the Protection Association in April 1947, he appealed for funds to those who would be adversely affected by the New Town. 'First there are the farmers: they would be sunk if the plan went through. Then there are the owner-occupiers; if the satellite comes they will lose their freeholds, and get 1939 value for their houses plus a maximum of 60 per cent. With them are the people with property in Stevenage, not living here but living by the rents as a form of investment; they will get 1939 value and nothing more. Then there are those who have lived here all their lives and want to go on living in the country, and not in a town the size of Watford [about 73,000].'

Deeply convinced of the righteousness of their cause, opposition leaders often found it difficult to refer to the Corporation or Ministry in other than bitter terms. At one inquiry, we sat between two prominent opponents who, throughout the morning and afternoon, were unable or unwilling to suppress a stream of invective, insult, and personal abuse directed against Corporation witnesses—'that sanctimonious ——', 'unctuous ——', 'son of a lady dog', etc.— which they muttered into our ears, to each other, and to themselves. 'My husband's violent', a housewife said. 'If ever the New Town is mentioned he starts throwing things round the kitchen, so I just keep quiet and we never talk of it.'

Any weapon was seized upon to club the New Town, and anti-Semitic talk was raised against known or imagined Jews on the Corporation or Ministry. 'A sheeny lawyer', was the way one of the town's most respectable citizens casually referred to a prominent planner, while the wife of a carpenter remarked, 'He's a Jew, you know, and they say he's got a big house out in the country not far from here and one or two others elsewhere' (this followed a reference to the houses due for demolition). A local paper printed the following artful inquiry: 'I was informed yesterday, on what seemed good authority, that one of the largest synagogues in England is to be built in the New Town. Is this likely? Could any of your readers inform me?'

We also heard, in surprising places, the most casual and unprintable charges of sexual perversion which served to indicate the degree of malice and contempt which some townspeople held for the planners (and, perhaps, for themselves).

Much personal animosity was directed against the Minister, especially after his town hall speech. 'I'd willingly do a month just to lay my hands on him', a 'modest young corn merchant' assured a London journalist. 'A distinguished local squire . . . asked, "D'you think it'd be any good if I planted a time bomb in his office?" '[1] Three and a half years later when Stevenage Young Conservatives discussed the New Town, they felt 'the Minister had made a very bad impression', and 'Local antagonism was influenced out of all proportion to the facts by the irresponsible remark . . . "You are going to get this New Town at Stevenage *whether you like it or not*".'[2] The nonagenarian maiden daughter of a local landowner, a devout Anglican, confessed privately, 'I find it hard to think well of one of His Majesty's Ministers'. A nationally known personage called the New Town planners 'fascists', while all a leading farmer could say upon hearing that the Government had won its case in the House of Lords was, 'This is a bitter blow. The Stevenage we love will never be the same. We are not against New Towns but we don't want to be interfered with. It isn't English at all.'

The operative word was 'English' for, to opponents, the New Town violated their traditional way of life and deep-rooted moral principles.

B. TRADERS—A SLIGHT CASE OF AMBIVALENCE

The attitude of traders to the New Town was more ambivalent than that of most other groups. As ratepayers, property owners, and, in general, conservatives, they shared the antipathy of these groups to the whole enterprise. But the New Town would be good for business—or would it? It was the difficulty of answering this question that made it difficult to determine where their ultimate interest lay.

In 1947 there were 126 shops and 22 licensed premises in Stevenage—a high average of about one shop per fifty townsmen. The ceaseless stream of traffic on the Great North Road helped sustain some of the shops, and they catered also to some thousand consumers from the neighbouring countryside. But most of the rural, and some of the local, trade went to Hitchin. The building of the New Town would redress this balance and, in all likelihood, enable Stevenage merchants to make further inroads upon Hitchin's sphere of influence.

'Stevenage would appear to have been in danger in recent years of being eclipsed by its neighbour, Hitchin, whose [commercial] hinterland almost surrounds its own. Its artificial expansion into a New Town will probably cause it to expand its hinterland again to some extent at Hitchin's expense.'[3]

[1] Mark Benny, 'Storm over Stevenage', p. 42.   [2] See note 3, p. 163.
[3] F. H. W. Green, *Spheres of Influence as Determined by the Study of Motor Bus Services* (mimeographed) (Ministry of Town and Country Planning, February 1949).

Two things spoiled this pleasant prospect and led traders to consider the New Town fraught with as much danger as promise: (*a*) the new shopping centre which the Development Corporation planned to build would compete with and probably dominate the established shopping area, and (*b*) the Corporation was expected to acquire the freehold of all commercial premises and thereby reap, in rent, much of the profit which the New Town would bring.

(*a*) Competition

At the Urban District Council's request, the Stevenage Chamber of Trade, the principal organization of local merchants,[1] held an emergency meeting on 12th October 1944 to submit its views for the development of a town plan. The minutes of this meeting record:

'It was hoped that . . . in any future development the character of the town would be retained. Considerable alterations would be necessary, but the large area covered by High St. and Albert St. [i.e., the chief existing shopping centres] would be sufficient to house all the business premises of a town of 30,000 population. . . . In any reconstruction, existing businesses to be given preference.'

But at the Ministerial inquiry of 8th October 1946, a witness for the Stevenage objectors testified that the existing shopping centre could not serve as the centre for the New Town:

'The depth of the buildings is insufficient. Over 100 ft. is the depth required for a main shopping centre. There are two island sites on the south giving a 70 ft. depth only—no, 42 ft. . . . and again, behind those sites the depth of these shops on the east is only 70 ft. . . . But the real point is that you cannot use the existing old cottage property, which it mostly is, for modern shops.'

Upon the latter occasion the objectors were trying to show how foolhardy was the Ministry proposal. When the proposal was accepted, they sang a somewhat different tune.

We have already discussed (pp. 125–7) the opposition to the location of the New Town centre just south of the High Street. From the traders' viewpoint, if the New Town had to have another shopping area it should be located as far as possible from the existing one. The Corporation, however, sought to concentrate estate values in a manner most advantageous to the New Town and profitable to itself, and it had its way.

The slowness of the New Town development brought an initial benefit to resident traders, for the population would increase faster

---

[1] In 1938, membership in the Chamber of Trade stood at sixty-one, but it sank during the war to a low of thirty-six in 1944, rising again to sixty-five in 1950. Not more than fifteen or twenty traders attended its monthly meetings, but the yearly dinner drew a goodly crowd.

177

than the construction of a suitable range of shops to cater for it. But eventually this process would be reversed and trade drained away from the old to the new centre, as a Corporation officer pointed out in a 1949 memorandum.

'The Corporation's tentative four year programme contemplates the erection of 8–12 shops by the end of 1952, in Neighbourhoods 1 and 2, and the beginning, at about the same time, of the erection of shops in the New Town Centre. During the period up to the end of 1952, the population, including the labour force will, it is anticipated, increase to double its present figure. The resulting increase in trade will benefit the traders and, in a limited way, increase the value of the shops and particularly the interests of freehold and leasehold owner-occupiers.

'All these increases in value are, however, likely to be temporary. When costs go down, restrictions on building are relaxed, and more shops are available, it is a reasonable assumption that there will be a general lowering of values. . . . The erection of shops in the New Town Centre . . . the resiting of the Railway Station near to the New Town Centre, with the 'bus station in close proximity and the diversion of the London Road [will draw trade from existing shops]. . . . The competition of the new and well fitted labour saving shops with the old and inconveniently planned existing shops and the introduction of new traders will also have their effect.'

Stevenage traders asked for preference in sites for New Town shops, but this the Corporation refused, stating that 'the main purpose of the New Town is to provide for population, industry and commerce decentralised from London'.[1]

(b) Corporate v. Private Profit

'. . . the letting of shops when the town is well established is one of the most profitable businesses which the agency can undertake, and one on which it must rely in order to meet its financial obligations in full.'

'The fundamental principle in fixing rents should be to obtain the highest amount which traders are able to pay consistently with their remaining successfully in business. The policy adopted by some estates of fixing rents on a cost basis cannot be justified; it makes a gift to particular traders of part of the real rental value of the shop created by the development of the town and the growth of population in the area served.'[2]

In the above passages the Reith Committee set out the financial principles which the Development Corporations subsequently endeavoured to implement. The principles applied to existing shops as much as to those which would be built. Indeed, the Corporations

[1] *Hertfordshire Express*, 14th May 1949. This was part of a formal reply by the Corporation's Chief Estates Officer to a set of questions submitted by the Chamber of Trade.
[2] Cmd. 6794, p. 7; Cmd. 6876, pp. 32–3.

regarded existing properties with a special ardour, for in no other direction could a sizeable revenue be anticipated during early years. Here was property which would yield an immediate return on the purchase price, and whose value would demonstrably increase. And so the Corporations early made overtures to the Minister for permission to purchase compulsorily existing commercial properties. However, because of the Government's programme of capital restrictions, he was under compulsion to restrict Corporation investments as much as possible, and therefore refused that permission time after time. Thus it was that free enterprise in Stevenage was extended for a period by courtesy of the Socialist Minister.

Traders were, nevertheless, anxious to know when the axe would fall and precisely what terms they could then expect from the Corporation. On 18th October 1948, the Chamber of Trade submitted five questions to the Corporation, including the crucial question, 'Will leases now in existence be continued in their present form, with option to renew where given in the terms of the existing lease? How will the new rentals be based?' Over half a year later, the Corporation replied:

'Leases now in existence will be allowed to continue in their present form, with an option to renew if the terms of the lease are not materially at variance with the terms of the Corporation's proposed lease, and provided that the rent payable under the lease is not substantially below the true rental value of the property, having regard to the altered circumstances created by the Corporation's proposals.'[1]

At the time of writing, it is impossible to go beyond this point at Stevenage. But it may be instructive to examine the leasing policy announced by the Crawley Development Corporation, first New Town Corporation to purchase the shopping centre in its area. The Corporation distinguished between freehold and leasehold owners. The former would be 'offered a 21 years' lease without breaks, with a right of assignment, though not to a different trade without the Corporation's consent, and . . . the rent should be based on the rental values used in settling the purchase price for the freehold'. Leasehold tenants would be offered varying terms, in accordance with prevailing terms of tenancy:

'(a) Tenants with leases having more than a year or two unexpired. Each case will be considered on its merits when the time for renewal arrives.

'(b) Tenants with leases having only a year or two unexpired. In general, they will be offered similar leases to those granted to owner-occupiers, except that the rent will be related to the conditions at the time of the negotiations. Should the planning of the central area have reached

[1] *Hertfordshire Express*, 14th May 1949.

the stage when it is definite that a particular property will be required for development purposes at a certain date, the length of lease granted in each case will be related to that date.

'(c) Tenants on weekly, monthly, quarterly or yearly agreements. When these are not protected tenants under the Rent Restriction Acts, each case will be considered on its merits.'[1]

Of the 106 shops (including eight owned by multiple firms) in and around Stevenage High Street likely to be first acquired by the Corporation, forty-three were freehold owner-occupied and the remaining sixty-three either leasehold owner-occupied or held on short tenancies.[2] If the Stevenage Corporation followed the Crawley precedent, local traders would evidently be offered a range of terms in general less exacting for owners, who had more to lose, than for tenants.

The prospect before traders was, accordingly, so various and uncertain that it was difficult for them to adopt a single outlook. One representative of the Chamber of Trade stated that older traders were less opposed to the New Town than younger ones, because they would not remain in business much longer in any case. The population of old Stevenage would inevitably increase, and optimists were convinced that, no matter what the Corporation intended, the High Street would always remain the most popular part of town just because it *was* unplanned—and because it had so many pubs. (The latter argument derived from the experience at Letchworth, from whose publess streets people flocked each evening to nearby towns better served in this respect.)

In opposing the New Town, one suspected that some small traders let their social aspirations (which led them to identify with the wealthier propertied classes) override their economic interests, while others let their tact override their honesty (publicly agreeing with the opposition, although privately convinced that their best interests would be served by the New Town).

Only the future could determine (too late, as always, for present usefulness) where the best interests of traders had actually lain.

C. NEW TOWN SUPPORTERS

In the nature of the circumstances, citizens in favour of the New Town had less opportunity or cause than opponents to make their attitude known. The Government initiated the project in response to national, not local, demands, and local approbation seemed irrelevant or gratuitous. Legal safeguards required that opponents be heard and

---

[1] *Report of the . . . Crawley . . . Development Corporation for the period ending 31st March,* 1950, p. 62.

[2] In 1948, according to a Corporation memorandum dated January 1949.

not that supporters come forward—indeed they could add little to
the well-documented case of Ministry and Corporation experts. It
was often when the New Town was most endangered that supporters tended to speak out. (There were indications, also, that
Ministry and Corporation curtailed some supporters in the early
stages—perhaps to placate the opposition—but, as time passed,
gained confidence and gave them a freer rein.)

(a) Industry, Jobs, and Houses

Whether the Council actively opposed or simply did not encourage the industrialization of Stevenage in the past, or industry
failed to develop for other reasons, was not quite certain. In one
case in 1905, the Council applied building by-laws so strictly that a
small manufacturer decided 'to entirely remove my business, with
all its plant and machinery, to a neighbouring town, where, I believe,
conditions helpful to the further development of the concern will
obtain'.[1] Similar episodes were said to have occurred after the First
World War. A firm of match manufacturers were coming to Stevenage in the 1920's, a trade unionist said, 'but the Council wouldn't
give them the facilities. These dear old widows and people like that
who go to the Women's Unionist and Conservative Association will
vote like that, but the real working-class are generally in favour of
the factories coming here.' 'We tried to get factories here at that
time,' another Labour informant stated, 'but people objected to it.'
In 1934, the Chamber of Trade complained to the Council 'that a
foreign firm searching for a factory site had recently applied in
Stevenage but were driven elsewhere as they could get no satisfaction'. An informant in close touch with the Council since the end of
the Second World War, stated emphatically, 'Certainly in my time
the Council did nothing to encourage industry in Stevenage, rather
the opposite'.

On the other hand, one informant (who was in favour of the New
Town and, one way or another, had been connected with the Council
and the local Labour movement for over twenty years) questioned
the accuracy of many of these rumours. To his knowledge, the only
factory the Council had dissuaded from remaining had been one the
medical officer closed down on sanitary grounds. As a few firms did
settle in Stevenage and gradually expanded during the inter-war
period, perhaps the difficulties of doing so were no greater than in any
other town of similar location, labour supply, and semi-suburban,
semi-rural characteristics. However, it rested primarily with the firm
to come to an agreement with a local landowner, and to make other
necessary arrangements. The Council had little power, and evidently lacked the incentive, to assist the process substantially.

[1] Newspaper report of the 29th May 1905 Council meeting.

Especially after 1939, it was the national and not local Government that exercised decisive control over manpower, fuel, raw materials, transport, prices, taxes, foreign exchange, etc., upon which industry's existence depended, and local industrialists therefore concerned themselves very little with the affairs of the Stevenage Council beyond making the necessary applications to it for planning permission for their development programmes.

A Council representative noted in December 1945, 'I was concerned this afternoon not to be able to give two young fellows assistance with a factory site. Something must be done to make more land available.' Four months later, local employers informed the Council they could use 1,767 houses during the next three years to house their workers, and urged that building begin immediately on a fifty-acre site. The Council, which had hardly begun its post-war housing programme (under which 188 permanent new houses were completed by 31st December 1950, a figure above the average for comparable Hertfordshire towns)[1] wrote to the Ministry of Town and Country Planning on 22nd March 1946 that it 'would appreciate some guidance as to what reply and information should be given . . .' The Ministry advised that employers should be told to wait and discuss their problem with the Development Corporation soon to be established.

Without the New Town, industry would probably have continued to grow slowly in Stevenage with the Council's uncertain co-operation, as had been the case ever since the First World War; but the New Town offered an unparalleled chance for immediate expansion and Government priorities that might otherwise be indefinitely delayed. At a 3rd April 1946 meeting with a Ministry officer, local manufacturers expressed unanimous support of the industrial provisions of the New Town plan, and, the following month, announced, 'After careful consideration . . . we agreed that the proposed [industrial] arrangement was the best that could be made in the circumstances', but carefully added, 'we do not feel that it comes within the province of our Group to deal with [New Town] matters other than those strictly concerned with industrial problems'.[2] 'The employers' bread is buttered on the side of the New Town, though they are not all in favour of the Labour Government', a Corporation informant commented. He estimated that the six Stevenage factories employing, in April 1948, 1,325 persons might employ 3,400 ten years later, if all went well with the New Town.

[1] In addition, twenty temporary houses were built by the Urban District Council and fifteen permanent houses were erected by private builders (Ministry of Local Government and Planning, *Housing Return for England and Wales, 31st December,* 1950, Cmd. 8138 (London, 1951), Appendix B, pp. 24–5).

[2] *Hertfordshire Express,* 25th May 1946.

Asked what would improve Welwyn Garden City from the indus-trialist's point of view, a Welwyn employer answered, 'Greatly improved housing facilities to attract labour, alternative shopping facilities, greatly increased amenities to draw residents to the area, improve communications. . . . and eventually to reduce rates and in-crease ancillary services required by industry'.[1] Stevenage indus-trialists had the same needs, perhaps to a greater degree, and, except for reduced rates, the New Town promised to fulfil all of them.

What was sauce for the gander was sauce for the goose. The Stevenage Trades Council, representing all local unions, unani-mously resolved in February 1946, 'We believe that the development of a Satelite [sic] Town at Stevenage . . . is in the best interests of the people of Stevenage; and as representatives of the organised workers of Stevenage pledge our wholehearted support and co-operation. . . .' One union forwarded to the Council on 19th February 1946 the following handwritten resolution passed 'unanimously' at a branch meeting:

'This Stevenage . . . Union, in view of the opposition expressed at a Public Meeting in Stevenage to the Abecombie [sic] Plan for a Satelite [sic] town in Stevenage re-affirm our considered opinion that such a Satelite Town at Stevenage is in the best interests of Stevenage as a whole; and by reasons of its Social, Educational and Industrial advantages commands the support of all workers and all who [have] at heart the interests of both local workers and those who will make up the new community. We therefore pledge our full support for the plan and urge that no avoidable delay be permitted.'

The Trades Council convened a conference, in October 1946, at which seventy-eight delegates representing fifteen local unions and other labour organizations unanimously supported the New Town, and urged that a committee representing workers' organizations in Stevenage and the London dispersal areas be established to help implement the plan.[2]

Soon after the Minister's Stevenage speech, which was broadcast over the BBC, letters like the following (the first, from a Coventry couple) appeared in the local Press:[3]

'As "natives" of Stevenage (we were born and bred there) we listened with disgust to the broadcast of the recordings made at the recent public meeting at Stevenage. . . . Had Stevenage, as envisaged in the new scheme, existed ten years ago, we should not have been forced to seek a new life elsewhere. . . . Proposed developments many years ago would have prevented the wholesale expulsion of the younger generation.'

[1] Purdom, *The Building of Satellite Towns*, p. 289. The statement was made in 1948.
[2] *Hertfordshire Express*, 19th October 1946.
[3] Ibid., 18th May and 1st June 1946.

'We workers have had enough of waiting for 'buses and trains to take us to and from our work. . . . There never has been enough factories to find jobs for us in Stevenage. I have had to seek, for the past 32 years, work outside the town. Must our children do the same? We hope not. . . . Beautiful flowers in boxes in the High Street won't get our living, so we ask [the Minister] to get busy with his bulldozers, and turn Stevenage into a lovely Satellite Town, with plenty of industry.'

Of an estimated 1,800 residents employed in Stevenage in March 1948, 672 were industrial workers; some 568 residents, many of whom were industrial workers, worked outside of Stevenage, journeying mainly to Welwyn Garden City, Letchworth, and Hitchin, because no work was available for them in Stevenage. The Board of Trade described Stevenage and Hitchin as 'to a large extent dormitories for Letchworth'.[1] Accordingly, when the Protection Association won the first court decision in February 1947, there was little jubilation at the workmen's Club and Institute. 'Not much chance of any victory celebration here', the club steward told a reporter. 'Most of our members wanted to see Stevenage enlarged and rebuilt.' A month later, when the appellate court reversed the decision, reactions were more cheerful. One aged member said, 'I think the majority of people want the New Town. At present quite fifty per cent of the workers, mechanics and people like that, have to go outside for a job.'[2]

After the Second World War, industrial production continued at a high level, the demand for local labour far exceeded the supply,[3] and overtime work at extra pay was generally available for those who wanted it. Unemployment in Hertfordshire had been far below the national average during the 1920's and 30's,[4] but workers remembered well these years when local factories were on short time and the indignities of charity were widely experienced, and naturally hoped that the increased industry of the New Town would decrease the likelihood of future unemployment. 'Not a bad idea', said a twenty-year-old railway porter when asked his opinion of the New

[1] The estimate of 568 Stevenage residents who left town to work is derived from the Corporation's March 1948 1 : 4 survey of all Stevenage households on the electoral register. The Board of Trade's characterization was made in a regional industrial survey issued by its Cambridge office in October 1949.

[2] *Hertfordshire Pictorial*, 29th March 1947.

[3] Only 162 persons were nominally unemployed in North Herts (3 in Stevenage) in October 1949, whereas employment exchanges listed 1,200 openings (report of Letchworth and District Employment Committee for the area including Letchworth, Hitchin, Arlesey, and Stevenage, *Hertfordshire Pictorial*, 11th December 1949).

[4] The percentage of all insured workers unemployed in England in 1928, 1932, and 1936 was 9·8, 20·6, and 12·0, compared to 3·2, 11·5, and 5·6 respectively for Hertfordshire (M. P. Fogarty, *Prospects of the Industrial Areas of Great Britain* (London, 1945), facing p. 18).

Town in April 1946. 'It will liven it up. They will need a bigger station.' A watchmaker, aged thirty, said:

'I feel everything will be extended to a great extent, and the place can do with it. I've only a small place in a side turning. It's the only place I can get. Same with where I live. We can do with the building extension, and the place livening up. There are only two jewellers here, and any place of any size needs three.'

Two housewives, aged twenty-five and fifty, expressed similar attitudes:

'A good idea. There should be more houses then, and better jobs for the men. Perhaps my husband will be able to get a job then, instead of having to go out of the district to work, as he does now.'

'Well, we don't know much about it. There's a lot of talk. I think it will be a benefit myself. If you've got a family, well, it's a good thing to know there'll be work for them.'[1]

Just how these hopes would be fulfilled no one could say with certainty. The main factor which dampened the ardour of even the strongest local advocates was that the New Town was not designed to provide jobs and houses for residents, but for migrants from London. Ever since the programme's inception, London authorities hounded the Ministry for news of when accommodation in the New Towns would become available for persons on their housing lists. Against the overwhelming needs of London, the Stevenage Council's housing list of 414 families[2] was puny, although presenting a disturbing local problem. The M.P. and other pro-New Town speakers at the Trade Union Conference of October 1946 asked that the first houses built by the Corporation be allotted to persons on the Council's waiting list,[3] but the Ministry was not receptive to the idea.

In 1949, the Corporation offered a few vacant plots to private builders and intimated it might allot a few houses to county school teachers and other key workers, but emphasized that its primary function was to serve the needs of London:

'When houses and flats are ready in considerable numbers it will be necessary to allot them so as best to assist the industrial, commercial and social development of the town. Some will go to those working in already

[1] Unpublished Mass-Observation report entitled *Stevenage* (typescript), 17th April 1946.
[2] As of January 1949. Two-thirds of the persons on the list were residents of Stevenage, and the remainder worked in Stevenage but lived outside. By June 1950 the number of persons on the housing list had risen to 526.
[3] Again at a regular meeting of the Stevenage Trades Council in February 1948, a member expressed the opinion that New Town houses 'should be shared between the old and new residents and not be allowed to cause ill feeling by one party building for the old residents and another for the new. This view met with approval on all sides' (minutes of meeting).

established industry—there are at present many key people working in Stevenage who cannot get proper accommodation in the town. But the main purpose of the New Town is to take industry and population from Greater London. To solve London's problem it is essential that jobs, as well as people, should move out of the area and into the New Town. . . .

'The process of dovetailing jobs and houses will probably . . . be somewhat as follows: an industrial firm will move [from any part of Greater London] to Stevenage bringing some—perhaps a quarter—of its employees, who will be allotted houses. It will recruit the balance of its employees from families coming in from . . . [six] North London [boroughs]. . . . Also from North London will come the additional labour to man the service occupations—transport, retail distribution, etc.—as they expand to keep pace with the needs of the growing population. In general, the subsidized houses will only be let to applicants who have got themselves a job in the New Town. . . .

'The non-subsidized houses, with higher rents and higher standards of space and amenity, will not necessarily all be let on the same principle, because it is important that a fair proportion of people in the higher income groups should be encouraged to live in the town.'[1]

Towards the end of 1950, local people who had put their names on the housing lists of the Development Corporation were being informed that 'for the time being at least, they have no hopes of being housed by the Corporation. . . . It is explained that . . . [the Corporation] would be failing in its duty to rehouse Londoners if it offered people from the Stevenage district any prospect of accommodation in the new town.'[2] The Corporation was thus in the position, in its housing policy, of catering to the middle- and upper-income groups upon whom, locally, the New Town inflicted financial and social injury, and who were its strongest opponents; while unable to serve local workers, the New Town's strong supporters.

(b) City Lights

There had always been persons discontented with Stevenage because of the limitations of small-town life. Opponents said scornfully, 'The only people in Stevenage who want the scheme are those who have been told by the Labour Party that it will mean plenty of work and cheap houses for them, and the youngsters, who want to see more cinema lights and skating rinks and anything else that will give them a cheap good time'.[3] But New Town supporters replied in kind, 'people talk feelingly of the two hundred years' old avenue of trees; I wonder if they include also the Avenue school with its

[1] Stevenage Development Corporation, *The New Town of Stevenage* (1949), pp. 35–6. The six north London boroughs or 'exporting authorities' with which the Stevenage New Town was linked were Hornsey, Wood Green, Tottenham, Edmonton, Enfield, and Hendon.

[2] *Hertfordshire Mercury* 8th, December 1950.

[3] *Hertfordshire Express*, 30th November 1946.

filthy playground. My small son and thousands of other kiddies like him are worth more to me than all the trees in Stevenage. . . .'[1] For the New Town would bring in its wake far more than cinemas (there were already two), skating rinks, and other glittering urban diversions regarded with such apprehension by conservative citizens. It would bring new schools (the two primary schools, built in 1834 and 1910, and the grammar school, dating from 1558, were overcrowded and ill-equipped);[2] a proper water supply (water pollution had been recurrent for many years and in May 1947 the Ministry of Health warned that 'the water supply in this district is liable to contamination at any time'); divert the heavy stream of vehicular traffic which passed through the High Street;[3] a new railway station and electrified service to London (at present, 'service has so deteriorated that passengers are beside themselves with joy when they arrive at work or home only five minutes late instead of twenty-five, thanks to the Late and Never Early Railway');[4] sorely needed civic buildings, improved shopping facilities, and, ultimately, after the New Town was completed, the reconstruction of old Stevenage (whose houses 'are for the most part sm. i, congested in their arrangement, lacking efficient sanitation and badly maintained')[5]—in short, all the general advantages of any large city and all the special material, social, and cultural advantages which a well-designed New Town of 60,000 could afford its inhabitants and a town of 6,000 could not.

In August 1945, before the New Town had aroused serious local attention, a Hitchin resident wrote to the paper:

'The town [i.e., Hitchin] is not overblessed with industrial concerns, mainly because the past and present members of our local Council turned their faces against any development of this kind as being likely to spoil the amenities of the town and destroy its old-world charm. . . . The majority of our boys and girls will have to seek work elsewhere when they come back from the Forces. . . .

'In the town there are hundreds of houses . . . without baths, in which the only facilities for washing dirty bodies is a tub of water heated over a gas-ring. . . .

[1] Letter, *Hertfordshire Express*, 1st June 1946.
[2] In 1949 the County Council added to these a magnificent modern secondary school.
[3] A 1938 traffic census showed 6,992 vehicles, including 467 bicycles, passing through Stevenage in sixteen hours, of which an estimated 80 per cent represented through traffic.
[4] Letters such as this (dated January 1946) from an irate commuter constantly appeared in the local Press.
[5] *Corporation Master Plan* 1949. The section referred to is the oldest part of town, lying east of the central High Street. The report continues, 'The bricks used in Stevenage at the period when this area was built were of poor quality and many have scaled on exposure to weather, settlement cracks are visible in the majority of these houses, and in many cases there is evidence of damp'.

'Would it not be a . . . boon to these future ratepayers of the town if all the land on the other side of the railway, and concealed to the great extent from the town, was set aside as an industrial area, surrounded by streets of small houses suitable for working people—with baths? . . .'[1]

What he said about Hitchin, a town of some 20,000, applied in almost all particulars to Stevenage.

(c) Labour Supporters

As has already been indicated, some Stevenage Conservatives supported the New Town, although they were fewer than Labour supporters. But just as the Protection Association, anxious to rally to its cause the widest possible segment of the community, disclaimed the label Conservative, so advocates of the New Town disclaimed the label Labour. A Labour councillor stated, 'the local Labour Party . . . stood aloof from the controversy and did not take any active part in the [May 1946] referendum'.[2] In March 1947, a Labour candidate for the Council said 'Although we favour the new town, we are not prepared to accept the plan hook, line and sinker. . . . we shall maintain every legitimate Stevenage interest'. His understanding of 'legitimate' differed, however, from that of the opposition. 'If elected we shall work our hardest to see that no hardship falls on owners of private property, but in any movement of social emancipation there is bound to be hardship to a minority.'[3]

Some criticism of the New Town plan was voiced by Labour Party leaders—notably, of demolitions, the Ministry's early failure to take the Council into its confidence, the reluctance to provide houses for local workers, and the intended acquisition of freeholds in the built-up part of town. But criticism was usually disarmed by overall approval of the New Town. Some independent Labour sympathizers supported the New Town and, at the same time, criticized the means the Government adopted to execute it, but local Labour Party leaders usually approved the means because they approved the end, and because the Labour Government had accepted responsibility for both. 'The Government has the last word in this matter', the Labour Council candidate told his town hall audience. 'If the Government says the new town is coming here it has the power to legislate; it has a majority in the House, and you put them there.'[4] It was 'presumptuous', a Labour councillor said at one Council meeting, for a Council representing only 6,000 people—'not much more than an overgrown village'—to advise Ministry experts on the course they should follow. Another Labour councillor stated frankly at the October 1949 Master Plan inquiry that experts could always be found

[1] *Hertfordshire Express,* 18th August 1945.
[2] Letter, *Hertfordshire Express,* 30th November 1946.
[3] *Hertfordshire Pictorial,* 25th March 1947.   [4] Ibid., 25th March 1947.

who disagreed with one another and he and the Trades Council trusted the Corporation and Ministry experts.

There was, therefore, truth in a machinist's remark that many workers supported the New Town 'because it's a Labour Party "do"', although the real division between New Town supporters and opponents was not so much between Labour and Conservatives as between progressives and conservatives, some of whom were inside the ranks of both parties.

D. THE DISINTERESTED

Something should be said about the many people who were neither for nor against the New Town, but merely indifferent to it.

Different individuals inevitably have different interests, as does any one individual over a period of time, which only compelling urgency is likely to upset—and surely history records many instances of persons who slept soundly or made love while panic raged about them. So no special explanation is really required for much of the indifference to the New Town: planning, politics, and the Brave New World interested only a varying portion of the population; the rest were more preoccupied with dogs, beer, gardening, poetry, their digestion, or their neighbour's wife.

To this general explanation, some factors specific to Stevenage may be added.

The crucial fight on the New Town was fought not in local assemblies, ballot boxes, and streets, but in judicial and Ministerial chambers where law and learned argument reigned supreme. There are moralists who draw comfort from the mass democratic process, but at best it is a gross and intermittent process with which, at most times (between elections), the State dispenses. Whatever may have been the nation's verdict in the General Election of July 1945, it was not a verdict on the *Greater London Plan*, the reports of the Reith Committee, the New Towns Act, or the Stevenage Designation Order: these policies had an intricate history of their own, and were formulated and implemented by professional politicians, civil servants, and prominent planners in accordance with *their* terms of reference. It would be an impractical democrat who insisted that a Government abstain from governing while constantly ascertaining the will of the electorate; but apathy is an obvious and rational corollary of the fact that the people's will is not and can not be determined on every important issue. And so Stevenage citizens commented on the New Town, 'People don't seem to have any choice about it'. 'We were not consulted. We are never consulted. It is nothing to do with us. What we do or think makes no difference. Why bother?' Indifference had bred indifference for so many years that many persons felt themselves powerless to alter the course even of events which closely concerned them; and, indeed, if they were not powerless to start with, this thought soon rendered them so. An opposition leader asked a friend what he thought of the New Town.

'He said that it would entirely ruin Stevenage . . . but that he refused to think about it, as it depressed him so; that he lived however in hopes that "something would turn up" to save the place. I asked him if he were doing anything about it; he said not, for . . . he looked to the officials to "get a move on".'[1]

Many persons ignored the New Town because they felt it would have little effect upon their lives or, in any case, their home and livelihood. Workers with secure jobs and homes often fell in this category, as did persons who owned no property, lived in areas unlikely to be disturbed by development, who had recently moved to Stevenage, or were planning to move away.

Ignorance helped generate apathy. Some patient attention to the meaning of signs and symbols was needed before the New Town plan could be understood, which not everyone was willing or able to give. At one Corporation exhibit[2] stocked with New Town maps, models, posters, and diagrams, an observer noted 'a large lady gazing helplessly at the maps showing contour lines, sewerage and water, saying, "This is what the New Town is going to look like. I don't understand it". . . . Another remark was, "I don't know anything about Town and Country Planning. Anyway they'll do it wrong."' Even the interested public could seldom find out as much as it wanted to know about the New Town, especially during the project's early days, when a greengrocer remarked,[3] 'The Stevenage people know very little about it. You'd have thought a few public meetings would be held to enlighten people. But nothing specific has been explained.'

Apathy also resulted from the excess of talk and dearth of action. The more than three years in which planners did nothing but plan made supporters and opponents alike lose heart.

E. SOME QUANTITIES AND COMPLEXITIES

Our discussion has attempted to clarify some factors which contributed to local opposition, support, and indifference to the New Town. Estimates of the numbers of persons involved have, for the most part, been omitted, because their significance is strictly limited: no end of quantitative estimates can be made and (as each is made at a

[1] Letter, *Hertfordshire Express*, 5th January 1946.
[2] Held at Knebworth in June 1949 and attended by hundreds of women, including the Queen.
[3] In April 1946, a month before the Minister's visit.

different time, in a different manner, and under somewhat different circumstances) no two are ever exactly comparable; nor is there reason to suppose that discrete, static quantities can adequately represent the continuous, shifting qualities of a living community. However, if these limitations are clearly understood, such quantitative estimates can serve a useful purpose, aiding both understanding and action.

The referendum of 18th May 1946 permitted electors to vote for one of three alternatives: (1) in favour of the New Town plan as presented by the Ministry, (2) in favour of the plan without demolitions and with compensation to property owners at prevailing market value, (3) against the plan. Of an eligible electorate of 4,810 persons, 2,523 or 52·5 per cent voted: 913 or 36·4 per cent of those voting and 18 per cent of the total electorate approved the first proposition; 282 or 11·2 per cent of those voting and 5·8 per cent of the total electorate approved the second proposition; 1,316 or 52·4 per cent of those voting and 27·3 per cent of the total electorate approved the third proposition; and 12 ballots were voided.

One newspaper interpreted these results as follows:

'Those in favour of either the Ministry's scheme or a modified one . . . total together 24·8 per cent of the electorate, against a figure of 27·3 per cent who are opposed to any change. . . . most of those who are against the scheme would surely have taken the opportunity of expressing their opposition. There was, we should imagine, more incentive to vote among those against the scheme, so that we can take it that almost half of Stevenage don't really mind what happens.'[1]

The assumption that opponents were more likely than supporters to vote seems reasonable, if only because the Protection Association conducted an energetic campaign for proposition (3) while no similar effort was made on behalf of the New Town; and it may be noted that the number of votes, 1,316, for the third proposition was about the same as the maximum membership credited to the Association. It is more problematical if the non-voting 47·5 per cent of the electorate should be counted as entirely indifferent to the New Town. Electoral lists are seldom up to date and, so soon after the war, some eligible persons (London evacuees and workers who had come to Stevenage from other parts of Britain and Ireland) were no longer living in Stevenage. Also 'Among those who did not vote were a large number of Stevenage ex-Servicemen who, although "demobbed", had not taken the precaution of seeing that their names were on the voting lists when these were being prepared'.[2] If we are not mistaken, these groups were probably more sympathetic to the New Town than other local residents. Since the Ministry did not

[1] Editorial, *Hertfordshire Pictorial*, 21st May 1946.
[2] *Hertfordshire Express*, 25th May 1946.

agree to abide by the results of a purely local referendum—indeed, tried to discourage the Council from holding one—it is also conceivable that many persons with decided opinions refrained from voting out of a feeling of futility. Nevertheless, the 52·5 per cent turnout of the electorate for a local poll was fairly normal for a local Government poll—at the March 1946 Council election, for instance, 57·4 per cent of the electorate voted, and, in 1947, 51 per cent.

The Council election of 30th March 1946 affords a far less reliable index of opinion. Although only three Labour councillors were elected as compared to six Independents (out of a field of nine Labour and nine Independent candidates), the existing balance of four Labour to eight Independent councillors was maintained. Independent A, who topped the poll, was a consistent New Town supporter, and Independent E shortly afterwards (in November 1946) changed his attitude from opposition to co-operation. The voting for successful candidates was as follows:

A	1,572	B	1,515
C	1,478	D	1,376
E	1,366	F	1,238
G	1,194	H	1,159
I	1,153		

Councillors B, C, and F were Labour men. Of the nine Independent candidates, four stood as 'Ratepayer Candidates' and most openly invited the support of New Town opponents; only one of this group, H, was elected. Four others, D, E, G, and I, stood as 'Independent Candidates' pledged to support the results of the subsequent referendum; all were elected. The ninth Independent, A, campaigned by himself. But too many extraneous factors (such as the personal popularity of candidates, their experience of public office, the local and national political and economic situation, etc.) entered into the election to permit one to interpret it merely as another referendum on the New Town. Over many decades, of course, Council elections did offer a gauge of the strength of Labour and Independent forces in Stevenage: the former never won a majority on the Council, although individual Labour candidates occasionally topped the poll. Competent partisan and non-partisan informants suggested that the solid bloc of Independent or Conservative voters was larger than the bloc of Labour voters, but neither sufficed to win a local election without support from a substantial group of floating voters who split their vote in accordance with the personalities and circumstances of each election.

Two small and methodologically unsatisfactory opinion surveys may supplement the findings of these polls.

On 10th April 1946 a Mass-Observation investigator asked three questions of fifty-one people (thirty-one men and twenty women) 'picked at random in the streets of Stevenage'.

'To the question "Did you know that Stevenage is going to become a satellite town?" every woman, and all but one of the men replied Yes.

'Asked how they felt about it, 57 per cent said that they thought it would be a good thing for Stevenage. . . .

'Opposition is definitely expressed by only 19% of the random sample, however, so that decidedly pro- and decidedly anti- account for only 76% of the whole. Of the remainder, 10% were indifferent, or didn't know, 8% were indefinite. . . . 6% . . . complained that they had no choice in the matter.

'Last of the three questions was "How do you think it will affect you personally?"

'31% expected, or hoped, it would be advantageously—better housing, sewerage, jobs, amusement, business.

'33% did not expect to be affected much, if at all.

'28% were indefinite or "don't know".

'8% expected disadvantage to result.'[1]

The second inquiry was conducted by a (female) employee of the Development Corporation, early in September 1947. The sample began with sixty-six interviews in every third house on one side of the streets east of the central High Street; 'to make up for the pre-dominance of women in this sample, a further 34 men were inter-viewed in the street'.

'Of the hundred people interviewed, 61 were women and 39 men; 36 were aged 30 and under, 64 were over 30; 54 were manual workers or their wives, 23 were traders or their wives, the remaining 23 being clerical, retired or miscellaneous.

'The interviewer began by saying "There is going to be an Information Centre opened in a few weeks to answer queries about the New Town: could you tell me what are the questions uppermost in your mind?"

'Of the 100 people interviewed, only 28 had definite questions in their minds, the most frequent being "Will people in need of houses, now living in Stevenage, be given houses in the New Town?" About a quarter of the questions were about what would happen to freehold properties, what type of leases would be arranged, etc. . . .

'From these interviews the Interviewer was able to form a rough idea as to whether the person interviewed was pro or anti the New Town, or neutral towards it. Of the 100 people interviewed, 54 were pro, 20 were anti, and 26 neutral. The proportions were somewhat different according to sex, age, occupation. This is shown in the following table:

[1] Unpublished Mass-Observation report, *Stevenage*, 17th April 1946. It is only fair to note that this report was undertaken for internal organizational use and not for publication; had publication been intended, a larger sample would have been secured. As they stand, of course, the percentages are of little significance because of the small number of cases.

| Attitude to New Town | Men | Women | Age | | Occupation | |
			Up to 30	Over 30	Manual	Other
	%	%	%	%	%	%
Pro	54	54	61	50	56[1]	38
Anti	28	15	6	26	9	33
Neutral	18	31	33	24	35[1]	29
	100	100	100	100	100	100

'It will be seen that women are more neutral than men: those under 30 are more pro and less anti than those aged over 30: and those who have manual occupations, or, where wives were interviewed, whose husbands have manual occupations, tend to be more pro and less anti than those in the remaining occupations.

'Of those in favour of the New Town, 26 gave as their reason that trade would be increased and more work brought to the spot. Twelve thought the town needed waking up, 12 that general living conditions would be improved and 10 that education and recreational amenities for the young would benefit. . . .

'Of those against the scheme 10 disliked the idea of change. . . . Five thought it a mistake to bring people out of the slums. . . .

'Of the . . . neutral . . . 10 appeared apathetic and gave their reason as not being personally affected by the scheme. Five had only recently settled in the town and had not yet formed an opinion.'[2]

Not only was this survey initially biased by the fact that the interviewer represented the Corporation (which possibly encouraged favourable replies from some neutral, and neutral replies from some antagonistic persons), but the classification of replies depended to a considerable extent upon the interviewer's subjective judgement.[3]

Nevertheless, it is noteworthy that results of the Corporation's survey—54 per cent pro, 20 per cent anti, and 26 per cent neutral—were very similar to those obtained independently by the impartial Mass-Observation investigator —57 per cent pro, 19 per cent anti, and 24 per cent indifferent or non-committal. Either this must be viewed as a coincidence and both surveys dismissed as unreliable (for which, as has been observed there is warrant, because of the procedures employed and the small

[1] These figures seem wrong: "Pro 67%" and "Neutral 24%" would be more consistent.

[2] *Relations of the Corporation with Stevenage Residents* (mimeographed), Corporation report, 9th October 1947.

[3] Judging from the neighbourhood in which the door-to-door interviews were held, it also appeared that the sample might be weighted disproportionately in the direction of the working class, but the occupational figures belie this inference.

size of the samples); or one may infer that the Council referendum did not accurately represent the prevailing division of opinion in Stevenage. It can be argued that people expressed their opinions to these interviewers more readily than they would go out of their way to record a vote in a formal poll at the Council offices; or, contrariwise, that honest and reliable opinions were less expectable in such personal interviews than on a secret ballot. On the basis of available evidence, it is not fruitful to decide between these viewpoints. The results of these surveys and the referendum reflected unreproducible and (what is worse) unknown conditions at so many vital points that, beyond these points of knowledge, their interpretation can only be speculative.

Clearly, there were in Stevenage sizeable groups favourable, antagonistic, and indifferent to the New Town who could be strengthened or weakened, marshalled or dispersed, by organized efforts and unpredictable events. At every moment the future was (sometimes more, sometimes less) open, and so many individuals inside and outside the community variously contended to close it that no one succeeded in exactly accomplishing his intention. The Protection Association achieved an early victory and the Corporation a later one; both groups pretended to act for a majority of the inhabitants, but neither was prepared to stop acting (or likely to stop pretending) if it did not.

Within particular groups of opponents and supporters, a degree of unity, of course, obtained; but it would simplify and generally falsify the picture to see even a small group as completely united and steadfast in its purpose, for defections and changes of membership constantly occurred. Few signs are more suspicious than the 'unanimous' vote of a large group.

Local farmers were perhaps the most convinced group of opponents, and, in May 1946, a public meeting of two rural parishes within the designated area 'unanimously' resolved that 'The residents of these two parishes are strongly opposed to the proposal to establish a satellite town in so far as any land in these two parishes is concerned'. The same month, the County Executive Committee of the National Farmers' Union 'unanimously' agreed to support Stevenage farmers' opposition, and a meeting of farmers held in the Stevenage town hall decided 'unanimously' to link up with the Residents' Protection Association.[1] Thirty-nine farmers signed an objection entered at the October 1946 inquiry in the name of Stevenage Farmers who 'collectively are the owners and/or occupiers of farms and holdings comprising approximately 5,000 acres out of the total of 6,100 acres included in the [designated] area'.[2] However, a 1946 estimate of the number of holdings within the area was 22

[1] *Hertfordshire Express*, 11th and 25th May 1946.   [2] See note 4, p. 133.

farms and 3 nurseries in their entirety, and parts of 80 other farms,[1] so that 39 represents a good portion, but only a portion, of the total.

Property owners were by no means unanimous in their opposition. Presumably owner-occupiers constituted the core of the opposition, but only 2,220 or 36 per cent of the 6,140 acres within the designated area were occupied by their owners.[2] Ownership of land was concentrated in few hands—5,261 acres (excluding the built-up part of Stevenage) were owned in 1946 by 173 individuals or groups, 3,966 acres or 75 per cent by 13 individuals or groups. Eight of the largest landowners were consulted by the Ministry and some—particularly absentee owners[3]—approved the plan before it was announced. The largest single owner, Gonville and Caius College, Cambridge, which held 1,250 acres, expressed willingness to sell all of its land to the Corporation, and some other owners were sufficiently wealthy and wise not to oppose the New Town for the sake of personal profit (Lord L, as we have noted, was an eminent figure in the town and country planning movement). In response to the 178 invitations to sell which the Ministry sent to property owners in April 1946, 76 replies were received: 12 indicated willingness to sell, 17 refused to sell, and 47 indicated willingness to sell subject to the settlement of various questions (principally, the basis of compensation and alternative accommodation).[4]

As near as we can estimate, in 1946 about 457 or 26 per cent of Stevenage families lived in houses they owned.[5] Owner-occupiers

[1] *Ministry Plan* 1946.

[2] Minister of Town and Country Planning, *Hansard*, 9th December 1946, vol. 431, col. 181 (written answer). Three thousand seven hundred acres were not owner-occupied, and the remaining 240 acres were owned by the local or national Government.

[3] Twenty-three owners living outside the designated area owned 2,496 or 46 per cent of the 5,261 acres. Of these twenty-three, five living in London owned 564 acres, fourteen in Hertfordshire owned 648 acres, and four living elsewhere in Britain owned 1,284.

[4] *Hansard*, 25th June 1946, vol. 424, col. 153 (written answer).

[5] This figure is derived from a 1946 Corporation 'Schedule of Owners and Occupiers in the Built Up Area of Stevenage', which lists 400 owner-occupiers (26 per cent) out of 1,512 houses and flats. The 1948 electoral register lists 218 additional houses and flats (of which a number were Council houses built in the intervening years); the assumption that owner-occupiers constituted 26 per cent of these houses yields a total of 457 for the entire urban district. This seems reasonably close to the mark: a 1949 survey of a national sample of 13,000 persons estimated that 32 per cent of British families owned their homes (J. W. Hobson and H. Henry (compilers), *The Hulton Readership Survey* 1949 (London 1949), p. 40), and the Corporation's 1948 survey of 961 non-Council houses in Stevenage concluded that 31 per cent owned their homes. It is difficult to get reliable and exact information. How, for instance, is one to classify the fairly numerous cases in which only one of a pair of owners lives in a house, a husband occupies a house owned by his wife, or vice versa? Nor can it be assumed that a common surname always indicates that an occupier is related to the owner. In

were concentrated in areas where opposition was strongest—in Fair-view Road, for instance, which became known as 'Objectors' Row', fifty-eight of the ninety-seven houses were (in 1946) owner-occupied. But even here, where all houses were due for demolition, numerous persons (often strongly pro-Labour) spoke out for the New Town. One stated, 'As an owner-occupier in the affected zone it would be hypocritical for me to say that I am overjoyed at the prospect of being moved. After all, one does get attached to a home into which much effort has been put'; but he was prepared to sacrifice his home for the good of the New Town. Another owner-occupier in this road was a member of the Development Corporation. A third (mellowed by beer) was positively gay when he showed us a letter he had just received from the Corporation confirming that his house would be demolished in 1952.

The owner of a house scheduled for demolition in another neigh-bourhood casually remarked, 'They may tear this house down in ten years, but I don't care, so long as they provide us with another house into which to move, as they've promised'. A lady over seventy, mother of an owner-occupier-farmer who stood to lose much by the New Town, cheerfully told a Corporation employee she con-sidered the scheme an excellent one for the rising generation; it was tiresome for her son to lose his property, but no doubt he would get over it.

One informant suggested that 'a lot of people with the opposition really want the New Town—it's a lot of bluff with them'; this was, he felt, particularly true of many traders who publicly opposed the New Town even though they clearly stood to gain during the initial years. It was, of course, likely that some people found it easier to donate than not to donate to the Protection Association, although approving of the New Town. Nor did membership in the Protection Association disqualify a person from humanity—i.e., multiplicity of motive, complexity of emotion, and capacity for change. There was, for instance, the case of the elderly gentleman who admired a Master Plan exhibit. 'But many people are still opposed to the Plan —the Residents' Protection Association, for instance', the Corpora-tion attendant remarked. 'The Residents' Protection Association. . . . Ah, yes,' the gentleman recalled with some difficulty. 'I'm a member.'

The same sort of comments can be made about groups of sup-

our calculation, we considered as an owner-occupier only an occupier whose surname *and* Christian name was the same as that of the owner. If the rule of common surname were adopted, our figure of Stevenage owner-occupiers would rise to 507 or 29 per cent. It is interesting to note that, in August 1949, an informant who was probably the single person best qualified to judge this matter, estimated that roughly 500 or 29 per cent of the 1,700 houses in Steven-age were owner-occupied.

porters and disinterested persons, although we will cite only one illustration.

After seventy-eight delegates at the Trades Council Conference of October 1946 'unanimously' supported the New Town, a townsman who signed himself 'Trade Unionist' suggested, in a letter to the Press, that the delegates spoke, in reality, only for themselves. A delegate replied,

'no one has claimed that the decision reached at the recent conference of Trade Unions was the opinion of every individual member. I would, however, strongly dispute your correspondent's statement—that it represented only the views of the delegates present. I represent a branch of 150 members, and was delegated at a well attended branch meeting which unanimously approved co-operation in the New Town scheme. At a subsequent meeting the delegate's report was adopted unanimously and action taken. If "Trade Unionist" is one of those who never attend branch meetings, nor takes an active part in his organization, he has no cause to complain if decisions are taken with which he may not whole-heartedly agree.'[1]

When a local union passed a resolution, in February 1947, urging the Ministry to proceed with the New Town despite the High Court decision, it took the pains to specify that out of 165 members, 130 signed the resolution, 7 abstained, 23 were absent from the meeting, and 5 were serving in the Armed Forces.

It has been mentioned earlier that some members of the Corporation's staff opposed the New Town (indeed, at least one member of the Corporation and several members of its staff had reportedly belonged to the Residents' Protection Association); many—at one time or another, one suspects, probably all including the Minister—were fed up with it. It distorts the picture equally to see any one individual as determined upon an 'attitude' to the New Town, for attitudes changed with the change of circumstance or mood, although preserving a degree of constancy which characterized each individual.

A well-placed informant said, in January 1949, that the opposition had quieted down; people realized the New Town was not coming so quickly, and some thought it might never come. A few months later, after the Corporation moved to acquire compulsorily a few plots in town, he noted a renewal of bitterness in the old quarters.

By any test in the world that divided people into the categories of 'opponents' and 'supporters', Mrs. G, a plain, hard-working, elderly working-class woman, would have been considered an unequivocal supporter of the New Town. In many hours' talk in front of the living-room fire and over dozens of cups of tea, this became so evident that we generally discussed other subjects, reverting to

[1] *Hertfordshire Express*, 30th November 1946.

the New Town only briefly, upon the occasion of some new development. One day, Mrs. G remarked that she loved the country so much she regretted the New Town would destroy it. Surprised, I asked did she really oppose the New Town. She replied that it might be all right for others, but not for her. I think Mrs. G had been quite sincere before, and that she then expressed a feeling that was no more or less sincere (it was not her fault if her feelings were complex or my perception limited).

A Corporation officer was well pleased with his friendly, even enthusiastic reception by a group of townswomen which he addressed on the New Town and which had a reputation of being neutral on the subject. Mrs. S, e.g., told him what a wonderful opportunity was offered to the rising generation, the scheme should be welcomed with open arms, etc. Mrs. S had been a professed antagonist of the New Town and (behind her back) Mrs. T now grew furious at her and called her a turncoat.

Women are not the only people who adapt their attitudes to their circumstances. Immediately after the High Court quashed the Designation Order, newspaper reporters contacted a local personage to learn his reaction. 'For one impudent moment', he recalled, 'I thought I might say that I considered it iniquitous that a great scheme destined to house and bring happiness to tens of thousands of people should be defeated on a legal technicality. Instead I replied that I had no comment to make.'

An Independent councillor elected on an anti-New Town programme, aroused criticism by subsequently voting for co-operation with the Ministry. He then issued a public statement:

'Up to November 9 [1946] I loyally supported every effort for Stevenage to expand normally, and not to have the New Town thrust upon it. I attended the public inquiry, and came away convinced that the objectors had made out an excellent case. . . . However, in spite of the positive objections, the Minister has sited Stevenage for a new town. . . . the only way we could continue the fight was by further liberal refreshers to counsels of hard cash, and while I had every sympathy with [this policy] . . . it was my firm conviction that we should be throwing good money after bad by further contesting the issue, by way of the High Court. . . . I voted in the best interests of the town, in an effort to avoid further useless expense. . . . Stevenage will gain more by negotiation with the Ministry than by continuing opposition.'[1]

This was a plausible argument, but plausible arguments can be given for many lines of conduct. Why did other Independent councillors not change their attitude at the same time? Why did this councillor change his attitude just then? Adequate answers to such questions would undoubtedly include subjective as well as objective con-

[1] *Hertfordshire Express*, 23rd November 1946.

siderations. And one can go on asking questions until there are no answers.

We cannot, in short, offer a simple, certain, or complete explanation of these interests, attitudes, and events. Society is a puzzle which cannot be completely solved because it is always changing and all the evidence necessary for the solution can never be in hand, being transmuted (not preserved) by recording, and diminishing every minute. Students of society leave one truth as fast as they approach another, and each world they discover is at the cost of worlds forsaken.

Part Three
The New Town Machinery

CHAPTER SIX

The Development Corporation

THE Stevenage Development Corporation, established 5th December 1946 by order of the Minister of Town and Country Planning in pursuance with the provisions of the New Towns Act, consisted of a chairman, deputy chairman, and six members. This public corporation financed by the Treasury had been recommended by the Reith Committee, in preference to a local government authority, a private limited liability company, or a non-profit housing association, as the most desirable type of agency to plan and develop a New Town. The Committee made the following suggestions on the constitution of such a corporation:

'(a) Appointments should be by the Crown, and members should be removable on certificate of the appropriate minister.

'(b) The governing body should consist of six to eight members.

'(c) Members should include persons who, among them, have experience of land development, of economic and social conditions and labour relations, of business and of local government, and appreciation of cultural requirements.

'(d) Some members should be chosen after consultation with the local authorities concerned, it being necessary to secure local contacts and goodwill, but it is essential that no member of the governing body should regard himself or act as a delegate of any other authority or organisation.

'(e) The object should be to gather together a group of people with varying qualifications who will work together as a team. The field of choice should not be restricted to "safe" men with established public reputations; we recommend that the field should be widened to include younger people with drive and imagination and a desire to render public service.

'(f) The term of office should be five years with staggered termination.

Members should be eligible for re-appointment but it should not be automatic.

'(g) The chairman should be of recognised public standing, and able to devote adequate time to the work. He and the other governors should be part-time.

'(h) It is desirable that some of the governors should live in the new town.

'(j) The chairman and other governors should be adequately paid.

'(k) The board should appoint the chief executive who should not be a member of the board.'[1]

These suggestions were generally followed by the Minister, although appointments, for three-year periods, were not staggered.

A. CHAIRMEN AND MEMBERS

In the three years after its formation, the Corporation had four chairmen, a circumstance that did not expedite its work. The first, Mr. ——, M.C., J.P., F.R.I.B.A., M.T.P.I., a prominent architect, resigned in August 1947 'because of the many other calls made on his time'. *The Architect* commented, 'the reason does not carry absolute conviction. Mr. —— is too big a man to throw up such an important position for petty reasons. In planning the New Towns is the architect given enough scope or is he but one of many conflicting voices?'[2] His successor, Sir ——, G.B.E., K.C.B., appointed October 1947, was a civil servant of long experience, principally in the Post Office, in which he had risen to a high position. Astragal observed:

'The appointment is not an informative one for the architects and planners who have wondered in the last few months what is happening at Stevenage. . . . A theory which the appointment naturally suggests is that the Treasury thinks Stevenage a new animal of a potentially disturbing kind and has put it to the Minister that a strong, safe hand on its bridle would be a good thing. . . . But . . . strength and safety are not enough. Stevenage stands for something new.'[3]

It was later said that Sir —— had accepted the post for twelve months only and, if so, he resigned punctually enough in October 1948. The third chairman, the Rev. ——, M.A., LL.B., was active in the local government of a Yorkshire city, where he had directed a large-scale slum-clearance campaign. He showed signs of making a forceful and excellent chairman when, unfortunately, he underwent an operation in May 1949 and died early in August. Mrs. ——, Ph.D.,

[1] *Interim Report of the New Towns Committee*, Cmd. 6759 (London, 1946), pp. 10–11.
[2] Editorial, *The Architect and Building News*, 29th August 1947, p. 164.
[3] *The Architects' Journal*, 18th September 1947, p. 249.

appointed in October 1949 to replace him, had been a former member of the London County Council, the Hertfordshire County Council, the Reith Committee, deputy-chairman of the Stevenage Corporation during its first year, and then chairman of the Peterlee Development Corporation.

Each chairman found his actions largely determined by the requirements of his situation, but managed also to impose his personality upon events. One was so austere he would not have a carpet on the floor of the board room, nor allow the room to be decorated; another redecorated the offices and installed flower boxes in the windows at considerable expense. One once cycled to the Corporation office all the way from London, rode regularly in the same crowded jeeps that took employees to and from the railway station, and was so unassuming that, visiting the Corporation upon one occasion, he was 'received with the deepest suspicion by —— who imagined he might have come to apply for a job as a building labourer'; others used the more private and comfortable cars that were at their disposal, and were more aloof in relations with the staff. 'Each new chairman', said an informant, 'means a new policy.' One chairman did much to improve relations with the Stevenage Council. The administrative ability of another was conceded, but it was asserted that he lacked initiative and enforced Government regulations to the letter, refusing to appoint senior officers to the staff and thus slowing the New Town's progress. 'He may have been a fine man, but you need someone with drive for a post like that', a Stevenage resident remarked. 'He said to me once, "Neither you nor I will ever see this New Town".'

The chairman received £1,500, the deputy chairman £1,000,[1] and ordinary members £400 annually for their part-time services, which required attendance at fortnightly meetings and various auxiliary committees, conferences, and consultations. The salaries afford a, rough index of the relative power and importance of each position. Constitutionally, the members were the final policy-making body (under the Minister and, of course, Parliament) for the New Town, issuing directives to the permanent staff and sanctioning or modifying suggestions which senior officers proposed. Theoretically, members could outvote him on any issue but, in practice, the chairman (and, to a lesser extent, the deputy chairman) exercised a great and often preponderant influence upon Corporation policy. Receiving a larger salary, he could devote more time to Corporation work and, as the Corporation's primary spokesman and most responsible member, had more occasion to do so. It was the chairman who made the vital top-level contacts with Whitehall officials, the Minister, and the

[1] Deputy chairmen appointed after May 1949 received £750 per annum (*Hansard*, 23rd May 1950, vol. 475, col. 1,823).

chairmen of other New Town Corporations, and was the main channel by which they communicated with Corporation members. In particular matters, of course, much of the chairman's power depended upon how his personality, knowledge, experience, intelligence, and generalship compared with that of other members, but his strategic position gave him a decisive overall advantage.

As of 1948–9, the deputy chairman was a leader of the co-operative movement, member of the Labour Party National Council, and director of a private housing society. The six other members were, respectively: the former director of building operations for a chain of department stores; a former member of the staff of the Labour Party responsible for its organization in the Greater London area; the mayor of a London borough; a Conservative member of another London borough council; the author of several books and editor of a journal on town and country planning; and a Labour member of the Stevenage Urban District Council and the Hertfordshire County Council.

Naturally enough, there were cliques and divisions of opinion among members of the Corporation, though informants were reticent on the subject. For example, an important change in the Master Plan was approved by Chairman A with the strong backing of members X and Y; Chairman B subsequently objected to this change, endorsing the original plan and, it was said, X 'was crushed when attempting to throw about his weight'.

Only one member of the original Corporation was a resident of Stevenage, a deficiency severely criticized locally. (The second round of appointments, in January 1950, partly remedied this complaint by putting three residents upon the Corporation.) Independent councillors and leaders of the opposition privately scoffed at the Corporation as an ineffective and inadequately qualified body, but their opinion seemed conditioned as much by their political and social outlook as by the objective merits and demerits of members. An accountant, for instance, criticizing the Minister's appointments, remarked, 'If you were going to pick someone to run the Corporation who would you pick? An accountant with wide business experience. Then a town planner, a builder, and so on. People with business experience, *practical* men. Instead of which they pick ——. What can he know about building a town?' (On the score of business experience, too, the new Corporation pleased local councillors more than did the original body. Four of the new appointments were company directors; the fifth was vice-chairman of the London County Council Housing Committee.)

The dispute about the ideal professional qualifications for town planning was a national one. Frequently (but, fortunately, not always) members of each profession—architects, engineers, administrators,

surveyors, lawyers, sociologists, etc.—could see only the virtues of
their own profession. When the New Towns Bill was before Parliament, *The Architect* editorialized, 'At least three of the proposed
members of each corporation should be architects. . . . the chairman
or deputy chairman should be an architect holding a town-planning
degree. And these conditions governing the constitution of the corporations *should be written into the Act, now.*'[1] William A. Robson,
however, asserted 'There is little doubt that by far the greater part
of an architectural training is of small use in the field of physical
planning, and that it omits much which is essential'.[2] The Institution
of Municipal Engineers said, 'The main structure of the scheme will
. . . be based on engineering considerations and if these are to be
properly applied the planner should have a detailed and practical
knowledge of these matters'.[3] The Association of Municipal Corporations considered it 'essential' that 'whoever is to be in general
charge of planning should be an experienced administrator', while
Nottingham University suggested that 'the university degree course
should be regarded as the soundest basis for the general education
of the planner. . . .'[4] 'This planner-who-is-he business', said *The
Architect* in a more sober moment, 'seems to be basically a struggle
for power. . . . each profession . . . thinks its members are the very
boys to boss the job of planning. But while they argue and hesitate
among themselves, the political lawyers and economists manœuvre
so that, as heretofore, the key positions and the power remains with
themselves to hold or to dispense.'[5]

A major criticism of the membership of the Stevenage Corporation was its political complexion. In 1949, six of the eight members
were Labour, and only two Conservative, supporters, and it was
contended (among local Independents and Conservatives) that
appointments were often political plums. When the new appointments were announced in December 1949, several Independent
councillors charged that one, in particular (that of Mr. R, a company
director who had been defeated as Labour candidate for the Council
in March 1949), was 'political'. ('Shocking', this member commented. 'Do they want one-party government? They didn't object
to Q's [a Conservative] appointment.') Labour councillors pointed
out that R's business qualifications were the equal of other members'.

The problem was not restricted to the Stevenage New Town. At

[1] *The Architect and Building News*, 24th May 1946, p. 119 (italics in original).
[2] In Gilbert and Elizabeth McAllister (eds.), *Homes, Towns and Countryside*
(London, 1945), p. 156.
[3] *Report of the Committee on Qualifications of Planners*, Cmd. 8059 (London,
1950), p. 36.
[4] Ibid., Cmd. 8059 (London, 1950), pp. 37, 38.
[5] Editorial, *The Architect and Building News*, 27th October 1950, p. 450.

Welwyn, it was said that the Corporation was 'predominantly Labour in composition'.[1] Questioned about the political composition of the Harlow Corporation, the Minister stated it 'consists of eminent persons of no political party. I do not know the politics of more than half the members of that corporation. I would guess that they are not the same as mine. But the members are not appointed on political grounds.'[2] And, replying to charges that he had appointed 'three "red-hot" Tories' to the Peterlee Corporation, he said, 'These are not political appointments. The last thing to do is to run this corporation as a political concern. These people are appointed purely on their suitability and on the contribution they can make to the building of the new town.'[3] Corporation chairmen, discussing the question at a meeting in November 1948, agreed with one chairman's statement that he would not object to an executive officer of any political party becoming a member of any Corporation provided a general balance was maintained and provided also that no member regarded himself or herself as being a delegate of their party.[4]

The charge of patronage was unlikely to be admitted by the party in power, or withdrawn by the party out of power. From the viewpoint of Corporation members, the basic trouble was that their status lay somewhere between that of the civil servant and the free citizen, and they sometimes thought it combined the disadvantages of both with the benefits of neither. 'Members of Development Corporations are, in fact, an unhappy race of hybrids. On the one hand they are limited in the exercise of the political activities which are the right of all citizens but Civil Servants . . . on the other hand they do not have the security of tenure enjoyed by Civil Servants proper.'[5] From the viewpoint of the Stevenage Council, the Minister had given its Labour minority representation on the Corporation, but failed to

[1] C. B. Purdom, *The Building of Satellite Towns* (London, 1949), p. 356.
[2] *Hansard*, 27th October 1949, vol. 468, col. 1,658.
[3] *The Times*, 2nd September 1949.
[4] On 23rd May 1950, a Conservative M.P. asked the new Minister of Town and Country Planning, Hugh Dalton, whether it was with his permission that the chairman of the Stevenage Development Corporation had actively engaged in party politics and whether he would issue instructions to prevent chairmen taking such action again in the future. Replying, the Minister agreed with his predecessor's rule that chairmen should be free to speak at political meetings outside the New Towns with which they were associated. 'It would be contrary to practice to impose unreasonable restrictions on persons holding part-time appointments, whatever their political party, to express their political opinions. I do not want to be unduly censorious in this matter. I agree that it should be done within reason and with some discretion, having regard to circumstances, but I am not prepared to muzzle them completely' (*Hansard*, vol. 475, cols. 1,830–31).
[5] Countess Russell, former member of the Harlow Development Corporation, 'New Town Corporations Swaddled in Red Tape', the *Daily Telegraph*, 30th May 1950.

recognize the rights of the Independent majority. Upon two occasions, he declined to accept the Council's recommendation for appointment to the Corporation of a capable Independent councillor who, several non-partisan and even Labour informants agreed, would have been an asset to the Corporation and a force in improving local relations. In defence of this action, local Labour spokesmen argued that the Minister could hardly be expected to appoint an opponent of the New Town; critics observed that there was no better way to turn an erstwhile opponent into a supporter than by giving him the responsibilities of office.

There was no significant difference in policy, according to one informant, between Labour and Conservative members of the Corporation (as of 1949). If a majority of Corporation members were Conservative, he believed it likely that more rigid economies would be introduced, some more expensive refinements of the plan eliminated, and all contracts probably let to private firms. Such a Corporation, in general, would presumably be more sympathetic to the needs and wishes of local property owners.

B. OFFICERS AND STAFF

The Corporation's programme was implemented by a full-time professional, clerical, industrial, and domestic staff totalling 96 at 31st March 1948, 133 at 31st March 1949, and 168 at July 1949. At 31st March 1949 it was composed as follows:

```
Administrative, professional, and technical    ..  55
        General manager    ..      ..      ..    1
        Administrative     ..      ..      ..    4
        Legal      ..      ..      ..      ..    2
        Finance    ..      ..      ..      ..    4
        Social development and public relations  2
        Architectural and planning        ..   16
        Engineering and surveying..        ..   23
        Estates    ..      ..      ..      ..    3
Clerical (including typists and telephonist)   ..  27
Industrial and domestic ..      ..      ..      ..  51
                                                    ___
                    TOTAL    ..      ..  133
```

A Chief Officer was responsible for the work of each department, and it was the General Manager's task to co-ordinate the whole. (The industrial and domestic staff was responsible for the upkeep and servicing of the Corporation offices, grounds, equipment, and canteen—not for building the New Town, which would be contracted out.)

Corporation meetings were customarily attended by Chief Officers or, occasionally, their deputies.[1] In theory, the Corporation made policy which Chief Officers and their assistants executed. When an Officer's work reached a stage where clarification of policy was required, he would usually approach the Corporation in some such form as 'I should be glad of the Corporation's instructions as to whether I should...' or 'Authority is requested to proceed with....' But that stage varied in each instance and, as it was also the Officers' duty to advise Corporation members on matters within their province (each being a full-time specialist in law, architecture, finance, engineering, etc., while the Corporation ranged broadly and briefly over all fields), Officers would inevitably form judgements which they sought to impress upon the Corporation. The line between advice and the formulation of policy was often difficult to draw. In one important case, the Minister backed an Officer whose advice (to delay the acquisition of shops) the Corporation had rejected, and persuaded the Corporation to reverse its policy, reportedly hinting, at the same time, that it would require special circumstances for him to favour the Corporation against an Officer if a difference of opinion arose on a matter within the latter's sphere of competence. But the Minister was a distant and uncertain aide while Officers and Corporations had to live constantly together.

It was not always easy. When the Corporation casually discarded proposals upon which Officers had worked long and ardently, the latter would seldom rejoice. Once, an informant reported, after architects had worked for almost a year on plans for workmen's hostels, 'The new chairman decided that the accommodation provided would be inadequate and anyway the buildings only temporary. So the plans have been scrapped . . . [though] ready to go out to tender.' Small matters might be equally aggravating: there was the case of the letter (communicating a Corporation decision to the Stevenage Council) which an Officer was obliged to draft in consulta-

[1] The following attendance record may be cited for the period from 7th June to 15th November 1949, during which eleven Corporation meetings were held:

Chairman	1
Deputy Chairman	11
Corporation Members A, B ..	11
C	10
D	8
E, F ..	6
General Manager	10
Chief Officers A, B	11
C, D	10
E	9
F, G	8
Deputy Chief Officers A, D, E, G	1

(The chairman's absence was due to illness and a gap between appointments; the poor attendance of member F, to illness.)

tion with a Corporation member and submit to the Corporation for its approval; and of the proposal that another Officer, who had presented a report (afterwards praised by the Minister) which he was quite competent to prepare, should approach a Government figure (unconnected with New Towns) and obtain his advice as to the most suitable person who could be employed to rewrite the report. Such behaviour reflected, on the part of some Corporation members, a lack of respect for certain Officers which was cordially reciprocated and resulted in one or two resignations-cum-dismissals.

We do not, of course, mean to make invidious reference to any individual or to the Corporation as a whole, but only to give some indication of the ruffled complex of human relations and emotions that underlay the apparently smooth surface of events. Nor, in such matters, is it easy—or even possible—to state many 'truths' upon which all observers agree; one can only present a number of changing and often contradictory attitudes and opinions. Thus one Independent councillor called a radio speech on the New Town by the Corporation chairman 'a bed-time story', 'complete nonsense', 'absolute drivel', and said 'the whole scheme is nothing more than a political racket'; whereas a Labour councillor described the same speech as 'quite a good text on practical Christianity, because it painted a picture of how the working-class people should live. . . .' X called Z 'a squirt, who picks everyone else's brains' whereas Y said Z, 'in particular, is a charming person, the sort of man who makes me feel confident and at ease'. E was 'practically paralysed with horror' upon learning of the proposed appointment of G, while F 'expressed great interest and enthusiasm for [G] and a desire to know him better'; and councillors, on grounds they believed reliable, said to the Minister, 'We *know* [G] is not well regarded at the Corporation', only to be told he had received a message of greeting and congratulation to G from Corporation members.

It seemed to one outside observer familiar with Corporation Officers that 'as a team, they get on well enough with one another'. This was not the outstanding impression that some inside observers formed. One had hoped, when he came to the Corporation, that it would work as a team, putting prejudices aside and tackling spiritedly the big job ahead; instead, he found the years at the Corporation an experience in frustration. 'It has been something like playing chess simultaneously on twenty boards, making one move on each board before one is free to make another.'

To the outside world, of course, Officers generally presented a united front; internally, however, there was a continual jockeying for power among them. The distribution of functions among departments was by no means sharp and border areas were often fiercely disputed. The General Manager filled the difficult role of adjudicator. The following comments by an informant, dated at about monthly intervals in 1948–9, illustrate some of the tensions between various Officers:

'[C] arrived. He . . . regards . . . [A's department] with alarm and suspicion. He is anxious to take over [some of A's functions] . . . he and [A] visited the General Manager together to try and sort out their various functions.

'[A] has been fighting to establish his position supported by [F] who has drawn out a definition of his functions for the Staff regulations.

'[A] had a talk with [B] and [E] suggesting it would be an asset if there could be closer collaboration between the Departments. [B] replied that it was difficult to co-operate successfully with anyone so egotistical as [A]. He had taken exception to one or two points in [A's statement] . . . which had been prefaced with "in my opinion".

'[A] had a three-hour conference with [B] and [E] which filled him with deepest gloom. . . . Any hopes of help from [E] were dispelled. He was also appalled by their attitude and criticism of . . . [their staff].

'[A] . . . had a conference on the subject with [B] and [E], neither of whom could supply any reason for suggesting . . . [their policy]. After which [B] sent a secret minute to the Ministry of Health stating that [A] had been highly unsatisfactory.

'The General Manager asked [A]'s advice on the control of [D]'s department which had been claimed both by [B] and [C], and was in favour of [C] taking it over. [A] was definitely not and privately expressed the opinion that if such a thing happened [D] would resign at once.'

Differences in professional outlook between architects and engineers, who made up the Corporation's two largest departments, were aggravated by the fact that the latter could undertake no construction until the former had finished their Master Plan which, for one reason or another (the engineers' explanations were caustic) was endlessly delayed. Gordon Stephenson remarks that 'in the building of new towns architects and engineers will have to work together once more if we are to achieve the unity in design which marks great building in all ages. One of the great tragedies of the nineteenth century is that by the end of the Victorian reign architects and engineers were "enemy brothers".'[1] It is doubtful if this unhappy tradition has been changed at Stevenage. Engineers charged architects with being visionary, impractical, and not facing up to (engineering) realities; any job was inevitably slowed up when an architect came on the scene; perhaps a house erected by engineers might not look so attractive but it would stand for ever, whereas anything built by an architect fell down at once; etc. Architects responded that engineers were interested only in economy and

[1] Gordon Stephenson, 'The Place of the Architect in the Building of a New Town . . .', *Architect and Building News*, 4th June 1948, p. 500.

standardization, lacked vision and were essentially mediocre types devoid of imagination. One informant claimed the typical engineer's personality, clothing, home, and wife were neat, conservative, and conventional, whereas the architect's were sloppy, modern, and unconventional; he reported a delightful discussion with an engineer whose

'attitude towards the architects is quite pathological. He admits that —— is a nice woman, but a bit "balmy" as she has the "same bug which afflicts all architects". You can even tell an architect a mile off by the way he dresses. I countered that some of the engineers' garments were a little eccentric, citing ——'s bright green battle dress and cycling socks, and that at least most clothes worn by architects were clean which could hardly be said of [another engineer]'s enduring trousers. Engineers are the race elect and architects scum. He was quite taken aback when I suggested that the architects—and some other people—might hold the opposite view.'

Efforts to bridge the gap between the groups were not uniformly successful:

'A dinner took place at [a Stevenage pub] . . . organised by [engineer G] when six of the engineers invited six of the architects to "promote closer collaboration". According to [architect H] the whole affair was extremely stilted. [G] made a heavy speech and the atmosphere was far from happy. . . . After the party [H] collected the architects and took them back to his house to drink wine, as he had had enough of bitter.'

Soon after the Corporation appointed a Chief Officer, he would usually ask for assistants to aid in the conduct of his work, and, if this were granted, other requests would generally be forthcoming as soon as they might judiciously be made:

'I wish to draw the attention of the Corporation to the inadequacy of the technical staff in my Department. Detailed planning, research work . . . and other work is now far behind-hand. Any further delay in the appointment of additional staff will have severe repercussions in the near future. It is essential that six appointments . . . should be made at the earliest possible date. . . . At the beginning of next year I shall be asking for further appointments. . . . The acute shortage of staff in my Department has now become a very serious matter. The time for planning and research prior to building is slipping away and very little has been achieved to date.'

Of course, as the work of the Corporation increased, there was need to expand its staff. But there seemed no natural limit to the process, for no matter how many persons were employed a case could always be made for employing others.

The staff increased steadily during the first three years,[1] although

[1] Thereafter a drop was recorded from 168 at July 1949 to 160 at 31st March 1950.

difficulties were experienced finding qualified personnel,[1] due partly to the full-employment situation and the scarcity of housing. (As of October 1949, the Corporation had not built a single New Town house, but had put up 32 temporary houses, bought 6 or 7, and planned to build 24 more for its staff. The country mansion and associated buildings and prefabs which served for office space no longer seemed sufficient, and it was hoped to acquire additional office space in Stevenage.)

There was obvious need to bring the staff up to a level commensurate with the Corporation's varied responsibilities; but that level also fluctuated in accordance with financial and political contingencies. There can be little doubt that sections of the Corporation were sometimes overstaffed, partly because the Corporation wished to be ready to go ahead when conditions—such as a lifting of capital restrictions and the Minister's approval of the Master Plan—permitted. (In January 1951, a well-informed observer stated flatly that the Stevenage Corporation 'is even now hopelessly overstaffed' and New Town Corporations in general 'are grossly overstaffed for the amount of work they have done'.)

Marked differences in the staffs of New Town Corporations suggested differences not only of circumstances, but also of policy and efficiency. The Aycliffe Corporation, for instance, 'decided not to appoint any Principal Officers to our staff until such time as our work warranted such appointments and an adequate return for the amount of salaries expended could be assured'. At the end of the first eight months of operations, its staff consisted of 'One Senior Clerk . . . and two shorthand typists'.[2] Table III indicates the extent of variation in the staffs of Corporations about which, it may be added, they were rather mindful.

It is, of course, difficult to draw a meaningful comparison between the staffs of different corporations from the published information, without taking into account variations in the use of consultants and in projects undertaken. In December 1947, the Minister referred New Town chairmen to the questions which he had recently answered in the House of Commons relating to the staffs of the Stevenage, Harlow, and Hemel Hempstead Corporations, and invited attention to his reply to a supplementary question in which he had given assurance that Corporations had been asked to adjust their staffs to the work which it would be possible for them to do in the near future;

---

[1] This difficulty extended, in 1947, even to some Chief Officers, who feared (partly because of the court action then in process) that the Corporation might soon wind up or substantially reduce its activities, and asked for compensation for loss of office in this eventuality.

[2] New Towns Act, 1946. *Reports of the . . . Development Corporations for the period ending 31st March,* 1948 (London, 1949), p. 14.

he had no desire to seek uniformity for its own sake in a matter of this kind, and a mere comparison of figures might well be misleading; at the same time Corporations should avoid wide divergencies unless good reasons could be given; the House of Commons had already displayed an interest in the matter and further questions could be expected.

TABLE III

DEVELOPMENT CORPORATION STAFFS[1]

New Town	Present Population	Pro-posed Population	Corporation Formed	Size of Staff*		
				3/48	3/49	3/50
Aycliffe	60	10,000	July 1947	3	21	48
Crawley	8,000	50,000	Feb. 1947	23	90	149
Harlow	4,500	60,000	May 1947	51	105	123
Hatfield-Welwyn Garden City†	26,000	61,500	June 1948	—	?	148
Hemel Hempstead	21,000	60,000	March 1947	74	177	175
Peterlee	200	30,000	March 1948	—	48	55
Stevenage	7,000	60,000	Dec. 1946	96	133	160

* Including professional, clerical, industrial, and domestic (a few of whom may be part-time).

† Hatfield and Welwyn Garden City are being planned jointly and the staffs are shared.

In connection with a renewed Government economy campaign, the Prime Minister asked the Minister, in November 1949, to invite New Town chairmen to undertake a review of their staffs—the Prime Minister wanted the reports to present to a Cabinet committee over which he presided. Anticipating this request, the Minister appealed again to Corporation chairmen in the latter part of October. Two or three years ago, he said, it had been hoped that each New Town would be built in a period of ten to fifteen years. On that basis building operations should now be reaching their peak, but in fact none of the New Towns was being built at anything like the speed which had been expected, though he thought that the staffs had been recruited on the basis of the original assumption. Even allowing for the impossibility of making a true comparison of the staffs of different Corporations, owing to the different circumstances in which they were operating, there still remained some very extraordinary discrepancies, and he thought it possible that some members of the

[1] Compiled from *Reports of the . . . Development Corporations* for the periods ending 31st March 1948, 1949, and 1950.

staffs of some Corporations were not fully occupied. Chairmen were urged to investigate the matter and report back in a few weeks. Five days later, the Stevenage Corporation deferred plans for staff expansion, and agreed that 'the present strength of the staff should not be increased unless absolutely essential'.

Replying to a question on 29th July 1949, the Minister had told the House of Commons that the Stevenage Social Development Department 'is responsible for the Corporation's public relations work and for their social research work which in view of the nature, magnitude, and complexity of their task is necessarily continuous and substantial'.[1] Now the Corporation discovered that the functions of this department 'are such that the greater part of them can be devolved on other departments', and decided to close it down.[2] The decision was convenient for several reasons, of which only one may be mentioned: the department was among the smallest in the Corporation. (Of its five members, two were relocated, and three left the Corporation.) At the same time, the Corporation announced that

'no appreciable reduction can be made generally in the existing staff without detriment to the short-term planning and construction programmes. Calculations indicated that at least 10 per cent of the time of the corporation staff was spent in preparing and submitting material for the many forms of control now in operation. It was in this field that there was the greatest scope for administrative economy'[3]

—thus adeptly throwing the ball back to the Minister.

Chairmen and Corporations apparently stood their ground fairly firmly against the Minister[4] on this matter. Instructions went obediently down the line, and reports came back up again solemnly reciting the vital tasks with which each staff member was occupied. This was not the occasion to mention the private letters which M wrote at work or the newspapers N and O read because there was nothing else for them to do, or the widespread demoralization, frustration, and sense of futility among the staff that so much time was spent accomplishing so little. Morale might be low and idleness extensive, but the ritual of signing in mornings and leaving not a minute before (or after) 5 p.m. was observed punctiliously, for labour was paid by time, not output.

The salaries of Chief Officers, ranging (in June 1947) from £1,500 to £2,000, with the General Manager receiving £2,500, were subject to much unfavourable local comment. '[A]'s an idealist', said a housewife who had recently met this Officer (there was a sardonic inflection to her voice). 'They didn't come here because of their

---

[1] *Hansard*, vol. 467, col. 186.   [2] *The Times*, 24th January 1950.   [3] Ibid.
[4] Or perhaps we should say 'with the Minister', since it was not reported at the time that the Ministry undertook a marked reduction of its own staff.

ideals', responded her husband, a businessman opponent of the New Town, 'but because of the £1,500 they're getting.'

A local paper reported:

'THEY WORK FOR FOUR FIGURES

'Four-figure salaries are being paid to chief officers of Stevenage Development Corporation, revealed Mr. Lewis Silkin, Minister of Town and Country Planning, in a written answer in the House of Commons this week. . . .

'——, chairman of the Corporation, receives £1,500 a year; ——, vice-chairman, £1,000.

'The five other members, of whom Mr. ——, a Stevenage Urban District Councillor, is one, receive £400 a year. They are given travelling and subsistence allowances.

'——, general manager of the Corporation, whose house . . . was bought and let to him by the Corporation, is paid between £2,500 and £3,000 a year.

'Other chief officers . . . can have subsistence allowances up to £1/13/6 when away for 24 hours on duty.'[1]

The reference to the councillor was significant, since councillors probably spent as much time on their job as Corporation members, and yet received no pay in keeping with the long tradition of English local government.

Complaints had a noticeable political tinge, coming often from Conservatives who did not criticize the far higher salaries offered to directors of private corporations.[2] But they came also from the Left, as a writer in the *New Statesman and Nation* made plain in comments which, while pointed at nationalized industries, applied with equal force to New Town Corporations:

'I wonder whether the Ministers concerned fully realize the reaction of the average worker in a nationalised industry to the announcements he is constantly reading of new appointments to Regional Boards? Many of these posts are part-time and very lucrative by working-class standards. . . . If the Minister selects a trade unionist or a Labour Councillor there is always bitter jealousy, and if he takes a Conservative business man there

[1] *Letchworth Citizen*, 27th May 1949.

[2] 'Almost every appointment to a top position in nationalised industry has been greeted by the Opposition with a cry of "Jobs for the boys", with the added inference that the fees and salaries for such positions are grossly inflated. . . . Yet the principle upon which these fees and salaries have been based is that, while the nationalised sector of industry remains small, it must be able to compete within reason for talent which might otherwise be attracted to lucrative jobs in private business. . . . Now the public sector of the national economy is at present about one-quarter the size of the private sector. But the total remuneration to members of public Boards is less than £700,000 a year. *The Economist* computes that Directors' emoluments in private industry amount to more than £36 million—about fifty times as much' ('Public and Private Directors', *New Statesman and Nation*, 26th November 1949, p. 604).

is violent political opposition. . . . The fact is that these jobs are the directorates of a new managerial society. . . . responsibility has been borne in the past in numerous local authorities by elected Councillors who never dreamt of demanding salaries. Now control has moved to remote regional headquarters, and the element of unpaid local democracy has entirely disappeared.'[1]

Corporation members' and Officers' salaries were certainly not excessive by prevailing standards for posts with this degree of responsibility and skill. Whether it was desirable or necessary, in building New Towns, to pay members after the style of directors of private corporations; to have so many members; or, indeed, to utilize such a Government-sponsored corporation responsible to no electorate (instead of a local-authority sponsored corporation, which the Reith Committee had also endorsed, or some other agency) is another matter.

The salaries and gradings of the staff, according to Corporation regulations, 'had regard on the one hand to equivalent scales in the Civil Service, and on the other hand to equivalent scales in Local Government service. . . . [and] the rates current in business practice'. Gradings were co-ordinated with other New Town Corporations, and approved by the Ministry. Typical rates were £312 for a shorthand-typist, £350–£800 for various grades of engineer, £140 for a male junior assistant filing clerk, £222 for a filing clerk, and £108–£308 for a female tracer in the engineering department.[2] Chairmen expressed the opinion that such rates were often insufficient to attract personnel from other areas.

C. HIERARCHY AND BUREAUCRACY

For all the idealism of its goal, the Corporation functioned with due regard for the privileges, responsibilities, and niceties of a conventional hierarchical organization. For example, regulations (similar to those in force in local government, the civil service, and private business) provided that

'Staff whose salaries are £1,000 a year or over are entitled to receive and required to give three months' notice to terminate their contracts of employment. . . . In the case of other staff paid monthly, the length of notice is one month. In the case of staff paid weekly, length of notice is one week.'

Two hours' notice 'at normal finishing time on Friday' sufficed for building maintenance staff. Officers with salaries of £750 and over were entitled to twenty-four days' annual leave with pay; the indus-

[1] Critic, *New Statesman and Nation*, 4th June 1949.
[2] These rates were in force at various times from 1947–49.

trial staff to twelve days after twelve months' service; and the canteen staff to six days after forty-eight weeks' service. Employees in receipt of salaries of £750 or more were entitled to claim first-class fares when travelling on Corporation business. Staff members took a Corporation jeep or public bus from nearby towns to and from work each day, but with a few exceptions such as the chairman noted above, Chief Officers and Corporation members drove their own cars (for which they received a special allowance) or were driven in cars provided by the Corporation. 'Much anger was vented on [Officer X]'s head', one employee remarked, 'as the Wolseley continues to deliver him and [Officer Y] from door to door daily and the bus starts from the —— [hotel] where the former is staying.'

At periodic staff meetings, the General Manager reviewed accomplishments and future plans, or another speaker lectured on a topic related to the Corporation's work. A Joint Committee of three Corporation and three staff members was formed to discuss problems of working conditions; when it first met in November 1947, according to an informant,

'[The Corporation chairman] appointed himself chairman. The agenda included housing, travelling, and billeting allowances, transport, and the five-day week. At the beginning of the meeting [the chairman] stated that only the first three points would be dealt with. All arguments raised by the staff were summarily dismissed—no concessions of any kind were made. From the staff point of view the meeting was a failure.'

Luncheon arrangements gave another indication of the relations obtaining between various staff levels. 'In the beginning', said one informant rather bitterly, 'everyone was supposed to eat together and mix democratically; the Corporation said it didn't want a special table to eat at. Then one day they put up separate tables and "reserved" notices appeared.' Corporation members ate the same food as everyone else, plus a bottle of beer (whether or not they paid for it themselves was a subject of speculation). Although seats were not prescribed, employees of each department usually sat together (there was also a visible grouping by age and sex), and Chief Officers ate at the same table with the General Manager in the centre.

The maintenance staff of about eighteen—including carpenters, electricians, messengers, canteen workers, cleaners, plumber, stoker, and night watchman—inherited in February 1947 from the Ministry of Supply, former occupant of the premises, reached a total of forty in March 1948 and sixty in July 1949. Overalls and work clothes, as well as speech and manners, marked them off from the white-collar staff on the few occasions when they mingled together, and the solicitude which some members of each group expressed for the welfare of the other did not bridge the gap between them. 'The division between industrials and non-industrials stinks', one (industrial) informant said flatly. The industrial staff did not eat together with administrative and professional employees; it was not clear if separate quarters had been requested by or imposed upon them. In March 1948, they resigned *en masse* from the Corporation's Sports and Social Club. 'They resented paying 3d. per week for which they considered they received little benefit, and also for tickets for the various social functions where the rest of the staff behaved "snootily"', commented a (non-industrial) employee. 'They also have no representation on the committee. It was suggested that [an industrial] be co-opted but he refused.'

The circuitous channels of bureaucracy helped safeguard the hierarchy of status and power, at the cost of some efficiency. Thus an informant reported that Officer D 'protested because I had asked [a member of D's staff] to put in the new houses on our . . . map. This he had done free hand and the job hadn't taken more than fifteen minutes. However I should have approached him "through the proper channels".' Or, during the summer months, a group of students worked at the Corporation. One day, Officer E,

'wandering round the kitchen after hours, came upon the students using the electric potato peeler. On inquiry he discovered that a request for the use of the same had not been registered through the "proper channels". The students had merely asked the canteen staff who had agreed and there had been an amicable arrangement. [E] delivered an admonitory lecture, and said he could not countenance such irregular behaviour. Potatoes must be peeled by hand for a fortnight when he would reconsider the position.'

Officers were apt to be sensitive about their authority. When some of A's staff consulted with B in the course of their work, A got into a temper about his assistants 'being abducted for secret meetings without his permission'. Miss L was on the verge of giving notice 'as she has received instructions [from Officer E] that she is not to go to the lavatory without permission!' 'The struggle over [M]'s body still continues between [Officer C]'s and [Officer D]'s Department. [C] has issued an ultimatum that [M] must decide which she will join before the end of the month. [D] wishes to shelve this as he hasn't sufficient work to keep her employed; neither, for the matter of that, has [C]. . . .'

Bureaucracy is nothing if not methodical. As the Corporation started completely from scratch, a vast amount of time and labour was devoted to setting up rules and procedures of all sorts—fixing salary scales, filing systems, messenger and mail services, conference schedules, routing internal reports and external correspondence, assigning (and delimiting) functions to each employee, equipping and arranging offices, etc. Up to a certain point, such systematization was obviously vital to efficiency. However, one suspects that that point was often passed, and it then reduced flexibility in meeting new situations, or created unnecessary rigidity in anticipation of needs which had not arisen and might never arise. Thus, in October 1947, an Officer reported:

'The Corporation have no Standing Orders and I should be glad of their instructions as to whether I should draft some for their approval. They need only be simple, nothing so elaborate as the Articles of Association of a Company or Standing Orders of a local authority being necessary. The items to be incorporated might include (1) appointment and constitution of committees and subcommittees and their functions; (2) arrangements for meetings; (3) procedure with respect to tenders and contracts.'

As the Corporation had managed to survive almost a year without Standing Orders, one wonders if an objective need suddenly arose at this juncture, or if the Officer was merely trying to keep himself occupied.

If this is a bad example, a better one is perhaps afforded by the lengthy Specification prepared as a preliminary to a request for sealed bids for a small contract for tree surgery on the Corporation grounds. One firm having previously done an unsatisfactory job on the trees, the Corporation wished to ensure success upon this occasion. Each tree was numbered and the required work meticulously described:

'The works consist of tree surgery in making good where bad lopping has been carried out and will entail cutting back damaged limbs to beyond wounds and bark strippings and dressings. . . . All saw cuts are to be properly made, using sharp tools. Where branch stubs are to be removed, they are to be trimmed back close to the parent limb or trunk so that the profile of the parent growth is maintained. Other cuts are to be made so that rain water cannot collect on the living wood. All cuts are to be chiselled off smooth to allow the Cambium to flow freely. . . .'

According to one of three Council or County representatives (either non-partisan or in favour of the New Town) who visited the Corporation frequently in 1947 and 1948, all three 'came away with the same impression, that the organisation there is huge, wasteful, without drive or direction . . . it is an expensive, inefficient, unstable organisation. . . . Why don't they get something built? . . . And the colossal expensive staff, what on earth do they do, muddling on, a self-sufficient hierarchy?'[1] To be sure, the Corporation was in the doldrums at the time, due to circumstances beyond its control. And later, when conditions improved, no matter how efficiently the Cor-

[1] These remarks were not continuous, but were made by the same person at different dates in 1947 and 1948.

poration operated, the Council, County, Ministry, and other Government departments which had to be consulted or obeyed, imposed interminable delays upon every action. But the Corporation must be held partly responsible for the fact that so little was accomplished during these early years. The long delay in completing the final version of the Master Plan from the preliminary draft which the Ministry staff had prepared even before the Corporation was created, was a notable instance, and there were others.

One illustration of the Corporation's tendency to procrastination is so trifling and innocent that it may be told with some specificity. This is the story of the seal and motto.

An authority states that 'The leading characteristics of a corporation are frequently summed up in the phrase that it has a name, a perpetual succession and a common seal. . . . The requirement of a seal is . . . important in order that there may be some means of authenticating the acts of a corporation.'[1] We cannot trace the earliest date at which members of the Stevenage Corporation considered the question of its seal, but the subject was discussed in April 1947, when the suggestion of another Corporation that a common symbol be included in the seals of all New Town Corporations was rejected and the chairman and deputy chairman were delegated to obtain the views of a local historian and the chairman of the Urban District Council on the subject. The (Corporation) chairman's suggestion for a coat of arms was approved in July 1947, and the following month, it was 'Agreed to apply to the College of Arms for a grant of Coat of Arms and to pay £160 therefore'.

The matter of the motto remaining outstanding, in August 1948 an Officer presented for the Corporation's consideration nineteen suggestions—seven in Latin and twelve in English—including 'Harmony', 'Harmony in All Things', 'In All Things—Harmony', and 'After Me Cometh a Builder'. Agreement could be reached on none. March 1949 the Officer volunteered that 'the Corporation might care to adopt his family motto', but this was respectfully declined and a decision again deferred.

In June, the coat of arms, minus motto, was publicly unveiled at a county rally attended by the Queen. 'It is becoming a matter of urgency to select a motto', the Officer observed, urging the Corporation to choose 'Firm and Foremost', 'At Unity in Itself', 'Quicquid Agunt Homines', or 'Ordinum Concordia'. At the same time, a note was sent to the chairman, absent because of illness, asking for his preference. He replied that he did not much like any of them and suggested 'Look to Thine End', a translation of 'Prospice Finem'. When it was suggested to the chairman that this

[1] Sir William E. Hart and William O. Hart, *An Introduction to the Law of Local Government and Administration* (London, 1938), p. 273.

motto 'might give rise to undesirable comment', he wrote back proposing 'Look to Thy Purpose' or 'Consider Thy Purpose'. At the meeting of July 1949, after entertaining various alternatives, the Corporation finally adopted the latter motto.

Such episodes, together with the overriding fact that the Corporation was unable to build one permanent house in over three years' activity, struck the observer's eye and contributed to the impression (certainly shared by many of the Corporation's staff) of inefficiency and waste. The Corporation's officers and staff were, for the most part, extremely competent professionally, and their work was undoubtedly of a high standard. However, in the period under review, it consisted exclusively of plans and surveys—forebodings, not accomplishments.

We do not wish to leave the impression that the Corporation was racked by internal dissension and so clogged with petty bureaucratic details as to be incapable of forceful, constructive action. Much of what we have described in this chapter would no doubt be true of many formative private or governmental organizations in Britain and elsewhere. The poor showing of New Town Corporations was due primarily not to mismanagement, but to the chronic shortage of capital (especially in dollars), labour, and materials from which the entire nation suffered at the time, and the lack of adequate Government priority (which will be discussed in a subsequent chapter). Finally, there were causes peculiar to Stevenage: the court action, the change in the chief architect and the frequent change of chairmen, the special problem of sewerage (see Appendix A), and the fact that—unlike the situation in some other New Towns—there was almost no land available locally with main services already installed upon which houses could be erected even before the Master Plan was approved. One sympathetic but independent informant summed the matter up as follows:

'Generally Stevenage has been too slow in getting off the mark. The root causes are I think (1) frequent changes of chairmen, (2) failure to appoint a General Manager until too late, (3) perfectionism—partly caused, no doubt, by the fact that Stevenage was the Ministry's first baby and much publicised—hence fussiness all round.

'In the early days with no General Manager the Corporation members waffled around. Staff appointments were made without co-ordination or proper salary scales and this took a lot of sorting out. The Corporation also got into trouble over the —— contract and, with a change of chairman, ran into the period of economic shut down. At the same time there was all the trouble about whose plan it was to be, and they got lost in planning (again a legacy of the Ministry interest) instead of finding some way of getting on with the job of building.'

Plans might be good enough in their way, but only houses could repay the national investment and the hopes of so many persons in the New Town. Fortunately, after so long a period of frustration and disappointment, the construction of substantial numbers of houses and flats was finally under way in 1950 and 1951, and the Corporation appeared to be making real progress towards its goal.

CHAPTER SEVEN

Council-Planner Relations

A. THE COUNCIL AND THE CORPORATION

THE Stevenage Council was a typical small local authority—the 'best people' thought little of it, but its members were generally proud of their voluntary work. Under the twelve councillors were the clerk and surveyor (who received from one-quarter to one-half the salary of Chief Officers on the Development Corporation) and, in May 1949, a staff of thirteen office employees plus about twenty-five labourers (engaged on the repair and upkeep of Council houses, the collection of refuse, the maintenance of the water works, roads, playing fields, and sewers).

The Council and its staff was probably no less or more efficient than other councils its size, but it had a good post-war housing record: 188 new permanent houses completed by 31st December 1950. Naturally, councillors compared this record and the comparatively small cost at which it was achieved with the mountainous Corporation's mousely production of twenty-eight houses at the same date. The Corporation, remarked one councillor in January 1950, 'have got some first-class technical men, but they haven't been able to do anything. Here they've spent two million pounds [the Corporation's total capital expenditure at 31st March 1950 was actually £457,061] and have nothing to show for it. Well, they say that the Treasury won't give them the money. I told [the Minister] that if he gave us four good engineers and a few second-string men, we'd put up all the houses he wanted.'

(a) 'Consultation'

The Council's legal rights under the New Towns Act were rather ambiguous. The Minister could not legally undertake certain actions such as issuing a New Town designation order, appointing Corporation members, or approving Corporation development plans, until 'after consultation with the local authority within whose district the land is situated, and with any other local authority who appear to him to be concerned'. But after the Town and Country Planning Act, 1947, the County and not the Stevenage Council became the local planning authority. It remained for the Minister to determine if the Stevenage Council was 'concerned' in a particular instance. Thus he did not feel obliged to consult the Council before making his second series of appointments to the Corporation in January 1950.

The Corporation's legal obligation to consult the Council derived less from the New Towns Act than from the fact that, under other statutes, the local government authority exercised many functions vital to the success of the New Town. But, within the restrictions of the Act, the Corporation had the privilege and responsibility of formulating and executing its own policy in such a manner as it might choose, and often enough it chose to act on its own in matters which (councillors felt) were also the Council's concern. For example, despite the precedent of April 1946 when the Ministry had stirred up violent opposition by failing to advise the Council of the dispatch to owners of invitations to treat for the sale of their property, the Corporation acted in the same manner three years later when, without previously notifying the Council of its intentions, it moved to acquire compulsorily a few plots of land in Stevenage. The Council 'received no information concerning the Corporation's proposal from the Corporation', it protested to the Ministry, 'and . . . they have informed the Corporation that they are of the opinion that a matter such as this . . . is one about which they should have been consulted before an Order and before serving notices upon individuals'.

In any case, as the final decision always lay with the Minister, 'consultation' with the Council could be a meaningless formality. It was patently that, in the Council's opinion, during most of the first three years. The Minister 'pays no attention to anything we say— he just goes through the motions required by law', an Independent councillor commented in December 1949, and this was also the substance of the Council's complaints against the Corporation. It took two to co-operate, the Council chairman told the Corporation. 'Don't let this consultation business be humbug, let it be real. . . . We are either in this scheme or we are not.'[1]

Corporation members and officers entertained councillors most cordially at various times (once, on 29th October 1947, when relations were anything but happy, councillors were received at the Corporation offices with sherry, roast chicken dinner, coffee, conversation, an inspection of maps, and short speeches by the chairmen of

[1] *Letchworth Citizen*, 3rd October 1947.

both bodies; Corporation officers held a farewell dinner for the Council clerk before he left Stevenage; etc.), but politeness and even sincere friendliness could not substitute for material concessions. 'Our relations with the New Town Development Corporation remain cordial', commented the Council chairman in April 1951. 'I wish at times they were a little more business-like than cordial.'[1]

The Council wanted to have some *say* in building the New Town; the Corporation believed that it was entitled only to express its opinion. The difference in outlook was exemplified in the Corporation chairman's offer, in April 1949, to meet periodically with the Council 'and explain in detail what the Corporation is doing and is planning'. These were the precise words with which the Corporation communicated the proposal to the Council. The minutes of the Council's Town Planning Committee (which considered the proposal), however, read, 'The chairman of the Corporation had offered to meet the Council or members of this Committee to *discuss* matters concerning the New Town. . . .' In a further communication three months later, the Corporation was obliged to specify that 'the Chairman's intention when he is able to take part in the proposed meetings is not to use them as an opportunity for asking the Council's consent to the Corporation's proposals, but only to inform the Council of the nature and extent of the Corporation's activities, present and prospective'.

Upon completion of the New Town, however, the Corporation was to hand over its functions to the Council (which, to be sure, would be in many ways a different and more important body then, representing ten times as many people). As the local government authority for most of the designated area, the Council was responsible for a housing programme of its own; for valuing,[2] levying, and collecting rates upon most of the property which the Corporation would build as well as that already present in Stevenage; for water, sewerage, refuse, and sanitation services, street lighting, local roads, public baths, certain town planning duties (delegated by the County Council after 1947), allotments, etc. Since the Corporation was vitally interested in all, and had authority in many, of these matters, a constant problem of overlapping powers was posed. Responsibility for most services throughout the designated area could legally rest with either Council or Corporation, provided both agreed upon the terms. When they could not agree, the final decision usually lay with the appropriate Minister (mainly the Ministers of Health and Town and Country Planning) or, sometimes, with Parliament itself, to

---

[1] *Hertfordshire Express*, 5th May 1951.
[2] After 15th February 1950, the Local Government Act, 1948, transferred to the Inland Revenue Department the Urban District Council's power to value property.

which appeal had to be taken. Such appeals involved time-consuming and sometimes expensive administrative and legal procedures, which it was in the interests of both parties to obviate, wherever possible, by amicable agreement.

It was difficult to achieve voluntary agreement during the first few years because of the fundamental hostility and distrust between the two bodies. Even after the House of Lords upheld the New Town Designation Order in July 1947, the Council's Independent majority wavered between co-operating with and opposing the Corporation. (They had wavered all along, first approving the New Town, then opposing it after the April 1946 Council election and May referendum, and, half a year later, adopting a favourable resolution on the chairman's casting vote.) In October 1947, an Independent councillor's motion that the New Town should be stopped (ostensibly because of capital restrictions)—'The continuation of this scheme is a travesty of justice and equity which has never been equalled'—was only defeated by five votes (three Labour and two Independents) to five (all Independents), because the new (Independent) chairman abstained from voting. 'The Council put a spoke in anything they can just for the cussedness of it', remarked a Corporation informant privately in November 1948, and his views undoubtedly represented the views of many Corporation officers and members.

From the viewpoint of Independent councillors, however, the shoe was on the other foot, and the Corporation, having won its court victory and confident of backing from the Ministry, consulted the Council only to the minimum extent required by law and good form, but was determined to have its own way in the end. Again and again the Council indicated a willingness to co-operate, but its overtures and recommendations were spurned. This was evidently the case in regard to the Master Plan:

'[In December 1947, the Council] . . . advised the Corporation of certain amendments that they considered desirable to the Ministry's plan, and expressed the wish that those proposed amendments should be made public. The Corporation . . . requested the Council to refrain from taking this step, stating that they themselves had various amendments to the plan . . . . [and that], by mutual co-operation, it might be possible to produce a plan which would receive the full support of both parties. The Council readily agreed to this very sensible suggestion. The first meeting to discuss the plan was held on February the 27th, 1948. The Corporation explained on that occasion that they had held the meeting at the request of the Council, but that they were not ready to consider the Council's proposals. . . . It was only after a number of requests by the Council that a second meeting was held on August 9th, 1948. You will appreciate the astonishment of the members of my Council who were present on that occasion when they were confronted with a new Master Plan, not for the purpose of consultation but presumably only as a matter of courtesy to the Council. . . . The Chairman of the Corporation made it quite clear on that occasion in his opening remarks that the Council's proposed amendments to the Ministry's plan had been carefully considered and had been incorporated where possible; and that the plan laid before the meeting was deemed to be final and that no further amendments would be considered. . . . These two meetings . . . were the extent of the co-operation which my Council were able to obtain on the preparation of the Master Plan.'[1]

When the Council surveyor first submitted his proposed amendments to the Ministry New Town plan at an evening meeting of the Council on 11th December 1946, an informant reported, 'His proposals were received without enthusiasm, almost without interest. [Councillor X] criticised them but declined to put any others forward. In the end when a vote was taken there were four for the amendments, [X] against, and [three councillors] abstained cynically.' Thus were adopted the Master Plan proposals which the Council championed determinedly (and futilely) for more than three succeeding years! We must infer that the proposals gradually assumed an importance they did not originally possess, becoming symbolic of the Council's prestige, which the Corporation Ministry and the Corporation did not regard too tenderly.

This was substantially how one informant explained the Council's stand at the Master Plan inquiry of October 1949. He said that what councillors really wanted was something to satisfy their egos. No serious proposal they had put forward had yet affected any major New Town policy. True, the Council had got favourable terms on the transfer of the water undertaking and the building of Sish Lane [linking the Great North Road and the first New Town development area. The Council agreed to widen and reconstruct it, upon receipt of a financial contribution from the Corporation] but it felt that the money did not come out of the Corporation's pocket anyway. If the Council got another member on the Corporation, the informant suggested, or if the Master Plan were changed as the Council had proposed at the inquiry, this would go much further towards gratifying councillors' wishes and winning their co-operation.

[1] Statement by the Urban District Council clerk at the Master Plan inquiry, 18th October 1949. The essential points of this version were corroborated by independent Council and Corporation sources. In a letter to the Council preceding the February 1948 meeting, the Corporation stated it 'would welcome discussion with the Council on this basis and within this framework' (i.e., within the limitations of the Master Plan as set forth by the Corporation). The Corporation's report to the Minister for the period 1st July–15th October 1948 noted that discussions on the Master Plan 'have now terminated and, unfortunately, in spite of modifications introduced to meet the Council's wishes, it has proved impossible to carry them with us. Their outstanding criticisms appear to us to be neither valid nor substantial.'

(b) Co-operation

The transference of the Council's water undertaking to the Corporation was quite a different story from that of the Master Plan. At the conference of Council and Corporation representatives held on 7th December 1948 to discuss the terms of this transfer, Councillor A was (according to a Council informant) 'severe and critical', concluding harshly, 'Well, what compensation do you offer us?' The Corporation's generous proposal 'dissolved [A]'s opposition and left us with little to say. . . . The general feeling when the Corporation people had gone was that it had been a business-like meeting and that it was a pity there had not been co-operation of this nature before.' Soon the Press reported:

'Full agreement has been reached between Stevenage Development Corporation and Stevenage Urban District Council as to the terms on which the Corporation will take over the Stevenage Waterworks. If they are approved by the Ministry of Town and Country Planning and the Treasury, the Urban District Council will give their consent and support to the necessary Order by the Minister of Health.'[1]

Of course, the outcome of negotiations depended upon how far each party was willing to compromise to achieve it. As the Corporation moved out of the doldrums of inactivity it became more anxious to conciliate the Council, while the Council, recognizing that the Corporation was there to stay, adopted a more conciliatory attitude.

With all due allowance for a tendency to prettify the picture, Press accounts during the first half of 1950 indicated considerable improvement in Corporation-Council relations. At a February meeting with the Council, 'The Corporation was particularly anxious to consult the Council as to where and how accommodation could best be temporarily provided for contractor's labour. After a very full and cordial discussion there was general agreement in principle between the Corporation and the Council.'[2] The following month, 'The Corporation . . . agreed to the majority of the Council's observations on the plans for the Monks Wood South Housing Estate' and the Council, 'Expressing appreciation of this', commended the remainder of another Corporation housing layout, and relaxed a provision of its building by-laws to enable the Corporation to proceed without delay on the first 259 houses of the New Town.[3] Although only a few months previously, when purchasing compulsorily sites for thirty-six houses in the built-up part of Stevenage, the Corporation had argued that there was no distinction in the designated area between the old town and the new—which may have been a true

[1] *Hertfordshire Express*, 22nd January 1949.   [2] Ibid., 25th February 1950.
[3] *Hertfordshire Mercury*, 31st March 1950, and *Hertfordshire Express*, 1st and 29th April 1950.

interpretation of the New Towns Act, but not one calculated to appease the Council—the Corporation now proposed that plans for the redevelopment of old Stevenage be prepared by the Council, and the Council surveyor drew up a tentative plan for the first redevelopment area.

Formerly there had been no regular contact between Corporation and Council, although joint meetings had been held from time to time. (The Corporation chairman's April 1949 offer to meet informally with the Council every three months was not implemented because of his illness and death.) Now monthly meetings took place and three joint sub-committees, equally representative of the Council and Corporation, were set up (May–June 1950) to consider problems in connection with the redevelopment of old Stevenage, housing, and refuse tips.

1. *The Role of the Chairmen*

The chairmen of Corporation and Council played an important part in determining the nature of relations between the bodies. A Corporation informant declared that one Corporation chairman 'rode them [the Council] a bit hard' and the Council had naturally responded in kind. According to an Independent councillor, the third Corporation chairman, the Reverend X, 'was the only good chairman they had.[1] He was a real negotiator . . . he got something settled because he was prepared to *give* something.' Another Independent councillor said:

'[X] was a good man. Why, this water order was being haggled over endlessly, and I said to him finally, let's meet and get this thing settled, and he said, fine, can you meet me at King's Cross, and sure enough, I met his train from Leeds, and we went over to the tea room at the station, and in ten minutes over a cup of tea the whole thing was settled; he said, you'll have a letter on Wednesday confirming the matter, and on Wednesday there was the letter.'

Upon this chairman's death, the Council wrote to the Corporation, 'Your Chairman had always shown concern to meet the Council's point of view and he had always been at pains to deal expeditiously with the matters which arose between the Council and the Corporation; his death is a great loss both to the Council and the Corporation'.

Although her appointment had been violently opposed by the Council, one of the first actions of the succeeding chairman was to meet the Council chairman and discuss ways and means of improving relations. An Independent councillor noted, in January

[1] This statement was made 7th December 1949, when the fourth chairman had only just been appointed.

1950, that the new Corporation chairman 'has been more than co-operative the past two months—she has been going out of her way to be co-operative, I'll say that for her'. A Corporation informant reported that the chairman experienced difficulty winning over some members of the Corporation to her views on co-operation with the Council, but a big improvement was soon noticeable; at one meeting with the Corporation, councillors even argued among themselves—a healthy sign of 'quarrelling within the family'.

It was the opinion of well-placed observers that the Council chairman exerted a similar influence upon the Council's attitude towards the Corporation. Mr. ——, M.B.E., J.P., London accountant, Independent councillor since 1946 and Council chairman since 1947, had never been a die-hard opponent of the New Town. Although elected on the Independent (but not the Ratepayer) opposition ticket in the spring 1946, in February 1947 he pledged to co-operate with the Corporation and make the best of the venture if the High Court ruled the Designation Order valid.[1] While other Independent councillors had minds of their own and could not be led anywhere like sheep, they respected their chairman's ability and integrity, and looked to him for leadership (the post was elective annually, by majority vote of councillors, so the very fact of re-election for four successive years, 1947–50, was a sign of the confidence in which he was held). From 1946 onwards, the twelve councillors might be divided into three groups: two to four Labour councillors (plus perhaps one Independent) were whole-hearted supporters, and a similar group of Independent councillors unbending opponents, of the New Town; a middle group of moderate Independents was more inclined to examine each issue on its merits. The latter group, and Independents who had no strong political convictions, limited Council experience, little knowledge of the legal, financial, and other technical considerations required to form an intelligent judgement on many issues, or who, for various reasons, had mixed feelings about the New Town, were most apt to follow the chairman's leadership. At the May 1950 Council meeting, one Independent councillor said to the chairman, 'I think we all realise that the happy relations we enjoy with the Development Corporation are due to your efforts, and by that I do not wish to take any of the credit away from . . . the chairman of the Development Corporation, for what she has done in this direction'.[2]

---

[1] When he made this pledge at the first meeting between the Council and the newly formed Corporation in London, 5th February 1947, the High Court hearing was expected the following week. He spoke then as a leader of the Independent councillors, being elected chairman that spring upon retirement of the former (Labour) chairman who held office for one year.

[2] *Hertfordshire Express*, 27th May 1950.

2. *Financial Factors*

Aside from the personal and political factors which have been mentioned, the tenor of Corporation-Council relations was determined principally by financial considerations. First, foremost, and always the Stevenage and County Councils sought to ensure that, both in the early stages of development when heavy capital investment was required in anticipation of demand and the final period when the Corporation would transfer debits as well as credits to the Councils, the income the New Town yielded would balance the increased expenses it entailed without throwing a heavy burden upon local rates. The Corporation was more interested in building a fine New Town than in the financial worries which it might bequeath to the Councils, although it recognized these worries and tried, if possible, to alleviate them. The limits of the possible were set by its own New Town policy and the financial restrictions which Ministry and Treasury placed upon its action. And, as has been noted (see pp. 159–60), up to 1950 the Ministry showed no eagerness to guarantee local Councils against the financial risks which a New Town brought. These risks were summarized as follows by one informant:

'(1) servicing capital expenditure incurred in advance of the increased rateable value that development will bring (i.e., "bridging the gap");

'(2) increase in maintenance costs during the period of development (also a gap-bridging problem);

'(3) the winding up problem (remember not only services but also assets such as houses, shops and factories go to the "appropriate local authorities"). This breaks down into worries about

'(i) whether the council's capital expenditure on services will leave a loan debt greater than it can service;

'(ii) whether maintenance costs will be too high when the planners have done with their "garden commons", etc;

'(iii) on what terms will the assets (houses, etc.) be transferred—cost or then value?

'Experience in Middlesex and Surrey between the wars showed there need be no worry about (3) (i) or (ii). But new towns are being developed at a time of very high costs and at Stevenage there is the special problem of the very expensive Rye Meads sewerage scheme which accounts for a lot in the County Council's attitude.'

To this general statement we need only add an account of some of the specific financial issues which concerned the Stevenage Corporation and the District and County Councils in the period under review.

(*a*) Two major issues involved the local water and sewage works, both of which had to be expanded to cope with the increased population.

The water works negotiations have already been mentioned; they

THE NEW TOWN MACHINERY

were successfully concluded and the works were transferred from
the Stevenage Council to the Corporation in the spring of 1950.
The Corporation agreed not to exceed the prevailing water charge
of 2s. in the pound of rateable value for the first five years after the
transfer; the following five years a rise up to 2s. 6d. was permitted;
and the consent of the Minister would have to be obtained before
the charge could go above 3s. Although the Council expressed
satisfaction with these terms, the Residents' Protection Association
protested at the future burden upon the rates and asked that the
period of the rate-freeze be extended from five to ten years.

Two separate projects were entailed in the expansion of the sewage
system—a short-term expansion of the town's existing works to its
maximum capacity able to cope with a population of 18,000 which
(the Corporation estimated in 1949) would satisfy the New Town's
needs until 1954; and a new regional works not only for the Stevenage New Town population of 60,000 but also for the 60,000 population of Harlow New Town, the New Towns of Welwyn Garden
City and Hatfield, and other expanded towns in the middle reaches
of the River Lee.

After lengthy negotiations, agreement was reached on the Corporation's financial contribution to the cost of extending the
Council's sewage works and maintaining it until the regional works
(at Rye Meads, Ware, Hertfordshire) was ready. Responsibility
remained vested with the Council, which commenced work on the
expansion of its works in 1950.

The regional sewage scheme presented far greater expenses and
problems—it was even uncertain if New Town Corporations had
sufficient powers to undertake so broad a project. In January 1949,
the County Council declined to sponsor suitable legislation (under
which it would have taken over the sewage powers of local authorities in the area, and delegated them to a committee upon which
representatives of New Towns and participating local authorities
would sit) unless the Ministry promised to provide a sum of not less
than £1,000,000 which the County Council estimated as the deficit
the scheme would incur beyond a reasonable proportionate contribution from the rates by local district councils. In June, the Harlow
and Stevenage Corporations thereupon received permission from
the Ministry, with the consent of the Ministry of Health, to proceed
on their own authority. In November 1949, the County Council
recommended that the entire £3,500,000 scheme be dropped and the
population of Stevenage New Town restricted to 18,000:

'In the first place, it was generally recognised that to transport sewage
effluent from Stevenage through miles of trunk sewers to a disposal works
at Rye Meads would be uneconomic. . . .

'Secondly, the majority of the authorities through whose areas the trunk sewers were to be laid already had efficient sewage disposal works, sufficient for their present needs and capable of dealing or being readily adapted to deal with their requirements, including anticipated increases of population for a considerable number of years. It was unlikely, therefore, that these authorities would willingly participate in such a scheme unless they were given an undertaking that the costs of their participation would be no greater than the expenses to which they would be put in running, and where necessary adapting, their existing sewage disposal works. This guarantee, of course, could not be given, and probably the only manner in which they could be persuaded to participate would be for the County Council to make up the difference by way of grant.

'Thirdly, the New Towns' Corporations are eventually to hand over to local authorities and the New Towns will then become part of the normal pattern of local government. It may well be that the financial burden that would be placed upon these towns to support this scheme would be more than they could reasonably be expected to shoulder. . . .

'The whole situation has been affected by two recent events:

'(1) Recognition of the financial position of the country and the call for every economy in public expenditure. . . .

'(2) The beliefs expressed by the Hatfield and Welwyn Garden City Development Corporations that if they were allowed to pump their sewage back into the Colne Valley Sewerage Board's system instead of being included in the Middle Lee Scheme it would result in a saving of something in the region of £500,000 capital expenditure and an annual saving of about £18,000.

'There can be no question that a very considerable saving in capital expenditure could be made if it were decided that Stevenage . . . should be confined to a maximum population of 18,000. . . . [This would] in no way hinder the sewage disposal scheme for the Harlow New Town. . . .

'It is difficult at this stage to estimate the amount of saving that would thereby be effected, but at a most conservative estimate it could not be less than £2,000,000.'[1]

However, in December 1949, the Minister of Town and Country Planning rejected this recommendation,[2] and in April 1951 the Minister of Local Government and Planning approved the Stevenage Corporation's proposal to construct its section of the regional sewage scheme.[3] The finances remained to be settled.

The Ministry and the Stevenage Corporation were seriously concerned about the expense entailed, and attempted to reduce it by investigating new and more economical methods for the disposal of

[1] 'Future of New Town of Stevenage', Report of the Hertfordshire Plannnig Committee, 4th November 1949.

[2] It took the Minister one word to answer Hertford M.P. Derek Walker-Smith's inquiry if he would limit the population of Stevenage New Town to 18,000 'in view of the heavy expenditure involved in sewage works for any larger population'. 'No' (Hansard, 7th December 1949, vol. 470, col. 158, written answer).

[3] Hertfordshire Mercury, 4th May 1951.

sewage effluent (as of 1950, it was uncertain if these would prove feasible). However, their primary allegiance was to the New Town programme, not economy, and their conviction that the Middle Lee sewage scheme was justified was reinforced by long-range regional considerations (detailed in Appendix A). The Lee had long served the mutually embarrassing functions of disposing of sewage effluent from its drainage area and supplying drinking water for London. As the population of the drainage area increased, these functions became increasingly incompatible, and some solution such as that which the Stevenage Corporation contemplated would, in all likelihood, sooner or later become necessary.

(*b*) It was a convenience to the Development Corporation to have the Stevenage Urban District boundary coincide with the designated area of the New Town, thereby simplifying its negotiations with local authorities. The Corporation made this request to the Stevenage Council in 1950. 'Before coming to a decision', it was reported, 'the Council is to obtain information as to the rateable value of existing properties in those parts of the rural districts to be absorbed, the services being provided, the estimated population, and the number of Council houses and other local authority property.'[1]

(*c*) As the Corporation's first housing estates approached completion, the financial aspects of 'unbalanced' (i.e., largely working class) *v.* 'balanced' development (that with a sufficient proportion of middle-class properties to make the whole development economic) came to the fore. The problem has been previously mentioned (see pp. 84-6), but may well be restated:

'High-class housing development brings high property values and a good rate revenue. The inhabitants of such property usually make few demands on the rates. They seldom require public assistance, often do not send their children to the public elementary schools, and do not avail themselves of the clinics or rate-aided hospitals. Moreover they, or most of them, pay their rates promptly. Housing estates of the working-class type are, on the other hand, of comparatively low rateable value, but necessitate the provision of the whole range of public services, free schools, free hospital treatment, and, in hard times, perhaps public assistance relief. Considerations such as these often have a very real effect on the willingness or hesitancy of local authorities to take over . . . areas where urban development has taken place.'[2]

The County Council and local councils affected by Hertfordshire New Towns repeatedly expressed their anxiety that New Towns be properly 'balanced', a goal towards which the Ministry and Corporations earnestly strove but which was difficult to achieve espe-

[1] *Hertfordshire Express*, 30th September 1950.
[2] W. Eric Jackson, *Local Government in England and Wales* (Penguin Books, Harmondsworth, Middlesex, 1949), pp. 48-9.

cially in early years, when four-fifths of all post-war housing licences went to relatively low space-standard Council housing, the rural labour shortage obliged Corporations to offer housing accommodation to building-trade workers, and high costs combined with the scarcity of materials and capital necessitated utmost economy in design and construction if houses were to rent at tolerable prices. As might have been expected, a Conservative member of the Hemel Hempstead Borough Council charged that 'The rateable values of the first houses in Hemel Hempstead [New Town] did not produce enough to pay for the services they were receiving. One neighbourhood unit had been completed and far from the balanced development that had been promised, they were all of the small type of houses.'[1] Similarly, both the Stevenage Council and the Corporation agreed that the first Stevenage New Town developments were 'of a lower standard than was desired. . . .'[2]

(d) Contrariwise, most of the *public* amenities—broad roads, many footpaths, pleasant landscaping, ample public garden and park space and community buildings—which the Corporation wished to introduce to raise New Town standards above the level of the conventional working-class housing estate threatened to raise maintenance costs for the local authority without yielding a corresponding increase in rateable value. Too little development had actually taken place in the New Town by the end of 1950 to work out these costs exactly, and the finances of the completed venture were even more problematical; but both the County and Stevenage Councils criticized the high space and road standards which the Corporation proposed in its Master Plan and early development plans. The County Planning Committee observed that the area of public open space provided in the Master Plan 'is nearly four times the minimum standard . . . laid down by the Greater London Plan' (the Minister subsequently asked the Corporation to reduce this standard), and 'there are relatively few roads in the country which have dual 30 ft. carriageways. The suggested provision of three such roads and of three single carriageway roads, merely to take the internal traffic of a town of 60,000 persons seems rather extravagant. . . .'[3] The Stevenage Council expressed its concern at the number of back footways in initial Corporation plans and was 'strongly of the opinion' that the Council should not be called upon to take over these footways in view of the expense of maintenance, scavenging, and lighting.[4]

It was impossible to anticipate the course events would take, but, as of March 1951, the Stevenage Council had not only held its own

[1] *Hertfordshire Mercury*, 4th May 1951.   [2] Ibid.
[3] Report of the County Planning Committee, 15th June 1949.
[4] Report of 30th April 1951 Council meeting (*Hertfordshire Mercury*, 4th May 1951).

but benefited financially from the New Town development. Whereas the rates of other local authorities in the county were going up and the County Council increased its rate for 1951–2 by 3d., the Stevenage Council was able to reduce its own rate for this period by 1d. Although the Council expected increased expenses during the year, this would be met from the increased rate income yielded by Corporation development which had cost the Council nothing to erect, but which it taxed like all other Stevenage property. 'If it were not for this,' a Labour councillor observed, 'we also would have had to put our rate up.'

The chairman of the Council's Finance Committee reported that 'Negotiations are slowly proceeding with the Development Corporation with the object of ensuring that expenditure in connection with the services to the New Town shall not be any burden on the ratepayers of old Stevenage. On the assumption that arrangements on these lines will eventually be concluded, expenditure in connection with the Corporation's estates has been excluded in calculating the rate levy.'[1] However, in April 1951 the Council broke off negotiations after the Corporation rejected the Council's proposal that the Corporation contribute to those specific services on which the expenditure per head increased in greater proportion than income per head, on the ground that this would be unduly advantageous to the Council. The Council chairman replied that if the arrangement proved advantageous to either side, it could subsequently be adjusted. 'I did wish to ensure that *this* Stevenage should not bear any of the cost of the *New* Town.'[2]

B. THE COUNCIL AND THE MINISTRY

(a) *The Dearth of Local Information*

The Ministry's failure to inform—much less consult—the Urban District Council on many important developments in the early days of the project contributed in no small measure to building up local ill-will against the New Town. From the end of 1945, 'it was continually the complaint of the Stevenage Council that insufficient consultation was taking place with them. Information leaked back that conferences were being held by the Ministry with the Railway Company, the Church authorities, agricultural interests, the County Council, and others, but the Stevenage Council received no direct information about progress and had no opportunity of expressing local views.'[3] According to a Ministry informant, these conferences

[1] *Hertfordshire Mercury*, 9th March 1951.
[2] *Hertfordshire Express*, 5th May 1951.
[3] G. V. Berry, 'New Towns—The Particular Case of Stevenage', Society of Clerks of Urban District Councils, (Report of) *Annual Meeting and Conference on 16th and 17th May 1947, Barnet, Herts.*

were 'purely informal and technical'—and, by inference, not the Council's concern. But the Council was disturbed. Occasional meetings took place at which Ministry officers supposedly gave the Council 'all the information at present available on the Satellite Town proposal'.[1] But somehow information did not keep abreast of events; or such was the Council's suspicion.

In February 1946, for example, the wife of a prominent citizen wrote the Council:

'My husband is a member of the —— Committee, and he was very surprised to learn from the Secretary last week that there is a plan in existence, and that it has been loaned to this Committee by the Ministry of Town and Country Planning. . . . I understand that this plan clearly shows the proposed extent of the new town boundary and the six zones into which it is proposed to divide the new town. . . . One is left with the uncomfortable impression that the information which the inhabitants of Stevenage are so keenly anxious to obtain is being deliberately withheld from them, and that they will eventually be presented with a scheme which it will be extremely difficult to alter.'

Inquiring at the Ministry, the Council clerk was informed by a senior Ministry officer:

'I can assure you that there is as yet no detailed master plan of the Stevenage proposals, and I think that you have seen all that we have prepared so far. If you would care to call in here when you are next in London, I shall be glad to assure you personally that nothing is being kept secret from your Council.'

On 12th March 1946, in reply to his parliamentary question, the Minister assured the district M.P. that local authorities were being consulted on the New Town development. But when this *Hansard* report reached Stevenage, a Labour councillor (who afterwards became a member of the Development Corporation, and was then chairman of the Town Planning and Development Committee) commented:

'it seemed evident that the Minister was unaware of the lack of co-ordination between the officials of his Ministry and the members of the Council. . . . most of the information the Council had received was from private sources. They did not know things had got as far as they had until, after pressing, through their M.P., for a deputation to be received by the Minister, a plan was sent to them under secret cover, which, they afterwards found, was being "publicly hawked" round Hitchin.'[2]

The following month, a citizen learned from the Council clerk

[1] This was the express purpose, for example, of a meeting at the Ministry London offices, 16th November 1945, between Ministry and Council representatives.

[2] Report of 25th March 1946 Council meeting (*Hertfordshire Express*, 30th March 1946).

that 'the information in the possession of my Council is still indefinite and I am not in a position to say for certain what land will be acquired compulsorily and where development is to take place'. A fortnight later, without warning, the Ministry dispatched to local property owners invitations to sell their property. 'They never gave us a tip they were going to issue that compulsory notice', a (Labour) councillor recalled. 'We were made to look like a lot of asses.' An informant who sympathized with the Ministry said, 'Similar letters are going out every day from Local Authority offices', but conceded:

'This was the mistake of insensitive lawyers. Lawyers are always ham-fisted! They should never have been sent in my opinion, but it should be remembered there was no Act, the project was urgent, and the procedure was being developed under Section 35 of the 1932 Act—a section which was in fact a "joker".'

Additional reasons given for Ministry secrecy at this stage were that it was necessary to avoid speculation in property (for this reason both Letchworth and Welwyn Garden City land had been acquired secretly by their developers), and 'the . . . detail of the New Town Plan was based on the provisions of the New Towns Bill, which was still being drafted. To divulge any part of the contents of this document before it was formally laid on the table of the House would offend a jealously guarded constitutional right.'[1] There was, also, obvious need for confidence during the course of negotiations to prevent disclosures which might embarrass the Government and jeopardize the success of the project. When the Council was consulted, it was difficult to prevent news leaking out to the public through one of the twelve councillors (indeed, councillors were morally and practically obliged to ascertain the opinions of at least some influential citizens and leaders of the principal local organizations). The course which the Ministry generally followed at this time had unfortunate consequences upon local opinion, but enabled it to pursue the project forcefully and quickly as seemed desirable at the time. It was not an ideal course, but what course was? It was not easy to reconcile efficient central planning and real local democracy.

(b) The Role of the Minister

The Minister was the arbiter who presided over the fate of the old and New Town of Stevenage. In the appointment of Corporation members, at public inquiries, development and redevelopment programmes, and most points in dispute between the Urban District or County Council and the Corporation, his word was final. Yet it was difficult, if not impossible, for Council representatives to make per-

[1] Mark Benny, 'Storm Over Stevenage', *The Changing Nation* (Contact Books, 1947), p. 44.

sonal contact with him, and they had to deal almost exclusively with Ministry officers. In this vital matter, the Council was far more badly served than the Development Corporation whose chairman and deputy chairman saw the Minister regularly (at least bi-monthly) at the Ministerial conference, and could arrange personal interviews as required.

The first meeting between Council and Minister, and the latter's only public appearance in Stevenage, on 6th May 1946, has been described fully in Chapter III. It produced a bad and lasting impression on all concerned. Receiving no conciliatory word from the Council majority (or the majority of his town hall audience), the Minister can only have felt they were being unreasonable and quite insensible to the national interest and the social idealism of the New Town project; at a London planning conference shortly thereafter, he spoke of the 'backwardness' of Stevenage citizens.[1] Independent councillors, on the other hand, were understandably offended. For months they had dealt with Ministry officers on an unequal footing and, despite frequent protestations and requests for an interview with the Minister, had not been (they were convinced) adequately consulted on developments. Now the Minister considered the whole project a *fait accompli*: if this was his idea of 'democracy' or 'consultation', they could not compliment him upon it. Labour councillors and others favourable to the New Town regarded the Minister's visit and the events leading up to it as an unfortunate failure in public relations. 'The Ministry had no imagination at all in the way they handled the Council', said one Corporation informant later. 'I was down to the Ministry and warned them several times [in the spring 1946] that they weren't going about it in the right way', said another informant. 'It was a tragic blunder . . . the local Council wasn't informed [especially before the dispatch of the invitations to sell in April 1946]. . . . I've told the Minister that he could have avoided a lot of trouble.'

The second meeting with the Minister took place at his initiative in October 1949, in connection with a Council protest against the projected appointment of the Corporation chairman. 'I don't imagine

[1] According to the notes of a Stevenage informant present at the 11th July 1946 conference of the Town and Country Planning Association, the Minister 'opened the proceedings and he made reference to Stevenage and to the backwardness of the people, he expressed the hope that the people of other places chosen as the sites for New Towns would see the project as a great adventure'. A printed version of the speech has it that the Minister said, 'I have every reason to hope that the more enlightened people of Sussex [where the Crawley New Town was to be built] will not regard our encroachment into their area in the same spirit as the, I suppose, rather more backward people of Stevenage' (Lewis Silkin, 'Building Our New Towns', *The Architect and Building News*, 19th July 1946, p. 39).

R   241

that the Minister will be influenced by the Council's observations,' one councillor had stated, 'but I feel that on a matter so important the Council's views should be placed on record.' Surprisingly, however, the Minister invited the Council to meet him, and a delegation of four councillors spent ninety minutes with him at the Ministry (on 25th October 1949)—the first formal personal encounter since May 1946. Councillors were reportedly impressed by the Minister's frankness and wish to improve relations with the Council, and voluntarily deleted an offensive paragraph from their resolution of protest later issued to the Press. According to the Council chairman, the Minister said he was keenly disappointed with the relations between Council and Corporation and pointed out how essential it was for the two bodies to work in harmony:

'Every member of the Council agreed with what the Minister said, but we did point out that it was wrong to imply, as he did imply, that this was due to any fault of the Council.

'We said that the New Town at Stevenage had got off to a bad start. He agreed, and we suggested that perhaps because of that, and because of the opposition to the New Town, the Minister and the Corporation were under a false assumption that everything put forward by the Council by way of criticism or suggestion, was put forward in a destructive manner.

'If the Minister would disabuse himself and the Corporation of this point of view and accept what the Council put forward to safeguard the interests of the people of Stevenage, the outlook might be better.

'The Minister accepted the fact that the Council represented the people of Stevenage and agreed that there was no reason why the Council should not safeguard the interests of the people of Stevenage and fully cooperate with the Corporation.

'I think on behalf of every member of the Council, I should say that the talk was very frank and informal, and if as a result of these talks the relations between the Council and the Corporation are not in any closer harmony the Minister will not be the only one who is disappointed.'[1]

Between these meetings, of course, the Minister retained touch with the Council by correspondence, reports from his staff and the Corporation, and some informal personal contacts. But all this afforded only a distant and partial view of the Council's needs and personalities, except for such impressions as survived from his explosive May visit. Stevenage was only one of many nameless places and problems demanding his attention—'I get 400 appeals a month, and I cannot visit every area', he once protested.[2] Considering how busy he was, the Minister displayed a surprising familiarity with details of the Stevenage situation, or was able to brief himself quickly and

[1] *Hertfordshire Express*, 5th November 1949.
[2] *Hansard*, 25th October 1949, vol. 468, col. 1,128.

well when he turned his attention to it. For the most part, however, 'the Minister' was, in effect, his staff:

'It need hardly be said that in the majority of cases the decision cannot be made by the Minister in person. It will be made by an Administrative Class officer . . . who will, of course, exercise his discretion within a framework of policy determined by the Minister. He may consult with . . . more senior officials. However, the number of appeals referred to the Minister for other reasons is by no means negligible. An appeal may involve strategic considerations, or an important conflict between national and local interests . . . or it may raise an issue on which the Minister's personal views are not yet known. Again, there is a tendency to refer to the Minister a case which is likely to arouse public criticism. . . .'[1]

The Minister was far more responsible for the Corporation's than the Council's activities—indeed, over most of the latter he exercised no control at all (this being the responsibility chiefly of the Minister of Health until January 1951) and had no legal responsibility. Hence, it was far more important for him to ensure a co-ordination of policy between Corporation and Ministry than between Council and Ministry. Ministry and Corporation policy conflicted at many points, as will be seen, but these were essentially internal and, for the most part, private conflicts such as every Government experiences. The conflict with a Conservative local Council was a regrettable but, to a certain extent, unavoidable political hazard for a Labour Minister. (The Ministry made frequent attempts to keep it private—inviting the Council, for example, to submit its views in private rather than at the October 1949 Master Plan inquiry—but failed, among other reasons because the Council feared its case would be weakened if not brought out into the open.)

In most instances when the Minister was called upon to decide between the Corporation and the Council—notably, the Designation Order and the Master Plan—he clearly favoured the Corporation. But the Ministry was not a rubber-stamp for Corporation decisions; it was more a forum at which the Corporation and other interested parties were obliged to present solid documentation for their views. We know of no instance in which the Ministry publicly sided with the Council against the Corporation, but it occasionally did so privately. A case in point was the Corporation's proposal to acquire a few scattered sites in the built-up part of Stevenage upon which to erect houses for staff accommodation. When this became known, much ill-feeling was aroused locally, which led, in October 1949, to

---

[1] S. A. de Smith, 'Appeals in Town and Country Planning Law', in R. S. W. Pollard (ed.), *Administrative Tribunals at Work* (London, 1950), p. 110. While de Smith's observations were made in regard to the procedure for planning permission appeals under the Town and Country Planning Act, 1947, their general substance is clearly applicable to the relations between the Minister and the Stevenage Council.

a Ministry inquiry at which the Council, the Residents' Protection Association, and most of the affected owners entered objections to the Corporation's compulsory purchase order. Ministry officers had intimated informally to the Corporation (in July) that they believed there was some substance to the Council's objection—that it was wrong for the Corporation to acquire the few sites in Stevenage on which it was possible for private developers to build. The Minister ultimately confirmed the Corporation's action by an Order dated 21st December 1949, but privately enjoined certain conditions favourable to the Council and one owner.[1]

If the Minister generally backed the Corporation, therefore, it was not because he was blind to the Council's proposals, but because these could not generally be reconciled with Government policy or the recommendations of his advisers.

(c) Representation on the Corporation

One of the Council's major complaints was the Minister's failure to give it adequate representation on the Corporation.

The New Towns Act provided that Corporation members

'shall be appointed by the Minister after consultation with such local authorities as appear to him to be concerned with the development of the new town, and . . . the Minister shall have regard to the desirability of securing the services of one or more persons resident in or having special knowledge of the locality in which the new town will be situated.'

In accordance with this provision (the Act being then in course of passage through the House of Commons) the Minister asked the Council for nominations to the Advisory Committee which, appointed in August 1946, was converted that December into the Stevenage Development Corporation. He formally consulted, also, the County Council, the principal London Councils whose housing needs the New Town was designed to alleviate, and, no doubt, other advisers.

The Stevenage Council submitted the names of two Independent and two Labour councillors (Mr. P, the Council chairman, and Mr. Q, chairman of the Town Planning and Development Committee), as well as six nominees from five local groups—the Chamber of Trade, National Farmers' Union (Hitchin Local), Industrial Employers' Group, Residents' Protection Association, and Trades Council.[2] The only one of these ten nominations accepted by the

---

[1] These conditions were that the Corporation reserve six plots for private developers and make six additional houses, which it would build, available to local teachers or other key workers nominated by the Urban District Council; the Minister also asked the Corporation to give greater security of tenure, at a lower rental than it had proposed, to one displaced owner.

Minister was that of Mr. Q, who thereby became the only resident
of Stevenage to sit on the Corporation during its first three years.
An Independent councillor commented that 'in view of the fact that
the chairmen of other [London Borough] Councils concerned had
been put on the Advisory Committee . . . it was a "snub" to the
Stevenage Council that their chairman was not', and the Council
passed unanimously a resolution declaring 'that more representation
should have been given to this district by the Minister of Town and
Country Planning on the New Town Advisory Committee and that
the position should now be remedied by the appointment of the
Chairman of the Council. . . .'[1]

Upon receiving from the Minister his list of proposed appointments to the Corporation, the Council asked (3rd December 1946)
to confer with him, expressing the opinion that 'the persons proposed . . . have not, in the majority of cases, the qualifications and
practical experience to inspire confidence in the success of the undertaking'. The Minister replied promptly, 'I am satisfied that such a
conference would not now serve a useful purpose. I am, therefore,
proceeding with the appointment of the members.' The Council
chairman (a Labourite and strong supporter of the New Town)
charged that the appointments did not take place after consultation,
as required by law. 'I myself hardly call what is going on consultation. It is rather stretching the imagination to call mere letter-writing
"consultation".' The vice-chairman (an Independent who had opposed the New Town) commented, 'I am not really surprised. It is
typical of [the Minister's] dictatorial attitude towards the Council
all along.'

In September 1948, the Council again asked the Minister to consider granting additional local representation on the Development
Corporation, but the second series of appointments (announced
January 1950 after expiration of the first three-year term of office)
pleased the Council little more in this respect. Three members were
now residents of Stevenage (two were Labour and one Conservative
sympathizers) but none represented the Council's Independent majority. Indeed, the Ministry did not even request Council recommend-

[2] The Council asked each of these groups to nominate one person, whose
name would be forwarded to the Minister. All apparently complied except for
the Employers' Group which insisted upon nominating two persons, stating,
'To agree . . . to limit ourselves to one nomination only would, in our opinion,
signify our acceptance and confirmation of the constitution and representation
of the Advisory Committee as proposed by the Stevenage Urban District
Council. . . . Our expressed disagreement with this proposed representation was
one of the main reasons for a dual nomination.'
[1] Report of Council 30th September 1946 meeting (Hertfordshire Express,
5th October 1946).

ations on this occasion, regarding circumstances as different from the initial establishment of the Corporation.[1]

The Council consistently opposed the Minister's choice of Corporation chairmen, and their private remarks in this connection were more forthright than their public ones. ('God help poor bloody-England', was a typical reaction to news of one appointment.) The protest against the appointment of the fourth chairman, Mrs. ——, was particularly strong and indicative of the conservatism of the Independent majority. In a resolution forwarded to the Minister, the Council expressed the view that a woman should not be appointed to this position, but rather a man 'with a wide practical business experience, whose ability, personality and tact will inspire the confidence and procure the co-operation of all parties concerned in the development of the New Town'.[2]

As the whole conception of the Development Corporation was that of a relatively independent *national* body with a bold new task, the Minister's reluctance to appoint to it more members of the conservative, often provincially minded and inexperienced local Council was understandable. Nevertheless, the Council was the authentic voice of the local electorate and the failure to give its majority any representation on the Corporation was a move away from the principles of local democracy—as was, of course, the Corporation's assumption of various powers over residents of the designated area which had previously been exercised by the Urban District and County Councils.

The Reith Committee's recommendation that 'Provision should be made for local authorities to initiate the creation of new towns if they desire to do so'[3] was not implemented by the Government

[1] The Ministry commented later that, had any name been suggested by the Council, it would have been given due consideration. In April 1950, the new Minister told the House, 'I am most anxious that there should be a fair proportion of local government representatives on the corporations, and I will be glad to receive their suggestions' (*Hansard*, 18th April 1950, vol. 474, col. 5).

[2] The personal statement of one influential councillor put even more explicitly what was probably then (October 1949) the dominant view on the Council: '. . . the Chairman of such an organisation as a New Town Development Corporation should be a person with wide practical business experience. The duties involve diverse negotiations on a large scale with commercial undertakings. Furthermore the Corporation are already considerably behind in their own scheduled programme and it will require a great deal of drive and energy to make up for the valuable time and money that has already been spent. . . . I am convinced that the Chairmanship of the Corporation is a job for a man and a "he-man" at that, one who has gained his experience in the hard and practical way of business.' After the appointment had been made, this councillor remarked, 'It's bad to have a woman as head of the Corporation—I don't think the men under her will talk to her as straightforwardly as they would talk to a man; there's always that little something that enters into their relations with a woman.'

[3] Cmd. 6759, p. 9.

'on the grounds that the creation of a new town was a matter of national concern, and that if local authorities sponsored a new town there might be extreme difficulty in obtaining the necessary co-operation between the authority exporting population and the authority at the receiving end. Further . . . the creation of a new town must entail the expenditure of large sums from the national revenue, and it is usual for a government to wish to control the use of money it is itself providing.'[1]

The possibility of electing locally some members of the Corporation was also investigated by the Reith Committee but no recommendation to this effect was made for the early stages of the development, presumably because (as the Committee states in regard to the final period when the New Town will be handed over to the local authority) 'continuity of policy in the management of the estate might be endangered by the changes of personnel natural to and proper in a publicly elected body. . . . When the major work of construction is completed, we suggest that it would then be appropriate to include on the governing body a minority of members— possibly two—resident in the new town and elected by the inhabitants by direct vote.'[2] However, discontinuity need be no greater under a system of elections for overlapping three-year terms (as on the Stevenage and other local councils) than under the prevailing system of three-year Ministerial appointments (with no overlapping). As we have seen, events produced four chairmen of the Stevenage Corporation in a period of three years.

(d) The Public Inquiry

An important, long-established safeguard against government by decree, the public inquiry was mandatory in some circumstances and optional in others under the New Towns Act in the event of objections to Ministry or Corporation orders. An inquiry into his proposed New Town Designation Order was therefore ordered by the Minister in October 1946, and other inquiries were later held into actions proposed by the Corporation. Hearings were usually conducted in the Stevenage town hall by a Ministry official (generally a civil engineer) who submitted a report which influenced, but did not alone determine, the Minister's final decision. The procedure and decorum which the inspector, witnesses, and spectators adopted approximated

---

[1] Peter Richards, 'The New Towns', *The Political Quarterly* (1951), vol. 22, pp. 240–1.

[2] *Second Interim Report of the New Towns Committee*, Cmd. 6794 (London, 1946), p. 21. Cf. F. J. Osborn (a member of the Reith Committee): 'Efforts should be made from the very beginning to associate the residents of the town with the complex business of its development by means of the direct election of a few members of the body taking charge of development. This will add to the vitality of the place, safeguard what is after all the most important interest, and fan the spark of civic pride' (*New Towns After the War* (London, 1942), p. 64).

in some but not all particulars that which is customary in an English court of law. The procedure was less formalized and the general atmosphere far less solemn than that of even the lowest court, but testimony was prepared and recorded with care, the inspector made every effort to be impartial, and legal counsel was often employed.[1]

At the first inquiry the Corporation had not yet been established and no Ministry spokesman, but only opponents of the New Town, testified. The Minister's subsequent decision to confirm the Designation Order came, therefore, as somewhat of a surprise to conservative local opinion which expressed considerable scepticism as to the purpose of the inquiry. One Independent councillor termed it a 'farce', while a prominent Conservative compared it to 'the Courts of the Star Chamber of Tudor and Stuart times'. The court action which the Residents' Protection Association subsequently pressed evolved in large measure upon the Minister's legal obligations at the inquiry—the Association maintaining that the Minister, having previously declared his intention to establish a New Town at Stevenage, was necessarily biased in considering the objections made at the inquiry; whereas the Minister stated in an affidavit that he had 'personally carefully considered all the objections', the inspector's report, and also a mass of related evidence (including the Barlow Report, the *Greater London Plan*, the reports of the Reith Committee, the opinions of other local authorities in Hertfordshire and Greater London, and of the Ministries of Agriculture and Health), and 'I came to the conclusion that it was expedient in the national interest that the proposed site should be developed as a new town'.[2]

Opponents contended that the Minister, in holding an inquiry and reviewing his inspector's report, should act in a judicial or quasi-judicial capacity, whereas the Government contended he was acting throughout administratively.[3] The substance of the argument was put in an interchange between the Attorney-General Sir Hartley

---

[1] At the October 1946 inquiry, the Stevenage Council engaged a barrister at the fee of 50 guineas on brief plus 25 guineas for each subsequent day, the local branch of the National Farmers' Union engaged one K.C. and the Residents' Protection Association another. At the 18th October 1949 inquiry, the Development Corporation was represented by its regular legal officer, the Stevenage Council by its clerk (an accountant with no legal training), and only the Residents' Protection Association employed a K.C. to state its case.

[2] Franklin *v*. the Minister of Town and Country Planning, *All England Law Reports* (1947), vol. 1, p. 616.

[3] Non-legislative functions of public authorities are conventionally classified as either *judicial, quasi-* (or 'not exactly') *judicial*, or *administrative*. The classification is not entirely satisfactory, and one authority notes that 'The indiscriminate use of the expression "quasi-judicial" is particularly confusing' (S. A. de Smith, 'The Limits of Judicial Review', *The Modern Law Review* (1948), vol. 11, p. 309).

Shawcross, representing the Ministry, and Mr. Justice Henn Collins in the High Court, 11th February 1947:

'The Attorney-General. The scheme of this Act . . . is not to make a man judge in his own cause, an affront to the elementary principles of natural justice, but to require him to hear publicly such objections that can be made in the knowledge that where objections possessing merit are made publicly Ministers will be afraid . . . to disregard them. . . . In this kind of legislation . . . the decision which he makes after hearing the objections that are presented is an administrative decision based on policy and not on evidence.

'Mr. Justice Henn Collins. It is devised for airing grievances only.

'The Attorney-General. Yes; to use colloquial language, an opportunity of letting off steam in public.

'Mr. Justice Henn Collins. If you are going to descend to colloquialisms what about "eye-wash"?

'The Attorney-General. As Ministers know, the opportunity of letting off steam in public is by no means a matter of "eye-wash". Ministers are very frequently very much affected by public demonstrations of this kind. . . . If a good objection is raised and disregarded, the next thing is the question in Parliament, and the next thing after that, if it is a really serious matter, is some adverse action by Parliament. That is the sanction here.'[1]

In his judgement of 20th February 1947, quashing the Designation Order, Mr. Justice Henn Collins stated:

'It is a commonplace feature of this class of case that a Minister should exercise both ministerial and quasi-judicial functions, and it is often difficult to draw a line between the two. . . . If I accepted the argument of the Attorney-General . . . that he acts throughout administratively . . . the result . . . is that an objector who may have everything at stake, has legislative permission to fulminate, but can do no more. . . . Although invited to state his case in public, he cannot secure that what he says will be weighed and considered on its merits, or, indeed, at all.

'[Under similar statutes] . . . it has been held time and again that the functions of the Minister concerned are quasi-judicial and not arbitrary. . . . To take any other view would reduce the provisions for objections, the holding of a local public inquiry, the report of the officer who holds it, and the consideration of that report by the Minister to an absurdity, because, when all has been said and done, the Minister could disregard the whole proceedings and do just as he pleased.'[2]

While the Court of Appeal reversed Justice Collins's ruling on the grounds that, even if the Minister had been biased in May 1946 (during his Stevenage speech), bias in October, November, and

[1] *In the High Court of Justice King's Bench Division, In the Matter of the New Towns Act, 1946 and In the Matter of the Stevenage New Town (Designation) Order 1946* (Sharpe, Pritchard & Co., London, mimeographed transcript of the proceedings of 10th–11th February 1947).

[2] *All England Law Reports* (1947), vol. 1, pp. 397–8.

December 1946 (during and after the public inquiry and at the confirmation of the New Town Designation Order) had *not* been proved,
it thereby sustained the Justice's view that the Minister was obliged
to act in a quasi-judicial manner.[1]

This interpretation of the statute the House of Lords rejected
decisively in a unanimous judgement delivered by Lord Thankerton:

'. . . no judicial, or quasi-judicial, duty was imposed on the respondent,
and any reference to judicial duty, or bias, is irrelevant to the present case.
The respondent's duties under [the New Towns Act] . . . are, in my
opinion, purely administrative. . . . the object of the inquiry is further to
inform the mind of the Minister, and not to consider any issue between
the Minister and the objectors. . . .'[2]

In effect, the House of Lords ruled that the balance of evidence submitted at a public inquiry need not determine the Minister's decision,
which might be based, in the final analysis, simply upon Government
policy. Or, as the Attorney-General had argued, 'It was the national
interest which was the overriding consideration. The Minister might
come to the conclusion that the objections in a given case were so
strong as to be virtually unanswerable, and yet that, in the national
interest, they must be put on one side.'[3]

The highest court's ruling on a question of law was, of course,
final (until the Law Lords elected to reverse themselves or Parliament modified the law); but it demonstrated—indeed, defined—the
unjust nature of the public inquiry so far as objectors were concerned.
'. . . it is idle to talk of natural justice in a case of this kind or of any
necessity for an appearance of justice', the Attorney-General said.[4]
The functioning of a representative democracy often requires that
injustice be thus done to a local group or minority so that the will of
Parliament may be efficiently served by the administrative process.
'Parliament should always be extremely reluctant to entrust either
Ministers or Ministerial Tribunals with purely judicial powers', the
Committee on Ministers' Powers had advised in 1932. 'It is in the
ordinary Courts . . . that justiciable issues . . . between Crown and
subject ought as a rule to be determined.'[5]

[1] See *All England Law Reports* (1947), vol. 1, pp. 612–20, and *The Times Law Reports* (1947), vol. 63, pp. 185–91.
[2] *Law Reports, Appeal Cases* (1948), pp. 102, 106.
[3] Before the Court of Appeal, counsel for the Stevenage objectors had argued precisely to the opposite effect: 'The question of national expediency was the last of the matters which he [the Minister] had to consider, for he could not approach the question until he considered the impact of the draft proposals on the interests of individuals affected by them' (*The Times Law Reports* (1947), vol. 63, p. 187).
[4] Before the House of Lords (*Law Reports, Appeal Cases* (1948), p. 95).
[5] The Committee added: '. . . when a public local inquiry is held as preliminary to a quasi-judicial decision by a Minister it is not reasonable or practicable that the inspector should be entirely bound by the practice of Courts of Law . . .

So the House of Lords legislated the legal issue (which was so ambiguous that four justices—one of the King's Bench Division and three on the Court of Appeal—had formed a contrary opinion), and the decision assumed considerable importance in legal circles, and experts, and the lay public, and the writer find much to commend in it. But it is doubtful if either Ministry or Corporation representatives or local citizens were entirely satisfied with, and if the latter, particularly, understood, the status of the public inquiry, which continued to retain judicial features and—as all sides wished and practical considerations demanded—to instil a confusing degree of justice into the administrative process. For the Lords could clarify the law but not the reality of that administrative process.

Four principles of natural justice have been enunciated and each remains a source of dissension in the inquiry system.

(1) '. . . *a man may not be a judge in his own cause.*'[1]

On this issue the Minister early adopted the viewpoint which the House of Lords eventually accepted:

'It has been criticised that I should constitute myself as judge and jury and that no man ought to be judge in his own court. That is an entire misconception of the functions of the inquiries. Before ever the inquiry is held I have to be satisfied, after consultation with any of the local authorities, that it is expedient in the national interest that the area should be developed as a new town.

'That is a responsibility which I think ought to be placed upon a Minister, but having satisfied myself it would be quite wrong to submit the whole thing to the judgment of an outside person who has no responsibility at all, and who may not have the knowledge or background or information to enable him to make a decision.'[2]

But the chairman of the Stevenage Council did not see the matter in the same light and, long after the House of Lord's verdict, persisted in his opinion that 'as the Corporation is sponsored by the Minister, when the Corporation is a party to the dispute it would be more in keeping with ordinary justice if the inspector was an independent

while his main function is to ascertain facts it is sometimes his duty to form his own views on public policy . . .' (Committee on Ministers' Powers, *Report* [presented to Lord High Chancellor], Cmd. 4060 (London, 1932), pp. 96–7, 101).

[1] Committee on Ministers' Powers, op. cit., p. 76.

[2] Report of the Minister's speech at Apsley (*Hertfordshire Express*, 23rd November 1946). In another speech that week at London County Hall, the Minister repeated this argument. The final decision about the site of a New Town, he emphasized, 'is a Ministerial and administrative decision for which the Government and I must accept responsibility. It would be quite inappropriate and alien to our system of Government responsibility to make these decisions subject to confirmation by an outside Tribunal' (*The Architect and Building News*, 29th November 1946, p. 161).

person'.[1] An American legal authority suggests that the situation 'is not very satisfactory from the point of view of ensuring public and professional confidence in the justice of administrative decisions'. (How the idea of justice obtrudes into this certifiedly administrative matter!) The fault, he believes, lies not with the House of Lords judgement, but with the New Towns Act, which 'expressly made the Minister the judge of his own order'.

'. . . the case does show the impropriety of such a concentration of functions in an Executive department. . . . Here surely is the type of case in which one would desire a separation of the functions of administrator and judge. If a complete separation is considered impracticable because of the possible harm to successful administration, there ought at least to be some form of "internal" separation within the department—along the lines of a separate tribunal within the Ministry . . . so that . . . objections . . . may be considered impartially before the order . . . is finally issued.'[2]

(2) '*No party ought to be condemned unheard; and if his right to be heard is to be a reality, he must know in good time the case which he has to meet.* . . .'[3]

The failure of the Government to state its case in favour of the New Town at the October 1946 inquiry placed local objectors at an obvious disadvantage, since they could not know exactly what they were objecting to. The Residents' Protection Association's counsel complained that 'we are missing on both sides that very valuable thing—cross-examination. . . . I do hope that . . . we may in future have some opportunity of really comparing the two sets of views. . . .' Questioned in Parliament as to

'whether he will give an assurance that, at future inquiries under the New Towns Act, he will arrange that his Departmental representatives will submit their case in public with evidence, so that objectors may have an opportunity for criticism and cross-examination'

the Minister replied, on 19th November 1946:

'I propose to arrange in future that in addition to my inspector . . . an officer of my Department will attend to explain the proposed project and the reasons which have led to it. He will be there to explain the proposal, but not to be cross-examined.'[4]

The New Towns Act specifies, 'If any objection is duly made to the proposed [New Town Designation] order and is not withdrawn, the Minister shall, before making the order, cause a public local inquiry to be held *with respect thereto* . . .' (our italics). Counsel for the

[1] Statement at the 30th January 1950 meeting of the Stevenage Urban District Council (*Hertfordshire Express*, 4th February 1950).

[2] Bernard Schwartz, *Law and the Executive in Britain* (New York, 1949), pp. 275–6.

[3] Committee on Ministers' Powers, op. cit., p. 79.

[4] *Hansard*, 19th November 1946, vol. 430, col. 93.

Stevenage objectors argued in court that this wording 'clearly indicated that the inquiry to be held by the Minister was to be into the proposed order. That could only mean one thing—namely, that the promoter had to justify the order in addition to hearing the objections thereto.'[1]

'[The inquiry] is a proceeding in which both parties must participate and evidence must be adduced in favour of the scheme to give the objectors the chance of cross-examining someone. It would be farcical if they could only indulge in shadow boxing and had only the right to fulminate in public.'[2]

All three courts, however, held that the italicized phrase referred not to the Designation Order but to the objections and, accordingly, that the Minister was not required to introduce at the inquiry evidence in support of his order. Lord Justice Oaksey observed that:

'In all the authorities which have been referred to [by counsel for the objectors] as shewing that at an inquiry there must be an examination of the case from both sides . . . there was what has been called a *lis*, that is to say, there were two parties contesting and the Minister as an outside party was deciding the contest. . . . [In the present instance] there is no obligation upon the inspector to insist upon having the case in favour of the [New Town Designation] order put forward by anybody on behalf of the Minister.'[3]

This might have decided the matter, but it did not, and soon the problem emerged in another form: should a Development Corporation give evidence at a Ministerial inquiry into objections to the Corporation's activities? The Minister privately expressed his view (in July 1949) that, while there was no constitutional objection to a Corporation being represented at an inquiry held by an inspector of another Department, it would probably be embarrassing in the case of an inquiry held by a Ministry inspector; Corporations were closely identified with the Minister in the public mind and their appearance at one of his inquiries might create the impression that he was unduly influenced by their representations; moreover, he might be embarrassed at having to decide against the views of a Corporation and thus seeming to inflict a public slight upon it; Corporations could make private representations to the Ministry on any matter at any time without impropriety, and this method was probably more appropriate. The chairmen of several New Town Corporations disagreed with the Minister's argument; one suggested that there might be strong local criticism if a Corporation did not appear at Ministry

[1] In the High Court (*The Times Law Reports* (1947), vol. 63, p. 143).
[2] Before the House of Lords (*Law Reports, Appeal Cases* (1948), p. 94).
[3] Lord Justice Oaksey's Court of Appeal judgement, 24th March 1947 (*All England Law Reports* (1947), vol. 1, pp. 617–18).

inquiries, since it would be known or inferred that representations had been made privately.

Thereupon the Minister evidently re-examined the subject, for a communication to Corporations in October 1949, 'Public Inquiries Relating to Master Plans', advised, 'While strictly speaking the onus is on those making representations to state their case, the Minister wishes that immediately after the Inspector's opening remarks the Corporation should, through an appropriate representative, make a fairly full statement explaining the conception of the Master Plan as a whole'. This, it was noted, was neither evidence nor in lieu of evidence, but merely to help those present understand the Plan. 'The statement should be an objective one and must not seek to deal in advance with any of the representations . . .'; after objectors put their case, cross-examination would be permitted by both sides. These instructions were carried out at the 11th October 1949 inquiry into a compulsory purchase order of the Stevenage Corporation, and at the Master Plan inquiry a week later. On the former occasion, the Ministry inspector told Corporation counsel, 'My view is that no legal obligation lies upon you to put in evidence, but it is helpful if you do it'.

The appearance of the Corporation certainly made for a livelier, more critical, and better balanced inquiry, although it was difficult to say which side benefited more from the opportunity of cross-examination. So far as positive testimony was concerned, Corporation experts spoke with an authority that opponents could muster only at great cost in money, time, and effort. At the first and most important inquiry, public opinion was so aroused that the Residents' Protection Association raised a considerable sum of money and managed to secure experts of recognized standing, but at the Master Plan inquiry three years later its resources and the general enthusiasm for its cause had so diminished that the Association presented no witnesses of its own, relying upon the testimony of the Stevenage Council surveyor and the cross-examination of Corporation witnesses.

It is notable that, despite the courts' unequivocal decision that neither testimony by nor cross-examination of Ministry representatives was necessary at an inquiry (neither occurred at the October 1946 inquiry), the Minister yielded to his critics on both points and, to that extent, voluntarily altered the character of the inquiry in a quasi-judicial direction. However the Minister did not yield an inch in regard to a very important matter—the private presentation by other Government Departments of their views on the subject of an inquiry. (As has been mentioned, the Ministry even tried—unsuccessfully—to persuade the Stevenage Council to discuss the Corporation's Master Plan privately at the Ministry, instead of at the October

1949 inquiry.) Derek Walker-Smith, the Conservative M.P. for Hertford, objected to these private

' "clearances" of other interested Government Departments. There should be no behind-the-door clearances. A Government Department should send a witness to the inquiry to give his evidence and submit himself to the test of cross-examination. That is the only proper way for these things to be done. I hope that the Minister will see his way to effect that improvement. . . .'[1]

But the Government did not intend to wash its linen in public. When another M.P. questioned the procedure at inquiries into the compulsory acquisition of agricultural land by a Government department—'Does the Prime Minister think that it is fair that Departmental views . . . should be given . . . in private, while those of other interested parties are given in public and open to cross-examination?'—Mr. Attlee replied somewhat obliquely, 'I think it is right that when a Government proposal is put forward the views of all the Departments should be ascertained and the thing agreed before it is put to the inquiry'.[2]

(3) *It may well be argued that there is a third principle of natural justice, namely, that a party is entitled to know the reason for the decision, be it judicial or quasi-judicial.*[3]

In the course of his argument before the House of Lords, the Attorney-General cited precedents to show that there was no obligation upon a Minister to explain the reason for his (purely administrative) decision.

'In those [cited] cases Ministers refused to disclose their reasons for their action, while the objectors put forward reasons, the only ones known to the public, suggesting that the Minister's conclusions were wrong and unfair. There was no appearance of justice in what was done. It was held [by the courts] that if the Minister was satisfied, the matter was a subjective one for him and that, unless it could be shown that he acted in bad faith, his decision stood.'[4]

However, following the Stevenage New Town Designation Order inquiry of 7th–8th October 1946, the Minister on 7th November, sent a letter—which was fully reported in the county Press—to the several local authorities and objectors concerned, discussing point by point the principal objections entered at the inquiry and explaining why he felt justified in disregarding them or what measures were planned to overcome the difficulties which he recognized they

---

[1] *Hansard*, 13th June 1950, vol. 476, col. 135.
[2] Ibid., 15th May 1950, vol. 475, col. 845 (the questioner was Conservative W. M. F. Vane).
[3] Committee on Ministers' Powers, op. cit., p. 80.
[4] *Law Reports, Appeal Cases* (1948), p. 95.

presented to the establishment of the New Town. Similarly, in March 1950, the Minister issued an explanation of his decisions in connection with the Stevenage Master Plan inquiry.

(4) '*Some judges have discerned a fourth principle of natural justice . . . that, when Parliament has provided for . . . a public inquiry, . . . held before an inspector appointed for the purpose by the Minister, as a means of guidance to the Minister . . . it is contrary to natural justice that the inspector's report upon the inquiry should not be made available to the parties so heard.*'[1]

The Committee on Ministers' Powers, which put forward the above recommendation where judicial or quasi-judicial functions were exercised by Ministers, found many arguments against publishing the inspector's report: the report is only one element which the Minister has to consider before making his decision; if the report were published it would lead to pressure to make the inspector's recommendation binding or to require the Minister to explain why he did not follow the recommendation (and there are often very sound reasons against both policies); and the value of the inspector's advice to the Minister would be reduced when it was no longer confidential. In favour of publication the committee found only one important argument: only thus could participants at the inquiry be satisfied that their case was fairly put before the Minister; and yet this argument weighed so heavily with them that the committee concluded, 'publication is right'.[2]

The chairman of the Stevenage Council felt the same way and urged that the inspector's report be made public. 'At the moment, one never feels happy that the Minister's decision follows the recommendation of the inspector.'[3] His view was supported by Walker-Smith in the House of Commons:

'. . . the parties should have access to the report of the inspector who holds the inquiry. In my view that is vital in order that it may be seen how nearly the decision of the Minister accords with the report of the man who actually heard the argument, saw the witnesses, and heard the cross-examination. . . .'[4]

Local criticism of the inquiry system partly stemmed, no doubt, from a failure to appreciate adequately that the inquiry came at the end (and not the beginning) of a long administrative process during which the major national factors for and against the advisability of siting the New Town had already been evaluated in Whitehall. The Abercrombie-Ministry proposal to establish a New Town at Stevenage was followed by inter-departmental meetings at which

[1] Committee on Ministers' Powers, p. 80.　　　　[2] Ibid., pp. 97–8, 103–5.
[3] *Hertfordshire Express*, 4th February 1950.
[4] *Hansard*, 13th June 1950, vol. 476, col. 135.

the Ministry made out and won its case before officials of the Ministries of Health, Transport, Agriculture, Labour, and the Board of
Trade; consultations with local authorities in London and Hertfordshire; and the preparation of a preliminary plan by the Ministry.
Only then did the Minister make the draft order setting forth the
designatory area and inviting objections at the local inquiry.[1] The
one step remaining before the appointment of the Development Corporation was the confirmation of the Designation Order, and it was
improbable that any fresh objection introduced at the inquiry stage
would prevent confirmation. 'If I find objections are sound, I am
bound to take them into consideration and either drop the scheme
or modify it', the Minister said truthfully, but a bit legalistically.[2]
His Chief Research Officer remarked more empirically, 'Unless some
rare error of judgement has been made it is extremely unlikely that
the project would be abandoned [after the inquiry]. It is possible
that he [the Minister] may decide to make alterations in the [New
Town] boundary line.'[3]

Thus, the public inquiry did not meet the ideal needs of either
justice or local democracy—but these were never its principal functions. The New Towns Act was designed to implement a national
policy and not to reform the machinery of executive government in
a judicial direction or so as to increase the influence of local opinion
upon the formation of national policy. The public inquiry merely
affords another instance of the degree to which the effective implementation of a national policy may be incompatible with the principles of justice and local democracy. The word *degree* must be
emphasized, since, as we have tried to show, the incompatibility is
anything but absolute.

[1] A review of these stages was given by Gordon Stephenson in a talk on New
Towns (*Architects' Journal*, 3rd October 1946, p. 251).
[2] From the Minister's speech at Apsley (*Hertfordshire Express*, 23rd November 1946).
[3] Gordon Stephenson, op. cit.

CHAPTER EIGHT

Corporation-Government
Relations

I N relations between the Corporation and other branches of the
national Government, including the Ministry of Town and
Country Planning, we come to the crux of the difficulties experienced in building the New Town. Local opposition by the
Residents' Protection Association or the District Council was embarrassing or irritating but, once the court action was lost, presented no
serious challenge to the Corporation: it might delay, but was unlikely
to defeat a New Town resolutely backed by the Government. The
Corporation was more concerned with the firmness of the Government's resolution and the effectiveness with which it was carried out.

A. MINISTERIAL CONTROL

As the Corporations saw it, the Ministry of Town and Country
Planning was their worst enemy as much as best friend. The Reith
Committee had assumed that a Corporation would

'be invested with sufficient powers to enable it to carry out its task free
from the administrative control and consequent interference which are
necessarily associated with full and direct government responsibility. The
appropriate minister . . . should have the power to give such directions as
he may from time to time consider necessary in the public interest in any
matter of major policy. Subject to that, the corporation must have freedom of action comparable with that of a commercial undertaking.'[1]

However, the New Towns Act was largely a Ministry product, and

[1] *Interim Report of the New Towns Committee*, Cmd. 6759 (London, 1946), p. 9.

the Minister did not propose to emasculate himself; at all crucial points final power rested in his hands, as the following citations show:

'the Minister may give directions to any . . . corporation for restricting the exercise by them of any of their powers under this Act, or for requiring them to exercise those powers in any manner specified in the directions. . . .'

'The development corporation . . . shall from time to time submit to the Minister in accordance with any directions given by him in that behalf their proposals for the development . . . of the new town, and the Minister . . . may approve any such proposals either with or without modification.'

'It shall be a condition of the making of advances to a development corporation . . . that the proposals for development . . . shall be approved by the Minister with the concurrence of the Treasury as being likely to secure for the corporation a return which is reasonable, having regard to all the circumstances, when compared with the cost of carrying out those proposals.'

'every development corporation shall provide the Minister with such information relating to the undertaking of the corporation as the Minister may from time to time require, and for that purpose shall permit any person authorised by the Minister in that behalf to inspect and make copies of the accounts, books, documents or papers of the corporation and shall afford such explanation thereof as that person or the Minister may reasonably require.'[1]

From the Government's viewpoint, such provisions were, no doubt, reasonable safeguards to ensure consistency of policy between its responsible member, the Minister, and his appointed agents. How strictly or leniently they should be enforced was largely a matter of individual judgement. The Corporations undoubtedly believed that the Minister was too strict. '. . . development corporations must obtain the Minister's consent for almost every significant action', the Hemel Hempstead Corporation observed.[2] '. . . the Ministry has scrutinised the activities of Corporations in the closest detail, and Ministry officials have attempted to impose their personal views on matters of minor policy', stated a former member of the Harlow Corporation,[3] and the Corporation itself put it on record that 'its progress has been unnecessarily delayed and its expenses unnecessarily swollen by prolonged scrutiny on the part of Ministry officials of matters of detail which might reasonably have been left to the Corporation's discretion'.[4] As C. B. Purdom saw it, the Minister

[1] *New Towns Act*, 1946, 9 & 10 Geo. 6, Ch. 68, Sections 2 (3), 3 (1), 12 (7), and 13 (7).

[2] *New Towns Act*, 1946. *Reports of the . . . Development Corporations for the period ending 31st March*, 1948 (London, 1949), p. 67.

[3] Countess Russell, 'New Town Corporations Swaddled in Red Tape', the *Daily Telegraph*, 30th May 1950.

[4] *Reports of the . . . Development Corporations for the period ending 31st March*, 1950, p. 103.

'has made himself the autocrat of the new towns, subject to the Treasury but otherwise with practically unchallengeable power. He has the first and last word on almost everything in the new towns with no appeal against him.'[1]

The initial idea of a public corporation, as exemplified in the Central Electricity Board established in 1926 or the British Broadcasting Corporation in 1927, had been to combine the advantages of public control and private enterprise. The public corporation 'provided a form of public management which did not mean putting socialized industries or services under the bureaucratic control of Government departments or of the Treasury, but equipped them with a more business-like and flexible form of management, and, thus, met the objection felt by so many people to' socialization on the score of bureaucracy'.[2] But New Town Corporations felt they had distinctly the worst of both worlds, and placed the blame more upon the Ministry than upon Parliament.

'The Corporations are spending public money, and a Minister must be able to satisfy Parliament that the money is being spent wisely. The Act that created Development Corporations expressly provided that certain of their activities need approval by the Minister. But from the fact that it placed on statutory Corporations the direct responsibility for building new towns, Parliament must be presumed to have intended that the degree of Departmental control must be different from what it would have been if the Department had been directly responsible for the enterprise.'[3]

One Corporation officer suggested that the root cause of the ineffectiveness of the New Towns organization was its failure to fix responsibility between Corporations and Ministry. There was almost nothing for which a Corporation was entirely responsible and for which the Ministry did not carry some vague share of responsibility. Not only Corporation plans, but also expenditure on both capital and revenue accounts was subjected to minute and detailed advance scrutiny by Ministry officials. The only matter of importance over

---

[1] C. B. Purdom, *The Building of Satellite Towns* (London, 1949), p. 482.

[2] G. D. H. Cole and Raymond Postgate, *The Common People 1746–1946* (London, 1946), p. 608.

[3] Harlow Corporation, *Reports of the . . . Development Corporation for the period ending 31st March*, 1950, p. 103. It is worth noting that the Reith Committee had assumed that a Development Corporation 'will be invested with sufficient powers to enable it to carry out its task free from the administrative control and consequent interference which are necessarily associated with full and direct government responsibility. The appropriate minister . . . should have the power to give such directions as he may from time to time consider necessary in the public interest in any matter of major policy. Subject to that, the corporation must have freedom of action comparable with that of a commercial undertaking' (Cmd. 6759, p. 9).

which Corporations had unfettered discretion was the selection of their staffs.[1]

The consequence of these rigid Ministerial controls was that, at worst, Corporations might be obliged to drop or alter a plan into which a vast amount of labour had been put; and, at best, delay and uncertainty (with all their deleterious effects upon morale and efficiency) were inevitable until the Ministry made its decision. Not only the Master Plan, but subsequent plans for every site and construction project, every purchase and capital investment down to cars and office furniture, had to receive Ministerial authorization, as the following examples illustrate:

(1) In 1947, when it was difficult to buy furniture, Corporations wanted to use the services of the Ministry of Works. Permission was first refused by the Ministry of Town and Country Planning; then it was granted with the specification that furniture must be obtained from no other source. When one chairman observed that this channel would not be able to provide furniture suitable for a boardroom, the Minister conceded that, if this were the case, the Corporation would be free to obtain it from other sources.

(2) Similarly, after the Corporations asked for permission to purchase cars (then in short supply) through the Ministry of Supply, the Minister of Town and Country Planning proposed, in February 1948, that they obtain their cars exclusively from this source. Several chairmen suggested that it was undesirable for the Minister to make himself responsible for such details; it would be sufficient for him to issue to Corporations a solemn injunction to be as economical as possible in the purchase and use of cars. However the Minister replied that he was in fact ultimately responsible for matters of this type and would have to answer questions concerning them in the House of Commons. They were, moreover, delicate matters on which public attention was then very much focused. It was the wish of the Government that Corporations should use the Ministry of Supply, and if he were to be their instrument in obtaining cars he would have to take responsibility for approving their requirements. He undertook, however, to reconsider the matter in the light of the comments which had been made. (His proposal was subsequently enforced and Corporations were no longer free to obtain vehicles other than through the Ministry of Supply—as Stevenage car dealers discovered and protested in August 1949.)

(3) In 1948, after the plans for a workmen's hostel had been prepared in detail, down to the contract documents, a difference of

[1] The Minister stated that 'the creation of higher posts [by Development Corporations] should have my prior approval'; junior appointments 'are subject to general budgetary control . . . [and] do not require my prior approval' (*Hansard*, 11th November 1947, vol. 444, col. 170).

opinion was discovered between the Stevenage Corporation and the Ministry. The Corporation felt that its standard of accommodation was the bare minimum which should be provided, if labour were to be attracted; the Ministry, anxious to reduce expenditure, suggested that the standard be lowered. The Corporation thereupon abandoned the scheme and decided instead to accommodate labour in permanent dwellings and temporary contractors' camps.

(4) In the summer 1949, a model of several Stevenage flats was seen by the Minister who commented that, while he appreciated the general layout, it was a dispersed one and might prove expensive. A Corporation officer responded that maintenance of the open spaces would cost only £500 per annum. The Ministry then proposed that, to make fuller use of the land, more flats and/or houses should be added, raising the density from 50 to 80–100 persons per acre. The chairman urged the Corporation not to alter the scheme and undertook to discuss it with the Minister as soon as possible.

(5) The Harlow Corporation proposed to erect a nine-storey block of flats. Since 'the Minister himself had urged us to avoid monotony and to be bold in all we undertook, the Corporation had no reason to fear that the proposal would be regarded, as it was, as inappropriate and reckless. . . . only the personal intercession of our chairman with the . . . Minister obtained . . . approval. . . .'[1]

Certain general principles of Ministry policy emerged in terms of which these decisions could be justified, such as the conservation of agricultural land and, above all, the pursuit of economy. Thus an informant who saw things from the Ministry's viewpoint commented that both the Stevenage and Harlow flats

'are examples of the financial irresponsibility of the respective corporations. They are luxury flats: (a) no one else in the country is allowed to build such flats, (b) they are not the kind of dwellings required in early stages. The Ministry has interfered too much in detail but it may be partly excused as the Corporations and their staffs as a whole have tended to get into an economic cloud cuckoo land. Nearly all the early developments are much too expensive and I imagine Ministry officers have been largely concerned in trying to bring down costs—which means interference in design details.'

In its scrutiny of Corporation expenditure, the Ministry acted as handmaiden of the Treasury. The New Towns Act prohibited the raising of loans by Development Corporations (other public corporations had been permitted to do this by Parliament) which had, accordingly, to rely for their financing exclusively upon Treasury grants repayable as returns accrued from development. Naturally the Ministry examined each Corporation plan carefully to ensure that a reasonable return was secured on the outlay involved. '. . . the

[1] Countess Russell, op. cit.

CORPORATION-GOVERNMENT RELATIONS

one standard by which . . . [Corporations'] efficiency can be gauged is the profit and loss account which has to be rendered each year to Parliament. . . . In the present state of the national economy . . . it is vital that the New Towns should be made to pay for themselves.'¹ This, the Corporations retorted, was too narrow a view of their task:

'The responsibilities of development corporations, for what may be called the community development side of their work and for setting a high standard of amenity in the widest sense in the new towns, clearly preclude them from making financial considerations their main object. Moreover, there is little evidence upon which it could be positively asserted that the development of existing towns taken as a whole has "paid" in the narrow financial sense. . . . Though it may well be that a development corporation, by tapping the land values created by it, can show a profit on developing its new town, the real test of its success is not to be measured solely by the state of its accounts, but also by results, which, while not reflected in its balance sheet, are from the point of view of the public quite as important, even in terms of money.'²

It was difficult to determine with certainty the point of view of 'the public', but evidently the Treasury and the Government were concerned more about a Development Corporation's balance sheet than about less tangible 'results'.

Ministry decisions could always be justified (by the Ministry); but they could not always be predicted (especially by the Corporations). 'When the Minister came down to Stevenage, none of us could predict which way he would jump, . . .' a Stevenage Corporation informant remarked. 'The Minister', said a well-qualified observer, 'is very ready to accept experimentation provided it has a substantial basis. He will approve anything that has a reasonable basis.' But alternate and equally reasonable lines of action were constantly available, and which course prevailed depended upon the special circumstances, personalities, and politics involved. To this extent no completely rational policy could be enunciated by the Ministry, and no completely rational choice was possible between rival Corporation and Ministry policies. The issue was simply decided by the stronger—or luckier—party.

Prudence sometimes dictated acquiescence by the Minister in a Corporation decision he disliked. But generally it was the other way round; and, indeed, the Minister's weapons were so potent they rarely had to be used and his informal recommendation was usually accepted by the Corporation as a command. The scurry and bustle that swept the Stevenage Corporation from top to bottom, the

¹ Editorial, 'New Towns Must Pay for Themselves', *The Architects' Journal*, 21st September 1950, p. 249.
² W. O. Hart (General Manager, Hemel Hempstead Corporation), 'New Town Development Corporations', *Public Administration* (1948), vol. 26, pp. 152-3.

special arrangement of luncheon seats, food, and wine, the special assignment and careful preparation of duties, the rehearsal of words before a rare Ministerial visit,[1] afford a measure of his importance. (And what was a noteworthy occasion for the Corporation was, we fear, less noteworthy for the Minister.) It is worth recording that when the Minister visited Stevenage in April 1949, he took issue with the Corporation on one major and one minor matter (the acquisition of commercial properties and the quality of a Corporation booklet), on both of which the Corporation thereupon reversed its attitude.

Some of the give and take between Corporations and the Ministry obviously depended upon the personalities involved. Chairmen who regarded themselves (and were regarded by many influential personages) as the Minister's peer or superior, were apt to view his recommendations as interference in their affairs. Nor did they place as much reliance upon the Minister's services as less-experienced chairmen. Acquaintance with high civil servants and familiarity with the machinery of government often enabled them to put their case directly to other Government departments. Some chairmen seemed able to get prompt and favourable decisions from the Minister, which gave their New Towns a pronounced advantage over others. '[Chairman X] can wring things from the Minister,' one informant remarked, 'and so can [Chairman Y]—he hasn't cared, he's just gone ahead and done things and he's got away with it. [Z] hasn't done that.'

The Corporations were not the only powers the Minister had to conciliate: there were the local authorities both in New Town and London areas, his own advisers, other Ministries, party leaders, spokesmen for the town and country planning movement, rural preservation societies, builders, quarriers, and every conceivable group interested in a particular case. To cite only Ministries, for instance, at the 20th September 1949 Inter-Departmental conference of technical officers to consider the Stevenage Master Plan, there were present representatives of the Ministries of Agriculture and Fisheries, Education, Fuel and Power, Health, Labour and National Service, Transport, and Works, the Board of Trade, the Post Office, and the Railway Executive. Each Ministerial decision was a semijudicial, semi-political judgement on the relative weight of (more or less) balanced and constantly changing evidence.

Were the Ministry more powerful and experienced, such decisions might have been taken in its stride: chips must fly before trees fall. But trees are not lightly felled in Britain, and the Ministry did not always help things along. It took, as a rule, inordinately long to make

[1] If our information was correct, the Minister visited the Corporation offices at Aston four times up to July 1950.

up its mind. Although the first draft had been prepared by the Ministry itself in 1946, and continuous consultations took place in ensuing years, the Ministry took eight months to approve the Stevenage Master Plan after its formal submission in the summer of 1949.

'The Harlow Corporation, having been constituted in May, 1947, submitted its Master Plan for the Minister's approval in January, 1948, being the first New Town to do so. Approval, with modifications, was received on March 15, 1949.

'Subsequent development proposals . . . have been detained by the Ministry for periods of not less than five months.'[1]

The Minister was aware of such facts, receiving many direct and indirect complaints on the score. In February 1948 he replied to one Corporation's complaint that some delay might be inevitable when statutory and administrative controls were unavoidable. (The Ministry staff 'don't consider themselves omniscient, as the Corporations do', said one informant. 'If they want to approve a new school, for example, they go to the Ministry of Education and get their views and it takes a long time to get them.') In July 1949, the Minister explained privately that there was a shortage of staff at the Ministry which could not soon be alleviated as he was under pressure to keep down the size of his staff; however, the importance of New Towns had been recognized by the creation of a separate New Towns Department in the Ministry which would gradually be expanded as more sites were designated.

In the light of the Ministry's insistence upon economy, the Harlow Corporation pointed out that Ministry delays

'can cost money in two ways. So far as they may be caused by examination of detail of no great importance they mean that the time of Departmental staff is being wasted, and so far as they impose an unnecessarily long gap between the completion of a plan and starting to carry it out, they mean that staff which is ready to get on with the job cannot do so except by anticipating approval, and so risking a waste of time and labour if approval should eventually not be given. . . . the five months' thought devoted by the officials of the Ministry to [two Corporation projects] . . . ended in acceptance of both, subject to slight modifications which effected a reduction of some £3,000 in programmes estimated to cost nearly two million pounds.'[2]

(The Corporations' debilitating experience, it may be interpolated, was not new. Bureaucracy has a long and not entirely noble history, and some of its most paralysing achievements lie in the field of public housing. In 1920, for example, a high official of the Ministry of

[1] Countess Russell, op. cit.
[2] *Reports of the . . . Development Corporations for the period ending 31st March*, 1950, pp. 103–4.

Health estimated that '20 weeks was the *minimum* time in which a [public housing] scheme could be approved';[1] while, in 1950, a London borough council had to approach the County Council and the Ministry of Health from four to six times for approvals and consents before commencing construction on a housing site.[2] '. . . there is probably no other industry in the country which is subject to so much control from three separate Ministries' as is housing, said the chairman of the Crawley Development Corporation. '. . . the machine is so complicated in some respects and it tends to be so stultifying that, if and when unemployment overtakes this country it is still as complicated, it will spell something like disaster. . . .')[3]

'The key to the whole business', said an informant sympathetic to the Ministry, 'is surely early informal consultations. These, for various and often childish reasons, the Corporations avoided.' However, the reasons were no more childish than the motives of men generally are. They reflected a natural wish for independence. When the Ministry attempted to encourage consultations and the exchange of information with Corporations, Corporation officers frequently suspected this was not just to expedite, but also to exercise surveillance over, their work. Consultation with the Ministry could be a devious form of command. (We have seen in the previous chapter that the Stevenage Council, whose power was less than the Corporations', was still more dissatisfied with the nature of Ministry 'consultations'.)

Thus, in November 1949, the Minister advised Corporations informally that it would be embarrassing for him to have to turn down development proposals after they had been fully formulated; the proper course was for Corporation technical officers to consult the Ministry staff at the earliest possible moment, before views on either side had time to harden; if the Ministry staff criticized a proposal in its early stages, that was not necessarily the end of the matter: the proper course for the Corporation, if they did not agree with the criticisms, was to take the matter up with the Department 'administratively' (i.e., the final decision lay in the hands not of the technical but the administrative branch of the Ministry, though administrative officers were advised by the technical staff). Again, in July 1949, Chairman X charged that approval in advance of quarterly revenue budgets, which the Ministry had recently instituted, could only be justified in terms of a distrust by the Ministry of the Corporations.

[1] E. D. Simon, *A City Council from Within* (London, 1926), p. 35. Italics in original.
[2] Holborn Borough Council report, *The Times*, 23rd February 1950.
[3] Sir Thomas Bennett, 'Experiences in Building Progress', *Architect and Building News*, 14th October 1949, p. 376.

The Minister replied that he had complete confidence that every Corporation was exercising a responsible control over its financial affairs, but he had his own duty to discharge and thought there was nothing unreasonable in asking how matters were progressing. All he proposed was that approval given by the Ministry to Corporation yearly budgets should not be an unqualified approval, but should be reviewed quarterly.

Fundamentally, there was a conflict not only of power, but also of function between Ministry and Corporation. The Ministry was a permanent branch of His Majesty's Government, charged by law 'with the duty of securing consistency and continuity in the framing and execution of a national policy with respect to the use and development of land throughout England and Wales';[1] the Corporation was a temporary agency which would be dissolved (its functions transferred to the local government authority) as soon as the New Town was completed. If Corporation members did not build quickly and well during their three-year tenure of office, they had wasted their time and public money, and failed in their purpose; whereas the Ministry's function was to ensure that the New Towns advanced at a speed and in a manner commensurate with the national welfare as determined by the Government of the day—that they did not, for instance, make undue demands upon capital, labour, materials, or land needed for other purposes. At times, economic vicissitudes obliged the Ministry to restrict the progress and endanger the success of the New Towns. The curtailment of capital investments in 1947 halted almost all land acquisition and construction in New Towns, and confined Corporations' activities mainly to drawing-boards and conference rooms. As economic conditions improved, the most stringent controls were lifted, but Corporations had still to eke along from year to year, coming constantly to Ministry, hat in hand, for their meagre allowance. Under these circumstances, tension inevitably developed between the Corporations and the Ministry.

One chairman protested vigorously to the Minister, in March 1949, that acquisition of land was the keystone of the entire New Towns programme, and he regarded the Ministry's go-slow policy as inadequate. Another chairman contended that psychologically, economically, and from the point of view of convenience, it would be best for Corporations to buy the whole of their designated area immediately; he had never been impressed with the argument that acquisition of land on a large scale was likely to be inflationary. The Minister replied there was general agreement that Corporations should ultimately own all the land in their designated area, but the implementation of that goal had to be modified owing to the country's economic difficulties. He noted that the Crawley Corpora-

[1] Minister of Town and Country Planning Act, 1943, 6 & 7 Geo. 6, Ch. 5, 1.

tion had been authorized to acquire the shops in its area and saw no reason why other Corporations should not submit similar proposals, but emphasized that he could never justify the acquisition of land purely in order to obtain the powers of landlord control. Accordingly he suggested that for the immediate future Corporations should rest content with the power to acquire (*a*) land needed for operations during the next two or three years, (*b*) shops and other property likely to increase substantially in value, (*c*) special and urgent cases. It need hardly be added that the Corporations did not rest content. The Hemel Hempstead Corporation, for example, publicly objected that

'Commercial property is likely to be the main source from which the Corporation must seek to regain any increase in values created by its development; and authority to purchase this type of property has not been granted in the absence of the Corporation being able to show a speculative rise in prices. The Corporation is of the opinion that this limited policy of land acquisition is unsatisfactory.'[1]

In their struggle with the Ministry, the Corporations would have been strengthened had they been able to maintain a united front, but this was by no means easy. A difference in individual problems (sewerage in one case, industry in another, court action in a third) militated against it, and the competitive spirit appeared as prominent as the co-operative. At one chairmen's conference, A asked B what his Corporation was doing in regard to industry, and was somewhat surprised when B thanked him afterwards for the opportunity to speak on the subject. Many other chairmen would have resented this 'interference', A remarked. A group of Socialist M.P.s observed that

'joint bulk purchase by . . . public agencies can effect enormous economies. . . . But we shall not get joint bulk purchasing unless we're prepared to tread on a few toes and to cut into the little empires of some of the empire-builders in the public service. So far we have not even persuaded the New Towns Corporations . . . to purchase jointly their common requirements.'[2]

Their comments about 'empire-builders' had a measure of truth (did the M.P.s not aspire to an empire of their own?), but oversimplified the issues.[3]

Nevertheless, a degree of concerted action was achieved by Cor-

[1] *New Towns Act*, 1946. *Reports of the . . . Development Corporations for the period ending 31st March*, 1949 (London, 1949), p. 98.
[2] A Group of Members of Parliament, *Keeping Left* (London, January 1950), p. 36.
[3] For instance, some New Town chairmen noted, bulk purchase tended to result in scarce materials lying idle and in the sometimes embarrassing necessity to take delivery of goods before building operations reached a stage when they could be used.

porations (more often between two or three neighbouring Corporations with friendly chairmen and common problems) and a number of committees were established on the officer and chairman level to discuss joint problems and co-ordinate policy: among others, Social Development Officers, Finance Officers, General Managers, and Chairmen met regularly at separate sessions. These conferences achieved much of value, but were hampered by mutual suspicions and a jealous regard by each group for its prestige and powers. Thus, several chairmen expressed concern lest the Social Development Officers' committee on social and economic research push Corporations into policy decisions they had not agreed upon (e.g., on the nature of New Town neighbourhood units and community centres); and the Minister, in turn, expressed concern that any policy made by Corporations should not embarrass him in dealing with problems outside New Towns.

With marked foresight, the Reith Committee, envisaging the state of affairs that subsequently developed, had recommended the establishment of a Central Advisory Commission to co-ordinate the work of Development Corporations and safeguard their independence from excessive Ministerial control.[1] This recommendation was never acted upon, among other reasons, presumably because the Ministry objected to a reduction of its powers. The conference of chairmen, vice-chairmen, Minister, and Ministry officers that first met in December 1946, attempted, with varying success, to serve a similar function in a manner more congenial to the Ministry. At the beginning, this conference concerned itself with astonishing matters such as the purchase of office equipment and cars, the salaries of staff members, and the like. The atmosphere was reportedly quite formal and there seemed to be a search for subjects which might safely be discussed. In July 1948, the conference reviewed its functions. The Minister remarked that the meetings had not operated as he had originally hoped; matters of detail were really not appropriate to a gathering of this nature, which he had convened originally to achieve an exchange of views on common problems. These sentiments were echoed by various chairmen, and a notable improvement in the significance of discussions followed. Indeed, they now threatened to become too significant for the Ministry's taste. Early in 1949, a morning conference of chairmen was convened which met *without* Ministry representatives, thus enabling Corporations to present a stronger front against the Ministry at the joint afternoon sessions. It appeared that the Corporations were moving in the direction of greater unity and independence of action

[1] *Final Report of the New Towns Committee*, Cmd. 6876 (London, 1946), pp. 62–4. Purdom (op. cit., p. 482) and a number of other authorities have also called for the establishment of such a body.

when the new Minister, Hugh Dalton, disbanded the conference soon after taking office in March 1950 (asking chairmen to meet him separately in the future).

B. GOVERNMENT DISCORD

There can be no doubt that the lack of co-ordination among different branches of the national Government seriously impeded the New Towns programme during its first four years. In relevant legislation introduced into the House, in the national allotment of building labour and housing, above all in the distribution of industry and housing within the Greater London area, the right hand of the Government did not know what its left hand was doing.

On 12th November 1948, a Bill was introduced in the House of Commons to place licensed premises in the New Towns under the control of the Home Secretary. Five days later New Town chairmen complained bitterly to the Minister of Town and Country Planning at not having been consulted in the drafting of this Bill which so obviously affected their interests. In a matter of this kind, the Minister replied, it must be for the Government to make up its own mind. He emphasized that the Corporations' views had been taken into account by the Government and had by no means been ignored; he was not, however, in a position to disclose confidential information once a decision had been made. Highly dissatisfied, chairmen met by themselves soon after and sent a delegation to present their views to the Home Secretary, which won for them a certain amount of control over New Town licensed premises, though less than they wished.[1]

At the end of 1946, the Ministry of Town and Country Planning had proposed that labour earmarked for New Towns in the London region should begin at 2,500 in June 1947 and rise to just over 40,000 by December 1951—a sizeable proportion of the national building force, which could have got the programme under way at proper speed.[2] Of course, nothing of the sort took place, and when the

[1] According to the Licensing Act, 1949, a local advisory committee of sixteen members would assist the Secretary of State's management of licensed premises in the Stevenage New Town: three would be members of the Development Corporation, five would be appointed by the Secretary of State after consulting the Corporation, and eight would represent various local bodies. 'The position of the Development Corporations is not wholly satisfactory. . . . the system of state management of licensed premises which has been extended to the new towns will impair both their social policy and their financial prospects. Any public control which was thought desirable could have been much better exercised directly by the corporations' ('London's New Towns', *The Economist*, 5th November 1949, p. 993).

[2] As of 31st December 1950, it was estimated that 199,400 men sixteen and over were employed in England and Wales on the construction of new permanent houses and flats and the preparation of housing sites (Ministry of Local

Government capital restrictions eased and, in the summer of 1948,
New Towns in the Greater London area were released from the
ceiling of 300 labourers which the Government had imposed the
previous year, they found themselves competing for labour with the
London County Council and local housing authorities—at a considerable disadvantage, because of the distance which labour had to
travel to reach the New Towns, and the lack of accommodation
there. The Harlow Corporation noted that 'The Ministry of Labour
. . . will not permit operatives living locally to be employed on New
Town development'.[1] The Ministries of Works and Labour advised
the Hemel Hempstead Corporation 'that the Eastern [i.e., the local]
Region is incapable of any material contribution; labour, they say,
must be drawn mostly from London'.[2] Likewise, the Stevenage
Corporation discovered that:

'There is in Stevenage and its immediate district no local labour which
can make any contribution to the Corporation's constructional programme
and . . . the Corporation has been informed by the Ministries of Works
and Labour that there is in the Eastern Region no more labour available
than is essential for the normal needs of the region. Experience in the first
engineering contract has confirmed this view as the whole of the men employed come from sufficient distances to qualify them for the payment of
subsistence and periodic travelling allowances. . . . As Stevenage lies a
considerable distance from sources of labour outside the Eastern Region,
e.g. from London, it is expected that the imported labour will not travel
daily but will have to live locally. This of course entails the payment of
subsistence allowances and the provision of living accommodation.'[3]

The effect of travel and subsistence allowances or the building of
local hostels for imported labour was to increase the per unit cost of
houses and, in turn, the level of their economic rentals, which
weighed against a policy of decentralization on immediate economic
grounds, as the *Economist* pointed out. 'The logical place to concentrate urban housing [if economy is desired] . . . is in the vicinity of
existing towns where a reservoir of labour exists which cannot easily
be transferred elsewhere. From the viewpoint of minimizing the
investmel programme while maximizing the output of houses, new
towns have a poor claim on national resources.'[4]

The Board of Trade did not encourage the movement of industry
to New Towns. Harlow Corporation, for example, reported in
March 1949:

Government and Planning, *Housing Return for England and Wales* 31st December
1950, Cmd. 8138 (London, 1951), p. 9). In 1946, of course, it had been hoped
to expand the building force far beyond this figure by 1950.

[1] *Reports of the . . . Development Corporations for the period ending 31st March*,
1949, p. 69.
[2] Ibid., pp. 97–8.   [3] Ibid., 1950, p. 183.
[4] Editorial, *The Economist*, 11th October 1947.

'It appears to be the present policy of the Government . . . that the Board of Trade must not approve the establishment of any industry anywhere other than in a Development Area, if it might equally well establish itself in a Development Area. If this is indeed so, the choice of Development Corporations will be so narrowed as to place them under a grievous handicap in attaining their aim, difficult enough in any case, of building up self-contained, balanced communities. Moreover, no firm can establish itself in a New Town . . . without a building licence, and it does not appear at present that the licence-granting authorities have any instructions to give any weight to the consideration that the establishment of a particular industry in a particular New Town may be an integral part of making the policy of that Town a success.'[1]

By March 1950, the Corporation was more dismayed:

'The past year has seen no improvement in the position and the Corporation is seriously concerned at the possibility of houses being available in considerable numbers without the necessary factories being there to provide work locally. A number of industrialists, suitable for introduction to the new town, are prepared to lease or build premises but so far, with one exception, it has not been possible to obtain the promise of a building licence.

'The exception was a building for a research association employing only 20 men.

'This is now the greatest problem unsolved. A solution is outside the powers of the Corporation. It is impossible to exaggerate the importance of finding one.'[2]

The London County Council stated that the decentralization of industry from central London and the 'supposedly accepted aim of preventing the further growth of industry in London' was being frustrated by the Government's insistence that the immediate increase of industrial exports take precedence over all other considerations.[3] By 1951 it was expected,

'there will be industrial employment available on the L.C.C.'s [post-war out-county housing estates] . . . for only 865 persons, compared with an estimated labour force of 8,600 persons and an eventual labour force of 21,000 persons. Only small, local factories have, in fact, been allowed to go. These "quasi-satellite" estates have thus become the very thing which the Council intended that they should never be—"dormitories". They are a fresh extension of what was called in the war years, when planning was much talked of, "the London sprawl".'[4]

If the eight New Towns in the Greater London area were to be self-contained, it was calculated that they would have to provide 68,355 new factory jobs when they were completed. At June 1950, however,

[1] *Report of the . . . Harlow . . . Development Corporation for the period ending 31st March,* 1949, p. 70.
[2] Ibid., 1950, p. 100.
[3] Editorial, 'London Housing', *The Times,* 5th August 1950.
[4] Geoffrey Hutchinson, letter, *The Times,* 23rd August 1950.

only 660 workers were employed in new factories licensed by the Ministry of Works in these New Towns.[1]

The Ministry of Health's system of allocating the national housing quota to existing local authorities left New Towns largely out in the cold until the summer of 1950 when the Ministers of Health and Town and Country Planning agreed upon a special—if small— housing allocation for New Towns. (Under the quota, Development Corporations were permitted to let contracts for 2,260 houses during the year, or just over 1 per cent of the national housing quota of 200,000.[2]) Some 76,300 houses were needed to complete the eight New Towns in the Greater London area. At 24th June 1950, only 154 houses had been completed and occupied, and 952 were under construction.[3] By contrast, the rate of building within the County of London at this time was 'about 10,000 houses [or flats] a year by the L.C.C. and about 5,000 and 1,000 by the boroughs and private enterprise respectively—a total of 16,000'.[4]

It was estimated in October 1948 that 'Twenty-three per cent of all new post-war houses of Greater London have been built inside the Green Belt' which Abercrombie and the Ministry of Town and Country Planning had hoped to preserve inviolate around central London.[5] The invasion was due largely to the high price of land in central areas and the failure of New Towns and country towns designated by the Minister to contribute materially to rehousing the population of London. The Socialist majority on the London County Council approved the Abercrombie plan, but could not ignore the immediate needs of its constituents for the sake of a distant advantage. Its housing programme required planning permission from the Ministry, but the Council managed to get it and its experienced and influential officers and politicians built up a housing machine far more potent than that of the New Town Corporations. Much might be said against the Council's housing programme from the planning point of view, but the Council was trying (and, as the New Town Corporations saw it, succeeding all too well) to alleviate overcrowding in central London in the only way then open to it.

'Cries about the disappearance of the Green Belt seem rather trivial against the mass of human misery in London resulting from the housing

[1] *Hansard*, 22nd June 1950, vol. 476, col. 157 (written answer by the Parliamentary Secretary to the Minister of Town and Country Planning).

[2] *Architects' Journal*, 7th September 1950, p. 229. See also 'Housing Allocation System, No Relation to . . . Dispersal Policy', *Manchester Guardian*, 9th December 1950.

[3] *Hansard*, 27th June 1950, vol. 476, cols. 209–10 (written answer by the Minister of Town and Country Planning).

[4] *The Times*, 4th August 1950.

[5] Editorial, 'How Goes the London Plan?' *Architect and Building News*, 29th October 1948, p. 351.

shortage. . . . Planning must accommodate itself to circumstances; as Mr. Gibson [chairman of the Housing Committee of the London County Council] put it, it must be "for the good of the people, and not only for the spiritual satisfaction of the planners". Housing estates in the Green Belt may be contrary to first principles. They are very definitely not contrary to the people's urgent need.'[1]

In June 1948, the Minister of Town and Country Planning informed New Town Corporations that he and the Minister of Health had met representatives of the L.C.C. and told them it would be necessary for the L.C.C. to regard New Towns in the London region as a partial solution of their housing problems. The L.C.C. had enough land for a building programme lasting five years or a little longer, and the Ministry of Town and Country Planning was refusing to allow them to acquire any more land. As this would result in the L.C.C.'s housing activities outside the County ending about 1953, the L.C.C. wished to be assured that New Towns in the London region would then be building 6,000 houses a year (which was its own rate of construction in 1948). The Minister of Town and Country Planning replied that no doubt Corporations would make faster progress if the L.C.C. were not competing with them for labour and materials.

In August 1950, the L.C.C. noted that the land available to it both inside and outside the county was running short, and again expressed concern at the slow rate of development of New Towns and existing country towns which were to take the surplus population of London.[2] It had yet received no guarantee that either the New Towns or existing towns would take a 'proper share' of residents from London. 'What practical working arrangement has the L.C.C. with any of the New Towns Development Corporations which are planned to take London's overspill population?' asked John Hare. 'None that I, as Conservative leader on the L.C.C. Housing Committee, have been told about.'[3]

Hoping for unified support for a programme endorsed by all parties, each New Town Corporation found itself merely another special interest group within a multifarious nation and Government, fighting a war of attrition against established powers which, pursuing ends of their own, were only partly interested (if not indifferent or hostile) to those of the Corporations. '. . . the New Towns Act gave to Development Corporations very wide powers; but

[1] Editorial, *Architect and Building News*, 4th October 1946, p. 3.
[2] The L.C.C. then had 750 acres inside and 1,200 acres outside the county, upon which 28,000 and 30,300 houses, respectively, were to be erected. By contrast, 165,000 families were on the Council's housing lists and new applications were being registered at the rate of 4,000 a month (*The Times*, 4th August 1950).
[3] Letter, *The Times*, 30th September, 1950.

unfortunately most of these powers already belonged to someone else.'[1] The work of the Stevenage Corporation was an endless series of negotiations with local, regional, and national authorities—the Stevenage Urban District Council, the neighbouring Rural and Parish Councils, the County Council, the London County Council and Borough Councils, the Metropolitan Water and Lee Conservancy Boards, and both regional and national offices of such Ministries as Health, Transport, Works, and Labour, the Board of Trade, British Railways, the British Electricity Authority, etc.— whose functions impinged upon the Corporation's at some vital point.

It was often difficult for a Corporation to know whether it was more efficacious to approach a Government department directly or through the Ministry of Town and Country Planning. The latter course might be roundabout, the former futile. The Minister said in July 1949 (perhaps in a benign mood) that he had no objection to Corporations establishing direct contact with other Government departments on any matter where the course appeared to be advantageous. But the most important policies could only be expedited at the Ministerial level, and here Corporations had to approach the Minister and wait patiently for his report, as the following examples indicate:

(a) In November 1949, the Minister agreed with chairmen that there were strong reasons for Corporations having power to sell houses on long leases and hoped to convince his colleagues of this. This was a matter of policy, which could not be determined at official level, and he proposed to take an early opportunity of having an informal talk on the subject with the Minister of Health.

(b) In connection with the Government's policy of decentralization, one chairman told the Minister, in July 1949, that he had been pressing to get a Government department to establish itself at his New Town; other chairmen agreed such movements should be encouraged. The Minister replied that he would discuss the matter with the Lord President of the Council.

(c) In the autumn 1949, the Minister conferred with the President of the Board of Trade about facilitating the movement of industries from London to the New Towns. The President was sympathetic, but asked for certain information, particularly relating to the industrial needs of the New Towns, before reaching a decision. A Working Party was accordingly set up to ascertain the facts.

It was in these top-level decisions that the status and power of the Minister within the Government was so important to the success of the New Towns. The Ministry of Town and Country Planning was a relatively new department created in February 1943 by the Coalition

[1] Countess Russell, op. cit.

Government, and Mr. Lewis Silkin was its second Minister, succeeding Mr. W. S. Morrison in July 1945. He was not a member of the Cabinet, which meant that at least seventeen Ministers outranked him (including, in particular, four with important functions relative to New Towns—the Chancellor of the Exchequer, the President of the Board of Trade, and the Ministers of Health and Labour), and the Ministry as a whole was small and inexperienced compared to others which, over the course of years, had grown to leviathan size and become powers of the first magnitude in the national life.

William Robson had foreseen, in 1945, the difficulties in store for a weak Ministry of Town and Country Planning in its relations with other departments.

'On the one side . . . would be arrayed a number of well-established departments possessing recognised constitutional responsibilities, long administrative experience and much technical knowledge in their particular fields; in close touch with the many powerful organisations of producers, traders, local authorities and other bodies whose interests are concerned in planning, and usually in frequent and friendly contact with the leading figures in those organisations.

'On the other side would be the lone figure of the Ministry of Town and Country Planning, regarded by its older fellows as a newcomer in the family of Government Departments, a mere infant in arms, inferior in powers, status and prestige to most of those with whom it would be in conflict on this matter. It would be disparaged as ignorant, theoretical and inexperienced.'[1]

Mr. Silkin, the only member of the Government who did not contest the February 1950 General Election, was subsequently elevated to the honourable retirement of the House of Lords, receiving a peerage in the Honours List of 8th June 1950. It will be interesting to see if his successor, Hugh Dalton—a Cabinet member and former Chancellor of the Exchequer, reputed in May 1950 to rank number five in the new Government hierarchy[2]—is able to speed up the New Towns programme.

Some persons argued that if the New Towns had been put under the Ministry of Health, long responsible for Government-subsidized housing, they would have made better progress. In January 1951, the Government took the bolder, and in some ways preferable, alternative of placing the housing responsibilities of the Ministry of Health under the authority of the Ministry of Town and Country Planning, which was renamed the Ministry of Local Government

[1] William Robson, in Gilbert and Elizabeth McAllister (eds.), *Homes, Towns and Countryside* (London, 1945), pp. 147–8.

[2] 'Since Mr. Hugh Dalton became Minister of Town and Country Planning his reputation, it is said, ranks No. 5 in the hierarchy. This means that if he wants to talk to a Minister lower in the batting order his colleague must come to him and not the other way round' (Pendennis in *The Observer*, 21st May 1950).

and Planning and would henceforth wield powers more commensurate with its original functions. The new Ministry would be responsible for: (1) housing and New Towns; (2) services such as water and sewerage; (3) planning and control of the use of land; (4) general oversight of the work of local government; (5) financial responsibility towards local authorities.[1]

Other critics (absorbing the teachings of Geddes, Mumford, and the Tennessee Valley Authority) suggested that a regional authority and not a central Government department like the Ministry of Town and Country Planning was the best instrument to execute the *Greater London Plan*. The 145 local authorities responsible, in 1946, for planning in the Greater London area were reduced to twelve by the Town and Country Planning Act, 1947, but development was still conducted by 181 separate local authorities and a large number of statutory undertakers.[2] The conferences, joint planning boards, and inter-departmental committees which the Ministry fostered to encourage co-operation among these local authorities were often unable to reach agreement, and generally lacked the power to enforce such decisions as they arrived at. A Ministry committee appointed to review this problem recommended in 1949 that, if the *Greater London Plan* were to be carried out, 'some kind of regional authority must be set up, possessing not only supervisory powers, but also . . . such powers of direction and of finance, if not indeed of execution, as may be necessary for . . . both planning . . . and development'.[3] However, such an authority would require important changes in the structure of local government within the region, not to mention sacrifices in the power of central Government departments, which the Government was unwilling, or unable, to undertake. On the contrary, the Labour Party declared in April 1949 that 'The framework of town and country planning is already in place. . . . Labour is satisfied that the powers it has placed in the hands of public authorities should be adequate for the job.'[4]

So far as the New Towns phase of the *Greater London Plan* was concerned, obviously the establishment of Development Corporations did not solve the problem of overlapping authorities and conflicting responsibilities, but it may be doubted if any merely organizational change would have effected major improvement in the situation. What was primarily lacking was sufficiently high

[1] *The Times*, 18th January 1951.
[2] Ministry of Town and Country Planning, *Report of the London Planning Administration Committee* (London, 1949), pp. 4, 15.
[3] Ibid., p. 10. On 3rd August 1950, it was announced that the London County Council had decided to oppose the creation of such a regional authority, on the grounds that it 'would dislocate the preparation of the London development plan by mid-1951' (*The Times*, 3rd August 1950).
[4] Labour Party, *Labour Believes in Britain* (London, April 1949), p. 22.

Government priority for the New Towns (and, for that matter, housing as a whole, since the total of 760,467 new houses and flats built in Britain from 1st April 1945 to 31st December 1950 fell far below the Government's 1946 programme of 4,000,000 houses by 1955 or 1957).[1] Had the Government unreservedly resolved to push ahead with New Towns and issued a clear-cut Cabinet directive to that effect, their initial schedule could no doubt have been maintained. This directive did not come because first the national economic crisis and then the international situation forced an expansion in the export and armament industries and a corresponding reduction in the New Towns programme. The contrast between the 275 men engaged in road and house construction at Stevenage New Town in June 1950 and the 3,000 men working twenty-four hours a day building Britain's first major atomic pile at the Sellafield Atomic Establishment, Cumberland, was instructive.

The economic arguments for and against New Towns (or, in a broader sense, housing development in rural as opposed to urban areas) have been referred to at various points in this book. The calculation is complex, and much depends upon the breadth of one's balance sheet—the span of years over which the reckoning is to be made, and whether it is restricted to the Exchequer, the Development Corporation, and the New Town, or extended to the finances of local authorities and ancillary agencies and services. Over a long period, the Minister of Town and Country Planning was no doubt right in asserting 'it is no more expensive to build a new town, than to build in the old bad way [i.e., in existing urban areas]'.[2] But, in the first years of the development, when expensive services had to be installed in anticipation of demand, labour imported, and an expensive Corporation established to supervise the whole process, it was more expensive to rehouse a given number of persons in a New Town than (if not in central metropolitan areas where the price of land was exorbitant, then) on the suburban fringe of existing towns.[3]

[1] 'The Government's housing programme contemplates the building of 4,000,000 houses by local authorities and private enterprise, in a period of ten to twelve years from the end of the war. . . . Under this programme building is expected to work up to a peak production of between 400,000 and 500,000 houses a year for six to eight years from the middle of 1949, in addition to repairs and other building work . . .' (*Second Interim Report of the New Towns Committee*, Cmd. 6794 (April 1946), p. 11). The rate of production actually reached by 1949 (and the revised quota which the Government set in 1950 and 1951) was less than half the above target.

[2] *Hansard*, 8th May 1946, vol. 422, col. 1,083.

[3] 'The greater part of the [New Town] investment will consist of expenditure on land, houses, roads, drains, services and local community buildings directly related to housing. This part will not differ greatly from that which would be incurred in ordinary suburban development; it should be somewhat less than in the building of suburbs on the fringe of a large city; and it will certainly be less,

This was presumably the economic factor which induced the Government to sanction a rate of building in existing urban areas that retarded the New Town programme (if the Government ever went into the precise economic calculation. Of course the economic factor was not the only immediate one: the political influence of existing urban areas on the one hand, and the strategic importance of decentralization on the other, may be mentioned; and 'long-range' economic factors can become immediate too).

Some planners reasoned that it would have been preferable to reduce the number of New Towns and proceed at a faster pace on a few sites.

'Since costs are high, it would have been more economic to limit the number of New Towns and allow those which continued to go full speed ahead. Economic arguments cannot justify the establishment of a multiplicity of towns, each with its own expensive staff, each admonished to go slow, and all compelled to do so by delaying tactics from the centre.'[1]

In October 1947, the Government considered the advisability of letting two of the four New Towns in the London area lie dormant and proceeding with the other two, but the proposal was discarded upon representations from the Ministry and Corporations. Since no increase in the maximum labour force of 300 men (to which the four New Towns were then restricted) was contemplated under this alternative, and such a force might suffice to build one New Town in about two hundred years, this was not exactly what proponents had in mind. In any case, their suggestion was strongly opposed by most New Town advocates who saw in it the death knell of the Abercrombie plan and their broader hopes.

The Government curtailed, but (as the reasons—and pressure groups—which had produced the policy still retained their force) was not prepared to eliminate the New Towns, and so the situation developed, not uncommon in politics, in which a programme was verbally endorsed while, in practice, little was done to foster it. 'The fastest possible progress will be made with the great adventure of the New Towns', the Labour Party promised in 1949,[2] and the

per family housed, than in congested centres redeveloped at high density. The investment in factories and commercial buildings, again, will be comparable with that in new buildings of the same classes in suburban situations. . . . On the other hand, the establishment of a new town necessitates the purchase of a large area of land that will not be developed at once, the provision of main roads, of main sewers and sewage disposal works, probably of a new water supply system and in some cases of new gas and electricity plants or new distribution centres. Schools, churches, and other public buildings have also to be provided, and to some extent in advance of full demand and use' (Cmd. 6794, p. 13).

[1] Countess Russell, op. cit.   [2] *Labour Believes in Britain*, p. 22.

Minister of Town and Country Planning declared, 'I am satisfied that the new towns are making as good progress as can be expected under present conditions',[1] when it was evident to all observers that the programme was lamentably retarded and these words could be true only if the realm of the possible and the actions of the Labour Government were identical at all points. 'If the Government thinks that dispersal is urgent and important enough to justify capital expenditure at the present time, then it should put its full weight behind the speedy development of as many new towns as possible', said the *Economist*. 'If it does not, then it had better suspend the whole programme. Half-measures are the one certainly wrong policy.'[2] *The Times* editorialized:

'The rival demands of the export drive, security, transport facilities, and social amenities create a painful dilemma. Even a Government which believes in planning for the future is being repeatedly driven to put the needs of the moment first. Whatever the choice made, nothing could be more calculated to cause confusion than the present situation in which some Government departments behave, and encourage local authorities to behave, as though the Barlow and Abercrombie reports are to be taken seriously, while other departments act as though those far-sighted documents had never been written.'[3]

Clearly the utopianism which carried the Labour Government to power in 1945 had faded during five years of office and harsh economic realities, and the tide of events which had brought a policy of decentralization to the fore threatened now to submerge it. In September 1950, Anderson Montague-Barlow, who had been chairman of the Royal Commission on the Distribution of the Industrial Population and responsible for its 1939 report, Patrick Abercrombie, author of the *Greater London Plan*, and Clement Davies, chairman of the London Planning Administration Committee which, in 1949, had recommended to the Ministry of Town and Country Planning the establishment of a regional authority for the planning and development of Greater London, reviewed the present status of their reports.

'What is the condition to-day? The Minister of Town and Country Planning is doing his best by amendment of Regulations to straighten out minor difficulties. But, broad and large, *it is not too much to say that these reports are now being almost entirely ignored*: for instance, new towns are being built, but Government departments refuse to encourage the transfer of industry to them; building effort is being directed to increasing instead of diminishing overcrowding at the centre; the L.C.C. and other authorities oppose the creation of a single regional authority; towns which it had

---

[1] *Hansard*, 27th October 1949, vol. 468, col. 1,660.
[2] *The Economist*, 5th November 1949, p. 993.
[3] *The Times*, 5th August 1950.

been decided did not admit of further growth have been stimulated by great industrial expansion, and so on.

'. . . Surely the time has now come when the Government, their departments, and particularly the Minister of Town and Country Planning, should decide and let the public know whether they have a policy at all in the matter, and, if so, what the policy is.'[1]

The search for and choice of a policy is the mark of the statesman, the planner, and the free man. But the historian may be excused for suggesting that it reflects events as much as it shapes them.

[1] Letter, *The Times*, 28th September 1950. Our italics.

Part Four
Review and Discussion

CHAPTER NINE

Review and Discussion

T HE problems of contemporary cities are the problems of
contemporary society, and if it is unrealistic to try to cure
the former without touching the latter, surely it is utopian
to attempt to cure everything at once. A combination of realism
and utopianism has, indeed, marked human endeavour in this field.

In 1801 the population of Britain was ten million; by 1901, as a
consequence of the Industrial Revolution (which, improving nutri-
tion, sanitation, and health, led to a fall in the death-rate), it had more
than tripled. The increase went into the cities and towns which
swelled over the countryside, transforming Britain from a rural
nation to the most highly urbanized nation in the world. Private
entrepreneurs built the new houses and factories mainly for their
own advantage, and the Government was not overly interested in
the general welfare because the general mass of people had no capital,
no property, no education, and no vote—that is, no economic or
political power (of which they or the Government were aware) to
change their condition or directly influence the Government. Although by present standards (and, in that day, by the standards of
men like Engels and Dickens) the abuses which nineteenth-century
housing inflicted upon the working classes were great, the earliest
reform movements had, therefore, less a political than a charitable
complexion. However, the physical and social dangers which slum
housing presented to the whole community were soon recognized
and the first Government interference with private building came in
the form of local by-laws prescribing minimum standards to which
buildings had to conform for reasons of public safety, sanitation, and
health. Parliament also sanctioned the building by local authorities
of houses for the poorest classes, but little was done in this direction

during the nineteenth century. Nor did the Government attempt to control the use to which land could be put, the choice resting with private developers, where this was not restricted by private covenants.

As the working classes assumed a greater share of power in twentieth-century Britain and the entire society underwent a shift towards a bridled (if not quite muzzled) capitalism, the State ventured further into the fields of housing and town planning. After the First World War an increasing proportion of housing for the poorer classes was financed or built by local authorities, which also exercised increasing control over land use under the authority of various planning statutes. During the first three decades of the century, these statutes were negative rather than positive in nature, local rather than national in administration and scope, and seriously hampered by the amount of compensation which local authorities had to pay owners whose property was adversely affected. The movement towards positive and effective central control over the nation's limited land resources was immensely furthered during the Second World War, when the State assumed control over industry, labour, materials, and practically everything else vital to the existence of the nation. The Minister of Town and Country Planning Act, 1943, which created a Minister 'charged with the duty of securing consistency and continuity in the framing and execution of a national policy with respect to the use and development of land throughout England and Wales', gave statutory recognition to this movement, but it remained for the first all-Labour Government seriously to implement this Act and carry forward the national planning and building programme in the years immediately after the war.

The modern metropolis was a vast snarl of people, buildings, goods, and traffic, from its newer industrial and slick suburban periphery, greatly extended by rapid underground and surface transport, through the older industrial and massive working-class quarters—those crowded foreign lands visited only by official representatives of the middle classes—to the sanctuaries of Commerce, Government, Society, and Culture. The foremost metropolis, London, was the worst of all so far as congestion, and the difficulty of relieving it, was concerned.

Two courses were open: to try and make the city function or to give it up as a bad job, and there were not lacking advocates and opponents of each course, pied pipers of salvation and sin, ready to lead all who would follow them to Eden or to Babylon. In their extreme forms (in which everyone would be housed in skyscrapers or farms) the urban and rural schools were equally impracticable, but more moderate versions—building flats in inner, and small houses-and-gardens in outer, London, and improving transportation facilities—were adopted by the national Government, the London County Council, and private interests.

The Garden City movement, launched by Ebenezer Howard in 1898 with the publication of *To-morrow: a Peaceful Path to Real Reform*, strove to combine the virtues of 'town' and 'country' in spacious, independent cities of restricted size to be built in the country around existing metropolises and drawing their population therefrom. The movement hoped first to stop and then reverse the growth of massive urban concentrations, but the process of urbanization could not be lightly arrested and, like other historical processes, seemed even to prosper upon opposition. Until 1946, only two small cities (Letchworth and Welwyn Garden City) fully exemplifying Garden City principles were founded in Britain, but the minimum garden-city space standard of twelve houses to the acre was generally adopted after the First World War—and was blamed by opponents for the 'ribbon development' along highways and the suburban extensions of cities which characterized inter-war development.

In 1946, the Garden City and national planning movements (i.e., the protagonists, respectively, of urban decentralization and of centralized control over land use) had sufficient influence and fortune to induce Parliament to pass the New Towns Act, which provided for the development of new self-contained towns by public corporations appointed by the Minister of Town and Country Planning and financed by the Treasury. The Act had the support of all political parties, serving to implement, in varying degrees, recommendations of the Barlow Report presented to Neville Chamberlain's Coalition Government in 1939, which called for decentralizing the nation's industry and population; the *Greater London Plan 1944*, prepared by Professor Patrick Abercrombie at the request of W. S. Morrison, Minister of Town and Country Planning in Winston Churchill's National Government, which advocated the relocation of over a million people from central London to a ring of new satellite towns and expanded old towns; and of the 1946 Reith Committee reports, which advised Clement Attlee's Labour Government upon the way New Towns should be developed.

Stevenage, Hertfordshire, a town of 6,500 thirty miles north of London, was designated in November 1946 by the Minister of Town and Country Planning as the site of the first New Town, which was to reach a population of 60,000, drawing inhabitants from over-crowded areas of London. By the end of 1949 eight New Towns had been designated and Development Corporations appointed in the Greater London region, and six elsewhere in England, Wales, and Scotland.

Abercrombie notes that 'The choosing of sites for new communities is always an exhilarating side of the planner's work'.[1] Stevenage

[1] Patrick Abercrombie, *Greater London Plan 1944* (London, 1945), p. 14.

was one of the sites he chose. 'It's all because Abercrombie put his finger on a map', said a Stevenage citizen later. 'And he probably never even saw it.' A handful of people (mainly officials at the Ministry of Town and Country Planning, one or two politicians, and two or three other persons) took the opportunity offered by the Abercrombie plan, the idealistic climate of post-war opinion and of a young Socialist Government, the nation's urgent housing needs and the great possibilities which the Government's ambitious housing programme then presented, to get the Stevenage New Town going even before the passage of the New Towns Act, and before the Reith Committee reports had any influence. They hoped, by a vigorous start, to channel a substantial part of post-war housing away from existing urban areas and into model garden cities such as Howard had envisaged. Ministry officers calculated in 1946 that the Stevenage New Town should be completed in ten years: 'During the war different and large-scale construction programmes have been completed in two years or less and the experience gained should increase the possibilities of solving many of the post-war difficulties of labour and supplies of materials. We have, therefore, assumed that, given the priorities and an efficient large-scale organization a ten-year programme is not unreasonable.'[1] Perhaps it was not unreasonable, but events proved the reasoning of the National Council of Social Service, in its 1944 report on *Dispersal*, more prophetic: 'Wartime experience shows that a new town can be built fairly rapidly, but it does not follow that a number of new towns could be built rapidly in time of peace.'[2]

At first the Stevenage District Council, local government authority for most of the designated area, was co-operative, but councillors became increasingly restive as the Ministry pushed ahead without consulting them as fully as they wished, and as growls of disapproval came from influential ratepayers and property owners. These turned into full-throated roars after property owners received invitations to sell on 'terms which prove acceptable to the Minister', with the inference that, if this were not done, their property might be acquired by compulsory purchase. When the Minister visited Stevenage in May 1946 to address a public meeting, he was greeted with outspoken and even violent opposition by local citizens who formed a Residents' Protection Association to defeat the New Town. The Association took its case to the courts where the Minister was eventually victorious; but the protracted legal action retarded the New Town development and, no sooner was a favourable decision reached, than, because of the national economic crisis, the Government ordered a virtual stoppage for one year in the building of New Towns in the Greater London region. Thus, although a consider-

[1] *Ministry Plan* 1946, p. 37.
[2] The National Council of Social Service, *Dispersal* (London, 1944), p. 42.

able staff had been recruited and planning continued during the interval, it was not until the end of 1948 that the Stevenage Corporation was free to proceed with the acquisition of much land and the letting of contracts. Internal delays, the difficulties of negotiations with powerful agencies of the local and national Government, and continued economic stringencies resulting from the rearmament programme thereupon supervened, so that the New Town made a very slow start indeed. On 31st December 1950, after more than four and a half years' activity by the Ministry, only twenty-eight houses had been completed.

The dominant traditions of Stevenage were conservative and rural, so it was natural for ratepayers, landowners, and farmers to lead the local opposition to a project which threatened to raise rates, abolish private ownership of land and homes, put many farmers out of business, and change the entire character of the district. Some opponents were naïve enough to believe that their interests and those of the whole community inevitably coincided, although only a minority of citizens were property owners or farmers; others tactlessly asserted that, where these interests diverged, the welfare of the majority should yield to that of the minority. 'Was it fair that the whole country should benefit at the expense of the few?' an opposition leader asked a meeting of the Residents' Protection Association.[1] However, no matter how selfish were their motives, opponents performed a distinct public service by subjecting the actions of the Ministry and the Development Corporation to the scrutiny of the courts, Ministerial tribunals, and national opinion, revealing very real problems and dangers therein, which New Town enthusiasts were inclined to overlook.

Let us examine some of the broad problems suggested by the Stevenage experience.

To begin with, there was the problem of conflicting local and national interests. The general trend in Britain during recent decades has been to augment the powers of the national Government over those of local authorities, and this, as we have seen, was also the history of town planning legislation. The experience was that small local authorities had neither the financial resources nor the technical ability to plan as well as a larger central authority, and were unwilling to concert a regional or national plan involving sacrifices of local advantage for the national welfare—an important reason why it was, and still is, so hard to execute a satisfactory plan for the Greater London region. An anarchist utopia might manage things otherwise, but the success of New Towns in 1946 hinged upon the concentration of sufficient powers in the hands of one agency (and, from evidence presented in Chapter VIII, one may conclude that

[1] *Hertfordshire Express*, 18th May 1946.

the powers granted by the New Towns Act remain inadequate in some respects, especially when divided between the Ministry and the Development Corporations).

However, the delegation of considerable power over local affairs to officials not responsible in any way to the local electorate laid the base for injustice to local interests and a weakening of local democracy. Both were evident at Stevenage and, if the New Town were to be built despite local opposition, were largely unavoidable. The sort of thing that might have been avoided was the Ministry's failure to consult fully the Stevenage Council, its attempt to discourage the Council from holding a public referendum on the New Town issue, its rejection of Council amendments to the Master Plan, and its failure to appoint a nominee of the Council majority to the Development Corporation.

It is paradoxical that a programme of decentralization should have had the immediate effect of injuring local democracy. Fortunately one may anticipate the opposite as the long-range effect after the New Town is completed and the Corporation hands over its remaining functions to the local authority. Likewise it is paradoxical that a programme designed to increase human happiness should initially have reduced it, bringing a sense of gloom and injustice to many local citizens. Here too one may hope that the good design will yet be achieved.

One informant was critical of the view 'That democracy means that everybody should be consulted about every detail and that the Stevenage Council should have had a say all along the line'. He felt that 'The Council should undoubtedly have been consulted more, and mistakes were made, some stupidly. But the tiny handful of people who got the thing moving were working day and night and could not possibly spend their time as public relations officers. Once the Corporations were set up it was a different matter. . . .' The success of the New Town programme obviously demanded (as far as anyone could see at the time) quick action by Ministry officials, whereas democracy demanded relatively slow action—the consultation of elected representatives and, ultimately, after a period of free discussion, the electorate. This is perhaps the most fundamental problem posed by the Stevenage experience: the extent to which efficient executive action is compatible with the democratic process. Those whose faith in democracy comes before all else must, if necessary, sacrifice efficiency and even success on its altar; but whose faith is so pure that he can offer this sacrifice gladly?

Ministry officials would not be bound by a decision of the Stevenage electorate (among other reasons) because the New Town was not for them but for the people of London. That, said this informant, 'was a very true and democratic point in the Minister's speech at the famous meeting [in Stevenage town hall, May 1946]—54,000 people out of 60,000 couldn't be consulted at the beginning and their welfare and happiness had to be considered'. What Minister of State is not concerned about the welfare and happiness of the people? It is the profession of a Minister to bear lightly burdens which would crush a saint. For what possible decision of this Minister could not win the support of 54,000 people out of the millions in London and the thousands of unborn whom the New Town would also serve?

In fact, no matter how altruistic the Minister's decision, it was, like most decisions in the vast bureaucratic apparatus of modern democratic States, never submitted by him to the judgement of the people—that is, the electorate—of Stevenage, London, or Britain. For better or worse, it is the bureaucrats and the planners who have taken over this function of advising Government upon policy and who, a good many historians and sociologists contend, now exercise final sovereignty over the State.

There are many who think that planning can be made a science, analysing objectively the needs of the people and the best means of gratifying them in any given historical situation; and, correspondingly, there has been much talk in both Britain and America about the need for social research to determine policy in planning and administration. What reasonable man does not prefer to act in the light of such knowledge as can precede action? If only foreknowledge could equal that of a latter day; if only there were *one* sociology to guide men in beneficent social action! Alas, there are as many sociologies as there are groups with different objectives to finance and support sociological research. Most sociologists agree, perhaps, on certain material and demographic facts; but, for the rest, they are as torn by passions and special pleading as any other body of men and there is no cause to bestow upon them, because of their profession, any confidence in the guidance of affairs which they do not merit as men.

We have described, in preceding chapters, some of the struggle for power between different groups of planners—the urban and rural groups, the house and the flat addicts, the Development Corporation and the Stevenage Council, the Ministry and the Corporation, and so on. This predilection for power and the planning of other people's lives, implicit in utopian (as in ideological) thought and explicit in the political action to which it leads, gives an authoritarian colour to the most benign utopia. In addition, as the anarchist Marie Louise Berneri noted, most nineteenth-century utopias appear authoritarian to the contemporary intellectual who, as a result of the contemporary experience, cannot share his predecessor's faith in the State. 'The majority of utopias assumed that the interests of the individual coincided with those of the State and that a conflict between the two was unthinkable. . . . The main trend of literature between the two wars has been one of extreme scepticism regarding the power of the State to transform society. . . . [Today] intellectuals are dreaming of avoiding the realisation of utopias and of returning to a less "perfect" but more free society.'[1]

It is strange how, in the foregoing quotation, anarchist now joins hands with orthodox capitalist doctrine. Likewise, it is strange how socialist and monopoly capitalist doctrines coincide in the New Town. For surely it is more a difference of name than substance that separates the social principles of, let us say, the Metropolitan Life Insurance Company's Parkchester development in New York City and the Ministry of Town and Country Planning's Stevenage New Town. In both there is to be found the same monopolistic ownership of land by one agency, the same leasehold restrictions on the freedom of the individual, the same lack of democracy in the appointment of the governing body, the same bureaucratic rule by remote officials. This is what Bellamy's and Howard's utopias have come to.

Must utopia, realized, always disappoint?

To be persuasive and practical (to persuade different kinds of people and to be practised in different times and places) a utopian idea must be relatively simple and generalized. But life is more complicated than any simple idea, and probably than *any* idea or image, one can have of it—'the inexpressible complexity of everything that lives' is how Tolstoy, for all his genius in expressing that complexity, put it. This is the rock upon which utopia, and reason itself, founders.

Where reason founders, only faith can carry on—faith in man, faith in his future, faith in life itself. Those who have this faith will be heartened even by the failure, and those who lack it will be disheartened even by the success, of the Stevenage New Town.

[1] Marie Louise Berneri, *Journey Through Utopia* (London, 1950), pp. 311, 310, 313.

Appendix A

SEWERAGE PROBLEMS

ABERCROMBIE concluded his review of the proposed Stevenage New Town site with the remark, 'Sewage would have to be dealt with independently of any centralised disposal works, but there is no special difficulty on this site'.[1] This view proved optimistic.

The Ministry's 1946 plan stated:

'Two sites only are available for a purification works to which the whole of the town can be drained by gravitation. These lie North and South of Stapleford. . . . The disposal of effluent into the River Beane may raise objections owing to the comparatively small flow in the river. . . . It may therefore be necessary to pipe the effluent as far as the Tumbling Bay on the River Lee East of the town of Ware. . . .

'The better alternative is a proposal for a large sewage works at Rye House, Hoddesdon, which eventually would deal with sewage from such places as Harlow, Stevenage, Hertford, Ware, Welwyn Garden City, and, possibly, Luton. This would be a long term project and for the short term it would be sensible not to lay the long and costly effluent pipe [to the east of Ware] but to build by stages a sewage works discharging effluent into the Beane [near Stapleford]. This works would be abandoned eventually'.[2]

At the public inquiry of 8th October 1946, the anticipated objections to the Stapleford proposal were strongly made by the Metropolitan Water Board, the Lee Conservancy Board, and the Lee Conservancy Catchment Board. The attitude of the Lee Conservancy Board, in particular, could in no wise be ignored, because under the terms of the Lee Conservancy Act, 1868, 'no new opening may be made into the river [Lee] or any of its tributaries to provide for the discharge of sewage . . . except with the consent of the Board. When

---

[1] Abercrombie, *Great London Plan*, 1944, p. 161.
[2] *Stevenage New Town. Report on Planning and Development Proposals* (Ministry of Town and Country Planning, 31st July 1946), p. 33.

giving such consent the Board may impose such terms and conditions
as they may think fit.'[1] The Board regarded the Ministry proposal
'with great alarm and strongly object to it'.[2] The proposed point
of discharge for sewage effluent was only three miles above the
Hertford intake of the Metropolitan Water Board, and it was felt
that placing this additional burden upon a river already overloaded
with effluent would pollute its water, which supplied one-sixth of
London's needs, to an unprecedented and dangerous degree.[3] While
the pollution danger could be overcome by piping the effluent to a
point below the Water Board's intake, this alternative would deprive
London of six million gallons of water daily which, in turn, would
have to be replaced by a pipe running from the Thames right across
London to the Lee. The Board was unwilling to impose upon
London taxpayers the £2,000,000 cost of the latter project which
would be incurred for the benefit of the New Town.

'Have you been able to find any evidence that this matter of the
water supply has really been considered in earmarking this site, or
rather the water supply of London has been considered?' the chief
engineer of the Metropolitan Water Board was asked by his solicitor.
'No, I do not think any consideration has been given to the water
supply of London,' he replied. 'In April this year some consideration was given to the supply of water to Stevenage and we were
consulted about that. . . . Speaking entirely from the point of view of
the water supply to London the Stevenage and Harlow sites are
about the worst that could have been selected from our point of
view.'[4] The evidence on this matter of prior consultation was not

[1] Evidence by Lee Conservancy Board at the 8th October 1946 Stevenage
inquiry.
[2] Ibid.
[3] The effluent would, of course, be chemically processed and purified before
being discharged into the river, but the Director of Water Examination for the
Metropolitan Water Board did not regard such effluent as a safe thing. He observed that 'In America generally speaking it is customary to draw water from
more highly polluted sources than would be accepted in this country. . . . over
a seventeen-year period, from 1920 to 1936, there were 399 outbreaks of water-
borne disease in America causing a total of 115,645 recorded cases of illness. . . .
Ninety-two of these outbreaks occurred in cities having water purification plants
and caused 65,000 cases of illness. . . . It has been the practice in this country
[Britain] since the days of cholera epidemics not to draw water from heavily
polluted sources. . . . As a result of that policy we have had, during a twenty-
seven year period only 21 outbreaks of water-borne disease. . . . if adjusted for
the difference in population this represents an incidence in the United States of
America of ten times that in Great Britain. I feel that the record of the U.S.A.
constitutes a grave warning to any who may hold that the existence of modern
water treatment plant justifies the use of highly polluted sources for providing
a domestic water supply.' (Evidence at the 8th October 1946 Stevenage inquiry.)
[4] Ibid.

entirely clear. One informant stated that 'The two water authorities [i.e., the Metropolitan Water and Lee Conservancy Boards] had, in fact, agreed to the site with Abercrombie. In private they later said they thought it would be just another paper plan so they didn't worry. Any plan translated into action makes people sit up and think again!' In his statement of 7th November 1946, following the Public inquiry, the Minister said:

'These [sewage] problems have been taken into account from the beginning and have been the subject of discussions with the Ministry of Health from an early stage and subsequently with the Metropolitan Water Board and Lee Conservancy Board. After carefully examining the representations made to him the Minister feels justified in going forward with the establishment of a properly planned community and will maintain close contact with the Ministry of Health and the statutory undertakers at every stage of the development. It has been fully recognised from the outset that every possible precaution must be taken to protect London's water supplies from any avoidable risk of pollution. The Minister has accordingly appointed a Consultant to examine the possibilities of a scheme which will apply to a much wider area than that of the immediate vicinity of Stevenage.'

The 'wider' scheme was the same one as the long-term works referred to in the Ministry's 1946 plan. All concerned agreed that this could satisfactorily solve the problem of sewage disposal, but not that of the diminished supply of London's water; and, as will be seen, the expense entailed raised serious financial complications.

It was the Minister's acknowledgment that he was taking advice on how to solve the New Town sewage problem which led Justice Henn Collins to squash the Designation Order on 20th February 1947, since he deduced from this proof of Ministerial bias. 'It is obvious that those [sewage] difficulties must be met before the scheme can go through. The Minister acknowledges that they have not been met, and that he is taking advice as to how it can be done. *Non constat* that any way will be found. And yet, with that fundamental problem still outstanding, the Minister confirms his Order.' The appellate court reasoned otherwise: '. . . the only objection of the Metropolitan Water Board and the Lee Conservancy Board to the project of forming a new town at Stevenage was really the question of expense, the question of bringing water from the River Thames into the River Lee; it was never suggested that it was an entirely impracticable scheme.'[1] (The implications of the sewage problem, which both courts held to be the crucial factor in the Stevenage case, were

---

[1] Transcript of the judgment *In the Supreme Court of Judicature. Court of Appeal. In the Matter of the New Towns Act, 1946 and In the Matter of the Stevenage New Town (Designation) Order,* 1946 (24th March 1947).

not pursued by the House of Lords who ruled that the question of Ministerial bias was irrelevant because the Minister was not acting in a judicial or quasi-judicial but in an administrative capacity.)

The Minister's technical consultant reported as follows on 4th March, 1947:

'The proposal to build new towns at Stevenage and Harlow merely emphasizes what has for long been a problem in the Lee Valley, viz., the inconsistency of the two main uses to which the river is put . . . as a conduit for treated sewage effluents, and . . . as the source of a substantial proportion of the water supply of Greater London. Quite apart from the two new towns, the problem has been becoming more and more acute as the growing population in the upper reaches of the Lee increased the pollution load, and the growing population within their own area increased the Metropolitan Water Board's demand for Lee water. . . . In their broad aspect your instructions ask us to devise measures not only to safeguard the interests of all the various present users of the Lee, but also to permit the development of the new towns without injury to the two irreconcilable purposes for which its waters are being used. We regret that we can make no recommendation on these lines, and we cannot endorse a future policy which would perpetuate the use of the river Lee for these conflicting ends. . . . No matter how . . . high the standards for the treated sewage effluents from both present and future sewage works, the effluents should either be removed from the Lee and discharged at a point below the intakes of public water supply, or alternatively, the use of the River Lee water for domestic purposes should cease entirely. . . .it would appear that one solution of the problem would be to construct sewers to intercept the sewage of the existing and proposed built-up areas and convey it for treatment to a suitable site, the effluent after treatment being discharged at some point below [the Metropolitan Water Board's intake at] Chingford Mill. This would not, however, be a real solution, because carried to its logical conclusion it would inevitably cause a serious decrease in the water available to the Metropolitan Water Board.

'Even if the Metropolitan Water Board can bear this loss . . . the river would still be an impure and improper source of drinking water since a river running through built-up areas such as the Lee Valley must always be liable to pollution from various causes quite apart from domestic sewage. The only right policy is complete abandonment of the Lee as a source of water supply.'

After issuing this sombre warning the consultant went on to suggest a central treatment works in the vicinity of Rye Meads, south of the Ware, which would serve Stevenage and Harlow New Towns as well as the New Towns of Welwyn Garden City and Hatfield and other towns in the middle reaches of the River Lee. £3,500,000 was the estimated cost of this scheme.[1]

[1] D. Balfour & Sons and J. D. & D. M. Watson, *Report on Upper Lee Valley Sewerage and Sewage Disposal*, 4th March 1947.

APPENDIX

This proposal was thereupon submitted to a working party set up by the Ministry of Health, with representatives of the Ministry of Town and Country Planning, the Metropolitan Water and Lee Conservancy Catchment Boards, and the Stevenage and Harlow New Town Corporations. While these technical and political deliberations continued, the Stevenage Corporation prepared to enlarge the existing Stevenage sewage plant to its maximum capacity, which could cope with a population of 18,000. It was hoped this would serve the New Town's needs until 1954.[1] The Corporation and the Stevenage Council agreed on the financial arrangements for this enlargement, on which work began in May 1950 (it was 75 per cent. complete by 31st March 1951.)

The Middle Lee scheme, however, ran into financial snarls. To implement the scheme, the Hertfordshire County Council was asked to sponsor legislation under which it would take over the sewerage powers of all local authorities in the area and delegate that power to a committee containing representatives of the New Towns and other participating authorities. This the Council declined to do, for three reasons: (1) the projected Rye Meads works would be uneconomic, (2) as local authorities had their own sewerage works, they could not be persuaded to contribute any more than their present expenses to the cost of the new works, (3) the ultimate cost, which would fall upon local authorities when the New Town Corporations were disbanded, was likely to be excessive.[2] Accordingly, the Stevenage and Harlow Corporations (the latter New Town needing this scheme even more desperately than the former) prepared to go ahead with the Rye Meads works themselves, under powers granted by the New Towns Act.

In November 1949, the County Council took the offensive, urging the Ministry to restrict the size of Stevenage New Town to 18,000, obviating the need for Stevenage participation in the Rye Meads project (although Harlow New Town would go ahead with its own works there) and, in turn, allowing the Welwyn Garden City and Hatfield New Towns to join the more economical Colne Valley sewage system. The total saving that could thus be effected was put at a minimum of £2,000,000.[3]

The chairman of the Stevenage Urban District Council commented that three years after the first public inquiry was 'rather late in the day' for the County Council to make this suggestion. Some people,

---

[1] *New Towns Act*, 1946. *Reports of the . . . Development Corporations for the period ending 31st March*, 1949, p. 134.

[2] *Future of New Town of Stevenage*. Report of the Hertfordshire Planning Committee, 4th November 1949. A more detailed extract from this report is given in the text, pp. 234–5.

[3] Ibid.

he said, might wonder why the Stevenage Council had not taken up the matter. 'We thought that matters such as water supplies and sewerage were matters which the Minister was quite sure of before he approved the scheme after the original public inquiry.'[1] The *Hertfordshire Mercury*, which did not generally side with the Ministry against the County Council, observed that the County had itself long had in mind a similar regional sewage scheme.

'No subject, we imagine, has been more fully explored. Why, therefore, should the County Council now be so diffident to admit the necessity for planning to solve the sewerage problem on a big scale?

'It seems futile at this stage to put forward the suggestion that Stevenage . . . should be limited to a population of 18,000. . . .

'If the County Council had agreed to promote a Bill in Parliament to carry out the proposed scheme it would have entailed the Council taking over the sewerage powers of all local authorities in the area. Even in the absence of New Towns surely this would have been a desirable project for it would have put an end to the growing fears of individual authorities failing to make adequate provision for sewage treatment except under pressure from a higher authority.[2]

However, the County Council's attitude seems to have been partly responsible for the Ministry's decision to re-examine the Stapleford proposal. On 10th January, 1950, it was reported to the Stevenage Corporation that

'the Ministry, being concerned at the heavy capital expenditure which would be involved in taking sewage from Stevenage to Rye Meads for treatment and disposal as part of a regional scheme were reconsidering the original proposal that treatment and disposal works for Stevenage should be located at Stapleford. . . . In the meantime, therefore, no further steps would be taken in connection with the proposal to lay a trunk sewer to Rye Meads and to build there joint disposal works with Harlow Development Corporation. The latter would proceed separately with the Rye Meads project. . . .'

The practicability of the Stapleford site depended, first, upon the finding of suitable gravel beds where the soakaway treatment of purified effluent might be adopted, and, secondly, the adoption of a means of filtration 'which would produce an effluent of sufficient purity to admit of its direct discharge into the river without objection from the river authorities.'[3]

After renewed investigation, it developed that the Stapleford site was not practicable, so the Ministry and the Stevenage Corporation

---

[1] *Hertfordshire Express*, 3rd December 1949.

[2] Editorial "Middle Lee Sewerage Scheme," *Hertfordshire Mercury*, 2nd December 1949.

[3] *Reports of the . . . Development Corporations for the period ending 31st March*, 1950, p. 179.

returned to the Rye Meads project. The thirteen and a half mile sewer from the edge of New Town would cost £1,350,000, and an undertaking was given the Metropolitan Water Board that, if it was not satisfied with the purity of the effluent, this would be piped further down the Lee below the point of the Board's water intake, at an additional cost of £1,500,000.[1]

The County Council worried about the 'serious position some [local] authorities would be in should they be forced into the trunk sewer with the loans for their own sewerage schemes unexpired'.[2] The Hatfield and Welwyn Garden City New Town Corporations, forced by the Ministry's decision to use the Rye Meads scheme rather than the more economical Colne Valley sewers, were exceedingly displeased. The Hatfield Corporation was 'greatly concerned over the cost of the Middle Lee Scheme and regrets that the less expensive [Colne Valley] scheme . . . could not be accepted. It is strongly felt that the capital expenditure involved can never be recovered out of the existing or future rateable value of the town. It seems that this is not a charge that Hatfield should be asked to bear.'[3] Sitting as the Welwyn Garden City Corporation, the same people said:

'we are not unmindful of the expenditure to be incurred under the Middle Lee Sewage Scheme and of the indication we received that no alternative to this scheme could be considered. It is a financial matter causing us concern. It is not for us to debate such factors as the national or regional health requirement, or the pollution of the River Lee, or the supply of drinking water to London that doubtless caused us to receive this view, but we are anxious to ensure that the town we have been charged to create shall be an economically sound proposition. This means that neither the local authorities nor the New Town Corporations should be required to bear more than their proper share of the financial burden in giving effect to national or regional policy decision.[4]

[1] *Hertfordshire Mercury*, 2nd February 1951.
[2] Ibid., 18th March 1951.
[3] *Reports of the . . . Development Corporations for the period ending 31st March,* 1951, p. 301.
[4] Ibid., p. 278.

Appendix B

A NOTE ON THE ACCIDENT AND BIAS OF THIS BOOK

To understand this book's limitations, the reader should know something about how it came to be written.

The writer came to London in September 1948 intending to conduct a functional anthropological study of a small English community, concentrating upon aspects of social stratification. Since the publication of the Lynds' *Middletown* in 1929, such studies have become increasingly popular among a group of American academicians whom some call 'social anthropologists' and others 'sociologists'. But they had not yet been undertaken in Britain, where anthropological field-work was confined almost exclusively to the colonies and social surveys still followed the practical, statistical, reformist tradition inaugurated by Patrick Geddes and Charles Booth at the end of the last century. (From 1937 onward, the directors of Mass-Observation had attempted, with varying success, to apply 'anthropological methods' to the study of modern Britain, but, after a brief flirtation, their relations with the academic world were largely severed and they turned increasingly to consumer research and opinion polling; nor did they ever produce a full-length community study. E. R. Roper-Power's excellent 1937 study 'The Social Structure of an English County Town' has, unfortunately, not been published. However, several students have recently done work in this vein, and studies are afoot in Scotland and Oxfordshire.)

Through a series of accidents which need not be related, and after consulting many authorities (too many, because their advice conflicted) and investigating various towns and villages in Herefordshire, Hertfordshire, and Kent, the writer finally chose Stevenage as a suitable site. The population of 6,500 was large for one student, but, in the course of planning the New Town of 60,000, officers of the Ministry of Town and Country Planning and the Stevenage Development Corporation had gathered a good deal of information about the old town, which they kindly made available. Also the location was convenient, for it was possible to live in London and gather background material there, while making the hour's journey to Stevenage as occasion demanded. So the writer set about work in the usual way, examining county newspapers, parish and Council records and the minutes of various organizations, attending all sorts of meetings, joining clubs, obtaining autobiographical essays from school children, and, above all, meeting and talking to people and writing down what they said—or, as it may be described more formally, conducting a series of interviews with local informants designed especially to throw light on prevailing class structure and attitudes.

Herbert Spencer tells of a Frenchman 'who, having been three weeks here, proposed to write a book on England; who, after three months, found that he was not quite ready; and who, after three years, concluded that he knew nothing about it'.[1] The writer's experience was similar. As the research progressed he was appalled by his ignorance of the English scene, his presumption in attempting to study it—almost all of it—single-handed, and the inadequacy of anthropological theory and method for this task. The ethnographer's ignorance of a primitive tribe becomes knowledge when displayed to a Western audience, but the English, unfortunately, are able to read what an American writes about them.

These and other considerations led the writer to narrow the scope of the research to three subjects and to investigate these along increasingly historical lines—i.e., all data (including, besides interviews, observations, and various documentary records in Stevenage, library and newspaper material on other towns and on England as a whole) were considered as necessarily biased and fragmentary evidence which first had to be evaluated for reliability and then juxtaposed with other relevant data to permit the exposition of such 'facts' and 'opinions' as the writer saw in these data. The three subjects were social class, local politics, and the New Town.

Social research is not conducted in a vacuum, but by specific individuals in specific situations, and its results are conditioned not only by what a student sets out to do but also by the opportunities which present themselves to him. For months the writer investigated records and interviewed persons at the Stevenage District Council and the Stevenage Development Corporation without being interested in the New Town. Later, he thought that local reactions to the New Town might afford insight into class relations and politics in old Stevenage. Then he felt it would be foolish and even irresponsible to neglect this opportunity to study at first hand the early stages of an

[1] Spencer, *The Study of Sociology* (New York, 1929), p. 91.

important social experiment. Finally he concentrated his attention upon the New Town and the sociological problems it posed.

Because of this back-handed approach to the subject, evidence from local sources and the Stevenage Council is generally strongest, it is somewhat weaker for the Development Corporation, and weaker still for the County Council, the Ministry, and other central Government departments where secondary sources had mainly to be relied upon. Social and ideological factors have naturally received more attention than psychological, political, legal, economic, or administrative factors.

The field of housing and town planning is an arena of important economic, political, and ideological conflicts, and for a sociologist to enter this arena as the blushing Ferdinand, the bull who would not fight, entered the bullring, is, to contestants and spectators alike, an astonishing and slightly ridiculous thing. Robert Merton, the Columbia sociologist, has thus reviewed his experience of American housing research:

'The type of housing to be built, the amount to be built, how it is built, for whom and by whom it is built—all these are matters involving great conflicts of interests and sentiments. . . . Some of the central issues have been joined: public housing versus housing privately financed in part or whole; ownership versus rental; the freestanding housing versus multiple dwellings; racial [for Britain, read *class*] segregation versus nondiscriminatory neighborhoods—around each of these pairs of alternatives are ranged large and important groups, more concerned with satisfying their interests than with having research establish the sociological, economic, and psychological consequences of alternative policies.

'The social psychologist bent upon entering into housing research, therefore, must know that he is forsaking the relative calm and peace of his academic laboratory for the strife and embroilments of the institutional battlefield. What is more, belonging to neither army, the social psychologist must be prepared to be caught in the heavy cross-fire. Little if any of his research work will be taken for what he intends it to be: scientific analyses. . . . Instead, each research finding will be taken as a sign of abiding allegiance or of desertion from one army or the other.'[1]

Judging from comments which readers have made about the manuscript, it is likely that a similar fate awaits this book. What is worse, although the writer does plead a scientific spirit, he cannot plead a scientific achievement, since he does not believe that sociology is much of a science or that the academic man is immune from special interest. The sociologist also eats, although it is another hand that feeds him. He has no special lien on the Truth. He has only an oppor-

[1] Robert Merton, 'The Social Psychology of Housing,' in *Current Trends in Social Psychology* (University of Pittsburgh, 1948), pp. 165–6.

tunity to observe events from his own vantage point and the leisure to report them to a busier public.

Little can be done about the uses to which others put one's work, but the writer wishes, in particular, to disclaim two inferences which some readers of the manuscript have surprisingly drawn.

It is far from his intention to hold up America as a standard against which the failings of British planning and democracy are to be judged. On the contrary, it is his sincere conviction that America has more to learn from than to teach Britain—both Labour and Conservative Britain—in these matters, and that in the maturity, tolerance, and integrity of its democratic process Britain is first among the great nations of the world.

Nor is he either an enemy of 'planning' (a word used by conservative propagandists to damn many virtues of the liberal twentieth-century state) or a proponent of 'free enterprise' (in which guise these same propagandists would preserve many vices of nineteenth-century capitalism). In America and Britain today one can no longer choose between 'planning' and 'not planning', but only between planning better and planning worse; between public and private planning; between the democratic control of political and economic power for the general welfare and the arbitrary exercise of that power for private advantage. But it is a poor liberal who can be satisfied with the measure of general welfare that the New Deal achieved in America, and a poor socialist who can be content with the measure of democratic control that prevailed in Socialist Britain. It is a naive man who believes that human plans are ever executed as designed—or are any the less necessary therefore.

The reader who keeps these prejudices in mind should be able to compensate for some errors of proportion that may have entered the text and, no doubt, to reconcile our observations with his own.

Index

(Notes are incorporated)

X   305

INDEX

Scott, Lord Justice, 33. *See also* Committee on Land Utilisation in Rural Areas
Sert, José L., 5
sewage problems, 51, 68–70, 72, 76, 125, 159, 233–6, 293–9
Sharp, Thomas, 88–9, 92, 102, 104, 112, 117–18, 120
Shawcross, Sir Hartley, 248–50
Sheepshanks, T. H., 32
shops, 36–7, 51, 155, 176–7, 180. *See also* traders
Silkin, Lewis, 15, 22, 27–8, 82, 109, 123, 143, 217, 241, 276. *See also* Minister of Town and Country Planning
Simon, E. D., 4, 24–5, 29, 45, 102, 150–1, 166, 265–6
Simon, R., 157
Sinclair, Robert, 22
Smailes, Arthur, 87
Smith, E. W., 5
Social Survey, 91, 106–8, 110–11
Socialists, *see* Labour
Society for Protection of Ancient Buildings, 138
soil, quality of, 135–6
Spencer, Herbert, 301
Stamp, L. Dudley, 33–4, 134–6
State, Secretary of, 270
Stephenson, Gordon, 34, 53, 79–80, 212, 257
Stevenage,
  history, 35–49.
  See also Development Corporation, Stevenage; Urban District Council, Stevenage; etc.; and individual subject headings
Supply, Ministry of, 261

Taylor, E. G. R., 32, 97, 99–100
Thankerton, Lord, 70
Tolstoy, 292
Tottenham Borough Council garden city proposal, 52, 109–10, 186
Town and Country (Interim Development) Act, 1943, 20
Town and Country Planning, Ministry of,

formation, 19–20
power in Government, 275–7
relations with, Development Corporations, 152, 179, 210, 215–16, 240–1, 243–4, 258–70, 275, 289–90; Hertfordshire County Council, 157–60, 233–8, 297–9. *See also* Hertfordshire County Council; Stevenage Council, 51–76, 225–6, 238–47, 288, 290
See also Minister of Town and Country Planning; other subject headings
Town and Country Planning Act, 1925, 13–14
  1932, 13–14, 16, 20 53, 56, 59, 63, 127, 240
  1944, 20, 65, 144, 148
  1947, 27–8, 133, 143–6, 150, 156–7, 167, 226, 243, 277
Town and Country Planning Association, 10, 58, 117, 131, 139, 241
town planning,
  acreage planned, 15
  legislation, 11–18, 88, 150, 286. *See also* individual statutes
Towndrow, F. E., 109, 123
Trade, Board of, 73, 110, 271–2, 275
traders and New Town, 52, 83, 98, 125–6, 129, 149–50, 174, 176–80, 197, 210, 267–8. *See also* Chamber of Trade; leasehold; New Town centre; shops
Trades Council, Stevenage, 48, 126, 183, 189, 198, 244
Treasury,
  control of Development Corporations, 204, 259–63
  and New Towns, 23, 31, 56, 71–2, 84–5, 157–9, 225
  See also economics
Tucker, Lord, 69
Tudor-Walters Committee, 117
Turnpike Act, 1663, 37
Tyrwhitt, Jaqueline, 5

unemployment, 184
Unwin, Raymond, 14

INDEX

Urban District Council, Stevenage,
chairman, 232
formation, 41
housing estate, 45, 163, 166–9, 182,
225. *See also* housing, Stevenage
and New Town, 52–63, 67–9, 75–6,
121–38, 165–6, 169, 225–7,
288, 290
plan, 62–5, 127, 129–30, 157, 167
political complexion, 41–3, 45–7,
58, 165, 192, 232
powers, 164–9, 225–7
See also individual subject headings
urban problems, 3–5, 285–6. *See also*
London, problems of
Uthwatt, Lord, 70. *See also* Expert
Committee on Compensation and
Betterment
Uthwatt Committee, *see* Expert Committee on Compensation and
Betterment
utopian thought, 95–101, 291–2
See also utopias; ideological thought
utopias, 5–11, 87, 291–2

Vane, W. M. F., 255

Veblen, Thorstein, 114, 146
village, atypical of England, 3. *See
also* rural cult

Walker-Smith, Derek, 235, 255–6
Walter, Marianne, 106, 108–9
war, affect on planning movement, 15,
25–6
Warner, W. L., 92–3
water supply, 40, 68–70, 72, 75, 174,
187, 230–1, 233–4, 294–6, 298
Watkins, Ernest, 14
Watson, J. D. & D. M., 296
Welwyn Garden City, 10, 14, 33, 54,
64, 89–90, 102, 111–12, 121, 123,
129, 149–50, 162–4, 167, 183–4,
240, 287, 293
Welwyn Garden City New Town, 24,
158, 208, 215, 234–5, 296, 297,
Williams, Rees J., 109
winds, prevailing, 36, 136–7
workers, attitude to New Town, 126,
171–2, 183–9, 194, 198
Works, Ministry of,
and New Towns, 261, 271–3
planning powers, 20, 168

313